Revitalizing Entrepreneurship Education

T0299950

Within mainstream scholarship, it's assumed without question that entrepreneurship and entrepreneurship education are desirable and positive economic activities. Drawing on a wide range of theoretical approaches and political-philosophical perspectives, critical entrepreneurship studies has emerged to ask the questions which this assumption obscures.

Students of entrepreneurship need to understand why and how entrepreneurship is seen as a moral force which can solve social problems or protect the environment, or even to tackle political problems. It is time to evaluate how such contributions and insights have entered our classrooms. How much – if any – critical discussion and insight enters our classrooms? How do we change when students demand to be taught "how to do it", not to be critical or reflexive?

If educators are to bring alternative perspectives into the classroom, it will entail a new way of thinking. There is a need to share ideas and practical approaches, and that is what the contributions to this volume aim to do and to illuminate new ways forward in entrepreneurship education.

Karin Berglund is Professor of Business with specialization in entrepreneurship at Stockholm Business School, Stockholm University, Sweden, and Visiting Professor at Linnaeus University in Växjö.

Karen Verduijn is a Senior Lecturer in Entrepreneurship at the Department of Management & Organization, Faculty of Economics and Business Administration, Vrije Universiteit Amsterdam, the Netherlands.

Routledge Rethinking Entrepreneurship Research
Edited by Alain Fayolle and Philippe Riot

The current focus on entrepreneurship as a purely market-based phenomenon and an unquestionably desirable economic and profitable activity leads to under-valuing and under researching important issues in relation to power, ideology or phenomenology. New postures, new theoretical lenses and new approaches are needed to study entrepreneurship as a contextualized and socially embedded phenomenon. The objective of this series therefore is to adopt a critical and constructive posture towards the theories, methods, epistemologies, assumptions and beliefs which dominate mainstream thinking. It aims to provide a forum for scholarship which questions the prevailing assumptions and beliefs currently dominating entrepreneurship research and invites contributions from a wide range of different communities of scholars, which focus on novelty, diversity and critique.

Rethinking Entrepreneurship
Debating Research Orientations
Edited by Alain Fayolle and Philippe Riot

Family Entrepreneurship
Rethinking the Research Agenda
Kathleen Randerson, Cristina Bettinelli, Alain Fayolle and Giovanna Dossena

Challenging Entrepreneurship Research
Edited by Hans Landström, Annaleena Parankangas, Alain Fayolle and Philippe Riot

Revitalizing Entrepreneurship Education
Adopting a Critical Approach in the Classroom
Karin Berglund and Karen Verduijn

Revitalizing Entrepreneurship Education

Adopting a Critical Approach in the Classroom

Karin Berglund and Karen Verduijn

LONDON AND NEW YORK

First published 2018
by Routledge
2 Park Square, Milton Park, Abingdon, Oxon OX14 4RN

and by Routledge
605 Third Avenue, New York, NY 10017

First issued in paperback 2020

Routledge is an imprint of the Taylor & Francis Group, an informa business

© 2018 selection and editorial matter, Karin Berglund and Karen Verduijn; individual chapters, the contributors

British Library Cataloguing in Publication Data
A catalogue record for this book is available from the British Library

Library of Congress Cataloging in Publication Data
A catalog record for this book has been requested

ISBN 13: 978-0-367-73535-7 (pbk)
ISBN 13: 978-1-138-21379-1 (hbk)

Typeset in Times New Roman
by Wearset Ltd, Boldon, Tyne and Wear

Contents

List of figures	viii
List of tables	ix
Notes on contributors	x
Foreword: teaching entrepreneurship is walking a tightrope	xiii
MALIN TILLMAR	
Foreword: critique, entrepreneurship, practice: a prolegomenon	xv
PASCAL DEY	
Prologue: looking to the future: how can we further develop	
critical pedagogies in entrepreneurship education?	xvii
DENISE FLETCHER	
Acknowledgements	xxv

PART I
Setting the scene — 1

Introduction: challenges for entrepreneurship education — 3
KARIN BERGLUND AND KAREN VERDUIJN

1 **Education or exploitation? Reflecting on the entrepreneurial**
university and the role of the entrepreneurship educator — 25
RICHARD TUNSTALL

PART II
On evoking — 41

2 **Entrepreneurship in societal change: students as reflecting**
entrepreneurs? — 43
JESSICA LINDBERGH AND BIRGITTA SCHWARTZ

3 **The reflexivity grid: exploring conscientization in entrepreneurship education** 62
LEONA ACHTENHAGEN AND BENGT JOHANNISSON

4 **From entrepreneurship to entrepreneuring: transforming healthcare education** 82
HANNA JANSSON, MADELEN LEK AND CORMAC McGRATH

PART III
On moving 97

5 **A space on the side of the road: creating a space for a critical approach to entrepreneurship** 99
PAM SEANOR

6 **Conceptual activism: entrepreneurship education as a philosophical project** 119
CHRISTIAN GARMANN JOHNSEN, LENA OLAISON AND BENT MEIER SØRENSEN

PART IV
On challenging 137

7 **Bringing gender in: the promise of critical feminist pedagogy** 139
SALLY JONES

8 **Entrepreneurship and the entrepreneurial self: creating alternatives through entrepreneurship education?** 158
ANNIKA SKOGLUND AND KARIN BERGLUND

9 **Between critique and affirmation: an interventionist approach to entrepreneurship education** 178
BERNHARD RESCH, PATRIZIA HOYER AND CHRIS STEYAERT

PART V
On dialogues 197

10 **Moving entrepreneurship** 199
KAREN VERDUIJN

11 On vulnerability and possibility in critical entrepreneurship education: mutual learning between students and teachers 211
ANNA WETTERMARK, ANDRÉ KÅRFORS, OSKAR LIF,
ALICE WICKSTRÖM, SOFIE WIESSNER AND
KARIN BERGLUND

Epilogue: critical entrepreneurship education: a form of resistance to McEducation? 228
ULLA HYTTI

Index 235

Figures

1.1	Towards a critical IFTA	15
4.1	Schematic illustration of the double diamond process map of DT	86
4.2	Preparing for role play, testing of prototypes and collecting user feedback	91
5.1	Searching	101
5.2	Playing and exchanging ideas	106
5.3	Forces at play	108
6.1	Juxtaposition I	123
6.2	Juxtaposition II	125
8.1	Course outline for entrepreneurship and the entrepreneurial self	166
8.2	Student's discourse at the start of the course	167
9.1	The contours of an entrepreneurial cluster or cracks in a community's soil?	184
9.2	Presentation on the relationship between creativity and freedom in the *Charlie Hebdo* tragedy	189

Tables

2.1	Different audience and student's perception	47
2.2	An overview of students' expectations of learning needs across five semesters	50
2.3	An overview of students' assessment of the course across three semesters	56
3.1	The reflexivity grid	76
4.1	Group project example – understand	89
4.2	Group project example – create	90
4.3	Group project example – deliver	92
5.1	The student voice	113
8.1	Learning outcomes in the EES course	165
8.2	Questions posed in relation to the three themes	168
8.3	Case description to "shaping the entrepreneurial self of a company"	170

Contributors

Editors

Karin Berglund is Professor of Business with specialization in entrepreneurship at Stockholm Business School, Stockholm University, Sweden, and Visiting Professor at Linnaeus University in Växjö.

Karen Verduijn is a Senior Lecturer in entrepreneurship at the Department of Management & Organization, Faculty of Economics and Business Administration, Vrije Universiteit Amsterdam, the Netherlands.

Contributors (in alphabetical order)

Leona Achtenhagen is a Professor of Entrepreneurship and Business Development at Jönköping International Business School, Jönköping University, Sweden.

Pascal Dey is an Associate Professor in Organization Studies at the People, Organization and Society Department, Grenoble Ecole de Management, France, and a Senior Research Fellow at the Institute for Business Ethics, University of St. Gallen, Switzerland.

Denise Fletcher is Professor of Entrepreneurship and Innovation in the Faculty of Law, Finance and Economics at the University of Luxembourg, Luxembourg.

Patrizia Hoyer is a Postdoctoral Researcher at the Research Institute for Organizational Psychology, School of Management, University of St Gallen, Switzerland.

Ulla Hytti is a Research Director in the Entrepreneurship Unit at the Turku School of Economics, University of Turku, Finland.

Hanna Jansson is Head of the Unit for Bioentrepreneurship at the Department of Learning, Informatics, Management and Ethics, Karolinska Institutet, Stockholm, Sweden.

Bengt Johannisson is Professor Emeritus at the Department of Organization and Entrepreneurship, Faculty of Economics and Management, Linnaeus University, Växjö, Sweden.

Christian Garmann Johnsen is Associate Professor at Copenhagen Business School, Denmark.

Sally Jones is a Reader in Entrepreneurship and Gender Studies at Sylvia Pankhurst Gender Research Centre, based in the Faculty of Business and Law, Manchester Metropolitan University, Manchester, UK.

André Kårfors is a master's student in management studies at the Stockholm Business School.

Madelen Lek is a project manager at the Unit for Bioentrepreneurship at the Department of Learning, Informatics, Management and Ethics, Karolinska Institutet, Stockholm, Sweden.

Oskar Lif is a master's student in management studies at the Stockholm Business School, Sweden.

Jessica Lindbergh is Assistant Professor in Business Administration at the Management and Organization section at Stockholm Business School, Stockholm University, Sweden.

Cormac McGrath is Lecturer and Researcher at the Department of Learning, Informatics, Management and Ethics at Karolinska Institutet, Stockholm, Sweden and Senior Lecturer at the Department of Education at Stockholm University.

Lena Olaison is Assistant Professor at Copenhagen Business School, Denmark, and Postdoc at the Life at Home and Sustainable Production research initiative at Linnaeus University, Sweden.

Bernhard Resch is a PhD candidate at the Research Institute for Organizational Psychology, School of Management, University of St Gallen, Switzerland.

Birgitta Schwartz is a Senior Lecturer and Associate Professor in Business Administration at the Management and Organization section at Stockholm Business School, Stockholm University, Sweden.

Pam Seanor is a Senior Lecturer at Bristol Business School, University of the West of England.

Annika Skoglund is Associate Professor at Uppsala University, Sweden, and Honorary Associate Professor at the University of Exeter Business School, United Kingdom.

Bent Meier Sørensen is Professor in Organizational Philosophy at Copenhagen Business School.

Chris Steyaert is Professor of Organizational Psychology at the Research Institute for Organizational Psychology, School of Management, University of St Gallen, Switzerland.

Malin Tillmar is a Professor at the Department of Organisation and Entrepreneurship at the School of Business in Linnaeus University, Sweden.

Richard Tunstall is Associate Professor of Enterprise at the Centre for Enterprise and Entrepreneurship Studies, Leeds University Business School, University of Leeds, UK.

Anna Wettermark is Assistant Professor of Management and Organization at Stockholm Business School, Stockholm University, Sweden.

Alice Wickström is a master's student in management studies at the Stockholm Business School.

Sofie Wiessner is a master's Student in management studies at the Stockholm Business School, Sweden.

Foreword

Teaching entrepreneurship is walking a tightrope

Malin Tillmar

As entrepreneurship researchers and university teachers, we are walking a tightrope that is at the core of the contemporary social and economic dynamics. On the one hand, many of us who are interested in entrepreneurship want to believe in the possibility of social change (Calas, Smircich & Bourne, 2009), and are interested in what entrepreneurs do (Gartner, 1988) and in which contexts entrepreneurship in a broad sense is possible. We may want to further this knowledge and understanding of the "productive" (Baumol, 1990), in the broadest sense, sides of entrepreneurship to our students. As academics with emancipatory knowledge interests (cf. Rindova, Barry & Ketchen, 2009) or with interactive research ambitions (Svensson, Ellström & Brulin, 2007), we may even wish to do that through engaged scholarship (Van de Ven, 2007) with an impact on the surrounding society.

Since "entrepreneurship" is a concept with strong positive connotations in the common and political debate, we do, however, need to be wary. If we are academics with a strong basis in the academic values of reflexivity and criticality (Humboldtian values), it is vital to safeguard these values – so also when we talk about entrepreneurship. As researchers and teachers in entrepreneurship today, 2017, we risk unintentionally, or even unreflectively, becoming tools in a top-down implementation of a neo-liberal agenda which includes entrepreneurialism and individualism. Against our better judgement, we are at risk of standing in classroom after classroom worldwide and conveying the message that everyone can turn their life around and is fully responsible for their own destiny and success – as if structures and context didn't matter. Yet we also know from entrepreneurship research that they do (Welter, 2011; Diaz, Brush, Gatewood & Welter, 2017).

It is, of course, possible to take the stance that entrepreneurship, including in the form of business ownership, is inherently good. It is also possible to take the stance that entrepreneurship – as a practice and as a concept – is inherently bad. As I see it, both of these stances compromise academic values. Personally, I am striving to understand and sometimes stimulate processes of social change, without enthusiastically encouraging people to start businesses if they may be better off not doing so. To take two examples, employees working in healthcare are not always less constrained when they start up a business than they are as employees (Sundin & Tillmar, 2010), and the issues faced by women entrepreneurs, for example in developing countries, are not necessarily resolved by starting businesses (Tillmar, 2016). These groups are nonetheless among those urged to start businesses by a multitude of entrepreneurship programmes. Immigrants are another of those groups that today receive "entrepreneurship training". This may lead to success. It may not (cf. Blackburn & Ram, 2006). Within academia, a nuanced and theoretically informed approach to what entrepreneurship is, and can imply, is of vital importance.

In other words, we really need to walk the tightrope without falling off on either side. But how? And how can we as academics support each other to find this balance? That is where this book comes in. It problematizes the entrepreneurialism discourse, without throwing the baby out with the bathwater. The contributions in the book provide inspiration and examples to help us make our entrepreneurship education more critical, avoiding what Hytti (this volume) calls the "McDonaldization" of education.

References

Baumol, W.J. (1990). Entrepreneurship: Productive, unproductive, and destructive. *Journal of Political Economy, 98*(5), Part 1, 893–921.

Blackburn, R. & Ram, M. (2006). Fix or fixation? The contributions and limitations of entrepreneurship and small firms to combating social exclusion. *Entrepreneurship and Regional Development, 18*(1), 73–89.

Calas, M.B., Smircich, L. & Bourne, K.A. (2009). Extending the boundaries: Reframing "entrepreneurship as social change" through feminist perspectives. *Academy of Management Review, 34*(3), 552–569.

Diaz, C., Brush, C., Gatewood, E. & Welter, F. (Eds) (2017). *Women's entrepreneurship in global and local contexts*. Cheltenham: Edward Elgar.

Gartner, W.B. (1988). Who is an entrepreneur? Is the wrong question. *American Journal of Small Business, 12*(4), 11–32.

Rindova, V., Barry, D. & Ketchen, D.J. (2009). Entrepreneuring as emancipation. *Academy of Management Review, 34*(3), 477–491.

Svensson, L., Ellström, P.E. & Brulin, G. (2007). Introduction – on interactive research. *International Journal of Action Research, 3*(3), 233–249.

Sundin, E. & Tillmar, M. (2010). The masculinization of the elderly care sector: Local-level studies of public sector outsourcing. *International Journal of Gender and Entrepreneurship, 2*(1), 49–67.

Tillmar, M. (2016). Gendering commercial justice: experiences of selfemployed women in urban Tanzania. *Journal of Enterprising Communities, 10*(1), 101–122.

Van de Ven, A.H. (2007). *Engaged scholarship: Creating knowledge for science and practice*. Oxford: Oxford University Press.

Welter, F. (2011). Contextualizing entrepreneurship—conceptual challenges and ways forward. *Entrepreneurship Theory and Practice, 35*(1), 165–184.

Foreword

Critique, entrepreneurship, practice: a prolegomenon

Pascal Dey

Critique, as Rosa (2009) reminds us, is a constitutive element of human practice. Whenever everyday life demands a decision, evaluation or justification, human practice is exposed to critique. This is no different for entrepreneurship, since where different ways of doing entrepreneurship exist there is always the possibility that entrepreneurship is done wrong (Harris, Sapienza & Bowie, 2009), i.e. in ways that are incommensurate with the advancement of the common good (Horkheimer, 1982). This book, *Revitalizing Entrepreneurship Education*, makes critique the central motto of entrepreneurship education. While the individual chapters, each in their own unique way, express a disenchantment with the "free enterprise model", which conceives of entrepreneurship exclusively in terms of economic finalities (Calás, Smircich & Bourne, 2009), they are worn by a general desire to move critique away from "gestures of pure negation" and towards changing entrepreneurship in the direction of greater justice, civic participation and societal emancipation (Horn, 2013). In this way, critique as it is employed in this book is never solely concerned with the nature and justification of good/bad or right/wrong entrepreneurial practice but with using education to liberate entrepreneurial practice from its ideological, political and economic enslavement. What is hence critically at stake is an understanding of critique as *emancipation* which uses education to intervene into common ways in which entrepreneurship is practised. Importantly, the book aims to challenge and transform not "only" the practice of entrepreneurship but also the very institution in which entrepreneurship is (mostly) taught: the contemporary business school. While business schools have variously been described as the place where knowledge and education is commodified, it appears legitimate to ask whether entrepreneurship education can amount to anything other than shallow "infotainment" associated with a (pro forma) qualification for the job market (Pfeffer & Fong, 2002). However, even if many business schools tend to subordinate knowledge and education to the principles of the market, this book by Karin Berglund and Karen Verduijn provides a perceptive analysis that alternative ways of teaching entrepreneurship do exist. Obviously enough, applying alternative approaches to entrepreneurship education might challenge, willingly or otherwise, business schools' institutional habits and imperatives. Crucial to teaching entrepreneurship critically is thus a willingness to take risks and an intimidation against negative ramification that might ensue. In a truly entrepreneurial fashion, teaching entrepreneurship differently and with a critical prospect presupposes the ability to turn the self into "a work of art". Such an aesthetic mode of self-formation is less about the cultivation of a new form of dandyism (Hadot, 1991) than about learning to live virtuously (Foucault, 1980), not by obeying to universal moral criteria but by destabilizing and creatively transgressing the way the business school wants us to act, thus redefining the realm of educational practice by our own rules.

References

Calás, E., Smircich, L. & Bourne, K.A. (2009). Extending the boundaries: Reframing "entrepreneurship as social change" through feminist perspectives. *Academy of Management Review, 34*, 552–569.

Foucault, M. (1980). *The history of sexuality, volume I.* New York, NY: Vintage.

Hadot, P. (1991). Reflection of the notion of the "cultivation of the self". In T. Armstrong (Ed.), *Michel Foucault: Philosopher* (pp. 225–232). New York, NY: Routledge.

Harris, J.D., Sapienza, H.J. & Bowie, N.E. (2009). Ethics and entrepreneurship. *Journal of Business Venturing, 24*, 407–418.

Horkheimer, M. (1982). *Critical theory.* New York, NY: Continuum.

Horn, D.M. (2013). *Democratic governance and social entrepreneurship: Civic participation and the future of democracy.* London: Routledge.

Pfeffer, J. & Fong, C.T. (2002). The end of business schools? Less success than meets the eye. *Academy of Management Learning and Education, 1*, 78–95.

Rosa, H. (2009). Einführung: Was ist Kritik? In R. Jaeggi & T. Wesche (Eds), *Was ist Kritik?* (pp. 7–20). Frankfurt a.M.: Suhrkamp.

Prologue

Looking to the future: how can we further develop critical pedagogies in entrepreneurship education?

Denise Fletcher

In this foreword, I contribute to discussions on the nature, purpose, meaning and form of revitalizing entrepreneurship education and I do this by thinking about the future and trying to envisage the societal changes that are likely to occur in the next five to eight years. At the same time, I have in mind two other issues which are important for shaping how entrepreneurship pedagogy might look like in the coming years. The first issue stems out of what I see as the increasing homogeneity of entrepreneurship programmes in business school curricula. The second relates to the co-created and "flourishing" visions of the 50+20 agenda[1] (positive social impact, disruptive innovation, social inclusion, scalability, flourishing, consciousness of connectedness) – visions which are both indispensable and inspiring for revitalizing entrepreneurship education.

In the coming decade, society will experience huge changes, which will have major consequences for the way we live, consume, interact and organize ourselves socially, economically and politically. The changes relate to, for example: (i) digitalization and our evolution towards a technology-immersed world; (ii) the use of robots (bots) as assistants and companions in households and workplaces; (iii) post-truth styles of communication enabled by social media; (iv) the craving for authenticity, meaning and purpose in human connections, jobs, occupations and careers but also in products, services that we consume and the social structures we live in; (v) flexible forms of working centred on projects that emphasize creativity; (vi) the shared or "maker" economy, which blurs (national/global, personal/work and producer/consumer) boundaries.

These societal, cultural and technological changes will have a significant impact on the form and organization of work activities. They will also impact entrepreneurial activities and more specifically the way these activities are expressed, performed and enacted. This means that business education in general, and entrepreneurship education in particular, should evolve to take account of (and also to anticipate) these changes and the new "demands" they will create.

For example, creative capabilities will be much in demand by employers as routine work tasks become automated. There is likely to be an increased demand for technologically competent and ICT-literate students with some skills in data analytics. A range of transferable professional skills and knowledge that enhance employability will be highly sought-after (i.e. social media management, pitching, public speaking, negotiation skills and emotional intelligence as well as participatory styles of management, leadership and diversity management). There is also likely to be a growing demand from organizations for students who are socially aware and who can analyse, synthesize, lead, envision and participate in (internationally) diverse teams to bring about social, business and organizational transformations. Above all, there will be a pressure for business education to be relevant, accessible, transparent and accountable to organizations, the general public and society at large (Donaldson, 2002; Pfeffer, 2009; Starkey & Tempest, 2009; Kieser, Nicolai & Seidl, 2015; Nicolai & Seidl, 2010; Fotaki & Prasad, 2015; Baden & Higgs, 2015; Alajoutsijarvi, Juusola & Siltaoja, 2015).

It is clear that entrepreneurship curriculum has a particular role to play in leading (critical) curriculum innovation. This is because, quite naturally, the cultivation of forms of innovation and enterprising skills or competencies is our core business. Also, entrepreneurship pedagogies are often premised on the practices of creativity, experimentation, exploration and discovery – all of which necessitate relevant and multimodal teaching methods, approaches, learning styles, tools and models. Programme directors, course tutors and business school leaders will not only be expected to respond to the needs of different stakeholders vis-à-vis global trends but also (and more challengingly) to anticipate and foresee what the demands/expectations might be. At the same time, we will need to *translate* these future needs into educational programmes that are socially/economically relevant and which prepare students appropriately for these new societal and technological challenges.

This takes me to my next observation, which is that the entrepreneurship curriculum is becoming increasingly homogenized in the sense, that beyond different institutional contexts, there is perhaps little difference between the content of an entrepreneurship course in Sweden, the UK, the Netherlands or Luxembourg. As the topic of entrepreneurship has become more popular, recognized and legitimized, so too have the "stock in trade" tools and concepts we use in the field (i.e. principles of effectuation, business canvas model, the business plan, elevator pitches, pivoting, the notion of opportunity, prototyping, etc.). This suggests that entrepreneurship programmes are facilitating generic skill sets which, although relevant for employers, are not necessarily oriented to the future needs/challenges of society. This also means that it is harder to set apart entrepreneurship programmes in different countries and ultimately suggests that the value of entrepreneurship education is less about content and more about the country-level ecosystem for entrepreneurship/start-ups and the opportunities for jobs, placements and network opportunities that this brings.

These observations have implications for the purpose, role and shape of entrepreneurship education in the future. What new fresh/innovative (and critical) learning experiences could be added to our curricula that stretch students to bring about market/product transformations in the media-savvy, technologically immersed society outlined earlier? Do the "stock in trade" tools of our teaching practice (the business canvas model, the business plan, the elevator pitch) have a future in entrepreneurship learning and teaching? How can we ensure that our teaching practices are well placed for anticipating societal and technological changes, especially when most of our research is retrospective and the explanatory modes post hoc? In short, what will help business schools and programmes differentiate their entrepreneurship education in the future and what role will critical thinking, theories and pedagogies play in this? I turn to a couple of refreshing examples from other fields of the management sciences where colleagues have presented alternative ways of thinking about business education.

At the level of leadership education, Collinson and Tourish (2015) present some new directions for "teaching leadership critically". In this essay, the authors are critical of the over-reliance on transformational models that stress the role of (usually white, male) charismatic people – models which overlook or downplay the dynamics of power, the influence of context and the significance of follower dissent and resistance. Their answer – to consider the pedagogical potential of an emergent, alternative paradigm questioning deep-seated assumptions that power and agency should be vested in the hands of a few leaders. They also offer a number of guiding principles from their experiences with students. These centre on: encouraging student participation and dialogue in courses; highlighting the importance of power in leadership practices as well as the multiple contexts and cultures through which leadership dynamics are produced; the paradoxes and unintended effects of leaders' practices; the damaging effects of over-conformity to destructive behavioural norms (i.e. the promotion of mono cultures that stifle critical feedback and the negative consequences of certain leadership dynamics (p. 590)).

Malcolm Parker (2016) also poses a refreshing set of questions concerning what a different sort of business school research and teaching agenda might look like (p. 150). He adopts a reformist agenda to demand a new way of thinking about organizing: "how can the discipline of management in both research and teaching stop being mere advocacy and become a proper field of enquiry?" (p. 150). His answer – a School of Organizing – which, rather than reducing everything to management or business, would take account of the different forms of organizing that exist in the world. The need to focus on organizing, he argues, is important because the problem of organization is not taken seriously enough and yet organizing features are very prevalent in all life and society, in cooperatives, markets, kinship groups, partnerships social movements, hierarchies, networks etc. He goes on to argue that we need multidisciplinary approaches to study these complex forms of organizing, which would be an "invitation to learn about organizing, all of it, not just management or entrepreneurship" and not as "sites for the production of global managerialism" or for showing inequality but "as a school for people who want to learn from other places, other times, other politics and to consider this for their own attempts to create organisations" (p. 154).

These are both passionate and convincing pleas and something for us to think about in the field of entrepreneurship where we have our own history of critically inspired viewpoints. Critical perspectives have been moderately influential in transforming our conceptions of entrepreneurship into ideological critiques that challenge received wisdom and knowledge about society, the economy and the various organizational, institutional and managerial practices. Such work usually involves a "questioning [of] established social orders, dominating practices, ideologies, discourses and institutions" (Alvesson & Deetz, 2000, p. 1) and it usually embodies an ideological and/or political-moral purpose. At a personal level, I recall being "blown away" by the early commentaries critiquing the concept of entrepreneurship in the late 1990s/early 2000s in the form of Nodoushani and Nodoushani (1999), Ogbor (2000) and Armstrong (2005). In these works, the authors deconstructed the ideological roots of entrepreneurship with its purported avant-garde and "anti-management lyricism" (p. 48). Ogbor (2000) was also concerned with "deconstruction in order to denaturalize or call into question the knowledge claims of the entrepreneurial texts/discourses, and to reveal how they present as inherently neutral the ways things are always done" (p. 607). Adding to these, Armstrong's critique (2005) also provoked a sceptical view of entrepreneurship by revealing the dysfunctional and ideologically controlling effects of the concept of entrepreneurship. Since then, many other studies have invoked critical modes or stances in entrepreneurship research (Jones & Spicer, 2005, 2009; Weiskopf & Steyaert, 2009; Steyaert & Dey, 2010; Spicer, 2012; Tedmanson, Verduijn, Essers & Gartner, 2012; Verduijn, Dey, Tedmanson & Essers, 2014).

These viewpoints offer something new and different – or, to use the words of Steyaert and Dey (2010), they enable entrepreneurship scholarship to stay fresh, pluralistic, reflexive and perhaps even dangerous. They are indicative of the post-positivist expansion of entrepreneurship research and "party on" calls for a richer, more multicontextual, multilevel, pro-social and compassionate approaches that advance comprehensive (inter)activity-based understanding(s) of the entrepreneurial phenomena (Shepherd, 2015). Such perspectives reflect a wish for transformational research and teaching that not only retains the vitality that engendered this domain of research in the first place but which also takes account of the grand challenges we face in the global world such as poverty and environmental issues (Shepherd, 2015). At the level of learning and teaching, however, critical perspectives are sometimes perceived by students as overly theoretical or too remote from their daily preoccupations. In addition, with the increasing instrumentality of students, they often find it difficult to see the need for critical perspectives as they can appear to counter their (hero) expectations of what it is to start a new venture.

To help overcome some of these challenges, I now sketch some preliminary ideas for a teaching and learning agenda for critical entrepreneurship. In outlining these ideas, I acknowledge our own home-grown "entrepreneuring" verb – a verb that can not only act as a conceptual attractor for research purposes (Steyaert, 2007) but also an attractor for a future critical learning and teaching agenda. I also have in mind Weiskopf and Steyaert's (2009, p. 15) conception of entrepreneurship as "critical engagement in the world" and also a set of motivations, themes and interests that facilitate this in an increasingly visual and digitalized learning and teaching context. The forthcoming list is not conclusive but offers some ideas for optimizing existing critical teaching practices and extending them further.

The potential for transformative (critical) entrepreneurship education

A starting point for facilitating critical modes of learning and teaching are the use of creative modes of curriculum design and assessment methods that develop engagement in entrepreneuring (i.e. negotiation, pitching, networking, stakeholder management, testing assumptions, bricolaging, pivoting, prototyping, etc.). These creative modes of engagement centre on learning oriented towards action, designing and problem-setting that opens up new pathways for bringing future-oriented visions, concepts and ideas into realization through interaction, stretching, staging and legitimizing. These modes of learning encourage students to cope with uncertainty, asymmetric information and to adapt and plan according to the changing and contingent environment.

Such engagement modes include any situation where students need to relate, engage, and interact in order to test assumptions, challenge expectations and validate hypotheses about potential future markets. This could be during: (i) interventions into entrepreneurial settings (i.e. incubators, social enterprises, start-ups, agencies, support organizations); (ii) interviews with local entrepreneurs, actors – by critiquing their discourses, policies, practices; (iii) placements in start-up companies, or work projects for start-up companies emphasizing problem-solving, process flow and designing solutions; and (iv) pitching exercises in incubator contexts, involving incubator managers, local entrepreneurs and investors. For tutors, creative engagement can be facilitated through the use of "real time" cases and/or video cases that take account of how "modern students are immersed in a visual society" (Tejeda, 2008, p. 434) and enable students to "elaborat[e] concepts/topic content" (Clemmes & Hamakawa, 2010, p. 562) or "tie … together" complex organizational processes (Proserpio & Gioia, 2007, p. 79). Other examples of visual learning modes are video pitches; video business plans; slide decks, role play and improvisations; the use of video diaries or visual mind maps; and narratives. Such modes encourage multimodal engagement (involving the emotions, listening and observation skills) and they also draw attention to the importance of body language, facial expressions and the nuances of "human interaction that can help to bring behavioural phenomenon into sharp focus" (Tejeda, 2008, p. 434), attuning us to be socially aware.

The benefit of these modes of engagement and interaction is that students are directly implicated in real-life organizing and entrepreneuring – making decisions, evaluations and judgements about what works or what needs adaptation, managing relations with diverse team members and stakeholders to realize future goals and tasks and, more importantly, taking responsibility for these actions. Through attention to process, practice, contingency, complexity theory, bricolage and design thinking, students can experience how entrepreneuring is a process that is non-linear and always contextualized and usually unfolding over time in incremental steps as one outcome provides the context for the next outcome or decision. Using such approaches, students can be challenged to *not* think of entrepreneurial outcomes and events as "properties" of alert individuals in the way of "possessive individualism" and instead they can conceive of them as the outcome of interactions, fragments of conversations and other contextualized experiences. They would then be able to understand embodiment (and the constraints or enabling aspects of embodiment) and also appreciate materialities (artefacts, prototypes, physical objects, narratives) – rather than just the personalities or actions of heroic entrepreneurs. They would also be enabled in understanding complexity, and appreciating the interconnectivity between one decision (or non-decision) and the outcomes and/or ethical dilemmas this generates.

Moreover, in these forms of critical learning and engagement the core principle is that students can observe, experience and identify what are usually presented as ordinary ways of perceiving, conceiving and behaving. They can hear talks from entrepreneurs or watch films, documentaries and podcasts to understand the multiple (and often contested) contexts in which entrepreneurial activities take place and look for areas of suppression, control, domination or loss of autonomy and voice (as well as examples of emancipation, self-expression and freedom to act). They can also be challenged to trace the influence of history, culture and societal forces in shaping their and others' behaviours. They can observe social positioning(s), dominant values at play, and how certain discourses permeate the way people act/interact and account for their behaviours. They can evaluate how entrepreneurial actions disrupt established routines and orders, whether this is through their own interactions with one another, looking for market opportunities or through engagement with stakeholders who give critical feedback. Furthermore, as they engage in future thinking to reflect on how new markets or services or institutional practices may become transformed, they can also become more alert to the ways in which entrepreneurial settings might be potential sites for power dynamics and control or which sites and contexts are more productive for participation and resolution.

In addition to active participation in events and practices, when hearing entrepreneurial accounts students can also be encouraged to adopt an active listening stance. Instead of listening to entrepreneurs in a passive mode, listening out for success and heroic stories, students can be assessed on their appreciation of the heterogeneity of entrepreneurial narratives while looking for patterns, mechanisms, discourses or materialities that disable, emancipate, constrain or limit. They can also start to be more aware of body language, facial expressions, impression management, staging and performance, as well as considering why entrepreneurs choose to construct their stories in the way they do. In forms of assessment, tutors can also use criteria that shows students sensitivity to the emotions, politics, ethical aspects, diversity issues and power asymmetries that have been involved in entrepreneurial experiences.

Already many of these approaches to learning are being practised in entrepreneurship education. However, and I speak as much to myself when I say this, perhaps there is scope to further develop and extend such practices. In so doing, this might help to normalize critical entrepreneurship learning (rather than seeing it as something radical or alternative). Engaging in these kinds of educational practices will enable us to differentiate our courses and exploit to the full the unique contextualized and situated experiences that our education programmes have to offer. At the same time, in true entrepreneurial spirit, we should have an eye to the future and be alert to the societal and technological trends that are coming. A more optimized critical entrepreneurship teaching agenda then could contribute to the flourishing principles of the 50+20 agenda – visions which target bringing out the best individual, organizational and systemic possibilities for the world. Embracing such visions and principles will help entrepreneurship programmes to ensure that they are producing locally anchored entrepreneurship programmes that are relevant for and anticipatory of societal needs. In addition, they will help to ensure that students have creative, flexible, diversity-sensitive, emotionally intelligent, authentic skill sets that foster social awareness and proactivity and which might engender positive social and organizational transformations.

Note

1 The 50+20 Agenda describes a vision for the transformation of management education in which the common tenet of being the best in the world is revised in favour of creating businesses that are designed and led to achieve the best for the world. See http://50plus20.org/5020-agenda.

References

50+20 Management education for the world (2017). *50+20 Agenda*. Retrieved from http://50plus20.org/5020-agenda.

Alajoutsijarvi, K., Juusola, K. & Siltaoja, M. (2015). The legitimacy paradox of Business Schools. *Academy of Management Education and Learning, 14*(2), 277–292.

Alvesson, M. & Deetz, S. (2000). *Doing critical management research.* London: SAGE.

Armstrong, P. (2005). *Critique of entrepreneurship: People and policy.* Basingstoke: Palgrave Macmillan.

Baden, D. & Higgs, M. (2015). Challenging the perceived wisdom of management theories and practice. *Academy of Management Education and Learning, 14*(4), 539–555.

Clemmes, B. & Hamakawa, C. (2010). Classroom as cinema, using film to teach sustainability. *Academy of Management Learning and Education, 9*(3), 561–563.

Collinson, D. & Tourish, D. (2015). Teaching leadership critically: New directions for leadership pedagogy. *Academy of Management Education and Learning, 14*(4), 576–594.

Donaldson, L. (2002). Dammed by our own theories: Contradictions between theories and management education. *Academy of Management Education and Learning, 1*(1), 96–106.

Fotaki, M. & Prasad, A. (2015). Questioning neo-liberal capitalism and economic inequality in business schools. *Academy of Management Education and Learning, 14*(4), 556–575.

Jones, C. & Spicer, A. (2005). The sublime object of entrepreneurship. *Organization*, *12*(2), 223–246.

Jones, C. & Spicer, A. (2009). *Unmasking the entrepreneur*. London: Edward Elgar.

Kieser, A., Nicolai, A. & Seidl, D. (2015). The practical relevance of management research: turning the debate on relevance into a rigorous scientific research program. *Academy of Management Annals*, 9, 143–233.

Nicolai, A. & Seidl, D. (2010). That's relevant! Different forms of practical relevance in management science. *Organisation Studies*, 31, 1257–1285.

Nodoushani, O. & Nodoushani, P.A. (1999). A deconstructionist theory of entrepreneurship: A note. *American Business Review* 17(1), 45–49.

Ogbor, J. (2000). Mythicizing and reification in entrepreneurial discourse: Ideology-critique of entrepreneurial studies. *Journal of Management Studies*, *37*(5), 605–635.

Parker, M. (2016). Towards an alternative business school: a school of organizing. In B. Czarniawska, *A Research Agenda for Management and Organization Studies*. Cheltenham: Edward Elgar.

Pfeffer, J. (2009). Renaissance and renewal in management studies: Relevance regained. *European Management Review*, *6*(3), 141–148.

Proserpio, L. & Gioia, D.A. (2007). Teaching the virtual generation. *Academy of Management Learning & Education*, *6*(1), 69–80.

Shepherd, D.A. (2015). Party on! A call for entrepreneurship research that is more interactive, activity based, cognitively hot, compassionate, and prosocial. *Journal of Business Venturing*, *30*, 489–507.

Spicer, A. (2012). Critical theories of entrepreneurship. In K. Mole & M. Ram (Eds), *Perspectives on entrepreneurship. A critical approach*. London: Palgrave.

Starkey, K. & Tempest, S. (2009). The winter of our discontent: The design challenge for business schools. *Academy of Management Education and Learning*, *8*, 576–586.

Steyaert, C. (2007). "Entrepreneuring" as a conceptual attractor? A review of process theories in 20 years of entrepreneurship studies. *Entrepreneurship and Regional Development*, *19*(6), 453–477.

Steyaert, C. & Dey, P. (2010). Nine verbs to keep the social entrepreneurship research agenda "dangerous'. *Journal of Social Entrepreneurship*, *1*(2), 231–254.

Tedmanson, D., Verduijn, K., Essers, C. & Gartner, W.B. (2012). Critical perspectives in entrepreneurship research. *Organization*, *19*, 531–541.

Tejeda, M.J. (2008). A resource review for diversity film media. *Academy of Management Learning and Education*, *73*(3), 434–439.

Verduijn, K., Dey, P., Tedmanson, D. & Essers, C. (2014). Emancipation and/or oppression? Conceptualizing dimensions of criticality in entrepreneurship studies. *International Journal of Entrepreneurial Behaviour & Research*, *20*(2), 98–107.

Weiskopf, R. & Steyaert, C. (2009). Metamorphoses in entrepreneurship studies: Towards an affirmative politics of entrepreneuring. In D. Hjorth & C. Steyaert (Eds), *The politics and aesthetics of entrepreneurship* (pp. 183–201). Cheltenham: Edward Elgar.

Acknowledgements

The idea of this book took off from a symposium with invited participants who, like us, had voiced their interest and concerns regarding how to educate entrepreneurship education, experiencing a gap between the entrepreneurship practices we studied and found in textbooks and what we felt was asked for in the classroom. During the process of the book a community of scholars united around the idea of revitalizing entrepreneurship education. This actually happened at different conferences, not least the 3E conferences we went to (in 2016 and 2017). All of these meetings have been of great value. We would like to thank all the participants who devoted their time, energy and knowledge, and in particular those who have contributed to the current book: a big and warm thank you. As well, we would like to thank the following reviewers, who have significantly contributed to the book by their constructive and detailed suggestions to the chapter's authors: Huriye Aygören, Dorota Marsh, Deirdre Tedmanson, Thorkild Thanem, Juliette Koning, Johann Packendorff and Eeva Houtbeckers. Last but not least we would also like to express our gratitude to our institutions, which have made this project possible.

.

Part I

Setting the scene

Introduction

Challenges for entrepreneurship education

Karin Berglund and Karen Verduijn

Introduction

The last decade or so has witnessed the rise of "critical" entrepreneurship studies (CES). CES questions dominant images and conceptualizations of entrepreneurship, entrepreneuring and the entrepreneur, and create room for other understandings and approaches. Generally, critical entrepreneurship scholars feel a need to connect entrepreneurship (more) to society (and not only to the economy), and to make students aware of this.

In this book we build on the presumption that it is timely to interrogate if and how CES contributions and insights have entered our classrooms. With students interested in the entrepreneurship phenomenon generally expecting merely the "conventional" (instrumental) approach towards the same, and for us to stipulate the importance of new venture creation with regard to our economy's health and vitality, some of us (i.e. entrepreneurship educators) might see the need to point at how entrepreneurship is broader than that, that there are multiple "versions" of it, that the entrepreneurial identity is a layered one, and not without its repercussions, and that entrepreneurship provides us with a Western world discourse that is classed, gendered, ethnocentric and thus excluding. Yet many new versions wish to tackle such issues, while paying attention to troublesome global developments, where contemporary neo-liberal displacements become entwined with entrepreneurship and blur boundaries between individuals, organizations and society. By shifting responsibility from society to the individual, thus bringing entrepreneurship in in new guises, it is no longer (solely) a question of economic and other *gains* but of taking (social, ecological and cultural) *responsibility*. However, when neo-liberal pursuits attempt to open up market society, the economic dimension is not pushed aside but spills over into and influences all the other aspects of life today. This provides a challenge and poses questions as to how to enact this in our classrooms and thus offer a *critical* entrepreneurship education.

We situate critical entrepreneurship education at the crossroads of "lower education" (preschool, compulsory school, upper secondary school) and higher education. While lower education has witnessed a striving to broaden the understanding of entrepreneurship by, for example, linking it to social and environmental issues, creativity and also democracy and politics (cf. Leffler, 2009; Holmgren, 2012), this broader view is rarely reported on in literature on entrepreneurship pedagogy used in higher education (for an exception see e.g. Hjorth, 2011; Barinaga, 2016). At the same time, in preparing this volume, we have come across many initiatives positing entrepreneurship as a broader phenomenon, and problematizing its different faces in our teaching. In experimenting with pedagogical purposes, approaches and content, the authors in this volume work with such issues as reflexivity, gender, the entrepreneurial self, responsibility, awareness, creativity and vulnerability. To further spur this kind of development, this book aims to make it clear why critical questions need to formulated, and how they can be enacted to evoke students' understandings of the plurality of entrepreneur*ing* (cf. Chapter 4 in this volume). Evoking students (and ourselves) to new entrepreneurial realities aligns well with a need to also challenge ourselves and our students to engage in a dialogue of what entrepreneurship (education) might become.

In this introduction we provide the reader with a short reminder of how entrepreneurship education is generally categorized in teaching "in", "for", "through" and "about" entrepreneurship. We also discuss some of the contemporary concerns of the field of entrepreneurship education. This is followed by an introduction to critical entrepreneurship studies and the questions that guide such efforts. Third, we discuss concerns expressed in critical pedagogy literature, especially in relation to the enterprising self, as well as some of those offered by the critical management education literature. Fourth, we sketch what this may entail for (critical) entrepreneurship education. We conclude by introducing the individual chapters in the book.

The *field* of entrepreneurship education

Entrepreneurship education (EE) has gained increasing attention and no longer interests only scholars in higher education but also teachers in elementary school, along with politicians, policymakers and education stakeholders. In a literature review, Alain Fayolle (2013) concludes that the field of EE is fragmented. There is little consensus on what unites EE, how the field (or area) should be defined, and what it contains in terms of theories, issues and teaching philosophy and pedagogies (also see Nabi, Linan, Fayolle, Krueger & Walmsley, 2017). Rather, at best diversity, and at worst fragmentation, seem to prevail. This may be an effect of the expansion of EE to broaden its focus and encompass more in terms of its objectives (O'Connor, 2013) and pedagogies (Nabi *et al.*, 2017). Kirby (2007) points to the need for entrepreneurship educators to "develop graduates who can be innovative and take responsibility for their own destinies not just in a business or even a market economy context" (p. 21). Thus, EE has transgressed from being limited to offering a place for students to learn about the creation of new ventures to inhabiting a space where it sets out to facilitate for (young) people to be able to "cope with uncertainty and ambiguity, make sense out of chaos, initiate, build and achieve, in the process not just coping with change but anticipating and initiating it" (Kirby, 2007, p. 23). It appears that EE is used for many different things, in different contexts, with different groups and for different reasons.

A division of EE into the categories "about", "for" and "in" was made by Jamieson in 1984. This division has spurred scholars to develop ideas relating to the diversity of and within entrepreneurship education. With reference to Henry, Hill and Leitch (2003), Taatila (2010) defines "for" as a preparation for self-employment/venture creation, and "in" as a form of management training for established entrepreneurs. To Kirby (2007), "for" is about developing the attributes of entrepreneurship in students, "through" is when the business start-up process is used to enable students to acquire both business understandings and entrepreneurial competences, and "about" refers to the traditional pedago-gical process of teaching students by providing them with academic knowledge about entrepreneurship. We adopt these four angles (in, for, through, about: IFTA) to shed some light on the diversity with regard to how entrepreneurship is thought of, shaped and practised in an educational context.

Within the scope of our introduction to entrepreneurship education, we want to highlight a few concerns voiced by entrepreneurship educators. First and fore-most, there is a growing awareness that entrepreneurship is more than "business making" (cf. Gibb, 2002; Kirby, 2007; Thrane, Blenker, Korsgaard & Neer-gaard, 2016). With entrepreneurship education initially focusing on new busi-ness creation, and doing so by adopting predominantly economic and business perspectives and models, we see a wider range of approaches being embraced, and a growing number of entrepreneurship courses and programmes adopting a "broader" definition of entrepreneurship (i.e. as more than business making). With this broadening of previously set boundaries, we also witness a call to con-tinue to wonder how entrepreneurship education can remain (or be made) *entre-preneurial* (cf. Kuratko, 2005; Fayolle, 2013; Hjorth & Johannisson, 2007). Experimenting with both ways to bring the various understandings of entrepre-neurship to the fore and in particular "where" to teach our courses seems to be a relevant theme. In experimenting with pedagogical approaches, emphasis is being placed on the creative-relational nature of learning (cf. Hjorth & Johannis-son, 2007; Hjorth, 2011), with reflections on not only our roles as educators and our (hierarchical) positions in teaching but also the relationality involved in engaging students as active (co)learners. In thinking about our roles as educators, we may feel the need to explore the relationship between education and *provoca-tion* (Hjorth, 2011), with less emphasis on "reproductive continuity" (i.e. the reproduction of knowledge) but with more room for *invention*, i.e. creating other concepts, allowing for new ways of understanding (ibid.).

Notwithstanding these developments and the variety of and in (designing) entrepreneurship education, there appears to be a striking consistency with regard to an assumed consensual aim for more and more students to start up a business (or, broadly, organization) either after or during the education. The idea of promoting entrepreneurship and entrepreneurship education is both omnipres-ent and pervasive (also see Nabi *et al.*, 2017), to the extent that students are not only educated for entrepreneurship but also *graduated* to do it. Pittaway and Cope (2007) write that there are "two distinct forms of output: first, to enhance graduate employability and second, to encourage graduate enterprise" (p. 485). When the assumption is "the more, the merrier", the ambition to broaden entrepreneurship education may falter as it is locked into its own narrow box where *performativity* rules (cf. Dey & Steyaert, 2007). The knowledge that counts is the knowledge that can be acted upon and measured in terms of success or failure, whereby learning for the sake of learning is by definition ruled out. It is this tendency to shift the "why" of education, or at least make it more one-sided, that is of concern to critical thinkers (Ball & Olmedo, 2013; Dahlstedt & Fejes, 2017). Entrepreneurship is transformed into a guiding principle for how we are to conduct our lives in accordance with the formula for "entrepreneurial freedom". This may involve starting a new business of the conventional type and taking a product to the market, or becoming self-employed and "living your dream": at best a "free life", at worst a life where you struggle to make ends meet, something you share with many others in a similar precarious situation. Or it could imply having to continuously ask yourself how to improve as if you were your own producer, marketer and seller (Berglund, 2013). Or it may involve engaging with others to come to grips with such societal concerns as inequality, social exclusion or environmental pollution, with entrepreneurship becoming the process of joint efforts to turn this problem into an opportunity where the two logics of solving a problem and thriving on the market may turn into a conflict. Entrepreneurial logic intervenes and turns stable employment into a process of *employability*; it compels us to engage in our personal development rather than to enjoy it; it moves political and voluntary action into the background as ideas for our collective good are offered through entrepreneurial paths. Thus, entrepreneurship (and the education that follows) is not simply one course among others to choose from, but has paved the way for how we can live the present. It is exactly this tendency, and the omnipresence of entrepreneurship and entrepreneurship education, from which there is no escape, not as students, teachers, children, adults or simply *humans*. This is of concern when entrepreneurial values underpin the idea of the contemporary citizen (Dahlstedt & Fejes, 2017). If entrepreneurship education is to remain vital, we cannot deny these problematics since entrepreneurship (and entrepreneurship education) are *everywhere*. As entrepreneurship educators we must embrace these problematics, ponder over them, use "other" theories to reflect on them, continue to pose new questions and invite our students to do so as well. So, to keep EE "fresh" we should remind ourselves of the *dangerous* side of it, in particular that which has seemingly become "untouchable" from interrogation. We can therefore no longer avoid the provocative questions (cf. Hjorth, 2011) but should instead use them to ask ourselves, and our students, whether there are other ways to live the present than the "conventional" entrepreneurial way.

We will return to IFTA in the fourth section to shed light on what a critical reflection of entrepreneurship can bring about in proposing "other" forms of in/for/through and about. But first we invite the reader to "enter" the field of critical entrepreneurship studies, for it is usually from the concerns raised in that field that educators start to think of raising critical awareness in relation to their entrepreneurship courses and/or programmes.

Concerns of critical entrepreneurship studies

This section offers an in-depth elaboration on critical entrepreneurship studies (CES), which builds on Denise Fletcher's short introduction to the subject. Having already witnessed two reviews of this field (Spicer, 2012; Fletcher & Selden, 2015), we can say without hesitation that it has expanded considerably since the early days of Nodoushani and Nodoushani (1999), Ogbor (2000) and Armstrong (2005). In line with Alvesson and Willmott's (1996) definition of critical management studies, critical entrepreneurship studies has set out "to challenge the legitimacy – and counter the development of – oppressive institutions and practices, seeking to highlight, nurture and promote the potential of human consciousness to reflect critically upon such practices" (p. 13), specifically in connection to entrepreneurship discourse (cf. Armstrong, 2005) and entrepreneurial practices (cf. Beaver & Jennings, 2005). Some milestones that we believe have shaped the field are the "movements books" by Daniel Hjorth and Chris Steyaert (2003, 2006, 2010), which together with special issues (Hjorth, Jones & Gartner, 2008; Tedmanson, Verduijn, Essers & Gartner, 2012; Rehn, Brännback, Carsrud & Lindahl, 2013; Verduijn, Dey, Tedmanson & Essers, 2014; Essers, Dey, Tedmanson & Verduijn, 2017) have challenged mainstream understandings and discourses of entrepreneurship.

CES offer insight into how entrepreneurial discourses have multiplied by expanding into new contexts (such as social entrepreneurship; see Ziegler, 2011), where entrepreneurship benefits values over and above economic values, where an understanding of entrepreneurship as socially constituted is shaped (Fletcher, 2006; Jack *et al.*, 2008; Korsgaard, 2011) and where entrepreneurs "other" than the stereotypical Western world self-made middle-aged man are given a voice (Banerjee & Tedmanson, 2010; Achtenhagen & Welter, 2011; Essers & Tedmanson, 2014; Ozkazanc-Pan, 2014). Critical scholars continuously testify to how entrepreneurship continues to pervade many areas of not only economic life but also social life, including the world of school (Berglund, Lindgren & Packendorff, 2017). Altogether, this expansion of entrepreneurship discourses is aligned with solutions for coming to grips with the shortcomings of conventional entrepreneurship such as its economic roots and excluding tendencies. Despite efforts to alter entrepreneurial discourses, it is recognized that they are entangled with a capitalist ideology and surely do not offer "solutions" to its crises (Costa & Saraiva, 2012; Marsh & Thomas, 2017), but may rather work as "prophylactic action" (Vrasti, 2009).

All in all, CES adopt and span a wide variety of theoretical approaches and disciplines. These are not limited to theories of political economy as influenced by post-Marxism or the Frankfurt School type of critical theory but include postcolonial views (Essers & Benschop, 2009; Essers & Tedmanson, 2014), non-entitative, processual stances (Nayak & Chia, 2011; Hjorth, 2013; Verduijn, 2015) and feminist theoretical perspectives (Calas *et al.*, 2009; Pettersson *et al.*, 2017), as well as political-philosophical perspectives addressing the enterprising subject (du Gay, 2004; Hjorth & Steyaert, 2010; Jones & Spicer, 2005; Berglund & Skoglund, 2016).

This has resulted in a vein of CES contributions that are *sceptical* about entrepreneurship studies, some of whom issue a firm "warning". Such contributions question dominant assumptions being attributed to the entrepreneurship phenomenon, its grand narratives and – more generally – the ideological distortions of mainstream entrepreneurship research (including its paradigmatic roots). Indeed, such contributions engage openly with the "dark sides" of and within entrepreneurship (such as the contradictions, ambiguities, tensions and paradoxes inherent in entrepreneurial activities; cf. Armstrong, 2005; Jones & Spicer, 2009; Costa & Saraiva, 2012; Olaison & Sorensen, 2014). Alongside this sceptical vein we witness a vein of contributions that form explicit *hopeful attempts* to "open up" our understanding of the entrepreneurship phenomenon to a more affirmative stance. Such contributions rearticulate entrepreneurship in the light of issues of societal production and emancipation (cf. Steyaert & Hjorth, 2006; Calas *et al.*, 2009; Berglund Johannisson & Schwartz., 2012; Al-Dajani & Marlow, 2013). Together, these veins form the "double-edged sword" that constitutes CES (also see Verduijn *et al.*, 2014), which needs to be reflected upon when critical entrepreneurship enters the classroom. Presenting entrepreneurship from a critical perspective simultaneously necessitates providing students with a space where it can be reconstructed. We will come back to how we can move from deconstructing entrepreneurship to reconstructing the same, but before doing so we will consult our "older" neighbours – critical management education and critical pedagogy – to see what lessons we can integrate in the emerging field of critical entrepreneurship education.

Learning from our neighbours: critical management education and critical pedagogy

Against the backdrop of the need to bring critical concerns to entrepreneurship education, we have turned to critical management education contributions as well as to critical pedagogy's writings on entrepreneurship and literature on the enterprising self to see if we can "borrow" some lessons for critical entrepreneurship education from them. To be sure, the critical pedagogy focus is not aligned with mainstream entrepreneurship education's concern of how to better train people in business making, or to become "entrepreneurs of the self", and stimulate (more) students to do so. Our attempt is by no means an attempt to arrive at a comprehensive overview of either critical management education or critical pedagogy literature. As stated, it is, rather, an attempt to learn from others who have already struggled with similar concerns for a longer period of time and have experience in bringing these concerns into their classrooms.

The concerns expressed in critical management studies typically translate into critical management education by means of a set of principles in relation to curriculum development (Choo, 2007a):

- The curriculum is expected to embrace humanistic and liberal studies and subsume cultural, social and political cognitive perspectives.
- It should not encapsulate only performance-related financial values or interests that are trapped in what Weber (1978) (in Choo, 2007a) called "instrumental rationality".
- The modalities of teaching and learning are expected to include an element of critical reflection to encourage students to question both hidden pedagogical assumptions and those that are taken for granted as received wisdom in both knowledge and practice.
- The critical reflection must provide students with opportunities to question what Argyris (1996) (in Choo, 2007a) called the "undiscussable"; that is, questioning coherent sets of values, beliefs and practices which are constructed and disseminated by lecturers to sustain their legitimate role as teacher, and the assumptions that are taken for granted and usually concealed during teaching.
- The methods of assessment are expected to be emancipatory, i.e. to support student empowerment and promote equal treatment and opportunity.
- The emancipatory process should also provide students with opportunities to identify and contest sources of inequality and treatment of minorities, and question the assumptions implicit in tutors' assessment methods.
- The learning environment is expected to be democratic and participative and have a collective focus.

Many CME contributions mention the particular problematic found in the context in which management education typically takes place, namely the business school/MBA programme (cf. Currie, Knights & Starkey, 2010). With a fair number of contributions signalling this and other significant barriers to introducing critical management education (such as – more generally, and not only pertaining to the business school context – institutionalized assessment rules and regulations, marketization of higher education, learning styles and cultural diversity of students; see Choo, 2007b), we also see attempts at rethinking management education (Beyes & Michels, 2011), with an emphasis on opening up and connecting to the "problematics of society" (Beyes & Michels, 2011), and to how institutions of management education can enact "other spaces", as productive forces.

In a similar vein, the ambition in critical pedagogy literature is to inform the reader about the power relations in play in the shaping of entrepreneurial students and teachers (Peters, 2001). The articles are descriptive (in contrast to normative) and take an analytical interest in how enterprise culture has come to govern education. Key concepts are not "idea", "business", "opportunity" and "discovery" but rather "governmentality", "enterprising self", "enterprising culture", "subjectivity" and "power". These are used by critical pedagogues and can be adopted to inform the student about critical issues that are part of the introduction of enterprise (and entrepreneurship) in schools. So let us start by introducing these analytical key concepts.

Neo-liberalism typically describes economic imperatives of enhancing privatization and de-regulating markets (Harvey, 2005). Critical pedagogy is not interested in the economic implications of this shift but in how an enterprise culture changes learners' and educators' relations to themselves as well as to others. Consequently, the pedagogical interventions developed, more broadly under the influence of enterprise culture, and more specifically within the framework of entrepreneurship education, are understood as a particular kind of governmentality which connects students and teachers to a capitalist logic and to the rationality of the market (e.g. Dahlstedt & Hertzberg, 2014). Governmentality refers to the productive power to govern through *mentalité*, e.g. "mind" (Foucault, 1978/1991). This mode of governing is not directed towards setting limits and boundaries but works *through* the individual by *producing* subjects, *forming* subjectivities and behaviour and *enhancing* the emergence of an organization of the social, which, assessed from an economic rationale, is seen to be more effective (Brown, 2003).

Neo-liberalism is inextricably linked to a need to foster *enterprising selves*. The enterprising self can, broadly, be described as a life form constituted by the autonomous, self-regulating, responsible and economically rational individual (Barry & Osborne, 1996). The enterprising self forms a subjectivity from which both the entrepreneur and the entrepreneurial student/teacher are given their contours. De Lauretis 1986 (in Ball, 2003, p. 227) defines subjectivity as "patterns by which experimental and emotional contexts, feelings, images and memories are organized to form one's self image, one's sense of self and others, and our possibilities of existence". In neo-liberal societies the enterprising self is further promoted by turning education into a personal and ethical investment of the individual (Peters, 2001, p. 60). The enterprising self informs us of the need to be(come) an ambitious person who takes responsibility by giving her or his life a specific entrepreneurial form (cf. Lemke, 2001). Thus, the enterprising self can be understood as a "template" from which various kinds of entrepreneurial identities are configured. Analytically, it informs us of the myriad of entrepreneurial becomings that can be constructed by combining, say, "education + enterprise + responsibility + creativity + freedom + opportunity + future". In this vein, entrepreneurship, as part of a broader culture of enterprise and neo-liberalism, will trickle down to schools, where enterprising selves can be fostered, shaped, affirmed and applauded (as we have described above).

The connection with a need for a more critical outlook on entrepreneurship education is easily made. Broadly, criticism is directed at what neo-liberal logic does to us, through an emphasis on entrepreneurship in policy (e.g. Connell, 2013; Dahlstedt & Tesfahuney, 2011) and curriculum (Dahlstedt & Hertzberg, 2014) and how it intervenes through enterprise culture (e.g. Peters, 2001; Down, 2009) and also through particular educational or training programmes (e.g. Bragg, 2007; Bendix Petersen & O'Flynn, 2007). The criticism expressed is that students and teachers alike are connected to the rationality of the market, with the activity and productivity of individuals being linked to global competitiveness and employability. With critical pedagogy insights, entrepreneurship in education not only signals the hopes for (more) new businesses and innovations, but also the seeking to prepare students for a society where they need to take responsibility to a greater extent than before. Bragg (2007), for example, has investigated how personal goals and aspirations are voiced in efforts to make students create opportunities for their futures and take responsibility for turning their ideas into action. This, as Bragg (2007) asserts, requires work on the self, involving both inspection of the self and self-criticism as these young people learn to strive for "endless potentiality" (cf. Costea, Amiridis & Crump, 2012). A similar story unfolds in Bendix Petersen and O'Flynn's (2007) study of how an award scheme is taken up by students in a prestigious Australian private girls' school. The award scheme is extra-institutional, but the school participates in organizing it with the aim of providing students with an opportunity to "accept a challenge" and "set a personal goal and achieve it". Along the way, students learn about themselves and "about qualities like responsibility, trust and the ability to plan and organize themselves" (p. 202). Placing this award scheme in the analytical frame of how neo-liberal governmentality fosters a particular enterprising self, Bendix Petersen and O'Flynn (2007) show how this programme actually constitutes a powerful technology of the self as it invites young girls "to desire and assess worthwhileness along entrepreneurial lines: to gaze upon themselves as malleable, flexible, always-improvable portfolios and learn to assess themselves as successful or failing accordingly" (p. 209).

In addition, responsibility is rolled down not only from global and national institutions onto the individual, but also from adults to children. The *citizen*, in many Western democracies, is still entitled to particular rights, but she is increasingly being processed to ask herself what she can do for herself, for her community, her organization (cf. Scharff, 2016). And children are invited to think about what they will be able to do for themselves in the future (Berglund *et al.*, 2017). If we made EE in higher education more critical, could we stimulate students to be creative in rethinking how responsibility could be "rolled back" without making the individual passive or expecting institutions to "solve matters"?

While most of the literature is interested in what neo-liberalism "does" to education, pupils and students, there are a few exceptions that discuss in what way the position of the teacher in particular has changed. Ball (2003) demonstrates how technologies of enterprise reform in the world of school produce new kinds of teacher subjects that are governed through performativity. In line with the principles of performativity, the teacher takes on the role of a performative worker who is expected to have a passion for excellence and performance competition. Education is then seen as a neo-liberal technology where "results are prioritised over processes, numbers over experiences, procedures over ideas, productivity over creativity" (Ball, 2003, p. 91). The teacher is no longer someone who first and foremost cares about knowledge dissemination and the student, but someone who highlights "front impressions" as presentations (Ball, 2003, p. 224). *Effectiveness* takes precedence, second-ordering honesty and ethical practices, and replacing authenticity with "plasticity" (Ball, 2003, p. 225). This may desocialize knowledge and knowledge relations, turning knowledge into an "object" instead of an embodied experience. Thus, the educational project is left hollow, challenging the very notion of academic work and education. Ten years later, Ball and Olmedo (2013) follow up on this study, in discussing teachers' possibilities to *resist* these practices of performativity.

In the critical pedagogy literature, entrepreneurship as *the* route towards freedom and creativity is problematized. Instead, we are invited to make a U-turn, whereby we discern how we are governed through entrepreneurial freedom. Desire turns into a technology that operates through the enterprising self and those governed are not so much obedient workers as they are to become reflexive knowledge workers. There is freedom to be gained. But using this freedom may also serve those in power and sustain dominant power structures. We should take this into consideration in the making of a more critical entrepreneurship education.

Contours for critical entrepreneurship education

In this chapter we offer our sketch of the contours for a field of a critical entrepreneurship education (CEE). What we have addressed so far is how we learn from EE how entrepreneurship has in fact opened up to embrace "more" in the sense of inviting students to take responsibility for themselves and others through learning how to solve problems (also see Dahlstedt & Fejes, 2017) but, more importantly, not to let all the positive connotations that build up entrepreneurship (education) to stand in the way of posing provocative questions (as with critical management education and critical pedagogy). Engaging in CEE could spur ourselves, as entrepreneurship educators, along with our students, to ponder whether there are other ways to live the present than the *standard* entrepreneurial way. As a next step we have consulted CES, to become aware of the need to integrate the *sceptical view* of entrepreneurship with the *hopeful* approach of "remodelled" entrepreneurship. In our interpretation, this implies an interplay between *de*construction and *re*construction. The following three principles may guide us to bring the interplay between deconstruction and reconstruction into our educational approaches, purposes and content:

1   **First**, we should assert that although the enterprising self operates through a productive power, which may be difficult to resist, there is always room for distance and resistance (cf. Ball & Olmedo, 2013). Resistance, however, requires us to learn "the rules of the game". From the perspective of critical entrepreneurship pedagogy, the game does not refer to "business making" but to the game of "governing through entrepreneurial freedom". As teachers, we could introduce students to the literature of critical entrepreneurship

studies, as well as to the concepts of critical pedagogy, helping them to understand the principles and providing them with a new perspective of how entrepreneurship may work. At first it may be enough to show them novel aspects of entrepreneurship and to help them digest the fact that there are also "dark sides" to it. In the next step they could become acquainted with the analytical concepts of, for example, neo-liberalism, governmentality and the enterprising self. Equipped with these analytical concepts they could, themselves, begin to analyse cases of their own interest and train their ability for critical reflection. In shaping their futures, this should help them to find more thought-out, aware solutions – for themselves, for organizations and for society.

2   **Second**, creativity should be prioritized over productivity and performativity. This may require involving students in play and becoming, and offering students a space for creative work that will not be assessed according to the "business scale", but that opens up for them to explore new perspectives, stories, connections and responsibility. Creativity could pave the way for curiosity, for motivation to learn (for the sake of learning) and for growing mutual relations with peer students from different societal collectives. If creativity is disconnected from the productivity expectancies, solving problems could be turned around to become a method for teaching and learning rather than the "productivity goal" of a student with such skills.

3   **Third**, resisting EE to propel neo-liberalism is different from past struggles as we then need to resist our *own* practices and confront ourselves at the centre of our discomforts (Ball & Olmedo, 2013). As EE educators we can learn about what it means to resist the neo-liberal educational practices foisted upon us. By recognizing how we are exposed to the productive power to perform we can slowly start to see a way to turn this into other directions (again, reconstruction). This can be done by enacting entrepreneurship education in line with the first and second recommendations (above) but we should not forget the importance of also discussing the matter with colleagues, of sharing ideas, of finding common strategies and of supporting each other in setting boundaries that may open up for another scene where we (teachers and students) can be engulfed by knowledge for the sake of knowledge, and aware that "the future" is not inevitable but part of our creations.

Based on these principles we can see the shape of a "field" in which EE and CEE are connected. Entrepreneurship education has been opened up from a narrow "business approach" to embrace a wider approach with the ambition to teach (young) people how they can manage life itself. This has involved a move from understanding the entrepreneur of the self to understanding entrepreneurship as a collective effort and as having social and societal consequences. Entrepreneurship changes from the idea of building one's kingdom to an understanding of engaging in an entrepreneurship for the other (cf. Jones & Spicer, 2009). This shows a need to move from understanding the doing of entrepreneurship from particular events where successful entrepreneurs are elevated and celebrated (e.g. *Dragons' Den*, entrepreneurship awards, etc.) in a "peacock kind of way" (Bill, Jansson & Olaison, 2010) to understanding the mundane practices of entrepreneuring where "worker ants" blend pleasure with struggles (Bill *et al.*, 2010) and where dialogue outclasses pitch and monologue at the scene (also see Denise Fletcher's prologue). These shifts require a move from "playing the rules of the business game" to understanding how the rules can be played *with* (Berglund & Gaddefors, 2010). Altogether this takes us towards new understandings of IFTA. We will now return to IFTA and see how it might incorporate a *critical* take on EE.

Taking named displacements into account we can sketch a shift with regard to IFTA. The "for" of EE changes from learning about starting up a business to nurturing students towards becoming aware decision makers. The "in" of entrepreneurship education changes from making business and business making to enacting entrepreneurship in some form (e.g. through projects, through NGOs, setting up an artistic performance, enacting flash mobs, social engagement and interventions, making films, etc.). The "about" of entrepreneurship education changes from adhering to the grand narrative to problematizing the same, perhaps with using the knowledge provided by critical entrepreneurship pedagogy. The "through" of entrepreneurship education changes from instructions and (business) tools to engaging with students in dialogue and critical reflection. Together this builds an "IFTA 2.0" (see Figure 1.1).

Introducing the book chapters

This section introduces the individual chapters in the book, and relates them to the contours that we have sketched. We can assure the reader that the various contributions offer a rich diversity of approaches, pedagogies and ways of raising questions that testifies to how homogeneity (see Denise Fletcher's prologue) becomes a matter of the past. Experimentation with criticality in the classroom is happening "out there", and many fresh and innovative learning experiences are offered by the contributors, including their honest accounts of the resistance and struggles they encounter in doing so.

First, from Richard Tunstall we learn more about how entrepreneurship has actually and effectively found its way into the very core of the university. In Chapter 1, *Education or Exploitation? Reflecting on the Entrepreneurial University and the Role of the Entrepreneurship Educator*, Richard sets the scene in an outstanding way by showing that entrepreneurship is no longer a marginal issue of providing students with a particular kind of education, but has turned into an issue of managing the university through university–business collaborations. One point he makes is that this sets the very idea of the university in motion. He begins by bringing us to a conference, held at a university, which has gathered prominent guests, including academic delegates, small business owners, university spin-off officers, innovation managers of major multinational corporations and a government minister. But uninvited, and less welcome guests, such as

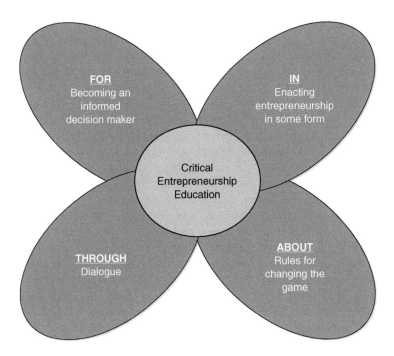

Figure 1.1 Towards a critical IFTA.

protesting students, have also gathered. Through rich empirical vignettes, Richard testifies to how this conflict unfolds over time and involves university staff, media exposure, and even a trial. With the legacy of the university being to enable students to develop their own reasoning skills in a milieu of academic freedom, entrepreneurship did not in this case pass by unnoticed. While some saw it as the redemption of a future for the (entrepreneurial) university, others saw it as the "evil" of capitalism and as the end of the university as it has always been regarded. Richard elaborates further on this dividing line and illustrates alternative ways of framing the purpose of education practice and the role of those involved. By taking the students' protests seriously he provides insight into how their expectations go beyond that of making a personal career, and are linked more to concerns about the very purpose of higher education. If we accept that entrepreneurship comes as part and parcel of our (entrepreneurial) society we cannot circumvent this topic in education, nor can we take it for granted. Rather, we need to think anew, for how it can be introduced without prohibiting criticism, protests and concerns, and without juxtaposing "academic freedom" with "the entrepreneurial university"?

In Chapter 2, *Entrepreneurship in Societal Change: Students as Reflecting Entrepreneurs?*, Jessica Lindberg and Birgitta Schwartz invite us to attend a course in which entrepreneurship is connected to various societal issues.

Introducing global issues through film, lectures and guest lecturers encourages critical questions among students. These questions are reflected upon from both "new" and "conventional" entrepreneurship literature. At the same time, students engage in solving a particular issue, and through an interplay between the literature and the local context they develop practices for societal entrepreneuring. For Jessica and Birgitta, the entrepreneurial learning process is, in addition to being experience-based (the students' projects), also and importantly a future-oriented thinking process.

Chapter 3, *The Reflexivity Grid: Exploring Conscientization in Entrepreneurship Education*, by Leona Achtenhagen and Bengt Johannisson, shares Jessica and Birgitta's concern for "the world at large". Leona and Bengt argue that reflexivity plays an important role in entrepreneurship education, whether it is in supporting students to become responsible entrepreneurs, or something "broader", that is to say training them to develop the intuitive insight they will eventually need to determine what is right and wrong both practically and ethically, and in various types of "concrete situations". They make a plea for a conscious pedagogical approach to advancing reflexivity, allowing students to conscientiously enact not only their own learning but to also contribute to the (local) world in which their learning occurs. They propose three different modes for enacting reflexivity, namely cognitive/emotional, hierarchy/network and being/becoming, and discuss these modes by offering two concrete learning situations as illustrative of how these modes for enacting reflexivity play out.

In Chapter 4, *From Entrepreneurship to Entrepreneuring: Transforming Healthcare Education*, Hanna Jansson, Madelen Lek and Cormac McGrath offer an intriguing insight into the world of healthcare and healthcare education. The chapter provides the reader with rich reflections on the struggles involved in introducing entrepreneurship education to that particular world, where the view of entrepreneurship as something *bad* is particularly pervasive among healthcare professionals (doctors, nurses, physical therapists, etc.). Interestingly, they connect education to what is perhaps a more general ability to learn and make sense of acquiring the ability to adjust certain practices, something they deem relevant, vital even, for the Swedish healthcare sector. This idea has invoked a particular take on entrepreneurship education, as they have proceeded to develop an EE course for their institution. Using Bourdieu's *habitus* to define, deconstruct and redefine what is meant by EE, they offer rich reflections on how they enact a pluralistic and nuanced conceptualization of EE in healthcare.

Taken together, these three chapters offer examples of how we can evoke students (and colleagues, as with Chapter 4). These chapters pointedly aim to generate responses, which for us would be a first move towards the kind of awareness that we see in our contours for a critical entrepreneurship education.

In Chapter 5, *A Space on the Side of the Road: Creating a Space for a Critical Approach to Entrepreneurship*, Pam Seanor offers a very personal story of how she struggles to bring criticality into her classroom. Her view on criticality is that of building awareness; there is never just one reality of entrepreneurship and of creating sensitivity for the differences in entrepreneurship. Pam meets considerable (varieties of) resistance, not only from students but also from colleagues. Her tactic has been – literally – to try to create space for her critical approach to entrepreneurship and entrepreneurship education. This chapter may be a good starting point if you are new to the life-world of the (critical) entrepreneurship educator. Pam raises interesting and relevant questions relating not only to the classroom but also to how to open up conversations with colleagues in allowing for "other" interpretations and conceptualizations of entrepreneurship, engaging them in a dialogue that might spur them on to realizing that they too can resist their own practices.

In Chapter 6, *Conceptual Activism: Entrepreneurship Education as a Philosophical Project*, Christian Garmann Johnsen, Lena Olaison and Bent Meier Sørensen provide us with insightful thoughts on how philosophy can challenge and invite students to rethink and re-enact entrepreneurship. The question they ask is how philosophy can become a productive force in the teaching of entrepreneurship in business schools. Through exploring their own practices and guiding the reader through two didactic approaches they have developed and experimented with, they provide us with a didactic approach tool which they call "conceptual activism". This approach implies deploying philosophical concepts in such a way that it sensitizes students to their own experiences and discourses on entrepreneurship. Christian, Lena and Bent take us on a tour to their classroom experiences where the two approaches are enacted. In one they use art and a mode of juxtaposition to evoke new "images" of entrepreneurship, and in the other the success/failure dialectics are problematized using Kristeva's concept of the abject. From these examples we learn how the teachers' own reflections on philosophy are translated to their interactions with students, who are challenged to unlock alternative viewpoints with regard to key features of entrepreneurship discourses, such as agency, creation, success and failure.

Chapters 5 and 6 together explicitly set out to *move* (understandings of) entrepreneurship, and entrepreneurship education. They do so by experimenting and offering new "thinking tools".

In Part IV we find three chapters that also set out to move students, but with explicit considerations with regard to how students can be challenged and moved out of their "comfort zones", so as to create room for distance and resistance.

In Chapter 7, *Bringing Gender In: The Promise of Critical Feminist Pedagogy*, Sally Jones gives an informed, insightful and detailed illustration of how she challenges, and sometimes provokes, students to reflect upon the gendered entrepreneurship discourse. By introducing entrepreneurship from a feminist theoretical perspective she involves students in making their own (gendered and other) presumptions visible, both to themselves and others. With the two concepts of "stereotype threat" and "stereotype lift" she invites the reader to reflect upon how teachers may reproduce a gendered, ethnocentric, racist and ageist entrepreneurship discourse. Yet, through employing different didactic approaches, she invites herself, together with the students, to not only reflect upon current gendered practices but also to reconsider how to alter those that they have come to find problematic. From Sally we learn that gendered entrepreneurship discourse requires reflection, and that that very reflection is underpinned by a critical awareness that can be used to analyse and become aware of not only gender but also other dysfunctionalities that entrepreneurship discourse may propel. "Bringing gender in" forced her to experiment with didactic approaches, which helped her and her students to challenge mainstream accounts and practices of entrepreneurship, and "beyond".

In Chapter 8, *Entrepreneurship and the Entrepreneurial Self: Creating Alternatives Through Entrepreneurship Education?*, Annika Skoglund and Karin Berglund discuss a critical entrepreneurship course entitled "Entrepreneurship and the Entrepreneurial Self" (designed for master's students). Entrepreneurship is brought into the course in relation to Foucault's notion of "productive power", and to how "freedom" has become linked to a creation of "the social" and "the economic", to (seemingly) open up possibilities for self-creation. Annika and Karin engage their students in critical reflections on political dimensions, human limits, alternative ideals and the collective efforts that are part of entrepreneurial endeavours. They provide the readers with a detailed description of how the course is set up, including the various assignments they have designed to engage the students in critical learning. The course addresses not only the emphasis being placed on the economic sphere in neo-liberal societies but also how this gives rise to "alternative entrepreneurships" in a way that witnesses how an abundance of entrepreneurial selves unfolds. Annika and Karin assert the need to interrogate this emergence of "rejuvenated and upgraded entrepreneurial selves" in a way that unsettles the spread of these alternative forms.

In Chapter 9, *Between Critique and Affirmation: An Interventionist Approach to Entrepreneurship Education*, Bernhard Resch, Patrizia Hoyer and Chris Steyaert also argue that it is not enough to "simply" question the optimistic politics of entrepreneurship education. Rather, this is an interplay between critique and affirmation, enabled by "an interventionist approach". Their interventions aim at disentangling and reassociating time and space, bodies and motions, people and materials, and we constantly add new elements to the equation in what they call "sometimes curious ways" to open up for unusual learning formats which push towards critical reflection as well as experimenting with aesthetic, material, spatial and embodied ways of learning. They offer a description and reflection of a course in which they set out to challenge some of the university's stabilized preconditions, take "critical walks", engage students in creative group performances, and invite them to move and dance. Patrizia, Bernhard and Chris illustrate how their interventionist pedagogy generates *affectual flows* that "may even result in a fumbling reinvention of teaching itself".

The chapters in Part V once again testify to how encouraging students to get out of their comfort zones and start to see and experience things differently takes time, and comes with discomfort, disruption and resistance – on the part of the students as well as the educators. It invites teachers to rethink their practices, and invent new ones. And it invokes the need to have dialogues.

In Chapter 10, *Moving Entrepreneurship*, Karen Verduijn engages students in dialogues on the fluid, ephemeral and indeterminate nature of entrepreneuring. The aim is to stimulate students' curiosity and to move them towards new understandings of what it means to enact entrepreneuring. This is accomplished – based upon process ontology – by introducing students to a film project where their assignment is to produce a film which questions dominant assumptions of the entrepreneur (as a particular person), of entrepreneurship (as a planned and manageable process) and of the result (as a predetermined goal). The approach challenges students' understandings of entrepreneurship and may at times, and with regard to students' previous educational experiences, appear uncomfortable and sometimes even incomprehensible. The approach thus moves students out of their comfort zones and introduces them to a new setting where educational concepts of examination, goals and results need to be reinterpreted. Apart from bringing the reader to the classroom to show in detail how this approach can enrich entrepreneurship education, Karen also addresses the struggles and turmoil it may bring about for the educators, and elaborates on how they form valuable learning experiences that can be brought back into the dialogue with students.

In Chapter 11, *On Vulnerability in Critical Entrepreneurship Education*, Anna Wettermark, André Kårfors, Oskar Lif, Alice Wickström, Sofie Wiessner and Karin Berglund emphasize the need to have mutual learning taking place in our classrooms. The chapter develops thoughts on vulnerabilities and possibilities in teaching entrepreneurship, and includes reflections of students who have taken the course, on which deliberate space is created for the "outing" of vulnerabilities, both the teacher's and the students'. The chapter continues with discussions on the *self*, as explained in Chapter 9. It offers an opportunity to witness how students take up critical notions about the self, in relation to other(s), and in doing so offers an inspiring example of how dialogue can be enacted, and student awareness fostered.

The epilogue, by Ulla Hytti, connects to the various chapters in the book by discussing how critical entrepreneurship education could take the form of resisting the tendencies towards a "McEducation", a tendency in which students are seen as consumers, with the right to have an entrepreneurship education. Ulla's contribution, as well as others in the volume, questions this tendency, and argues that bringing in the "why" may prove a way forward.

Together, the contributions provide us with a platform from which we can start to meet the challenges that entrepreneurship education faces in contemporary society, and a basis from which to continue to bring criticality in the classroom, whether through evoking and/or through moving and/or through challenging and/or through having dialogues with students. With this volume we would like to affirm to other entrepreneurship educators that we no longer have to experiment in isolation but that in sharing our thoughts, concerns and ideas of a critical entrepreneurship education we have a community to learn from and with, which serves to break up our sense of isolation.

References

Achtenhagen, L. & Welter, F. (2011). "Surfing on the ironing board" – The representation of women's entrepreneurship in German newspapers. *Entrepreneurship & Regional Development*, 23(9–10), 763–786.

Al-Dajani, H. & Marlow, S. (2013). Empowerment and entrepreneurship: A theoretical framework. *International Journal of Entrepreneurial Behaviour & Research, 19*, 503–524.

Alvesson, M. & Willmott, H. (1996). *Making sense of management: A critical introduction.* London: SAGE.

Armstrong, P. (2005). *Critique of entrepreneurship: People and policy.* Basingstoke: Palgrave Macmillan.

Ball, S.J. (2003). The teachers' soul and the terrors of performativity. *Journal of Educational Policy, 18*(2), 215–228.

Ball, S.J. & Olmedo, A. (2013). Care of the self, resistance and subjectivity under neoliberal governmentalities. *Critical Studies in Education, 54*(1), 85–96.

Banerjee, S.B. & Tedmanson, D. (2010). Grass burning under our feet: Indigenous enterprise development in a political economy of whiteness. *Management Learning, 41*(2) 147–165.

Barinaga, E. (2016). Activism in business education. In C. Steyaert, T. Beyes & M. Parker (Eds), *The Routledge companion to reinventing management education* (pp. 298–311). Abingdon and New York, NY: Routledge.

Barry, A. & Osborne, T. (1996). *Foucault and political reason: Liberalism, neoliberalism, and rationalities of government.* Oxford: University of Chicago Press.

Beaver. G. & Jennings, P. (2005). Competitive advantage and entrepreneurial power: the dark side of entrepreneurship. *Journal of Small Business and Enterprise Development, 12*, 9–23.

Bendix Petersen, E. & O'Flynn, G. (2007). Neoliberal technologies of subject formation: A case study of the Duke of Edinburgh's Award scheme. *Critical Studies in Education, 48*(2), 197–211.

Berglund, K. (2013). Fighting against all odds: Entrepreneurship education as employability training. *Ephemera: Theory and Politics in Organization, 13*, 717–735.

Berglund K. & Gaddefors J. (2010). Entrepreneurship requires resistance to be mobilized. In F. Bill, B. Bjerke & A.W. Johansson (Eds), *(De)mobilizing entrepreneurship – exploring entrepreneurial thinking and action* (pp. 140–157). Cheltenham: Edward Elgar.

Berglund, K., Johannisson, B. & Schwartz, B. (Eds) (2012). *Societal entrepreneurship: Positioning, penetrating, promoting.* Cheltenham: Edward Elgar.

Berglund, K., Lindgren, M. & Packendorff, J. (2017). Responsibilising the next generation: Fostering the enterprising self through de-mobilising gender. *Organization*, 1350508417697379.

Berglund, K. & Skoglund, A. (2016). Social entrepreneurship: To defend society from itself. In A. Fayolle & P. Riot (Eds), *Rethinking entrepreneurship: Debating research orientations* (pp. 57–77). New York, NY: Routledge.

Beyes, T. & Michels, C. (2011). The production of educational space: Heterotopia and the business university. *Management Learning, 42*, 521–536.

Bill, F., Jansson, A. & Olaison, L. (2010). The spectacle of entrepreneurship: A duality of flamboyance and activity. In F. Bill, A. Jansson & L. Olaison (Eds), *(De)mobilizing the entrepreneurial discourse: Exploring entrepreneurial thinking and action* (pp. 158–175). Cheltenham: Edward Elgar.

Bragg, S. (2007). "Student voice" and governmentality: The production of enterprising subjects. *Discourse: Studies in the Cultural Politics of Education, 28*(3), 343–358.

Brown, W. (2003). Neo-liberalism and the end of liberal democracy. *Theory and Event, 7*(1).

Calas, M.B., Smircich, L. & Bourne, K.A. (2009). Extending the boundaries: Reframing "Entrepreneurship as Social Change" through feminist perspectives. *Academy of Management Review*, 34(3), 552–569.

Choo, K.L. (2007a). Can critical management education be critical in a formal higher educational setting? *Teaching in Higher Education, 12*(4), 485–497.

Choo, K.L. (2007b). The implications of introducing critical management education to Chinese students studying in UK business schools: Some empirical evidence. *Journal of Further and Higher Education, 31*(2), 145–158.

Connell, R. (2013). The neoliberal cascade and education: An essay on the market agenda and its consequences. *Critical Studies in Education, 54*(2), 99–112.

Costa, A.S.M. & Saraiva, L.A.S. (2012). Hegemonic discourses on entrepreneurship as an ideological mechanism for the reproduction of capital. *Organization, 19*(5), 587–614.

Costea, B., Amiridis, K. & Crump, N. (2012). Graduate employability and the principle of potentiality: An aspect of the ethics of HRM. *Journal of Business Ethics, 111*, 25–36.

Currie, G., Knights, D. & Starkey, K. (2010). Introduction: A post-crisis critical reflection on business schools. *British Journal of Management, 21*, 1–5.

Dahlstedt, M. & Hertzberg, F. (2014). In the name of liberation. Notes on governmentality, entrepreneurial education, and life-long learning. *European Education, 45*(4).

Dahlstedt, M. & Tesfahuney, M. (2011). Speculative pedagogy: Education, entrepreneurialism and the politics of inclusion in contemporary Sweden. *Journal for Critical Education Policy Studies, 8*(2), 249–274.

Dahlstedt, M. & Fejes, A. (2017). Shaping entrepreneurial citizens: A genealogy of entrepreneurship education in Sweden. *Critical Studies in Education*, 1–15. doi: 10.1080/17508487.2017.1303525.

Dey, P. & Steyaert, C. (2007). The troubadours of knowledge: passion and invention in management education. *Organization, 14*(3), 437–461.

Down, B. (2009). Schooling, productivity and the enterprising self: Beyond market values. *Critical Studies in Education, 50*(1), 51–64.

Essers, C. & Benschop, Y. (2009). Muslim businesswomen doing boundary work: The negotiation of Islam, gender and ethnicity within entrepreneurial contexts. *Human Relations*, 62(3), 403–423.

Essers, C. & Tedmanson, D. (2014). Upsetting "others' in the Netherlands: Narratives of Muslim Turkish migrant businesswomen at the crossroads of ethnicity, gender and religion. *Gender, Work & Organization, 21*, 353–367.

Essers, C., Dey, P., Tedmanson, D. & Verduijn, K. (Eds) (2017). *Critical perspectives on entrepreneurship. Challenging dominant discourses*. New York, NY: Routledge.

Fayolle, A. (2013). Personal views on the future of entrepreneurship education. *Entrepreneurship & Regional Development, 25*(7–8), 692–701.

Fletcher, D.E. (2006). Entrepreneurial processes and the social construction of opportunity. *Entrepreneurship & Regional Development 18*, 421–440.

Fletcher, D.E. & Selden, P. (2015). A critical review of critical perspectives in entrepreneurship research. In H. Landström, A. Parhankangas, A. Fayolle & P. Riot (Eds), *Challenging the assumptions and accepted research practices in entrepreneurship research*. London: Routledge.

Foucault, M. (1978/1991). Governmentality. In G. Burchell, C. Gordon & P. Miller (Eds), *The Foucault effect – studies in governmentality with two lectures and interviews with Michel Foucault* (pp. 87–104). Chicago, IL: University of Chicago Press.

du Gay, P. (2004). Against "enterprise" (but not against "enterprise", for that would make no sense). *Organization, 11,* 37–57.

Gibb, A. (2002). In pursuit of a new "enterprise" and "entrepreneurship" paradigm for learning: creative destruction, new values, new ways of doing things and new combinations of knowledge. *International Journal of Management Reviews, 4*(3), 233–269.

Harvey, D. (2005). *A brief history of neoliberalism.* Oxford: Oxford University Press.

Henry, C., Hill, F. & Leitch, C.M. (2003). *Entrepreneurship education and training.* Aldershot: Ashgate.

Hjorth, D. (2011). On provocation, education and entrepreneurship. *Entrepreneurship & Regional Development, 23,* 49–63.

Hjorth, D. (2013). Absolutely fabulous! Fabulation and organization-creation in processes of becoming-entrepreneur. *Society and Business Review, 8,* 205–224.

Hjorth, D. & Johannisson, B. (2007). Learning as an entrepreneurial process. In A. Fayolle (Ed.), *Handbook of research in entrepreneurship education, volume 1* (pp. 46–66). Cheltenham: Edward Elgar.

Hjorth, D. & Steyaert, C. (Eds). (2010). *The politics and aesthetics of entrepreneurship: A fourth movements in entrepreneurship book.* Cheltenham: Edward Elgar.

Hjorth, D., Jones, C. & Gartner, W.B. (2008). Recontextualising/recreating entrepreneurship. *Scandinavian Journal of Management, 24*(2), 81–84.

Holmgren, C. (2012). Translating entrepreneurship into the education setting: A case of societal entrepreneurship. In K. Berglund, B. Johannisson and B. Schwartz (Eds) *Societal entrepreneurship: Positioning, penetrating, promoting* (pp. 214–327). Cheltenham: Edward Elgar.

Jack, S., Drakopoulou Dodd, S. & Anderson, A.R. (2008). Change and the development of entrepreneurial networks over time: A processual perspective. *Entrepreneurship & Regional Development, 20*(2), 125–159.

Jamieson, I. (1984). Schools and enterprise. In A.G. Watts & P. Moran (Eds), *Education for enterprise* (pp. 19–27). Cambridge: CRAC, Ballinger.

Jones, C. & Spicer, A. (2005). The sublime object of entrepreneurship. *Organization, 12*(2), 223–246.

Jones, C. & Spicer, A. (2009). *Unmasking the entrepreneur.* London: Edward Elgar.

Kirby, D. (2007). Changing the entrepreneurship education paradigm. In A. Fayolle (Ed.), *Handbook of research in entrepreneurship education* (pp. 21–45).

Korsgaard, S. (2011). Entrepreneurship as translation: Understanding entrepreneurial opportunities through actor-network theory. *Entrepreneurship & Regional Development, 23*(7–8), 661–680.

Kuratko, D.F. (2005). The emergence of entrepreneurship education: Development, trends, and challenges. *Entrepreneurship Theory and Practice, 29*(5), 577–598.

Leffler, E. (2009). The many faces of entrepreneurship: A discursive battle for the school arena. *European Educational Research Journal, 8*(1), 104–116.

Lemke, T. (2001). "The birth of bio-politics": Michel Foucault's lecture at the Collège de France on neo-liberal governmentality. *Economy and Society, 30*(2), 190–207.

Marsh, D. & Thomas, P. (2017). The governance of welfare and the expropriation of the common: Polish tales of entrepreneurship. In C. Essers, P. Dey, D. Tedmanson & K. Verduijn (Eds), *Critical perspectives on entrepreneurship. Challenging dominant discourses.* New York, NY: Routledge.

Nabi, G., Linan, F., Fayolle, A., Krueger, N. & Walmsley, A. (2017). The impact of entrepreneurship education in higher education: A systematic review and research agenda. *Academy of Management Learning & Education, 16*(2), 277–299.

Nayak, A. & Chia, R. (2011). Thinking becoming. Process philosophy and organization studies. *Philosophy and Organization Theory Research in the Sociology of Organizations, 32*, 281–309.

Nodoushani, O. & Nodoushani, P.A. (1999). A deconstructionist theory of entrepreneurship: A note. *American Business Review, 17*(1), 45–49.

O'Connor, A. (2013). A conceptual framework for entrepreneurship education policy: Meeting government and economic purposes. *Journal of Business Venturing, 28*(4), 546–563.

Ogbor, J.O. (2000). Mythicizing and reification in entrepreneurial discourse: ideology-critique of entrepreneurial studies. *Journal of Management Studies, 37*, 606–635.

Olaison, L. & Sorensen, B. (2014). The abject of entrepreneurship: Failure, fiasco, fraud. *International Journal of Entrepreneurial Behavior & Research, 20*, 193–211.

Ozkazanc-Pan, B. (2014). Postcolonial feminist analysis of high-technology entrepreneuring. *International Journal of Entrepreneurial Behaviour & Research, 20*(2), 155–172.

Peters, M. (2001). Education, enterprise culture and the entrepreneurial self: A Foucauldian perspective. *Journal of Educational Enquiry, 2*(2), 58–71.

Pettersson, K., Ahl, H., Berglund, K. & Tillmar, M. (2017). In the name of women? Feminist readings of policies for women's entrepreneurship in Scandinavia. *Scandinavian Journal of Management, 33*, 50–63.

Pittaway, L. & Cope, J. (2007). Entrepreneurship education: A systematic review of the evidence. *International Small Business Journal, 25*(5), 479–510.

Rehn, A., Brännback, M., Carsrud, A. & Lindahl, M. (2013). Challenging the myths of entrepreneurship? *Entrepreneurship & Regional Development, 25*(7–8), 543–551.

Scharff, C. (2016). The psychic life of neoliberalism: Mapping the contours of entrepreneurial subjectivity. *Theory, Culture & Society, 33*(6), 107–122.

Spicer, A. (2012). Critical theories of entrepreneurship. In K. Mole & M. Ram (Eds), *Perspectives on entrepreneurship. A critical approach*. London: Palgrave.

Steyaert, C. & Hjorth, D. (Eds). (2003). *New movements in entrepreneurship, volume 1*. Cheltenham: Edward Elgar.

Steyaert, C. & Hjorth, D. (Eds). (2006). *Entrepreneurship as Social Change (Vol. 3)*. Cheltenham: Edward Elgar.

Taatila, V.P. (2010). Learning entrepreneurship in higher education. *Education+ Training, 52*(1), 48–61.

Tedmanson, D., Verduijn, K., Essers, C. & Gartner, W.B. (2012). Critical perspectives of entrepreneurship research. *Organization, 19*(5), 531–541.

Thrane, C., Blenker, P., Korsgaard, S. & Neergaard, H. (2016). The promise of entrepreneurship education: Reconceptualizing the individual–opportunity nexus as a conceptual framework for entrepreneurship education. *International Small Business Journal, 34*(7), 905–924.

Verduijn, K., Dey, P., Tedmanson, D. & Essers, C. (2014). Emancipation and/or oppression? Conceptualizing dimensions of criticality in entrepreneurship studies. *International Journal of Entrepreneurial Behavior & Research, 20*(2), 98–107.

Verduijn, K. (2015). Entrepreneuring and process. A Lefebvrian perspective. *International Small Business Journal, 33*(6), 638–648.

Vrasti, W. (2009). How to use affective competencies in late capitalism. In *British International Studies Association (BISA) Annual Conference, University of Leicester* (pp. 14–16).

Ziegler, R. (2011). *An introduction to social entrepreneurship.* Cheltenham and Northampton, MA: Edward Elgar.

1 Education or exploitation?

Reflecting on the entrepreneurial university and the role of the entrepreneurship educator

Richard Tunstall

Act 1, Scene 1: The university disrupted

It is a bright summer morning on campus. Semester has ended and conference season has begun. This conference is no different to any other. There is a registration list, name badges are handed out, old relationships rekindled over questionable coffee and delegate lists scanned for new people to meet.

We sit comfortably, dressed in suits in an air-conditioned lecture theatre within a glinting new glass and steel campus building, dedicated to a historical local luminary who inspired a national social movement. The topic today is entrepreneurship and innovation, and I attend as a researcher, but academic delegates are few in number. We sit alongside small business owners, university spin-off officers and innovation managers of major multinational corporations listening to a keynote from a government minister, who explains the importance of the conference to the national agenda for university–business collaboration. So far, so normal, yet not a traditional university event by any means.

Suddenly, there is an ear-piercing shriek as the lecture theatre doors burst open. The minister stops mid-speech and backs away as six students walk across the stage unfurling a large banner which poses one question to us:

Education or exploitation?

At first delegates seem shocked by the stage invasion and air horns, but become relaxed and good humoured as all the signs of a student protest in progress become clear.

STUDENT PROTESTOR [Shouting from the lectern]: We are here today to protest against companies involved in some of the most horrendous human rights abuses! Exploitation of the planet and animals! And government ministers who are colluding with big business! This is not what elected representatives are supposed to do! There are some of the most horrible companies around today! There was a terrorist attack yesterday! Nine people killed! Companies here are killing far, far more people than that every single day!

Making cluster bombs! Making bombs and tanks! And guns! That are used to oppress people! Used to destroy the planet!

SMALL BUSINESS OWNER DELEGATE: Why are you here?

STUDENT PROTESTOR: To protest against multinationals

SMALL BUSINESS OWNER DELEGATE: So where did that Goretex coat come from that you're wearing? And those Nike shoes?

STUDENT PROTESTOR: I got them from a charity shop

ALL DELEGATES: [*Laughter*]

SMALL BUSINESS OWNER DELEGATE: Look. We are having a conference. You've made your point now. Can't you leave and let us get on with it?

STUDENT PROTESTOR: We are exercising our right to protest. [*Begins shouting again*] We are here to protest! Multinationals are killing the planet … (etc.).

The shouting continues. Uniformed university security appear and attempt to escort the protestors out. One female student drops to the floor and is picked up, dragged screaming. The doors close. The government minister regains his place at the podium.

GOVERNMENT MINISTER: Well at least when I was involved in student protests I took the time to get my facts right. I'd be a lot more worried about nano-technology if I were them, it is far more potentially harmful than GM crops.

ALL DELEGATES: [*Laughter*]

Despite continued sirens outside, the conference continues. The noise stops and the protests are forgotten about as the formalities of the conference return. We look forward to our glass of wine at the vice-chancellors welcome reception.

Notwithstanding the convivial nature of the occasion, the discussion at the reception return to the conference invasion. The idea of a student protest reso-nates with some delegates as part and parcel of being on a university campus, yet for others it is a frustration that the serious work of the university–business conference has been disrupted in this way.

During the conference, I find myself torn between my role as researcher of entrepreneurship on the one hand and my role as entrepreneurship educator on the other. My understanding of the positive intention and importance of the con-ference, versus my sympathy with the student's request to be allowed to speak and engage, created a sense of personal dissonance. This was particularly sym-bolized by that student banner:

Education or exploitation?

What is the purpose of the university? To educate and disseminate knowledge for the sake of knowledge, with no prior assumptions of the consequences or relevance to the outside world? To generate research impact through innovation and ensure the industry potential of students, so as to maximize competitiveness in the global economy (Down, 2009; Dahlstedt & Hertzberg, 2012)? The protestors' question directly engages with these alternative perspectives of the purpose of the university, traditional versus entrepreneurial. It was through the organized protestors invasion of the formal event that these alternatives collided. Through their direct action protesting the presence of commercial interests on campus and their banner, the protestors highlighted their argument that the ideals of traditional university values were under threat. For my part, as a participant in the conference engaged in both entrepreneurship research and education, the protest illustrated the apparent contradictions inherent in entrepreneurship education at universities. The protest therefore provides us with the occasion to look critically at alternative ideals of the university and the extent to which these ideals compete, and further consider the implications and tensions this creates for entrepreneurship education. The conference was a place where the legitimacy of market-related activity in universities was questioned. As an entrepreneurship educator and researcher, this also raised questions about my own practice(s). On the one hand my role as an academic is to critically examine entrepreneurship and its consequences, engaging students in this as part of their academic studies within the university. On the other hand, my legitimacy in teaching entrepreneurship is tested on the basis of my prior business experience, where an emphasis on practical knowledge and market-relevance is expected and where questions are asked about whether it is academics or business owners who are best placed to teach these topics. Business people at alumni events and parents at university open days may perceive entrepreneurship education as a primarily practical exercise requiring business practitioners to lead it, and therefore ask, as Farny, Frederiksen, Hannibal and Jones's (2016) students ask of academic faculty, "How can you then lecture on the topic?" (p. 519).

Act 1, Scene 2: The traditional values of universities

Before the conference took place, protest websites presented it as a meeting place for unethical multinational corporations. The university was portrayed as seeking to make deals with these actors by exploiting knowledge in a way which undermined the traditional purposes and activities of the university.

In the scope of this argument, the emphasis on entrepreneurship education becomes *education about entrepreneurial exploitation*, where entrepreneurship is a subject to be studied dispassionately as a remote object, as one of the canon of topics which a business school student reads during the liberal engagement of the student in their overall intellectual development. In this sense, I might position myself as a traditional university academic, teaching a speciality subject. Here I am asked to provide my course as part of a management student's curriculum within management studies and it is vital that the subject can be considered appropriate to be taught as an academic field.

Entrepreneurship is relatively new as a field of study and much academic labour has sought to establish entrepreneurship as a disciplinary science which can hold its own within business and management studies (Wiklund, Davidsson, Audretsch & Karlsson, 2011; Zahra & Wright, 2011). Yet this is not uncontentious, as the push towards academic legitimacy has had an institutionalizing effect (Aldrich, 2012) tending to privilege normative science where individual entrepreneurs as economic actors are emphasized over perspectives and paradigms which might provide alternative intellectual tools to study the subject (Pittaway & Tunstall, 2016). This can cause challenges for educators when teaching entrepreneurship in a traditional academic mode, where the demands of the disciplinary science are countered by students' demands that certain topics or famous entrepreneurs are considered and that industry and employability relevance be included in the classroom (Farny *et al.*, 2016). Answering these challenges requires not only a change in pedagogy but a change in priorities for the university towards those of the entrepreneurial university.

Act 1, Scene 3: Supporting the entrepreneurial university

The disrupted conference was officially instigated to promote corporate venturing, entrepreneurship, innovation and collaboration between universities and industry. Delegates included small firms, university technology commercialization officers and members of the innovation units of multinational firms. By hosting the conference, the university was presented as entrepreneurial, and therefore an equal partner in economic activity with industry and government.

> The Conference was certainly a valuable experience for policy makers, practitioners and researchers as there was a rich and varied source of entrepreneurial experiences and above all the willingness to share and exchange views and ideas.
>
> (University events website)

The concept of the entrepreneurial university originates in the perspective that universities are remote and disengaged from the needs of society. By becoming entrepreneurial, universities are seen to engage by assuming their role as contributors to the knowledge economy in a "triple helix" of university, government and industry (Etzkowitz, 2003; Etzkowitz & Leydesdorff, 2000) through intellectual property creation and subsequent development (Perkmann & Walsh, 2007). As a key element of the triple helix, the entrepreneurial university may be seen a key creator of new knowledge, through patents, licences and spin-off firms developed on the basis of faculty research (Etzkowitz, 2003; Etzkowitz & Leydesdorff, 2000; Perkmann & Walsh, 2007). This approach acts as a key element of government regional development policy (Etzkowitz & Leydesdorff, 2000) as well as an important aspect of industry open innovation strategies, through which commercial businesses seek ideas external to their firm to develop new innovations (Chesbrough, 2006).

The conference was in this sense an embodiment of entrepreneurial university activity and attracted significant attention. In addition to corporate multinationals and government ministers, the university vice-chancellor appeared later that evening at a welcome reception to speak on the importance of university–

business collaboration and the role of the university in providing innovations from research, employability from education and the importance of cultivating campus entrepreneurship. Through discussions and presentations, the event was positioned as an example of the triple helix in action.

> The responsiveness of the university sector to innovation and venturing was exemplified by the work of [the] university, portrayed by the Vice Chancellor.
>
> (University events website)

This indicates that, beyond specific economic activities such as IP innovation and spin-out venturing, there was something within the unique nature and purpose of this specific university which made it a particularly valuable partner. Similarly, the concept of the entrepreneurial university is often seen to focus attention on openness to change in otherwise bureaucratic university processes and towards the exploitation of opportunities for innovation across the university (Gibb & Hannon, 2006).

In our dialectic of "education or exploitation?" the entrepreneurial university emphasis on entrepreneurship education becomes "education for entrepreneurial exploitation", where education acts as a mechanism to exploit students' capacity for innovation as an internal knowledge resource, through which they become entrepreneurs (Dahlstedt & Hertzberg, 2012), and to exploratively generate new partnerships with commercial firms. Here my role as an entrepreneurship educator is no longer to be an expert on the academic discipline of entrepreneurship; indeed, from this perspective disciplinary knowledge is viewed as no longer privileged but an entrepreneurial resource which may be obtained anywhere inside or outside the university. Instead my role is to act as the guide on the side, not the sage on the stage (Löbler, 2006), coaching and facilitating student learning which is self-deterministic, abandoning traditional assessment by examination or research dissertation and instead helping students to fine-tune their business plans and pitches to enable them to launch start-ups while further assisting them in shaping their identity as future entrepreneurs to carve out their niches in the global economy (Smyth, 1999; Löbler, 2006; Farny *et al.*, 2016). This alternative approach to university teaching is often presented as a modernizing innovation for university education. This innovation is argued to be essential to the relevance of a university to the modern economy and to student expectations of their experience as consumers of knowledge in a crowded space. Here universities must compete against other providers for their market share and academic educators must shift their mode of operation from knowledge creators and disseminators to professionalized service providers (Olssen & Peters, 2005).

Act 1, Scene 4: Debating the entrepreneurial university

While the perspectives presented through the official conference programme and counter-conference protest websites on the role and legitimacy of the entrepreneurial university competed in their outlook on the consequences of change, they both represented the entrepreneurial university as an approach which engendered movement from traditional university activities to a more industry-focused approach. While there was a shared acknowledgement of this change, the two differed in how they presented the underlying purposes, intentions and potential outcomes of this change.

The protestors directly drew on the idea of a university as an institution for the advancement or betterment of knowledge to develop their argument that the shift in modes for the university was an erosion of pure academic principles and values. Here they proposed that this erosion was caused by the entrepreneurial university, through the pursuit of business and market investment activity and the interference of government and corporations, leading to a creeping spread of managerialist thinking within universities:

> As universities are forced to rely on external funding to a greater and greater extent, the face of the Academy is changing. Increasingly decisions are made by faceless bureaucrats, and traditional values such as "academic freedom" are eroded by business plans and links with multi-national corporations, who expect returns for their investments.
>
> (Protest website)

In a wider context, the event was described as a significant indication of the wider marketization of universities, deliberately engendered and sustained by powerful multinationals and national government, with detrimental impacts on subjugated universities and increasing attempts to subvert faculty and students so that they might become more entrepreneurial and market-focused. This was noted by one mainstream national newspaper commentator:

> Central to [the national government's research and innovation policy] document was that universities must work much closer with business and indeed must behave more like business. The plan was bursting with policies and funding programmes to expand not only corporate sponsorship of research, but also entrepreneurial activities amongst academics themselves. The corporate venture conference which was the target of the protest at [the university] was one manifestation of this policy.
>
> (National newspaper)

The proponents of the conference conversely presented the changing mission of the university as a necessary, positive development. This modernizing perspective exhibited similar concerns to protestors in bemoaning bureaucracy in universities, but argued that this is endemic in the very same traditional institutions and values that the protestors sought to protect. The proposed solution was to instead seek to create new opportunities for generating innovation across the university by disrupting the existing order (Gibb & Hannon, 2006) and offer empowerment to previously restrained faculty by allowing them to behave entre-preneurially (Etzkowitz, 2003; Perkmann & Walsh, 2007). Conversely, this modernizing tone has been argued to act as a strategic ploy by university leaders to influence external and internal stakeholders (Mautner, 2005) and du Gay (1996) notes that, in an organizational context, entrepreneurialism is used as a way to gain power over employees by giving them the impression they have the creative capacity to create change, yet limiting this within the strategic aims of the organization.

The debates illustrate two different conceptions of the purpose of a univer-sity, the goals of research and education and the expectations which should be placed upon university faculty and students. At the same time, the arguments illustrated a related set of concerns regarding avoiding bureaucracy within universities, engendering academic freedom and developing pedagogies which enable students, albeit these were framed from entirely different perspectives on the purpose of these activities. The conference and counter-protest therefore provide the opportunity to compare these arguments as they were directly employed by university faculty and students in their everyday practice. But the conference was just the beginning.

Act 2, Scene 1: University values on trial

After university security took the protestors out of the building, allowing the conference to proceed, the protestors continued their protest outside. This was a surprise to delegates when we took part in our conference break, but when police arrived the protestors dispersed. The excitement over, the conference continued and we looked forward to the vice-chancellors wine reception.

After the conference, delegates exchanged emails to follow up on their earlier conversations at the conference. Through this email discussion it became appar-ent that this had not been the end of the story for the protestors at all. The univer-sity had pressed charges against their students. The case went to trial and was recorded verbatim by an underground university counter-magazine. Further coverage was provided by national newspapers, student associations and left-wing organizations:

> Six students … could be jailed for staging a protest on university premises against "the commercialisation of university research".
>
> (National Newspaper)

> [Charged with] "Momentarily disrupting a conference"? In my day students would have been disrupting things for a lot longer, where's their staying power?
>
> (Online cartoon sketch)

The official university communication channels and official conference media provided no coverage of these events.

During the trial and subsequent retrial at a regional court the student protestors and a range of university staff were called to speak. During these trials the prosecutor put forward the case that the protest had been an illegal trespass of a private event. The defendants countered that as the protestors were students their presence was legal. As these arguments were presented, the protestors themselves sought to use the trial as an opportunity to continue their argument by putting the entrepreneurial university on trial. Two key arguments emerged about the entrepreneurial university: the legitimacy of commercially related activities and the role of students in universities.

Act 2, Scene 2: What is legitimate in a university?

The student protestors, defending, particularly focused their arguments on the legitimacy of their protest and further proclaimed the illegitimacy of entrepreneurship and research commercialization at universities. They suggested that education and exploitation were mutually exclusive, and that the encroachment of enterprise meant that academic integrity was under threat:

> Because of his own research [a post-graduate student protestor] had been concerned to hear about the conference, because of its implications for the independence and freedom of research. Such concerns were widely held amongst his colleagues and other scientists.
>
> [A student protestor] was "concerned about the impact of the privatisation of the university on the objectivity and direction of academic research."
>
> (University counter-magazine)

A university faculty member, speaking in the protestor's defence, noted his surprise that the students had been arrested, yet also expressed sympathy for the legitimacy of the conference:

> The witness [university professor] was then asked about his statement that the commercial involvement in university research was "fraught" and if he also thought that the use of university premises for commercial purposes, especially common outside term time, was also controversial. He replied, "Yes, but less so. Universities have to make money." He said this issue was less significant than issues of academic integrity.
>
> (University counter-magazine)

In addition to students and academic faculty, a number of university support staff were cross-examined. One member of staff, when asked about university commercialization, suggested that this was completely legitimate but acknowledged the right to protest:

Asked about the appropriateness of corporate links to the university, [the head of security] replied, "We live in a capitalist society", adding that he respected the opposition view being voiced by the [protestors], and would have supported a peaceful demonstration.

(University counter-magazine)

These arguments illustrate diverse perspectives on the legitimacy of commercial activity at universities among those involved. Where commercial activity was presented as illegitimate, the primacy of academic integrity and independence above contractual profit-seeking activities were used as a discursive vehicle to challenge the purpose of the conference. Where the conference was defended, this was on the basis of the primacy of profit-seeking activity as the expected norm and the hierarchy of university management governance, along with the expectation of individuals to act according to their contractual roles as employees within a corporate organizational system. Each sought to justify their behaviour as ensuring that the obligations of the university were fulfilled to those it served. In this sense the conference, student protest and trials illustrate the different perspectives and frequently emotive debates about the underlying purpose of the entrepreneurial university and universities as a whole (Mautner, 2005; Gibb & Hannon, 2006; Perkmann & Walsh, 2007; Barnett, 2011; Collini, 2012).

The differences in perspective on the university as a system, with their own internal consistencies, illustrates how the arguments employed were based on different discourses inhibiting incompatible arguments. For proponents of the liberal university the university was an idea, part of a noble tradition following Humboldt (1810) and Newman (1852) of free speech and independent thought, unfettered by base economic concerns. The protestors diverged from this traditional understanding by emphasizing freedom of speech for students, which has been argued to be related to, but not the same as academic freedom (Connolly, 2000), instead emphasizing how the local historical context of the university legitimized their actions.

For the proponents of the entrepreneurial university, while the conference aims portrayed the university as an entrepreneurial university integral to an eco-system of regional economic and industrial development (Etzkowitz, 2003), the participants in the conference and the university's legal defence team went further by framing it as a professional organization which competitively offered services into the market, thus positioning it as an entrepreneurial organization seeking to compete (Miller, 1983; Covin & Slevin, 1991) where opportunities are sought and exploited (Gibb & Hannon, 2006), justified by wider acceptance of capitalism as a desirable social good (Berglund, 2013). The trial illustrated that, to some extent, the concept of an entrepreneurial university, as an instrument of economic development through innovation, education and knowledge services, is directly aligned with neo-liberal market connotations. As the head of security put it, "we live in a capitalist society".

Act 2, Scene 3: The role of students in the university

It was noted during the trial and the subsequent wider media debate that this particular university had a history of student activism in the 1960s, of which many associated with the university were proud, including campus-based protests and blockades. This was referred to specifically within the trials as an activity that today, while not necessarily approved of, was at least viewed with respect as part of a legitimate student right to engage in critical debate and open access on campus as a member of the university:

> Defence Lawyer: "This was an attack on the culture of openness and public space which traditionally prevailed in universities and as [a university manager] had said, such events were common in universities (and elsewhere) 20/30 years ago."
>
> [A student protestor] said he hadn't been aware that delegates were paying to be there, but that would have made no difference to his view that he had a right to protest inside the conference. It was a conference held at a university in a public building with a government minister present. Normally protests at the university by students are tolerated, and "people don't over-react."
>
> (University counter-magazine)

In these arguments, the point was made that the traditional values of the university around research and education extended to the right for freedom of speech and open dialogue. These values were proposed to have primacy not only in interactions between members of the university but also in the use of material space on campus. It was noted by the defendants that the building in which the conference took place was named after a local founder of a national social movement known for activism, philanthropy and concern for social responsibility. Consistent with their framing of the role of a university, they emphasized how the building's name was a material expression of the values of the liberal university. From this perspective they positioned the role of students as free thinkers and their rights to engage in dialogue and protest and to move freely across buildings as members of the community who could critically engage in any context with debates and arguments.

Yet, in direct response to the defence lawyer's reference to open-access rights, the prosecution lawyer firmly portrayed the university as a contractually defined entity, which may give or deny licence to students and commercial users as it wished:

> He stated that [the university] had complied with its code of practice on the day of the corporate venturing event. [The lawyer] stated that the demonstrators were trespassers within the terms of the law on aggravated trespass. Although they had a license to be on university premises, they exceeded the terms of the license by protesting in a way that interfered with the rights of the delegates.
>
> (University counter-magazine)

These arguments firmly positioned the university as a business, relating back to wider rhetorical framing of the university as an entrepreneurial undertaking which seeks to generate competitive commercial value. In this context, the student's role was as a consumer who is provided education services and therefore has rights which are limited to the terms indicated by the university in the provision of that service.

These alternative explanations of the role and rights of students point at differences between the values of the university, with a liberal philosophy focused on the development of intellectuals who engage in the betterment of society, or a neo-liberal philosophy whereby students act as customers who engage in a contract for the use of services as part of an overarching market system where financial return on investment is prioritised.

Act 3, Scene 1: Rethinking entrepreneurship education: the yes, the no and the becoming

At the trial and subsequent retrial of the protestors, the prosecution succeeded in arguing that the legal licence of the university to host commercial conferences superseded the moral arguments of open access to all campus buildings from the defendants, and the final judgement of the court was that the student defendants be given suspended sentences, which were extended at the retrial. Through this legal verdict, the argument for the legitimacy of profit-seeking activity in the corporate entrepreneurial university was confirmed. Yet, while this was the final verdict of the court, this was not the final word in the media articles which followed, where one of the protestors commented on the verdict:

> Student Protestor (in local newspaper interview): "We remain proud of what we did and we still believe that the moral victory is ours. As far as we and our supporters are concerned, it has been the university's ethics that were and are on trial, and again and again they are being found guilty."

Despite the conclusion of the trial and final verdicts, the contrasting discourses remained intact and intractable. It is worth then considering how these discourses connect to the literature on entrepreneurship education.

Entrepreneurship education literature tends to put forward a view of entrepreneurship as an aspirational good which should be promoted across all educational levels and within all schools and faculties in universities (Farny *et al.*, 2016), this "Yes"[1] approach proposes that entrepreneurship education's primary purpose is to encourage students to learn to behave as entrepreneurs and launch start-up businesses for personal gain (Hannon, 2005). Conversely, views of critical entrepreneurship education acknowledge and often systematically investigate the role of power, meaning and legitimacy in the entrepreneurial university and entrepreneurship education and what this means for students and educators (Fournier, 1998; Olssen & Peters, 2005; Bragg, 2007; Connell, 2013). Despite this, there is a tendency to set up the entrepreneurial university as a definable set of assumptions which are dominant and enforced by institutions and government, with the only solution being disobedience or protest to seek to preserve liberal ideals. This "No"[1] approach however ignores investigation into the specific systems and processes which sustain the entrepreneurial university and the ways in which alternatives could be organized. It further ignores local context and seeks to generalize about the pervasiveness of capitalism and its effects as an entirely negative force. The "No" is valid, but also self-perpetuates by acting as an outsider to the mainstream, positioning critical entrepreneurship education as a periphery activity, which is provided to a special class of the disaffected and marginalized (Hannon, 2005). In perpetuating "Yes" and "No" arguments, both sets of assumptions about entrepreneurship education serve to support and strengthen the internal consistency of their arguments but do not seek to engage with alternative conceptions of universities, students, education and entrepreneurship and how these systems might look when applied to entrepreneurship education. It does not seek the engage with the "becoming"[1] and what might be. As identified through this case, this requires us to take our analysis of entrepreneurship education beyond pedagogy to consider the overarching purposes of entrepreneurship education, its formulation and practice in the lived experience of those who participate and the interests of those would seek to develop it.

Postscript: the becoming

The conference, protest and trials illustrated the importance of understanding how the entrepreneurial university is understood and enacted. Universities are different, and entrepreneurship within universities, including entrepreneurship education, is not neutral. The differences expressed illustrate alternative ways of framing the purpose and practice of education and the role of those involved. The trial illustrates that in the case of the specific university where the conference and protest took place, it was not possible to identify one objective rationalization of the universities' purpose, instead multiple explanations, values and interpretations existed and collided at the conference and subsequent trials. Similarly, Jain, George and Maltarich (2009) found that university scientists' engagement in technology transfer activities were required to assume a commercial role identity, but that they attempted to assimilate this into a hybrid role by working to simultaneously maintain their academic personas. While Heinonen and Hytti (2010) indicate that not all students will want to engage in one single form of entrepreneurship education and Hannon (2005) notes how alternative aims and purposes may drive different forms of entrepreneurship education, the trials illustrated that student expectations go further than simple topic selection and personal career goal motivation, to deeper concerns about the purpose of higher education, the role of students on campus and the different valuing of university provision.

While a key element of debate in the student protest was the legitimacy of academic research commercialization activities, it also engendered a different form of university entrepreneurship. Once the protest and the university's decision to press charges were made public, a number of protest and mainstream media websites provided commentary on the event and the subsequent trials. Among these, an underground internal university online magazine was launched by university faculty members in response to the prosecution of the students by university management, one that set out to provide a different voice for the university staff than the one provided by those who instigated pressing charges on behalf of the university. This initially set out to show the discontent by faculty for the student protestor's arrest as well as a general discontent with university management, which subsequently became the focus of the developing magazine:

> The last few months have been interesting ones for many of us in the University community. It will have escaped the notice of few that certain events have given rise to remarkable levels of distrust, anger and resentment as well as, more positively, the awakening of a certain solidarity and activism.... The prosecution of the [protestors] and the peculiarly heavy-handed approach to the reform of our corporate governance should be seen as symptoms of much wider developments that have been subtly spreading their tentacles for some years now.
>
> (Counter-magazine opening editorial)

While not an act that came out of a specific research project nor intended to be commercialized, this counter-magazine can be viewed as an entrepreneurial act, albeit unofficial and underground *skunkworks*. The counter-magazine sought to indicate an alternative to the dialectic of traditional university versus entrepreneurial university and the ways in which individual roles are positioned within them, by means of the reappropriation of managerial language and the assertion of an alternative form of institutional legitimacy and moral authority:

> One of our aims is to contribute to the University's tradition of being a democratic and open institution. Universities are communities based upon the open sharing of (and disagreeing with) opinions, and in our view they flourish best when the traditions of dissent and open discussion are respected and encouraged. More widely, we hope also to contribute in some small way to the task of enhancing that sense of community and collegiality that has been sadly diluted in recent years. In sum, we could do worse than ... adopt as what our esteemed managers would call our "mission statement" an adapted clause in our now often-forgotten Royal Charter: "The object of [this publication] shall be to advance knowledge, wisdom and understanding by teaching and research and by the example of its corporate life."
>
> (Counter-magazine opening editorial)

This launch can then be seen as a world-making act (Spinosa, Flores & Dreyfus, 1997) and as an alternative form of social-political entrepreneuring, which through entrepreneurial action generated a culturally linked output from the university academic community to the wider public. While not the official purpose of the conference, it may be said that the event itself stirred university faculty to engage directly in entrepreneuring in order to make a difference.

To some extent, this is not at odds with the concept of academic entrepreneurship, as making a difference is often the reason why academics become involved in entrepreneurship, rather than financial reward (Perkmann & Walsh, 2007), and the online magazine intended to directly influence the development of change in the institution (Gibb & Hannon, 2006), but these perspectives are usually explicitly related to profit-seeking outcomes. The counter-magazine allows us to see how entrepreneurship in universities may be seen as *enabling* via social change: a civic outcome of the critique, development and advancement of knowledge. Relating entrepreneurship to the process of social action, rather than financial outcomes, puts the purpose of entrepreneurship in universities, and entrepreneurship education, in a new light.

As Fenwick (2008) emphasizes, enterprise itself as a concept remains unsettled and ripe for challenge. So too does enterprise and entrepreneurship education. This does not therefore give us a sense that an option can be simply chosen but instead that the interaction of contested terrains sets the scene for an approach where overlapping interests combine. This generates a concept which is inherently political, in which the competing pressures of the political context of university management, culture, student expectations, government pressure and industry expectations combine to set a theatre in which the direction is unclear but should not be seen as uncontentious.

As was the case with the counter-magazine and has been emphasized by entrepreneurship theory, opportunities may be created as well as exploited. Through reflecting on entrepreneurship education, its purpose and goals and the wider context in which it is carried out, there is the opportunity to shape it into something which has the freedom to challenge assumptions of university teaching and curriculum. To create new ways to tackle the interface of teaching, research, society and economy. To create alternative voices and new ways of doing.

Note

1 Weiskopf and Steyaert (2008) put forward related concerns about the study of entrepreneurship and approach this through Nietzsche (1986) to propose a *Yes*, *No*, and *Becoming* of entrepreneurship studies. Here I extend this to entrepreneurship education.

References

Aldrich, H.E. (2012). The emergence of entrepreneurship as an academic field: A personal essay on institutional entrepreneurship. *Research Policy*, *41*(7), 1240–1248.

Barnett, R. (2011). *Being a university*. Abingdon: Routledge.

Berglund, K. (2013). Fighting against all odds: Entrepreneurship education as employability training. *Ephemera*, *13*(4), 717–735.

Bragg, S. (2007). "Student voice" and governmentality: The production of enterprising subjects. *Discourse: Studies in the Cultural Politics of Education*, *28*(3), 343–358.

Chesbrough, H.W. (2006). Open innovation: A new paradigm for understanding industrial innovation. In H. Chesbrough, W. Vanhaverbeke & J. West (Eds), *Open innovation: Researching a new paradigm* (pp. 1–14). Oxford: Oxford University Press.

Collini, S. (2012). *What are universities for?* London: Penguin.

Connell, R. (2013). The neoliberal cascade and education: An essay on the market agenda and its consequences. *Critical Studies in Education, 54*(2), 99–112.

Connolly, J. (2000). The academy's freedom, the academy's burden. *Thought & Action, 16*(1), 71.

Covin, J.G. & Slevin, D.P. (1991). A conceptual model of entrepreneurship as firm behaviour. *Entrepreneurship: Theory and Practice, 16*, 7–25.

Dahlstedt, M. & Hertzberg, F. (2012). Schooling entrepreneurs: Entrepreneurship, governmentality and education policy in Sweden at the turn of the millennium. *Journal of Pedagogy, 3*(2), 242–262.

Down, B. (2009). Schooling, productivity and the enterprising self: Beyond market values. *Critical Studies in Education, 50*(1), 51–64.

Du Gay, P. (1996). *Consumption and Identity at Work*. London: SAGE.

Etzkowitz, H. & Leydesdorff, L. (2000). The dynamics of innovation: From national systems and "mode 2" to a triple helix of university–industry–government relations. *Research Policy, 29*(2), 109–123.

Etzkowitz, H. (2003). Innovation in innovation: The triple helix of university–industry–government relations. *Social Science Information, 42*(3), 293–337.

Farny, S., Frederiksen, S.H., Hannibal, M. & Jones, S. (2016). A CULTure of entrepreneurship education. *Entrepreneurship & Regional Development, 28*(7–8), 514–535.

Fenwick, T. (2008). Whither research in enterprise? A response to Salaman and Storey. *Organization, 15*(3), 325–332.

Fournier, V. (1998). Stories of development and exploitation: Militant voices in an enterprise culture. *Organization, 5*(1), 55–80.

Gibb, A. & Hannon, P. (2006). Towards the entrepreneurial university? *International Journal of Entrepreneurship Education, 4*, 73.

Hannon, P.D. (2005). Philosophies of enterprise and entrepreneurship education and challenges for higher education in the UK. *International Journal of Entrepreneurship and Innovation, 6*(2), 105–114.

Heinonen, J. & Hytti, U. (2010). Back to basics: The role of teaching in developing the entrepreneurial university. *International Journal of Entrepreneurship and Innovation, 11*(4), 283–292.

Humboldt, W. (1810). On the internal and external organization of the higher scientific institutions in Berlin. In *From Absolutism to Napoleon, 1648–1815, German History in Documents and Images*. Retrieved 28 February 2014 from http://germanhistorydocs. ghi-dc.org/sub_document.cfm?document_id=3642.

Jain, S., George, G. & Maltarich, M. (2009). Academics or entrepreneurs? Investigating role identity modification of university scientists involved in commercialization activity. *Research Policy, 38*(6), 922–935.

Löbler, H. (2006). Learning entrepreneurship from a constructivist perspective. *Technology Analysis & Strategic Management, 18*(1), 19–38.

Mautner, G. (2005). The entrepreneurial university: A discursive profile of a higher education buzzword. *Critical Discourse Studies, 2*(2), 95–120.

Miller, D. (1983). The correlates of entrepreneurship in three types of firms. *Management Science, 29*(7), 770–791.

Newman, J.H. (1852/2009). *The idea of a university*. Dublin: Ashfield.

Olssen, M. & Peters, M.A. (2005). Neoliberalism, higher education and the knowledge economy: From the free market to knowledge capitalism. *Journal of Education Policy*, *20*(3), 313–345.

Perkmann, M. & Walsh, K. (2007). University–industry relationships and open innovation: Towards a research agenda. *International Journal of Management Reviews*, *9*(4), 259–280.

Pittaway, L. & Tunstall R. (2016). Is there still a heffalump in the room? Examining paradigms in historical entrepreneurship research. In H. Landström, A. Parhankangas, A. Fayolle & P. Riot (Eds), *Challenging entrepreneurship research (Routledge Rethinking Entrepreneurship Series)*. Abingdon: Routledge.

Smyth, J. (1999). Schooling and enterprise culture: Pause for a critical policy analysis. *Journal of Education Policy*, *14*(4), 435–444.

Spinosa, C., Flores, F. & Dreyfus, H.L. (1997). *Disclosing new worlds: Entrepreneurship, democratic action and the cultivation of solidarity*. Cambridge, MA: MIT Press.

Weiskopf, R. & Steyaert, C. (2008). Metamorphosis in entrepreneurship studies: towards an affirmative politics of entrepreneuring. In D. Hjorth & C. Steyeart (Eds), *The politics and aesthetics of entrepreneurship*. Cheltenham: Edward Elgar.

Wiklund, J., Davidsson, P., Audretsch, D.B. & Karlsson, C. (2011). The future of entrepreneurship research. *Entrepreneurship Theory and Practice*, *35*, 1–9.

Zahra, S.A. & Wright, M. (2011). Entrepreneurship's next act. *Academy of Management Perspectives*, *25*(4), 67–83.

Part II
On evoking

2 Entrepreneurship in societal change

Students as reflecting entrepreneurs?

Jessica Lindbergh and Birgitta Schwartz[1]

Introduction

The focus on entrepreneurship has been seen as a positive economic activity (Tedmanson, Verduijn, Essers & Gartner, 2012), not only bringing about innovations in the business and at the market but also as a way to develop societies (e.g. Berglund, Johannisson & Schwartz, 2012). However, entrepreneurship education in business schools is still mainly related to more conventional forms of entrepreneurship, with a focus on starting a company based on the innovation of a new product or service (Fiet, 2000; Gartner & Vesper, 1994; Gorman, Hanlon & King, 1997; Henry, Hill & Leitch, 2005). Accordingly, students learn how to start a company, find a customer demand and make their company profitable and successful on the market. Not on our course. We aim to give the students a broader awareness of the societal issues that today's society is facing, frequently caused by the traditional economical reasoning, such as growth and more efficient production processes. The issues that are targeted are pollution, poor working conditions and overconsumption, but also other societal issues more related to integration, and mental health.

In this chapter, we describe a course in which we try to involve the students in developing knowledge of how to find solutions to problematic societal issues through entrepreneurship. One way that we visualize societal issues to the students is with the help of film material that presents the activities of different stakeholders in the production of consumer goods, such as shoes and clothing. We believe the students can quite easily relate and identify to such goods as consumers. Please come with us to the classroom where one of our lectures is being given.

The students enter the classroom for a lecture on entrepreneurship and context. At the beginning of the lecture, the teacher tells the students that she will show a documentary about the clothing and shoe industry in India. Before the film starts, the students are given different roles as stakeholders, i.e. suppliers, retailers, customers, NGOs and workers. The teacher also presents a number of questions for the students to reflect upon while watching the documentary, such as the actors' responsibilities and what opportunities and hindrances there are to changing the situations of workers and farmers. The film begins with some interviews with large Swedish retailers explaining that their clothes and shoes are produced in India and how much they know (or don't know) about their suppliers and how their products are produced. In the next scene, we follow the reporter to India and we see child labour, workers suffering from severe health problems, and how the pollution of water caused by the Swedish companies' local suppliers creates toxic drinking water and destroys farm land. The reporter interviews factory owners, workers, farmers and NGOs about these problems. In the next scene of the documentary we jump back to the Swedish context and the reporter confronts the retailers about the appalling working conditions and environmental consequences. The students watching the film see different responses. Some of the retailers are very honest and reflective on the Western world's exploitation of workers in developing countries, while others relate to the problems from a business perspective and how to handle the problems by controlling the suppliers using codes of conduct.

After the film, the students are asked to discuss their stakeholders' responsibilities, opportunities and hindrances in this situation and to come up with solutions. The students suggest, for example, increasing the *control* of suppliers, and NGOs doing *voluntary* work to help their workers. But they also see many hindrances to change for the actors, such as lack of laws, regulations and norms that ensure workers' rights and protect the environment. The students' solutions are often grounded in their own cultural context. They see great difficulties in making an impact as a single customer. Instead, they argue that customers need to organize themselves into larger groups in order to be a stronger force for changing the situation.

The solutions suggested by the students have difficulty breaking free from stakeholders' existing logics, as presented in the documentary, and therefore there is little discussion on new ways of creating change. Instead, the solutions emphasize more of the same, i.e. stronger institutions to enable more control and stronger NGOs. It is clear that this is a documentary that upsets some students in various ways. This is evident not so much in that they voice it in the classroom but rather that they come forward during the break to discuss it with the teachers. Other students seem to be more aware of the problems, as a result of similar documentaries and/or personal experience as a volunteer in a developing country. In relation to this lecture we always end up discussing their own decision-making while shopping. Very few students believe that they can influence producers and retailers and they also explain that "doing good" is very expensive for poor students.

After a break, the lecture continues with the presentation of a research project about a social entrepreneur who produces organic and fair trade cotton clothing and bags in India with the aim of solving the environmental and social issues presented in the film. The students meet the entrepreneur's struggle to combine her social mission with running a for-profit company, all with the purpose of presenting the complexity of doing societal entrepreneurship.

With this episode, we wanted to bring the reader into the classroom to get an idea of what the students are asked to discuss and reflect upon in relation to entrepreneurship and societal change. Today, several kinds of entrepreneurship are evolving related to how individuals, organizations and nations try to solve problematic issues in society and change society with regard to, for example, social and environmental issues. This is defined in this chapter as societal entrepreneurship (Berglund *et al.*, 2012). In order for students to understand societal entrepreneurship and for us as teachers to encourage students or comply with students' societal engagement, there is a need to widen entrepreneurship education, i.e. to take more than simply the economic aspects into consideration. To accomplish this task students must embrace a broader view of entrepreneurship. For example, what success factors related to conventional entrepreneurship and enterprising, such as growth and profit maximization, can have consequences for society, such as social problems and environmental problems (Söderbaum, 2000, 2009). As the lecture also highlights, the difficulty for entrepreneurs following their social or environmental mission entails a struggle for themselves and their enterprises when striving to survive on the market (Smith, Knapp, Barr, Stevens & Cannatelli, 2010; Berglund & Schwartz, 2013).

For that reason, we find that it is important that entrepreneurship education allows the students to study and reflect upon dark and bright sides of conventional entrepreneurship and societal entrepreneurship. This is done by studying literature and real cases as well as working in student projects. In these projects the students reflect on their own entrepreneurial process, and the challenges and risks of their own solution, when trying to organize how to solve a social or environmental problem in society. In class, the students in the group project assignment also learn from each other when reviewing and discussing each other's projects. Similar to Rae's argument (1999), our aim is to combine the three sources of entrepreneurial learning: formal (theoretical learning), active (practical learning) and social (learning from others).

The purpose of the chapter is to describe our process of developing and teaching a course in societal entrepreneurship and how the students appear to receive the course and to learn. In this chapter, we illustrate how we strive to combine formal, active and social learning (Rae, 1999) on an undergraduate course of 7.5 ECTS credits given during a period of 4.5 weeks for bachelor's students in business administration and how the students understand and experience the topic and course. This is done by problematizing how students perform their project assignment and also how students understand entrepreneurship at the beginning of the course and their evaluation of such experience at the end of the course. We have material from five courses given during the years 2014–16, including notes of student expectations collected during the course introduction and evaluation in written forms from three course occasions collected on the final day of the course.

Our intentions with regard to the course

The overall aim of the Entrepreneurship in Societal Change (ENSO) course is for the students to understand societal entrepreneurship and to express how it may be enacted in various contexts. In addition, the course focuses on the interplay between entrepreneurship and societal change, i.e. to what extent entrepreneurship plays a part in changing society. During the course we discuss and study conventional business entrepreneurship and societal entrepreneurship, with a particular interest in societal entrepreneurship and the challenges these entrepreneurs meet. Such entrepreneurship focuses not only on growth and profit as a success factor but also includes other factors deemed equally important, such as finding new solutions for creating a common good, fighting poverty, maintaining cultural heritage, and implementing a transition to a more environmentally sound society.

The students are assessed by means of three assignments: a group project, which is worth 30 per cent, a review of another group report, worth 10 per cent, and a final written exam, worth 60 per cent. These assignments are related to our pedagogical underpinnings of how to teach and help students to reflect upon entrepreneurship and societal change and can be compared to Rae's (1999) discussion on entrepreneurial learning as referred to in Edwards and Muir's (2005) article. Rae argues (1999) that entrepreneurial learning stems from three sources, namely theoretical learning (formal), practical learning (active) and learning from others (social). The sources can be translated into activities that we do on the course, such as providing theoretical understanding through diverse literature and lectures, gaining practical experience both through the project and through learning from the others by sharing their projects with the other course participants, as well as guest lecturers who share their experience of social entrepreneurship. These activities should not be seen as isolated and unrelated to each other but rather as part of a learning cycle, where different practices are important for the understanding of theory and vice versa (Kolb, 1984).

The learning goals on the course and assessed by the three assignments can also be related to Rae's (1999) three sources of learning – formal, active and social. The learning goals related to gaining knowledge and understanding relate to both formal and active learning, such as:

- Identify, describe and explain forms of entrepreneurship in relation to contexts and societal change (formal).
- Recognize different entrepreneurial contexts (active).

Learning goals for skills and abilities relate to all learning sources but mainly to active and social sources, such as:

- Apply perspectives from management and organizational theories in order to investigate the challenges of doing entrepreneurship for societal change (formal and active).
- Identify entrepreneurial challenges and suggest solutions regarding environmental or social problems with focus on societal change (active, social).
- Show ability to plan and execute, individually and in a group, a defined entrepreneurial project (active and social).

The final theme of learning goals related to judgement and approach relates to all three sources of learning and is expressed as:

- Critically analyse and evaluate different forms of entrepreneurship in relation to context (formal, active, social).

The audience of entrepreneurship education

Entrepreneurship education and training have different content and perspectives in programmes and courses (Henry *et al.*, 2005). These variations depend on the nature of the target audience (students at college or university, potential entrepreneurs, business owners) as well as the expectations from students or the fact that there are different target markets for these courses (Gorman *et al.*, 1997). Some audiences believe that what should be included in potential entrepreneurship courses is a more practically oriented "how to start your own business". But they also mention issues such as marketing, entrepreneurship, business planning, management and financial management and how to assess one's own entrepreneurial skills, which could improve one's chances of success (Le Roux & Nieuwenhuizen (1996), referred to in Henry *et al.* (2005)). These audiences relate to the categories of specific and broad audiences in Table 2.1 below, where the differences between audience and student perceptions of entrepreneurship education are presented. As we can see, there are different audiences. The "specific audience" wants to start a business and to have an insight into how entrepreneurs act and create value. The "broad audience" is more interested in how to develop their entrepreneurial mindset for how to think and learn and to identify, evaluate and organize opportunities (Nielsen, Klyver, Rostgaard & Bager, 2012). There is yet another kind of audience that does not relate to entrepreneurship at all, or that is sceptical towards business. This unaware/sceptical audience is not aware

Table 2.1 Different audience and student's perception

Perception/ audience	*Specific audience*	*Broad audience*	*Unaware/sceptical audience*
Career ambition	Have real ambition to start a business	Has ambition to work with entrepreneurial issues	Want employment
Overall rationale	To understand start-up processes	To develop an entrepreneurial mindset	To understand what it means to be enrolled as part of an entrepreneurial working force
Learning needs	Seeking practical and instrumental skills	Seeking an ability to identify, evaluate and organize opportunities	Understanding the consequences of living in an entrepreneurial era

Source: Nielsen *et.al.*, 2012; Berglund 2014.

beforehand of what entrepreneurship is and is more sceptical in the sense of questioning the role of business in society. They do not aim to start their own business; rather, they want to be employed in other types of organizations (Berglund, 2014).

Our audience and their expectations of the course

So, what kind of audience do we meet on the course? The students that can choose this course are on programmes within business administration, business administration and political science, and business administration and IT. The course is not mandatory for any of the student categories. It is also open for students taking free-standing courses, of whom a majority are exchange students, primarily from Europe but also a small number of students from Asia and North and South America. The students are generally in their second or third year of bachelor's studies. The number of students has fluctuated between semesters but a total number of 250 students have been first-time registrants on the course (of whom 45 per cent are exchange students) and a total of 235 students have actually completed the course.

The course is presented to potential students on the school's web page, and as soon as the students have been enrolled on the course they can download a study guide presenting the course. On the first occasion when the course is introduced, the students are given a lecture on sustainable development and its relation to high- and low-income countries and the three societal sectors, i.e. private sector (market), public sector (state) and the non-profit/voluntary sector (civil society), before they are asked to state their expectations of the course and write them on Post-it notes. The following questions are asked to find out about the students' expectations of the course: *What do you want to achieve, get out of, learn from this course? What do you expect from the teachers? What do you expect from your fellow students?*

The material on student expectations has been gathered from five semesters, starting with spring 2014 and ending with spring 2016. Over this period of two years we have been interested to find out what kind of preconception the students had about entrepreneurship in general, but also more specifically about entrepreneurship in societal change. Over the years the results have helped us to better understand our audience and to be able to set the stage for introducing several forms of entrepreneurship to the students. In the following table, Table 2.2, we present an overview of the students' comments regarding their expectations in respect of the first question, what to learn on the course. The statements are not to be seen as individual responses but as general areas of expressed expectations regarding the course (i.e. we do not quantify how many individuals can be related to each statement).

In an attempt to understand the students' expectations, we can see that the students fit the criteria of an anticipated audience as defined by Nielsen *et al.* (2012), i.e. a specific audience whose aim is to acquire the skills to set up a business, and a broad audience with an interest in gaining an entrepreneurial mindset. We can also to some extent find wishes/reasoning similar to that referred to in

Berglund's (2014) third group of audience, the unaware/sceptical audience. However, since the students have made an active choice to enrol on the course, as it is not mandatory for their programme, we perceive that the expectations do not imply that the students are sceptical to entrepreneurship but rather that they are interested in the interplay between society and business in general. Hence, we choose to call them the analytical audience. In Table 2.2 below, we have placed the students from different semesters into three categories that capture the different audiences in Table 2.1. In the first category, we look for different statements referring to the skills of setting up a business (specific audience). The second category captures statements about an entrepreneurial mind set (broad audience) and the third category captures statements that aim to better understand the consequences of living in an entrepreneurial era, which we call a reflective stance (analytical audience).

The fifth time the course was given, prospective students had had time to speak and ask about the course before it started. The presentation on the course's web page, as well as the format and content in the introductory lecture, remained the same. Perhaps we can therefore assume that some of the students' expectations at a later stage are more in line with what the course actually covers in regard to entrepreneurship in societal change. This might also be the reason why there is a greater emphasis on learning about sustainable development, social entrepreneurship and societal change and the role of entrepreneurship in society in the later semester than in the first. In the first semester, the students' primary focus was to learn *for* entrepreneurship, such as setting up their own business (Jamieson, 1984). However, the expectations of learning entrepreneurial skills have been consistent over time despite its very brief focus in the course presentation on the web (one sentence at the end) as well as little emphasis on such skills, i.e. how to set up a business, for the project work. In the next section, we explain how we organize the course.

In the classroom

The course has several underpinnings, both theoretically and practically, that the students experience through the literature as well as in an actual project. The main course literature is a book, *Entrepreneurship in Theory and Practice: Paradoxes in Play*, written by Nielsen *et al.* (2012), illustrating the "messy and paradoxical" nature of entrepreneurship by using different entrepreneurial cases. These are discussed using different types of theories and, as such, explaining how different theoretical lenses present different types of paradoxical theoretical reasoning. It is a textbook whose primary target group is undergraduate students and it is structured in four themes: entrepreneurship and the entrepreneur, the entrepreneurial process, the entrepreneurial content and the entrepreneurial context. We have also taken these themes as the structure of our course. The book aims to take a broad view of entrepreneurship and presents the reader with different perspectives on entrepreneurship and its outcomes. It does not, however, in any way discuss the dark sides of any type of entrepreneurship.

Table 2.2 An overview of students' expectations of learning needs across five semesters

Expectation/semester	Spring 2014	Fall 2014	Spring 2015	Fall 2015	Spring 2016
Skills (specific audience)	• Learn the bases of entrepreneurship (not specified) • Learn how to write a business canvas • Be responsible entrepreneurs • Contribute to something good • Achieve sustainable thinking	• Find new solutions to societal problems • Learn how to implement ideas effectively • Write a business canvas • Learn how to tackle entrepreneurial challenges	• Learn how to tackle societal problems • Make a societal change	• Learn tools to make changes in home country • Gain applied practical knowledge • Learn how to start a business	• Start a new business • Create a new idea • Deal with small business issues
Entrepreneurial mind set (broad audience)	• Get inspiration to new ideas • Be more courageous	• Gain entrepreneurial thinking • Get determination to realize own ideas • Learn that entrepreneurship is not only for profit but can be "good"	• Learn how to be more socially and environmentally oriented in business • Understand problems and challenges of entrepreneurship • Find new ways of problem-solving	• Learn tools to identify opportunities in a responsible manner • Develop an entrepreneurial mind set • Prepare for serendipity • Generate innovative solutions • Gain an awareness of societal problems and possibilities in entrepreneurship	• Learn about decision-making when faced with multiple options

Reflective stance (analytical audience)				
• Learn how entrepreneurship affects society • Understand not only big corporation logic • Understand this evolving phenomenon • Learn how it may differ in different cultures	• Learn entrepreneurship's effect on society and vice versa • Learn about different kinds of entrepreneurship forms	• Learn how to affect corporations to be more socially responsible • Take a global view of entrepreneurship	• Understand different forms of entrepreneurship	• Learn what entrepreneurship demands from us humans • Learn how social entrepreneurship impacts standard of living around the world • See entrepreneurship in a societal context

Students find the book easy to read and we believe that one reason is the very fact that students are the target group and it follows a traditional business discourse. The course literature is also based on articles, some of which are referred to in the book by Nielsen *et al.* (2012). The thinking is that the students also need to read the original articles, not only other authors' interpretations of them.

To balance the more conventional view on entrepreneurship we use an additional course book with more context-specific dilemmas that societal entrepreneurs encounter. The book is called *Societal Entrepreneurship: Positioning, Penetrating, Promoting* by Berglund, Johannisson and Schwartz (2012) and focuses on entrepreneurs acting in and between different society sectors, i.e. the public sector, the private sector and the voluntary/non-profit sector. The book also shows how the sectors' different logics influence and challenge entrepreneurs and sometimes even create dark sides of entrepreneurship. Students find this book a bit more challenging; the reason could be that its primary target is other academic scholars, even though both students and reflective practitioners are included in the book's target groups.

Defining the problem and the entrepreneurial solution

In order to make the students reflect on societal issues through more than reading relevant literature and being assessed by means of a written exam, they must also create their own entrepreneurial project in groups of four to five students. The students participate in a collective entrepreneurship process, where they identify an environmental or social problem in an industry or society and define how different actors, from different societal sectors, handle or cause this problem. The aim of the investigation is to find a solution and choose an entrepreneurial form that they will work with in order to solve the issue. This process is initially quite irritating and frustrating for the students, since they themselves have to define a problem they think is important enough to work with. In addition, they also need to define and organize a solution. We know this process takes time, since they first need to decide on a problem and then also dig a lot deeper into the reasons behind the problem and map all the actors connected to the problem. In this process we also tell the students that they cannot copy an existing idea but that it is fine to improve an existing idea and translate and/or redesign it into their chosen context. Nonetheless, some students find the initial creative process very difficult. On one occasion, a group actually plagiarized an existing societal entrepreneurship, the idea as well as the organization, which we interpret as a desperate action. The groups that seem to struggle most with the aim of their idea are those that start out by finding an existing product, often on the Internet, and then try to find the societal problem that the product could help to solve. In contrast, the groups that start by identifying the societal problem (which they are encouraged to do) do better in developing an idea to solve, or at least improving the problematic issue they focus on. The solutions or ideas are also more often related to organizing services rather than developing or innovating a new product for sale, or a new charity.

For the project, we tell them that they can choose to start a business, or a non-profit voluntary organization (NGO), or to be an *intra*preneur in a public organization or company. Most often the students choose an NGO as the organizational form, instead of a for-profit initiative. The argument is generally that they do not think that they will gain legitimacy for their organization if it has a for-profit aim. They do not think that the collaborating organizations and/or donors would trust them if they made a profit for themselves. This view has changed somewhat since we introduced a guest lecturer from a for-profit social enterprise who discusses the issue of making money when doing social entrepreneurship. She questions the view in today's society that it is OK for companies and their CEOs to make a lot of money from contributing to societal problems, while a CEO of an NGO is not expected to earn a high salary. Her experience as a social entrepreneur gives her a greater legitimacy and seems to change the view of some students on trustworthiness in relation to for-profit. So, on subsequent courses, we saw more student projects that chose a for-profit form, even though some groups stress that in order to be trustworthy their goal is not profit maximization.

The student groups are supervised on two occasions during the course where they discuss how they develop their idea and what challenges they struggle with, both in relation to their idea development and also if they have any collaboration problems among the group members. Since there is a mix of international and Swedish students the societal problem can vary widely according to context, and sometimes cause confusion and tensions on how to describe the problem as well as finding a solution. We frequently see that one or two students eventually dominate the definition of a societal problem and solution. Consequently, in addition to struggling with the process of defining a problem and solution, the other students in the group also struggle to grasp the context in which this problem and solution will be situated.

On the five times we have held the course, we have recognized that the societal problems the students have chosen to work with are often related to their own contexts, such as finding accommodation (e.g. housing for students), difficulties finding jobs, renting out products that are expensive for students or only needed when studying, promoting social issues in schools, or cheap but healthy food for students. The Swedish students have often chosen a problem in Sweden; exchange students have also chosen Sweden but often look for ideas already established in their home countries and then try to translate these ideas to the Swedish context (e.g. selling or producing juice from an unattractive fruit, or exchanging flats between exchange students). The reverse is also common, i.e. that Swedish sustainable solutions are translated to another context related to group members' home countries, for example a project on recycling water bottles in Thailand.

Becoming entrepreneurs for societal change

During the course we give two workshops. In the first, the entrepreneurial learning source is based on social interaction in which students learn from each other

(Rae, 1999). The groups present the problem they will solve and their entrepreneurial idea to the other groups and are given both written and oral comments by another group and by us. In this workshop exercise, the ideas are also discussed in relation to their choice of organizational form, which sector logics to handle and the context in which they will situate their organization and idea. The students are very active in the workshop and take the assigned consultancy role seriously. They can be very creative and critical of each other in developing the ideas further. At this workshop we can see a transformation taking place and students "becoming" societal entrepreneurs when defending their entrepreneurial idea. The first workshop's exercises also relate to Rae's (1999) formal learning source, since the reviews and discussions might also contribute to their theoretical understanding.

At the second workshop, we emphasize the active entrepreneurial learning source (Rae, 1999) and the groups work actively on a business model canvas in order to investigate their customers/users, their competitors, collaborations with other actors, costs, financial sources etc. This is an activity that the students engage in with enthusiasm, since the business model canvas tool seems to help them structure their discussions when identifying the different steps in developing their ideas. On this occasion, the financial issues become more evident for the students regardless of which organizational form they chose. This is also when the tension between revenues and social mission becomes obvious.

The process of distancing

The final project report emphasizes the formal entrepreneurial learning source (Rae, 1999). The students are asked to distance themselves a little from their entrepreneurial process by reflecting on their project work when writing the report. They should reflect on their own collective entrepreneurial process with the help of the course literature, such as, for example, their experiences of using a business canvas when developing the idea, and also how they experience their process was created or discovered or both, etc. In addition, the students need to reflect not only on which practical and organizational challenges they need to overcome in the context in which they will act and in relation to different society sectors and their logics, but also if their idea of solving a pressing issue could cause other unwanted societal problems.

The students seem to have some difficulty reflecting on their own entrepreneurial process and their own idea and how to organize their solution. Some groups are better at this than others. The analysis of the entrepreneurship form they have chosen often relates to the legitimacy issues we discussed previously (for-profit vs non-profit) but some reports discuss how their idea could benefit from a specific form. This is often discussed from a user perspective or in relation to collaborators and funders. But two-thirds of the students' project reports often lack an analysis of the entrepreneurship form in relation to the context and the society sector(s) in which they have chosen to act. Also, there is no mention of how to deal with the logics of different sectors when collaborating with other organizations from other sectors and how this challenges their solution and idea. As mentioned earlier, we find that the students have a problem with the process of distancing in the project report. There might be several reasons for this, such as time pressure or being able to go back and forth between theory and practice in the same report. This is similar to Gartner and Vesper's (1994) findings that show the difficulty students have in analysing their own actions and thoughts while undertaking activities of developing, for example, a business plan.

In the process of distancing, we ask the students to reflect on critical risks that may come with their project idea. The discussions vary from economic to societal risks that their projects can have and cause. If the students choose the form of a for-profit enterprise, their discussions of risks are related more to profitability, market, competitors, prices and costs. If they choose the form of an NGO initiative instead, they explain the risks as related to legitimacy issues and collaboration problems. There are examples of discussions and reflections of when *their own idea* could cause other societal problems or consequences, such as, for example, safety risks for refugees and volunteers and the risk of exploiting refugees due to unequal power relations (e.g. project on immigration). Other projects discuss risks related to their for-profit organizational form: the solution might cause the same effects that the idea is intended to solve, the students might stop their studies and start work instead (e.g. project on unemployed students) or the project providing food coupons to homeless people might create a black market (e.g. project on food to homeless people). Other risks related to voluntarism as explained by the students were that Western people do voluntary work without much concern for the local community's genuine needs (e.g. project on education of children in India). These latter issues are related more to the students' need to reflect on the more problematic consequences and challenges of their idea and working process, and not only if the idea would be successful from a profit and market perspective. These reflections are also related to the social learning source (Rae, 1999) since the students need to discuss these matters with each other. But they are also related to an active learning source (Rae, 1999) since they investigated practical issues and the risk of unintended consequences when conducting interviews with potential users of their idea.

Students' evaluations of course outcome

Over the years we have collected the students' evaluations of the course outcome. However, in the first two semesters we let the students discuss and review the course together in class. Even though the students did discuss both positive and negative experiences (in need of improvement) of the course, not all students were involved, so we decided to do this exercise in written form in subsequent semesters. In spring 2015 for the first time we asked all the students to write down their perceptions regarding the course outcome. Before they replied, they also received a short update on the expectations they stated on the first day of the course. All the students' replies are summarized in Table 2.3,

Table 2.3 An overview of students' assessment of the course across three semesters.

Semester/assessment	Spring 2015	Fall 2015	Spring 2016
Positive experiences?	• Learning entrepreneurship and business with a creative perspective • Being inspired about entrepreneurship and starting business • Learning to be a more socially aware citizen • Learning how to become an entrepreneur or start a business that is profitable and social • Achieving a project that could be real • Learning a lot about theory and application of entrepreneurship • Mixing theory with real-life practice • Being more confident to present entrepreneurship ideas in the future • Good learning how to develop an opportunity – project planning helped to think outside the box • Learning different ways to look at entrepreneurship; getting a deeper view of the social part • Project was a substantial part of the learning process and helpful for future job assignments • Feeling empowered to tackle challenges in home country	• Learning that entrepreneurship is more differentiated than expected • Reflecting on entrepreneurship as an individual vs collective phenomenon • Learning about the social view of entrepreneurship • Discovering that entrepreneurship is a way of thinking rather than a fixed way of doing	Majority met their expectations, though five did not. **Majority:** • Learning how companies can mix profit and sust./social issues • Learning that entrepreneurship can take on several organizational forms • Learning to combine theory and project and how those benefitted from each other for creating an understanding • Learning about the complexity, challenges and time-consuming efforts of entrepreneurship • Learning how to work in teams, and teams with different cultural backgrounds • Learning about sustainability and social issues and to be more aware of those **Group project:** • Perceived the project as realistic, as an entrepreneurial attempt • Liked working with students with different cultural backgrounds • Liked that the projects target sustainability and social issues

| Improvements needed? | • More academic than expected
• Executing or enacting some of the aspects in the projects
• More knowledge on how to create a start-up
• Learning more how to do market research and how to contact partners
• Weighing of the grading of project vs exam | • More academic than expected
• Executing parts of the project
• More guest lectures from different society sectors
• Giving more support to the project | **Five students:**
• Too few legal aspects
• Too little theory
• Too little discussion on understanding the social challenges of today
Group project, all students:
• Too time-consuming
• Too demanding to be a realistic project (e.g. realistic financial numbers, scan potential competitors, reflecting of organizational needs etc.) |

in which we present both input on positive experiences and necessary improvements.

In the spring of 2016 we also used an additional survey that is general and mandatory for all the courses given at the institution. Slightly less than half of the class responded. The survey asked the students to rate the extent to which they had learned the stated skills in the course on a scale between 1 (to a very small extent) and 5 (very high). The first question asked if the students had acquired the knowledge and understanding to "Identify, describe and explain forms of entrepreneurship in relation to contexts and societal change". Over 70 per cent of the students rated this 4 and 5, suggesting that they perceived they had learned this very well or well. We also asked the students to assess their knowledge and understanding regarding to "Recognize different entrepreneurial contexts". We received similar results there: 72 per cent estimated that they had learned it very well or well during the course. Regarding skills and abilities in relation to "apply perspectives from management and organizational theories", over 60 per cent estimated that they learned it very well or well. Also, over 60 per cent estimated that they learned "to identify entrepreneurial challenges and suggest solutions" very well or well, and over 60 per cent estimated that they learned the "ability to plan and execute an entrepreneurial project" very well or well. Finally, we also asked the students to rate their assessment regarding the learning outcome of judgement and approach as how well the course has taught them "to critically analyze and evaluate different forms of entrepreneurship in relation to context". This time, 72 per cent of the students assessed they were doing very well or well in this matter. In spring 2016 we could follow how the previously expressed frustration with regard to the project seemed to take a different turn, at least for some of the students. Since a majority of the respondents were positive to their learning outcomes we are inclined to believe that they had accepted our intent to combine formal, active and social entrepreneurial learning sources.[2]

Regarding the students' own assessment of their learning during the course, it is clear that the project does indeed give the students a sense of having experienced a realistic entrepreneurial attempt. Further, working together in teams, often with team members from different cultural backgrounds, was highlighted as a positive outcome of the project. We also found that the students reflected on how they made use of the literature to know what steps to take in the project and vice versa, and how the project activities helped the students to understand the theoretical arguments. Hence, the literature and practical activities were perceived by the students to be complementary sources to understand the theory as well as execute the project. In line with Rae's (1999) reasoning, where it is possible to outline three sources (formal, active and social) for entrepreneurial learning, we also find that the students mention the importance of the literature and the practical struggles of formulating a social problem, as well as the team-work activities, as key contributors for their learning process. And this process, we believe, provides the students with a broader perspective and understanding of entrepreneurship.

Our own reflection of analysing the course

In our work analysing the course and systematically looking into students' expectations and evaluations over the years, we have learned more about what kind of audiences we are trying to educate. Despite the fact that we emphasize in the course syllabus and in the introduction lecture that this is not a course in how to start your own business, we meet these expectations from the students every year. Hence, their expectations may be less influenced by the course information received prior to the course start than their own preconceptions of entrepreneurship and entrepreneurship education. It seems that we have some difficulties in diverting from the dominating entrepreneurship discourse, emphasizing what entrepreneurship is and how it could be taught.

So, the question we could ask ourselves is: is it possible to expect all groups and students to be reflective regarding entrepreneurship in relation to societal issues and to learn what we are aiming to teach when they have different expectations? Some students are more focused on specific skills with regard to how to start up and run a business, while others are more in the category of an analytical audience. We have experienced that all students were able to identify a societal problem to be solved but only half of them could reflect on how their own solution and organizing might contribute to other societal problems. On the other hand, after the course the students themselves seemed to be of the opinion that they had learned what we ask for in the learning goals, and stated that they now reflected more on sustainability issues and the role of entrepreneurship and different forms of entrepreneurship. We interpret this as their ability to identify and problematize the societal issue they will solve. However, having the ability to question how their own entrepreneurial solution might create new problems may be more difficult if the initial expectation is that entrepreneurship is the only solution and can only be positive (i.e. specific and broad audience) and they do not see how entrepreneurship can play a role in contributing or causing problems.

Indeed, the students do acquire skills useful for entrepreneurship, but the group project is grounded in a more traditional academic logic. They are expected to present a written report that is assessed on the basis of their ability to make a theoretical analysis based on the course literature, their critical ability to analyse and the ability to write a report in a more academic style. In addition, they need to be active in seminars and be able to organize and present the project orally with a focus on subject content rather than visual content. Of course, these can be important entrepreneurial skills, but they are also typical generic skills common in the majority of academic courses.

A further concern regarding their ability to reflect, in relation to context, might be that the group project assignment is completed during a short period of time, only 4.5 weeks. In order to be able to make a proper analysis they probably need to experience their ideas in a real setting. Now they only have time to plan "how to execute" an idea, which also makes it possible for them to analyse the use of the business canvas or reflect on whether the idea was created or discovered. Perhaps our ambition with regard to the course can only be fulfilled with another form of pedagogy and within a longer time frame, where they have the time to test their ideas in a real setting. The students are also assessed through two more assignments, a review of another group's project and a written exam. Gartner and Vesper (1994) argue that entrepreneurship instructors have a propensity to fill a course with as much knowledge and experience as possible and that there is a limit to how much material and how many experiences can be absorbed in a given amount of time. That might be true in this case as well.

Conclusion

We argue that it is important to encourage the students to reflect on entrepreneurship regardless of whether it is conventional entrepreneurship or societal entrepreneurship that are considered in some regards as the "good forms" of entrepreneurship, e.g. social, societal, cultural and ecological. To conclude, we do believe in the main idea of the course since we see that many of our students do manage to take the time to reflect over entrepreneurship and its role in society.

To reach an understanding about, through and for entrepreneurship we have organized our course using different sources for learning as also argued by Rae (1999). By combining the process of reading and acting entrepreneurially collectively we can see a varying degree of a sense of achievement on the part of the students. Some are very enthusiastic and even feel empowered to take on societal challenges through entrepreneurship, whereas others still feel a sense of frustration with the course, perceiving it to be too academic. According to Rae (2000), entrepreneurial learning is a process where knowing, acting and making sense are interconnected. Part of such a process is then to construct stories of "who they want to be" (p. 151). Hence, besides being experience-based, the entrepreneurial learning process is also a future-oriented thinking process. With that said, time is an important factor for us when assessing entrepreneurial learning, and a next step of interest would therefore be to follow up on our early students. What learning appears, if any? What do they take from the course into their present work life? Is there a change in learning experience compared to the initial assessment of the course?

Getting answers to those questions might give us an idea of whether it is possible to teach about, through and for entrepreneurship in a more reflective manner. It is our hope that presenting several stories of entrepreneurship, including bright and dark sides, gives the students more informed ways and opportunities of constructing "who they want to be".

Notes

1 Authors are presented in an alphabetical order and have contributed equally to the text.
2 If, on the other hand, we are critical of this form of evaluation, it does not really tell us anything about how well the students have learned the outcomes, since we already evaluate that through their examinations.

References

Berglund, K. (2014). *Entrepreneur/ship ... Part 1. Course lecture: Entrepreneurship in societal change*, Stockholm Business School, Stockholm University, 20 February 2014.

Berglund, K., Johannisson, B. & Schwartz, B. (2012). *Societal entrepreneurship: Positioning, penetrating, promoting.* Cheltenham: Edward Elgar.

Berglund, K. & Schwartz, B. (2013). Holding on to the anomaly of social entrepreneurship: Dilemmas in starting up and running a fair-trade enterprise. *Journal of Social Entrepreneurship, 4*(3), 237–255.

Edwards, L.J. & Muir, W.J. (2005). Promoting entrepreneurship at the University of Glamorgan through formal and informal learning. *Journal of Small Business and Enterprise Development, 22*(4), 613–626.

Fiet, J.O. (2000). The pedagogical side of entrepreneurship theory. *Journal of Business Venturing, 16*, 101–117.

Gartner, W.B. & Vesper, K.H. (1994). Experiments in entrepreneurship education: successes and failures. *Journal of Business Venturing, 9*, 179–187.

Gorman, G., Hanlon, D. & King, W. (1997). Some research perspectives on entrepreneurship education, enterprise education and education for small business management: a ten-year literature review. *International Small Business Journal, 15*(3), 56–77.

Henry, C., Hill, F. & Leitch, C. (2005). Entrepreneurship education and training: can entrepreneurship be taught? Part I. *Education + Training, 47*(2), 98–111.

Jamieson, I. (1984). Schools and enterprise. In A.G. Watts & P. Moran (Eds), *Education for Enterprise* (pp. 19–27). Cambridge: CRAC, Ballinger.

Kolb, D.A. (1984). *Experiential learning: Experience as the source of learning and development.* Englewood Cliffs, NJ: Prentice Hall.

Nielsen, S.L., Klyver, K., Rostgaard, M. & Bager, T. (2012). *Entrepreneurship in theory and practice: Paradoxes in play.* Cheltenham: Edward Elgar.

Rae, D. (1999). *The entrepreneurial spirit.* Dublin: Blackhall.

Rae, D. (2000). Understanding entrepreneurial learning: a question of how? *International Journal of Entrepreneurial Behaviour & Research, 6*(3), 145–159.

Smith, B.R., Knapp, J., Barr, T., Stevens, C.E. & Cannatelli, B.L. (2010). Social enterprises and the timing of conception: Organizational identity tension, management, and marketing. *Journal of Nonprofit and Public Sector Marketing, 22*(2), 108.

Söderbaum, P. (2000). Business companies, institutional change, and ecological sustainability. *Journal of Economic Issues, 34*(2), 435–443.

Söderbaum, P. (2009). Making actors, paradigms and ideologies visible in governance for sustainability. *Sustainable Development, 17*, 70–81.

Tedmanson, D., Verduijn, K., Essers, C. & Gartner, B. (2012). Critical perspectives of entrepreneurship research. *Organization, 19*(5), 531–541.

3 The reflexivity grid

Exploring conscientization in entrepreneurship education

Leona Achtenhagen and Bengt Johannisson

Introduction

Entrepreneurship education has witnessed a shift from teaching *about* entrepreneurship in different forms towards encouraging the action- and activity-based training of students *for* entrepreneuring through business plan writing on fictitious or concrete ventures to enacting these ideas in real life. For example, Ollila and Williams-Middleton (2011) describe ways in which a venture creation approach allows students to "test the waters" while reflecting on real-life situations and while exploring entrepreneurial behaviours (see also Williams-Middleton & Donnellon, 2014). Though there has been a growing focus on simulating or experiencing entrepreneurial behaviours through entrepreneurship education, little space has been given to students' reflexivity in positioning themselves as learning subjects beyond educational settings. Yet very often questions posed by our students in the classroom, for example when listening to entrepreneurs telling them about their venture journeys, start with a "why" statement, clearly expressing their desire to engage with reflexivity. Reflexivity is then not only understood as a kind of generalized self-awareness (Swan, 2008, p. 393) but also as a concern for the world at large (Swan, 2008, p. 394).

We thus argue that reflexivity plays an important role in entrepreneurship education, whether in supporting students in becoming responsible entrepreneurs or in training them to develop the intuitive insight eventually needed to determine what is right and wrong both practically and ethically in various types of concrete situations. Situated knowing differs from the general and formal knowledge that academic education typically provides. The ancient Greeks did not only recognize Aristotelian *episteme, techne* and *phronesis* but also *mētis*, or cunning intelligence (Letiche & Statler, 2005). While the two former modes refer to scientific knowledge and to skill proficiency, the latter two recognize knowledge as situated, experientially acquired and embodied. Mētis concerns a knowing of how and when to apply rules of thumb, or street smarts, for instance when enacting a venture, and phronesis represents practical wisdom on ways to act judiciously in a particular situation (Flyvbjerg, 2001). This is the kind of knowing that we associate with entrepreneuring (Johannisson, 2011, 2014).

Getting students to acquire and practise mētis and phronesis in an academic context that otherwise promotes episteme and techne calls for a conscious pedagogical approach to advancing reflexivity. Mētis and phronesis bring students out of their traditional roles as passive recipients of scientific knowledge and advice delivered by teachers. This is what Freire (1970, 1998) refers to as a "banking system", referring to a metaphor of students as containers into which educators place knowledge. Instead, students are expected to take responsibility for their own learning by becoming personally involved and by using their curiosity to build new knowledge and to enforce their entrepreneurial identity. In this chapter, we will explore modes of reflexivity this challenge triggers and how these modes capture students' experiences in different learning contexts.

In doing so, we draw considerably on Paulo Freire's work. Since his notion of "conscientization", originally published in his *Pedagogy for the Oppressed* (1970), mainly concerns developing (Latin American) countries, we instead relate to his notion of "epistemological curiosity", the focus of his last book *Pedagogy of Freedom* (1998). Epistemological curiosity refines spontaneous or ingenuous curiosity through reflection: "one of the fundamental types of knowledge in my critical-educative practice is that which stresses the need for spontaneous curiosity to develop into epistemological curiosity" (Freire, 1998, p. 83). This development builds from the students' concrete experiences with the world.

The remainder of this chapter is structured as follows. We open by arguing for a pedagogy that allows (business school) students to conscientiously enact not only their own learning, but to also contribute to the (local) world in which their learning occurs. Next, we propose three different modes of enacting reflexivity – cognitive/emotional, hierarchy/network and being/becoming. We then present and empirically illustrate two alternative pedagogical paths to the enhancement of reflexivity and use these to illustrate examples of reflection along the three modes. Taking the first road forces students out of their comfort zones and of their view that entrepreneurship represents just another form of management and economic value creation. We refer to this path as the "catharsis approach". The second path originates from contemporary students' familiarity with social media and from its potential for the creation of an entrepreneurial identity. We refer to this path as the "blogging approach". Based on our findings, we develop a "reflexivity grid". By capturing cognitive and socio-emotional effects, this grid presents different forms of reflexivity of relevance to responsible (would-be) entrepreneurs. One dimension of this two-dimensional grid covers the proposed modes of enacting reflexivity, while the other dimension concerns in which (personal, academic or global) communities of practice reflexivity can be located. Using this grid, we present various types of activities that may be used as part of an entrepreneurship curriculum to support different aspects of reflexivity. We conclude the chapter by discussing further challenges confronted when facilitating activities aimed to enhancing reflexivity.

Getting started – making students enact their own learning

Entrepreneuring and different forms of knowledge

We associate entrepreneuring with generic human faculties such as curiosity, creativity and care – for oneself and for others through social (inter)action. As relentless action and interaction are at the core of entrepreneuring, it is best viewed as a process of creative organizing or as *entrepreneuring* (Steyaert, 2007; Johannisson, 2011), which, as experientially enacted, is closely related to learning (Hjorth & Johannisson, 2007). To capture this through a pedagogy of entrepreneurship, we claim (by paraphrasing Mahatma Gandhi) that "there is no road to entrepreneurship; entrepreneuring is the road".

Entrepreneurship education – whether in focusing on hands-on skills for venture creation or on entrepreneuring as an approach to professional/public and personal/private life – requires a pedagogy that allows students to acquire mētis and phronesis and not just formal knowledge captured through episteme and techne. The commonly used pedagogical tool of business plan writing encourages the focus and internal consistency of a roadmap generation that is of no value when travelling into an unknowable future (see Chia & Holt, 2009). It fails both at encouraging students to develop improvisation skills through the hands-on enactment of venture ideas (= mētis) and in favouring prudence in guiding actions and their outcomes (= phronesis).

Practising entrepreneuring calls for versatile competencies. Lazear (2004, 2005) suggests that the enforcement of non-cognitive skills such as social skills might help aspiring entrepreneurs create a resourceful personal network that allows them to align their professional identities with other identities marking their life-world. Among individuals who recognize the world as becoming (Chia, 1996), and here we include entrepreneurs and university students who are about to craft their identities and careers, reflexivity is then as much an existential issue as a work-related project. Yet, with comparatively little experience to drawn on, students cannot typically trust the embodied knowledge that they bring to the university because it still appears as what Freire addresses as "ingenuous" curiosity and knowledge. Thus, universities have the opportunity or even responsibility to provide an arena in which students' experiential learning as an outcome of curiosity, playfulness and emerging passion is designed to train and advance their practical reasoning or "actionable knowledge" (Jarzabkowski & Wilson, 2006).

Drawing on Weber (2003, 2005), we argue elsewhere that entrepreneurship education at business schools can fruitfully coach students in developing their entrepreneurial selves (Achtenhagen & Johannisson, 2013, 2014). Such identity work requires that students – individually and collectively – take charge of their own development. In the university setting, students can be encouraged to activate their immediate social worlds, and namely, their peer students, in this construction endeavour, creating a training ground for students to acquire core entrepreneurial capabilities. Self-organizing not only supports entrepreneurship as creative organizing, but solidarity and democracy as well (Spinosa, Fernando

& Dreyfus, 1997). This in turn renders students aware of other values than economic ones such as social, ecological and cultural values. In line with our concern for supporting students in developing their entrepreneurial selves, we thus view socially and environmentally responsible projecting as important dimensions of the process of entrepreneuring (Steyaert & Katz, 2004).

Identity work self-organizing also bridges students' professional and private lives. Today, international programmes are found in many business schools, as very diverse student cohorts provide social and cultural variety that can be used to complement traditional teaching resources (see Achtenhagen & Johannisson, 2013). This can save personnel and financial resources, and most importantly provide a more dynamic and potential context.

Introducing three modes of reflexivity

An education in entrepreneuring that aims at benefiting both students and society triggers student experiences along different modes of reflexivity, which in themselves present dualities in that they have two opposing poles. We identify three such modes and label these dualities as "from cognitive to emotional engagement", "from a hierarchic to a networked order" and "from a concern for the present situation (as *being*) to an orientation towards the future (as *becoming*)". These modes are discussed in more detail in the following.

Between cognitive and emotional reflexivity: more or less explicitly, academic literature rather normatively presents critical management research as a cognitive activity whereby the researcher's own understanding and values are integrated into thorough investigations of what is taken for granted by others (Alvesson & Deetz, 2000; Alvesson & Sköldberg, 2009). While such an approach questions the status quo of received knowledge, it appears to be too distanced from a practice approach (Schatzki, 2001; Chia & Rasche, 2010). A practice approach instead highlights reflexivity as not only a cognitive project but (also) as a social and emotional activity (Swan, 2008) and, in the context of entrepreneuring, even as an existential endeavour (cf. Johannisson, 2011) relevant to the crafting of an entrepreneurial identity.

If reflection is merely treated as a mental process, it may in turn prevent hands-on action rather than triggering it (see Brunsson, 1985), which obviously would run counter to the notion of a more action-based pedagogic approach to entrepreneurship education aimed at encouraging entrepreneurial drive (see Florin, Karri & Rossiter, 2007). Kyrö, Seikkula-Leino and Mylläri (2011) suggest that effective action-based entrepreneurship education should be based on developing key competences and propose that affection (relating to values and attitudes; see Gibb, 2002) and cognition (relating to declarative knowledge and procedural skills) should be combined with conative factors. Conation refers to aspects of motivation and volition (see English & English, 1958; Snow, Corno & Jackson, 1996). Similarly, such combined capacities have been recommended as the means of explaining moral thought and action (Hannah, Avolio & May, 2011), which are crucial in the endeavour of training responsible entrepreneurs.

However, as Messick (1996, p. 353) has noted, it is "exceedingly difficult to articulate educationally relevant processes fostering both personality and intellect, primarily because these overarching concepts are extremely complex as well as vague and amorphous". The challenge of combining social/emotional features of reflexivity with the entrepreneurial dimension of experimenting is further amplified when educating young and rather inexperienced persons who are crafting their identities.

Between hierarchical and networked reflexivity: reflexivity can materialize as a formal and hierarchically structured – i.e. designed – activity typically organized by a teacher with fixed expectations regarding the form of results to be delivered and leaving little space for dialogue. The opposing pole of this duality is reflexivity as triggered spontaneously and as emerging from conversations with peers through multiple dialogues or polylogues. Related to responsible entrepreneurship education, the organizing of opportunities for reflection is an outcome of negotiations between groups of peers, whereby everyone can contribute with their "slice of genius" (Hill, Travglini, Brandeau & Stecker, 2010) that all human beings possess. In such networked and reflective educational settings, the role of the teacher necessarily changes from that of an instructor to one of mentor and/or role model in reflectively elaborating on their own professional academic competencies while engaging with students as a mentee, addressing not only educational issues but also existential challenges. Here, a promising dialogue can only emerge if students do not submit to their teachers altogether. In intercultural settings, with students for instance socialized into unquestionable seniority principles, establishing such dialogue requires extra care (see Achtenhagen & Johannisson, 2013).

Reflexivity between criticizing what has been and appreciating what may become: reflexivity is often associated with a thorough examination of what "has been" and of what "is", so that those who are privileged are revealed while those who are marginalized are recognized. From a more conservative stance, this is mainly about correcting what retrospectively appears to be mistaken. However, reflexivity can also be associated with looking for coincidences that can be turned into opportunities and further enacted into real events – the trademark of entrepreneuring. Some argue that the ultimate vision of entrepreneuring is to create new worlds (Spinosa *et al.*, 1997). Focusing on reflexivity as part of an entrepreneurship curriculum calls for careful consideration of how it is enacted. Eriksen (2011) notes the importance of being concerned with student self-development and how such "making of capable selves" could be achieved. However, while he along with Schön (1983, p. 276) differentiates between "reflection-in-action" and "reflection-on-action", we suggest that a practice approach could bridge this divide. As a practice, entrepreneuring surfaces as processual, founded in an ontology of becoming (Chia, 1996) where improvisation and the use of analogy jointly invite reflexivity while space for new organizing and arrays of action is created (Johannisson, 2011).

Alternative pedagogical approaches for enhancing reflexivity

We have in the context of academic education experimented with two contrasting ways of stimulating epistemological curiosity and reflexivity among (business) students in a course setting. The first approach is based on the assumption that any student as a human being has a dormant potential to reflect on intellectual, practical and existential issues but that there may be barriers to such processes that must first be removed. The dominant management ideology of the business school setting and limited experience with or resources for interactions with local constituencies outside of the university hinder the crafting of a responsible entrepreneurial mindset. Students will then need help to escape ideological restrictions and the associated "banking system" (Freire, 1970) of knowledge provision. This can only be accomplished by exposing students to a radical experience through a "catharsis approach". The second approach aims at stimulating reflexivity by drawing upon unique capabilities that contemporary students as "digital natives" have, thereby recognizing them as competent citizens. As noted by Freire (1998, pp. 36–37), it is important to recognize students' capabilities, and we thus decided to articulate their digital skills (cf. Spinosa *et al.*, 1997). According to Berglund and Johansson (2007), it is important to enact concrete "situations" to accommodate conscientization processes, and thus we next reflect on business school education ventures facilitated at two universities in southern Sweden that have adopted two different approaches.

Conscientization[1] through emancipation[2]

The rationale for and the design of a catharsis approach

From the mid-1970s, Linnaeus University has offered a bachelor's programme in Entrepreneurship and Business Development (EBD). Over its first two decades of operation, a focus was placed on intense internships held in small firms through which students individually for two years socialized into the entrepreneurial milieu by working closely with owner-managers and by completing assignments translating between academic knowledge (episteme and techne) and practical knowing (mētis and phronesis) as applied in the firms. This model was then succeeded by a programme involving less intense practice in student teams and in different firms over the study period. This focus on practice in and concern for entrepreneurial values and behavioural norms is considerably reduced in the current EBD programme. One of the authors was however asked to draw attention once again to the original premise of the bachelor's programme and to organize a training context that would facilitate student experiences with entrepreneuring as a hands-on practice extending beyond for-profit venturing. As the students had already been colonized by management ideologies communicated through a traditional academic episteme format, shock therapy was deemed required to convert the students. It turned out to be convenient to integrate this educational challenge with a research and development project aimed at adding a social dimension to the traditional triple helix constellation: the university, political body and business community.

The SOcial Regional Innovation System (SORIS) project, which ran from January 2014 to January 2015, was financially supported by a state agency, a regional political body and the university. It was also backed by a loosely coupled network organizing the regional social economy that involved work-integrating social enterprises as well as voluntary organizations and social activists. The formal project owner was Macken's Friends, a non-profit association supporting one of the work-integrating social enterprises. A steering committee for the project was established, including resourceful and committed persons originating from the public, private and non-profit sectors. One of the authors, who also initiated SORIS, became the project leader and orchestrated the everyday operations of SORIS together with a project assistant.

With the formation of SORIS in February 2014, the project leader informed the programme's 37 first-year bachelor's students (all Swedish speaking) on entrepreneuring as a practice in general and as applied to SORIS in particular. They were then invited to participate in the enactment of three social ventures and were accordingly asked to self-organize into groups (one for each venture). The first venture, SNI (Social Network Innovation), aimed at establishing a tighter network between work-integrating social enterprises in the region. An experienced consultant who was also the chairperson of the board of one of the social enterprises became SNI's process leader. The second venture, Gottfrid's Barn, focused on energizing an emerging social venture in the tourism industry. SORIS acted as a temporary incubator for the venture mainly by providing mentoring support. Its initiators, themselves excluded from the labour market, remained as SORIS process leaders. The third venture, Växjö Young Competence (VYC), aimed at creating a staffing company offering young people's competencies to private- and public-sector employers. A hard-core economist who later became a social activist, the originator of the venture idea, became VYC's process leader.

The three social ventures were run sequentially from March to May 2014 lasting one month each and were reported at an innovation forum held at the university at the end of the month. Process leader(s) and student representatives then jointly and in public presented proposed measures for enacting the ventures whereby they were scrutinized by a panel of (regional) experts. Roughly one week after the forum, the students were individually examined through brief written reports whereby they were asked to reflect on personal and professional experiences gained throughout their involvement in SORIS and to position the latter against contrasting images of entrepreneuring. According to several scholars (e.g. Steier, 1991; Ellis & Bochner, 2000; Alvesson & Sköldberg, 2009), the basis of reflexivity is to reflect on one's own impact on experiences created. This applies to students as much as it does to researchers and practitioners.

Evidence of reflexivity achieved through emancipation

In exploring our conclusive individual examination of the undergraduate students involved in SORIS to identity their ways of reflecting, we had two foci. The first concerned the students' understanding of the entrepreneurial processes that they had co-enacted. We then asked them to use contrasting logics of "causality" and "effectuation" to structure their interpretations of their experiences, explicitly referring to Shane and Venkataraman (2000) and Sarasvathy (2001) (for details, see Johannisson, 2016a). Our second focus involved exploring illustrations related to the three proposed modes of reflexivity – the emotional/cognitive mode, the hierarchy/network mode and reflections regarding the being/becoming mode – as identified above. Below we provide some quotes related to each of these.

Reflexivity in the cognitive/emotional mode:

> As a student you are expected to remain seated, to raise your hand and to ask or answer questions. This is why I experienced SORIS, whereby decisive steps forward were taken as a bit of a clash. Instead of doing what was being told I was expected to find solutions and tasks on my own. In jobs outside of the academic world I have taken initiative, but somehow it is easy to assume the role of a student and to not look for solutions to problems oneself.... During this project I was exposed many new ideas on entrepreneurship – which probably was the intention. There have been many question marks down the road but as Bengt Johannisson has explained, that is a major part of entrepreneurship. Find/create solutions where there are question marks rather than asking new questions. I am thinking of what to create.
>
> (Male student – SNI)

> However, towards the end of the project (a few days before the innovation forum) I found a prime mover, the motivation that was needed to finish the project. I was not at all motivated when considering it as an assigned task that had to be accomplished.... Then, I experienced a kind of revelation that made me think something like: *Although for long I have considered this to be an unrealizable venture that is very laborious, I do not want to do a bad job and not for my own sake or for the university's sake but because this is about Mary and Paul's lives. Even if I am not fully committed to the venture and perhaps think that what they say about it is ridiculous, it remains incredibly important to them. I am not going to do a half-hearted job just because I do not see what they see in Gottfrid's Barn.*
> (Female student – Gottfrid's Barn, italics in original; the names of the social entrepreneurs have been changed)

Both students recognize the need to hold back short-term personal interests when engaging in social entrepreneuring. The male student notes his concern for his own entrepreneurial career, which brings him close to the cognitive pole. The female student in contrast reveals her emotional stance and demonstrates a sense of solidarity with the initiators of the venture.

Reflexivity in the hierarchy/network mode:

> [I]t has not been clear who pulls the strings. Rather than having a process leader who assigns tasks, several persons have taken on the role of leader, which has made the students suffer.... As a result of this ambiguous leadership we on one hand were told that we were free to create and to be innovative and to work in an entrepreneurial way but on the other hand were given instructions to follow. This in my mind does not stimulate creativity. Instead, it caused much confusion and inefficiency and many redundant work.
>
> (Male student – VYC)

> It did not feel right to change the information given because then it would not appear as a serious project, which would had made it more difficult to attract the firms.... For sure we have participated in and developed a process and even if VYC's objective has remained the same – and appreciated by many as interesting and excellent – this ambiguous invitation may make the venture uninteresting in the end. My philosophy is to nurture my contacts and I do not want to confuse people with changed information.
>
> (Female student – VYC)

Both students show that they have experienced problems in dealing with the ambiguities and paradoxes that they associate with the VYC venture. This suggests that the students feel locked into a hierarchical structure with few opportunities to break out and establish a networked structure with other students. To a great extent, this perceived imprisonment within a given structure is self-imposed given the process leader's explicit ambition to practise democratic leadership.

Reflexivity in the being/becoming mode:

> Although we collaborate a lot with [commercial] firms in our program, it has been a very interesting experience to visit these social ventures, which are so different. It has been exciting to meet these real enthusiasts who fight to improve the living conditions of other people although their very limited financial resources put a spoke in their wheel.... However, my personal contribution could have been more significant it was always like that. I still have the feeling that I am at the beginning of becoming an entrepreneur. It is difficult to create my own initiatives while I'm still a beginner and always have the feeling that I have to check with somebody else because I do not know what should be done. Many of us do not dare let ourselves go even if that is the very idea.
>
> (Female student – SNI)

I have learned a lot in terms of launching a venture, like in terms of the need for preparations and of the importance of personal networks.... By activating contact with the entrepreneur while being involved in Gottfrid's Barn, I strengthened my relation to him. I am convinced that if I maintain this contact, we will collaborate in the future. Additional contacts of this kind will dramatically increase my opportunities to start a business or to carry out innovative projects.

(Male student – Gottfrid's Barn)

In reflecting on their involvement in the projects, both students seem to feel that they have had a learning experience that has helped them imagine their own entrepreneurial careers. The female student underscores the importance of engaging personally while the male student communicates the need to recognize that entrepreneuring is a relational exercise. Clearly, both students in their reflections have adopted a "becoming" mode.

Not very surprisingly, multiple tensions dominate the students' reflections on their participation in SORIS. Nevertheless, the quotes bear witness to important lessons regarding the students' own understandings of entrepreneuring and of what it takes to practise it both with respect to their own personal development and regarding their interactions and responsibilities within and across boundaries of the academic context.

Conscientization through articulation

The rationale for and design of a blogging approach

The second case draws upon some of the students' unique capabilities to practice and enhance their reflexivity as part of an adequate pedagogy for responsible entrepreneurship education. Given that today's students are "digital natives", it was natural for us to develop an approach that would make use of this familiarity as a social and cognitive asset. The approach involved blogging activity following through the entire introductory master course entitled Entrepreneuring: Person and Process at Jönköping International Business School. As its name indicates, the purpose of this course was to invite students to develop their entrepreneurial selves based on a hands-on, practice-oriented approach. The blogging activity was coached and channelled through oral and written instructions that noted the importance of reflexivity for responsible entrepreneuring and through a number of guiding questions posed by us, the educators. In an earlier paper, we presented the findings of a blogging experiment that approached student reflexivity through individual tasks (see Achtenhagen & Johannisson, 2011). Here, we aim to examine the social dimension of reflexivity.

For a highly international cohort of master's students, we thus adopted a relational design to capture entrepreneuring and entrepreneurial learning as a collective phenomenon. Using diversity (in terms of prior experiences and cultural backgrounds) as a criterion, the students were assigned to groups of four to five students. In addition to writing their own blog entries on various assigned topics, students could post additional entries on different entrepreneurship-related aspects of personal interest to them, and they were asked to comment on one another's blog entries. In turn, different levels of reflexivity could be captured first through individual reflections on the different course sessions, the course literature, and the students' prior experiences and second through reflexivity among equals, creating an arena for exchange and mutual learning. The instructions clearly communicated that students should not summarize readings and class sessions but should instead link the readings, class activities and their own experiences to provide their own thoughts on these linkages. Students were explicitly invited to question what they had heard and read.

Evidence of reflexivity achieved through blogging

Below we provide examples of students' blog entries to illustrate how they capture the three different modes of reflexivity introduced above.

Reflexivity in the cognitive/emotional mode:

> The guest lecture given by KL was very exciting. You can tell from his lecture that he is very passionate about what he is doing. He showed that acting differently from what people expect makes you memorable.... He mentioned that everyone is dreaming about something and that it is motivating to pursue your dreams. I found it interesting that in his opinion, while honesty in a company is crucial, lying to your competitors is okay. Do you agree with him or do you think this is contradictory?
>
> (female German student)

> Hi, I agree with you that he is a man full of energy and indeed it is a good tip to act differently from others to be remembered. He mentioned passion as being important to becoming the best at what you are doing. However, he claimed that a person still can be good at what he is doing without having passion for his job. However, he could not imagine that for himself. But I think it is not always possible to work directly in a job you have passion for. It takes some time to see if you have the passion for a given job. After having discovered that your passion for your job is not strong, it might not always possible to change jobs for various reasons. What do you think about this issue? To answer your last question, I do not think it is contradictory, as you are competing against one and working with the other. Internal lying is very inefficient and usually affects profits negatively. External lying (what he did was in my opinion more misleading) is okay if not done too often. If a competitor asks what your current strategy is, of course you are not going to tell him. You have two options: lie or do not answer the question. Also, the competitor should know not to trust everything a competitor says. But what do you think about this issue?
>
> (male Dutch student)

In my opinion it is a very difficult question whether lying is the best way to "confuse" or "mislead" a competitor. I think that once you get used to telling lies, maybe it is very tempting to lie internally as well. Is lying externally consistent with what we have learned on being a moral person? Aren't there other ways of "misleading" a competitor, like avoiding answers or changing the topic and so on? I of course agree with you that you cannot tell your competitor your strategy and so on. But I have difficulty agreeing that lying is okay if not used too often. Who defines "too often" and how do you differentiate between people you can lie to and people you cannot lie to?

(female German student)

This discussion between the students illustrates two aspects of relevance to this chapter. First, it demonstrates how the students reflected on what they had heard during the guest lecture from a local entrepreneur in relation to their own experiences and opinions on entrepreneurial behaviour. Second, it shows how this mutual interaction was used to negotiate an agreement on what is right and wrong as evident from the discussion on moral behaviour. Both of these aspects illustrate students' attempts to train their phronesis and mētis.

Reflexivity in the hierarchy/network mode: the following reflective discussion illustrates how the students negotiated a common view of the contents of a lecture challenging mainstream views on entrepreneurship and introducing them to the concept of entrepreneuring largely based on Johannisson (2011). While the students had been explicitly encouraged to challenge received views, the discussion below illustrates the students' struggle in coming to terms with whether they had bought into what they learned or not.

My view on entrepreneurship is in li ne with professor BJ's because I think that everyone can become an entrepreneur with certain qualities like risk-taking, innovativeness and persistence. It was really interesting when he compared children with entrepreneurship. Have you ever thought about that? I never had, and I think it is really fascinating. He said that "Entrepreneurship is learning, learning is entrepreneuring." I think that he wanted to make sure that we all start to think like entrepreneurs and not be afraid of our ideas or limits.... I think this can mean that we should try to experiment in our life in order to learn from this. BJ said that children model experimental behaviour, as they continuously want to change things and therefore are naturally born to be entrepreneurs.... I have learned that entrepreneurship is an everyday activity, which means that it's a process that goes on continuously.

(female Iranian-Swedish student)

I would like to comment on your thoughts about children. I also found that view very interesting. BJ said that he does not try to teach people to become entrepreneurs, and instead he tries to make them stay entrepreneurial. What he, as you wrote, meant by that was that everyone is born as an entrepreneur and the challenge is to keep them like this. I agree that it is true because childhood is all about discovering and learning new things. Children have this curiosity to see and learn how new things work. It is that curiosity that drives them to learn new things and to progress in life. Among grown-ups, I believe that having this curiosity could have a powerful effect on the entrepreneurial market.

(female Swedish student)

Hi! I agree with you that being curious can help you to develop but can also influence personal growth opportunities [smiley face icon]. So I think from now on we should be very curious about everything we can learn as much as possible.

(female Swedish-Iranian student)

Hej, I absolutely agree that everyone could become an entrepreneur and could learn the skills needed. I believe that it is good if you already have some of the skills needed to be a good entrepreneur, but it is possible to develop them if you do not possess them yet.... I admit that I haven't thought of children as being entrepreneurs. However, don't you think it is some different kind of entrepreneurship game? I mean, sure children have their ways of achieving their goals, but they also have the advantage of having nothing to lose. They could try and fail and it is not a big deal. On the other hand, if a businessperson is as courageous as children are, he/she would probably fail very fast and would not be able to give it another try soon. These are my comments for now. I enjoyed reading your entry ☺.

(male Russian student)

The discussion above illustrates how epistemological curiosity (Freire, 1998) can emerge also in a peer-based setting in which newly acquired insights are tested and refined.

Reflexivity regarding being/becoming: the examples of reflexivity shown below illustrate considerations regarding how entrepreneuring is enacted.

In the reading, some ideas remain puzzling to me. One of them concerns the difference between an idea and an opportunity. When does an idea become an opportunity, and why isn't any idea always an opportunity?

(female African student)

Hey, maybe I can help with your first question: what is the difference between an idea and an opportunity? Well, Barringer & Ireland (2010) define the difference as follows: In order for an idea to become an opportunity, it needs to meet several criteria. An idea by itself is just a thought, not an opportunity. Only when an idea is linked to a product that creates value for its buyers and is attractive, timely, and durable does it turn into an opportunity. So I take this to mean that Zuckerberg had the idea of creating a social network, but it was also an opportunity. It was created at the right time during a period of increased ICT use. It was an idea that he would be able to "sell" for a long time, and it was very attractive to customers because it created value by means of simple and fast communication to (most) corners of this planet. On top of this, it was attractive for Zuckerberg himself because a lot of money was going to be involved. Does that help clarify the difference?

(female German student)

[response from African student thanking the German student for her post…]

I agree with you that experience may not be necessary for all entrepreneurs to succeed with their start-ups. Nonetheless, I do believe that experience is helpful in terms of anticipating what needs to be done, when it needs to be done and how it needs to be done. In your example on Zuckerberg, it is necessary to acknowledge … [continues].

(male Austrian student)

These excerpts illustrate the academic reflexivity process of becoming through mutual learning among peers. An important aspect of this emerging reflexivity is the openness to dare to say which subject-related aspects are not yet quite clear and the openness to take on explanations from fellow students. The process of explaining theories to peers including the search for examples that explain the subject at hand deepens understanding of the subject matter even if just for explanation purposes.

The "reflexivity grid" – a proposed integrated framework

Both cases confirm that there is not just one but at least three modes of reflexivity that are activated when students encounter mētis and phronesis as situated and experientially acquired knowledge. These modes of reflexivity also constitute one axis of what we refer to as the "reflexivity grid", which is summarized in Table 3.1 below. The second axis of the grid concerns *where*, i.e. in what context, reflexivity "takes place". Through both of our two pedagogical approaches, we identified three different yet coexisting contexts or "communities of practice" (Wenger, 1998) that students temporarily belong to while participating in an entrepreneurship education programme. These contexts are their personal community, academic community and global community. A "personal community" (see Wellman, 1982) is a network constituted by a student's interpersonal relations. The relations that students bring upon joining a study programme are highly influenced by the students' socio-cultural backgrounds. For example, in a number of blog entries students reflected on their families' expectations regarding their entrepreneurial behaviours. The "academic community" is the temporary social cluster to which students are invited while enrolled at a

Table 3.1 The reflexivity grid

Mode/community	From cognitive to emotional	From hierarchical to networked	From being to becoming
Personal	Live encounters with entrepreneurs who as role models tell of their career experiences	Genuine dialogues and informal organizing within peer groups	Dialogue on the enforcement of the entrepreneurial self
Academic	Arousing experiences that invite students to recognize their entrepreneurial selves	Invitation to question teachers and texts vs subordination (in relation to gender, age and responsibilities)	Transfer of accumulated knowledge or self-organized understanding as a result of peer dialogue
Global (physically, socially, mentally)	Inviting activism as a personal commitment to different issues	Challenging the dominance of for-profit entrepreneurship and subordination to institutions	Envisioning how entrepreneurial venturing can contribute to a sustainable world

business school or university. To a great extent it is populated by course mates, but other participants include academic staff and university stakeholders. In the case of SORIS, student teams assigned to social ventures clearly constituted such a community. The "global community" is the universal setting wherein a student participates as a citizen with both rights and obligations regarding social, environmental and moral issues. The global community does not recognize any boundaries in physical, social or mental space (Hernes, 2003). For example, throughout the blogging exercise, international students frequently described to their fellow students how insights gleaned from class had translated into their respective home contexts.

Social processes related to the three communities overlap and interact as students craft their identities and entrepreneurial selves. Membership in all three communities must be considered when identifying events whereby reflexivity may sediment into situated knowledge that we associate with mētis in regard to practical coping and with phronesis in regards to moral judgement.

The reflexivity grid integrates different aspects of reflexivity along proposed dimensions and provides examples as to how these dimensions might be captured in an educational setting – from inspirational meetings with entrepreneurs via reflective blogging to participation in (social) venture projects. These examples together with vignettes reported through the cases can jointly guide academic teachers who wish to creatively imitate our approach(es).

Concluding remarks

Echoing Freire's advice to recognize ourselves as constant learners, in this chapter we encourage academic colleagues to expand ways of enhancing reflexivity among (business school) students. However, even more fundamental is approaching students as co-teachers and as co-learners.

> The more my own practice as a teacher increases in methodological rigour, the more respect I must have for the ingenuous knowledge of the student. For this ingenuous knowledge is the starting point from which his/her epistemological curiosity will work to produce more critically scientific knowledge.
>
> (Freire, 1998, p. 62)

We experience both the SORIS and the blogging case as appropriate mutual learning settings. Another conclusive lesson intentionally created but enhanced by serendipity is the sociality of entrepreneurship as both a practice and learning process. Socializing is today as much associated with close personal relations – in an educational context involving students and teachers – as it is with intense digital relating. This reveals the entrepreneurial self of the future.

The blog entries demonstrate this through a clear pattern: the designed event is represented by tasks given to the students to write about, but the discussion and interactions take place in response to individual posts. Furthermore, additional posts created outside the task structure of guiding questions are more improvised and effectuated (see Chia & Holt, 2009). They illustrate the students' negotiations towards developing a clearer stance in determining for themselves what to consider right or wrong. In the case of SORIS, students were pushed into normality as in a "psychic prison" (Morgan, 2006) as much as many of the students had ideas that did not fit into SORIS's format and that therefore were considered dysfunctional. During SORIS's operation, students were also strangers to one another, as their previous programme courses had been delivered as traditional academic lectures. This experience explains the students' awkwardness in terms of organizing their efforts in the SORIS programme. It also underlines how crucial it is that students are invited to experience entrepreneuring as relational and to become aware of the importance of collaboration in rendering entrepreneuring in the interest of society.

Our experience with blogging as a pedagogical approach to enhancing different dimensions of reflexivity shows that student familiarity with social media creates opportunities for identifying new ways of making students take charge of their own learning and of developing their reflexivity along different dimensions. At the same time, the blogging exercise offers educators opportunities to themselves practice entrepreneuring by experimenting with new pedagogical approaches to teaching and evaluating, serving as an entrepreneurial way of developing academic education. It is close at hand to invite readers to design student tasks whereby blogging carries a polylogue on the creation of social values like those aimed at through the SORIS project. Identifying was to grade reflexivity fairly however remains as a challenge to be addressed (cf. Francis & Cowan, 2008).

In spite of our broad approach, several contextual factors that condition student behaviour and (thus) the outcomes of blogging tactics are not considered. Additional impacts not considered here include the students' contemporary social lives, the broader academic setting in which an entrepreneurship programme occurs and regional communities and their stakeholders. In our mind, these aspects invite further inquiry. For example, combining blogging as one of many ICT-based approaches can create room for building a learning community among university students across universities and national borders. Additionally, the blogging polylogue can easily be extended to include constituencies outside of the academic setting (e.g. practising entrepreneurs). Such interactivity may help us construct translations between formal education and experiential learning. This was practised in SORIS but certainly along a different and much more laborious, yet much needed, road. Perseverance is required not only in regard to developing epistemological curiosity and an entrepreneurial self but also in terms of entrepreneuring itself.

Notes

1 Although the concept of "conscientization" is not easily applied to a Western society like Sweden, we have maintained it as a conceptual attractor, as it is so closely associated with Paulo Freire.
2 This subsection draws extensively on Johannisson (2016b).

References

Achtenhagen, L. & Johannisson, B. (2011). *Blogs as learning journals in entrepreneurship education – Enhancing reflexivity in digital times.* 21st Scandinavian Academy of Management Conference, Stockholm, August 2011.

Achtenhagen, L. & Johannisson, B. (2013). The making of an intercultural learning context for entrepreneuring. *International Journal of Entrepreneurial Venturing, 5*(1), 48–67.

Achtenhagen, L. & Johannisson, B. (2014). Context and ideology of teaching entrepreneurship in practice. In S. Weber, F. Oser & F. Achtenhagen (Eds), *Entrepreneurship education: Becoming an entrepreneur* (pp. 91–107). Rotterdam: Sense.

Alvesson, M. & Deetz, S. (2000). *Doing critical management research.* London: SAGE.

Alvesson, M. & Sköldberg. (2009). *Reflexive methodology. New vistas for qualitative research* (2nd edn). London: SAGE.

Barringer, B.R. & Ireland, R.D. (2010). Getting financing or funding. *Entrepreneurship: Successfully launching new ventures.*

Berglund, K. & Johansson, A.W. (2007). Entrepreneurship, discourses and conscientization in processes of regional development. *Entrepreneurship & Regional Development, 19*(6), 499–525.

Brunsson, N. (1985). *The irrational organization.* Chichester: John Wiley & Sons.

Chia, R.C.H. (1996). The problem of reflexivity in organizational research: towards a postmodern science of organization. *Organization, 3*(1), 31–59.

Chia, R.C.H. & Holt, R. (2009). *Strategy without design. The silent efficacy of indirect action*. Cambridge: Cambridge University Press.

Chia, R.C.H. & Rasche, A. (2010). Epistemological alternatives for researching strategy as practice: Building and dwelling worldviews. In D. Golsorkhi, L. Rouleau, D. Seidl & E. Vaara (Eds), *Cambridge handbook of strategy as practice* (pp. 34–46). Cambridge: Cambridge University Press.

Ellis, C. & Bochner, P. (2000). Autoethnography, personal narrative, reflexivity: Researcher as subject. In N.K. Denzin & Y. Lincoln (Eds), *Handbook of qualitative research* (2nd edn, pp. 733–768). Thousand Oaks, CA.: SAGE.

English, H.B. & English, A.C. (1958). *A comprehensive dictionary of psychological and psychoanalytic terms*. New York, NY: Longmans, Green.

Eriksen, M. (2011). Facilitating authentic becoming. *Journal of Management Education, 36*(5), 698–736.

Florin, J., Karri, R. & Rossiter, N. (2007). Fostering entrepreneurial drive in business education: An attitudinal approach. *Journal of Management Education, 31*(1), 17–42.

Flyvbjerg, B. (2001). *Making social science matter. Why social inquiry fails and how it can succeed again*. Cambridge: Cambridge University Press.

Francis, H. & Cowan, J. (2008). Fostering an action-reflection dynamic among student practitioners. *Journal of European Industrial Training, 32*(5), 336–346.

Freire, P. (1970). *Pedagogy of the oppressed*. New York, NY: Continuum.

Freire, P. (1998). *Pedagogy of freedom: Ethics, democracy, and civic courage*. New York, NY: Rowman & Littlefield.

Gibb, A. (2002). In pursuit of a new "enterprise" and "entrepreneurship" paradigm for learning: Creative destruction, new values, new ways of doing things and new combinations of knowledge. *International Journal of Management Review, 4*(3), 233–269.

Hannah, S.T., Avolio, B.J. & May, D.R. (2011). Moral maturation and moral conation: A capacity approach to explaining moral thought and action. *Academy of Management Review, 36*(4), 663–685.

Hernes, T. (2003). Organization as evolution of space. In B. Czarniawska & G. Sevón (Eds), *Northern light – organization theory in Scandinavia* (pp. 267–289). Malmö: Liber.

Hill, L.A., Travglini, M., Brandeau, G. & Stecker, E. (2010). Unlocking the slices of genius in your organization. In N. Nohria & R. Khurana (Eds), *Handbook of leadership theory and practice* (pp. 611–652). Cambridge, MA: Harvard University Press.

Hjorth, D. & Johannisson, B. (2007). Learning as an entrepreneurial process. In A. Fayolle (Ed.), *Handbook of research in entrepreneurship education: A general perspective* (pp. 46–66). Cheltenham: Edward Elgar.

Jarzabkowski, P. & Wilson, D. (2006). Actionable strategy knowledge. A practice perspective. *European Management Journal, 24*(5), 348–367.

Johannisson, B. (2011). Towards a practice theory of entrepreneuring. *Small Business Economics, 36*(2), 135–150.

Johannisson, B. (2014). Entrepreneurship: The practice of cunning intelligence. In P. Braunerhjelm (Ed.), *20 Years of entrepreneurship research – from small business dynamics to entrepreneurial growth and societal prosperity* (pp. 109–119). Stockholm: Swedish Entrepreneurship Forum.

Johannisson, B. (2016a). Limits to and prospects of entrepreneurship education in the academic context. *Entrepreneurship & Regional Development, 28*(5–6), 403–423.

Johannisson, B. (2016b). Practicing entrepreneurship and citizenship – social venturing as a learning context. In L. Lundgaard Andersen, M. Gawell & R. Spear (Eds), *Nordic perspectives on social entrepreneurship* (pp. 93–112). Abingdon: Routledge.

Kyrö, P., Seikkula-Leino, J. & Mylläri, J. (2011). Meta-processes of entrepreneurial and enterprising learning: Dialogue between cognitive, conative and affective constructs. In: O. Jarl Borch, A. Fayolle, P. Kyrö & E. Ljunggren (Eds), *Entrepreneurship research in Europe: Evolving concepts and processes* (pp. 56–84). Cheltenham: Edward Elgar.

Lazear, E.P. (2004). Balanced skills and entrepreneurship. *American Economic Review, 94*(2), 208–211.

Lazear, E.P. (2005). Entrepreneurship. *Journal of Labor Economics, 23*(4), 649–680.

Letiche, H. & Statler, M. (2005). Evoking metis: Questioning the logics of change, responsiveness, meaning and action in organizations. *Culture & Organization, 11*(1), 1–16.

Messick, S. (1996). Bridging cognition and personality in education: The role of style in performance and development. *European Journal of Personality, 10*, 353–376.

Morgan, G. (2006). *Images of organization.* Thousand Oaks, CA: SAGE.

Ollila, S. & Williams-Middleton, K. (2011). The venture creation approach: Integrating entrepreneurial education and incubation at the university. *International Journal of Entrepreneurship and Innovation Management, 13*(2), 161–178.

Sarasvathy, S.D. (2001). Causation and effectuation: Toward a theoretical shift from economic inevitability to entrepreneurial contingency. *Academy of Management Review, 26*(2), 243–263.

Schatzki, T.R. (2001). Introduction: Practice theory. In T.R. Schatzki, K. Knorr, Cetina & E. von Savigny (Eds), *The practice turn in contemporary theory* (pp. 1–14). London: Routledge.

Schön, D.E. (1983). *The reflective practitioner: How professionals think in action.* New York, NY: Basic.

Snow, R.E., Corno, L. & Jackson, D.N., III. (1996). Individual differences in affective and conative functions. In D.C. Berliner & R. Calfee (Eds), *Handbook of educational psychology.* New York, NY: Macmillan.

Shane, S. & Venkataraman, S. (2000). The promise of entrepreneurship as a field of research. *Academy of Management Review, 25*(1), 217–226.

Spinosa, C., Fernando F. & Dreyfus, H.L. (1997). *Disclosing new worlds: Entrepreneurship, democratic action, and the cultivation of solidarity.* Cambridge, MA: MIT Press.

Steier, F. (1991). Introduction: Research as self-reflexivity, self-reflexivity as social process. In F. Steier (Ed.), *Research and reflexivity* (pp. 1–11). London: SAGE.

Steyaert, C. (2007). Entrepreneuring as a conceptual attractor? A review of process theories in 20 years of entrepreneurship studies. *Entrepreneurship and Regional Development, 19*(6), 453–477.

Steyaert, C. & Katz, J. (2004). Reclaiming the space of entrepreneurship in society: Geographical, discursive and social dimensions. *Entrepreneurship & Regional Development, 16*(3), 179–196.

Swan, E. (2008). Let's not get too personal: Critical reflection, reflexivity and the confessional turn. *Journal of European Industrial Training, 32*(5), 385–399.

Weber, S. (2003). A framework for teaching and learning "intercultural competence". In G. Alred, M. Byram & M. Fleming (Eds), *Intercultural experience and education* (pp. 196–212). Clevedon: Multilingual Matters.

Weber, S. (2005). *Intercultural learning as identity negotiation.* Frankfurt: Peter Lang.

Wellman, B. (1982). Studying personal communities. In P.V. Marsden & N. Lin (Eds), *Social structure and network analysis* (pp. 61–80). Beverly Hills, CA: SAGE.

Wenger, E. (1998). *Communities of practice. Learning, meaning and identity*. Cambridge: Cambridge University Press.

Williams-Middleton, K. & Donnellon, A. (2014). Personalizing entrepreneurial learning: a pedagogy for facilitating the know why. *Journal of Entrepreneurship Research, 4*(2), 167–204.

4 From entrepreneurship to entrepreneuring

Transforming healthcare education

Hanna Jansson, Madelen Lek and Cormac McGrath

For some, entrepreneurs are inventors or champions of technology, whose new ideas transform the world in radical ways, and entrepreneurship education (EE) is a way of promoting and stimulating the qualities those individuals have. This view of entrepreneurship is one we have encountered many times in our teaching practice, where entrepreneurship is often synonymous with starting a business. For others, EE falls under a broader definition of entrepreneurship and does not necessarily focus on starting a new business but is an activity focused on creativity and the development of one's own practice. This view resonates more with our own view of entrepreneurship and is in focus in this chapter, where we share how we endeavour to integrate a broad view of entrepreneurship and healthcare entrepreneuring in a course on service innovation within healthcare.

In our context, a world-leading research-intensive medical university, EE is a practice faced primarily with two challenges. One challenge lies in establishing entrepreneurship and EE as valid parts of the different educational programmes within the university so that EE, too may be considered a key value for healthcare professionals. The second challenge is brought about by establishing a pluralistic notion of entrepreneurship that does not sell the grand narrative of modernity, or the narrative of raw capitalism, but has to find a middle ground that is multifaceted and nuanced. In this chapter we describe how we go about developing a robust and inclusive notion of EE that challenges some of the traditional notions of healthcare education through adopting a critical approach to the concept of entrepreneurship. To this end, we introduce Bourdieu's concept of habitus as a sensitizing device, which we believe enables us to become aware of and question some of the prejudices that exist around the notion of entrepreneurship in healthcare contexts. Furthermore, we use principles of design thinking to describe how we design a course, Idea to Service Business – Transforming Healthcare (I2S), which aims to promote a critical approach to entrepreneurship in the medical and healthcare education context. In this chapter we also introduce the concept of "healthcare entrepreneuring" as a way of capturing the aforementioned critical approach.

Setting the stage

The scene for this chapter is a medical university that offers a wide range of medical and healthcare education programmes, most of which lead to a professional qualification such as medical doctors and nurses. The close connection to healthcare contexts could ideally promote entrepreneurship as a means to bring value from research to patients. As a case in point, the university has a long tradition of significant innovations, such as the pacemaker, the gamma knife and recent innovations in point-of-care diagnostics (Karolinska Institutet, 2013). These innovations have in common that they are highly technological inventions, which can be developed and sold under patent protection. Even though research has benefitted from the close connection to healthcare, innovation and education have traditionally been kept apart and the potential of connecting these two has not been fully realized. In part, this is because healthcare education is not typically driven towards the development of innovations or services and products. For example, most researchers at a medical university do not work on projects leading to the development of highly technological products that can be patented, and most students are not trained in entrepreneurship.

Since 1998, Karolinska Institutet (KI) has been part of the Stockholm School of Entrepreneurship (SSES), a collaborative effort between KI, the Royal Institute of Technology, Stockholm School of Economics, Stockholm University and the University College of Arts, Crafts and Design (Konstfack). Through SSES, students at the member schools are offered courses focusing on different aspects of entrepreneurship. Each school contributes with their core focus, some with more traditional EE including management and business methods and knowledge and some, like KI, with a particular context – healthcare – and the particular rules that apply there. Still, most programmes at KI do not include entrepreneurship courses from SSES in their programme syllabus and we perceive the reason for this to be that the traditional healthcare programmes at KI are not ready for or maybe even susceptible to the traditional notions of entrepreneurship. Our experience suggests that students and researchers in the medical and healthcare context generally identify more with healthcare and the patient perspective than with for-profit life science industry and drug development. However, everyday and mundane practices in healthcare involve both learning and sense making, which Johannisson (2011) views as integral to entrepreneuring. The ability to learn and make sense in order to adjust some practices is continuously pressing in the Swedish healthcare sector, which during the last decade has been exposed to privatization and public retrenchment. We thus realized that in order to bring out the full potential of entrepreneurship and to reach the students and researchers in the medical context we needed a new and more specific focus for our courses and introduced healthcare entrepreneuring as a way of emphasizing the processual nature of entrepreneurship.

Habitus

We identified a need to define, deconstruct and redefine what is meant by EE and the *entrepreneur* in the context of medical and healthcare professional education (Gartner, 1990). Previous research has suggested that there are different, potentially incommensurable discourses within EE (da Costa & Silva Saraiva, 2012; Kenny & Scriver, 2012). Entrepreneurship is often described in idealized or demonized forms. On the one hand, the idealized entrepreneur is depicted and promoted in policy documents at campus, national and trans-national policy levels. One such example is the Bologna agreement, which stipulates that entrepreneurship is a European value that should be sought after and implemented in higher education. This understanding of entrepreneurship, with its focus on innovation and unbounded creativity, is somewhat naïve, and represents a grand and perhaps neo-liberal narrative of modernity (Berglund & Johansson, 2007); it may be too broad and lacking in substance. On the other hand, the demonized entrepreneurship is reduced to a greedy person interested simply in making money, which in our case is in the context of state-subsidized healthcare systems. Entrepreneurship is reduced to a form of raw capitalism, where moneymaking endeavours stand above other values such as the duty of caring for patients, ethics etc. Our experience suggests that this view of entre-preneurship as something bad is particularly pervasive in the medical and healthcare profession context. However, it may be a specific Swedish or Scan-dinavian perspective, due to the fact that healthcare is state-subsided in Sweden and there is a willingness to pay a high level of taxes for healthcare services for the broader population (Eckerlund, Johannesson, Johansson, Tambour & Zethraeus, 1995).

Traditionally, MDs and other healthcare professionals are socialized into a profession that cherishes values such as safety, competency and proficiency (Jaye & Egan, 2006). Medical and healthcare curricula are designed to promote these values, and little attention is dedicated to different forms of entrepreneur-ship today. In this chapter, we use Bourdieu's concept of habitus as a sensitizing device to delineate the types of challenges that are expressed through different assumptions and prejudices that keep new and emerging concepts and discip-lines such as EE outside the curricula. Habitus focuses on ways of acting, feeling, thinking and being. It emphasizes how history is an integral part of human identity. Furthermore, habitus defines, indirectly, not only the choices people make but also how people may subsequently act. Habitus is acquired through a process of acculturation into certain social groups such as social classes or our peer groups, and also the working place. In terms of the healthcare system where many of the students will finally work, it may be the case that entrepreneurship has never been a part of the collective identity, or a part of the joint enterprise. Habitus, as a sociological concept, is as much about explaining the structure of the social world as about explaining the mechanism that ensures its transformation, and also the reproduction of behaviour (Reay, 2004) or, as Bourdieu writes,

Habitus is a kind of transforming machine that leads us to "reproduce" the social conditions of our own production, but in a relatively unpredictable way, in such a way that one cannot move simply and mechanically from knowledge of the conditions of production to knowledge of the products.

(Reay, 2004)

Normally, one may not be consciously aware of habitus in our everyday environment, as it is essentially never articulated explicitly; instead, it is part of the fibre of the everyday experience. Habitus becomes evident first in the context of an alien or new environment. According to Mutch (2003), habitus allows one to identify an explicit link between patterns of thought and social conditions. Consequently, the particular forms of habitus are formed in specific social conditions and become part of the fabric of those social conditions. Thus, habitus is not necessarily a set of rules and principles, but rather the embodiment of rules and principles, which are defined socially by inhabitants in different fields. It is this embodiment of assumptions and expectations that we choose to target in the I2S course.

Habitus must be viewed in relation to Bourdieu's other concepts: capital and field (Brosnan, 2010). Academia is itself a field and within academia, medical and healthcare schools may also be viewed as fields, with different disciplines, cultures etc. (Albert, Hodges & Regehr, 2007). In each field, different notions compete for access and acceptance. Students bring with them different forms of capital – cultural, economic, social and symbolic capital – but the field itself also has a capital and a set of rules that are articulated tacitly. Power within a field or discipline is culturally and symbolically created. Furthermore, it is maintained through the interplay of agency and structure (Brosnan, 2010). The main way this happens is through socialized norms or tendencies that guide behaviour and thinking (Wacqyabtm, 2005). Thus, in order for EE to make an impact and establish itself as a legitimate aspect of healthcare education, social and political agency must be questioned. The activities outlined in this text are a part of questioning the field of medical and healthcare education as a way of addressing the two main challenges outlined above: (i) putting entrepreneurship on the agenda for medical and healthcare education and (ii) promoting a pluralistic and nuanced notion of entrepreneurship.

Design thinking

When looking for a new approach to promote a multifaceted notion of EE, going beyond research-based highly technological product development, problem-solving methods inspired by the work of designers caught our interest. Design thinking (DT) is a method for innovation that puts the user needs in focus. Unlike other problem-solving methods, where the solution is typically in focus, DT concentrates on the challenge or problem. The problems addressed are often so-called "wicked", open-ended and difficult to solve problems, such as societal and health-related challenges. DT is described as:

A methodology that imbues the full spectrum of innovation activities within a human-centred design ethos. By this I mean that innovation is powered by a thorough understanding, through direct observation, of what people want and need in their lives and what they like or dislike about the way particular products are made, packaged, marketed, sold, and supported.

(Brown, 2008)

DT is focused on the early stages of innovation and involves practical work with personas, prototyping and role play while working in an iterative way, alternating between problem and solution (Carlgren, 2013).

The double diamond metaphor is a way to describe the process (Design Council, 2005). It consists of four different phases: (i) discover a challenge, (ii) define specific needs, (iii) develop ideas and (iv) deliver solutions. The double diamond is used to illustrate how the design process is either diverging or converging. At the beginning of the process, one expands the perspective to discover all the possible angles to the challenge at hand, before narrowing down the perspective and defining specific needs (insights, what needs to be done) to continue working. When the second diamond begins, the perspective is again diverging when as many diverse ideas as possible are developed. To be able to deliver a final solution, the perspective needs to be narrowed down, going for only one or two solutions. A slightly modified version also incorporates the DT steps as described by the "d.school", the Institute of Design at Stanford University (d.school, 2009). In this model, the second diamond covers three steps; ideation, prototyping and testing. Here we emphasize an iterative approach of DT (Figure 4.1).

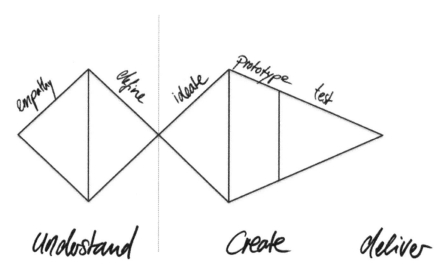

Figure 4.1 Schematic illustration of the double diamond process map of DT.
Source: Cecilie Hilmer, co-course director 2016.

A twofold approach

This chapter presents the design and development of the course I2S where the concept of healthcare entrepreneuring is intended to signal the transformative focus of our critical approach to entrepreneurship and EE. Further, the concept is used to identify the processual and lived experience of entrepreneuring as something that is enacted on a daily basis as opposed to something that is done to an organization or individual (Johannisson, 2011). The verb form entrepreneuring signals the active involvement of students in creating knowledge and an awareness of the active development of ongoing practices but also lends itself as an invaluable theoretical concept for professionals in healthcare contexts that does not always lends itself to predictability and pre-existent goals (Steyaert, 2007). Consequently, healthcare entrepreneuring is characterized by students working with creative tools and methods to transform (i) a shift in their thinking around what it means to study at a medical university and (ii) the shift in practice that is brought about by the newly found focus on services and development of one's own practice. I2S is designed to look beyond the biomedical industry, represented by big pharma and bio- and med-tech companies that focus on intellectual property and patents. The objective is to explore different ways to improve healthcare, and this idea of improvement is a core concept throughout the course. We aim to get the students to understand, from day one, why healthcare improvements are needed and how the healthcare context is different from other types of organizations, and further and perhaps most importantly we wish for them to see the opportunities to engage in entrepreneuring as an everyday activity (Johannisson, 2011). We believe that this may be experienced by the students as taking a step away from the expected trajectory many healthcare students have (Jaye & Egan, 2006).

The overall aim with I2S was to develop a course that (i) is based on a broad and inclusive definition of entrepreneurship, challenging the traditional perception of entrepreneurship in the given context, and (ii) reaches out to other students than those who want to start up a business or work within the life sciences. The purpose is to lay the foundation for creativity, innovation and action, aiming to broaden the perspectives of innovation and entrepreneurship and the students' future occupations.

Idea to service business – transforming healthcare

The I2S course was developed at KI and the Unit for Bioentrepreneurship, with the aim of introducing students to the concept of service innovation and development of one's own practice within the healthcare sector. The objectives are to (i) introduce students to the context of healthcare from a service innovation perspective, (ii) provide effective design tools and basic entrepreneurial tools, and (iii) to broaden their perspective on career alternatives (industrial, private etc.). The course is a 7.5-ECTS course at master's level, and was offered for the first time in 2010. For the course to be interdisciplinary, it has been taught in collaboration with SSES since 2013 with students from all five member schools.

The course is conducted as part-time study, two evenings per week over a period of two months. Theoretical lectures are provided in combination with practical work, inspirational talks and individual literature studies, for each learning objective. Most evenings are divided into two sections: a theoretical part, covering specific concepts such as service design and project planning, and an interactive part, where the students experiment and gain practical experience. Some sessions focus on the translation of concepts whereby invited guests share personal stories from working in the field. The core focus of the course is not to give the students knowledge and experience about a specific method or theory. Instead, the focus is to create and work with opportunities specific to the health-care sector. To guide the students through the process of service innovation, design and entrepreneurial tools are provided. The course will now be described following the DT process: (i) understand, (ii) create and (iii) deliver – three critical steps taking us from entrepreneurship to entrepreneuring – when transforming healthcare education.

Understand – knowing, unknowing and knowing again

The first step is to explore the present situation, in this case the course and service innovation within healthcare. Following a brief introduction to the course aims and learning objectives, the students elaborate on their preconceptions of concepts and expectations of the course in group discussions. What is their understanding of entrepreneurship, service innovation and the different practices within healthcare? What do they know about healthcare and life science? What prior experiences do they bring with them and what do they expect to learn? The final list of expectations is linked to the introduction of the course format and content. To get a head start in practice, the first evening ends with a guest sharing her/his own experience of starting up a service-based project or company within healthcare. The students are encouraged to critically reflect on the story and consider their own experience in relation to the experience of the invited guest.

Many students come to the course with a traditional view on entrepreneurship, that it is about starting up high tech companies and earning as much money as possible. Even though these students have applied to a course about service innovation within healthcare, many choose a picture of money or a man in tie and suitcase when asked to illustrate entrepreneurship. By introducing the first step, the students become more aware and "embrace" a broader definition of entrepreneurship. Likewise, their understanding of healthcare contexts and practices develops, going beyond trauma situations in the casualty department commonly depicted in TV series and the media to more commonplace events like a nurse instructing a patient on how to administer their medicine.

Defining the scope of the course is part of the first step. Emphasis is put on group formation and collective decisions have to be taken. What should the focus for the group work be? How do we collaborate and communicate in teams?

To guide the students, there is an introduction to what a project is and, since the course targets students other than healthcare professionals, we talk about inter-disciplinary teams. What is it like to work in a multidisciplinary group? What is the difference between interprofessional and intraprofessional work settings and practice? The students get the tools to put together a simple group contract, and all groups have to choose a group leader. The student's hand in a short written proposal, outlining the challenge they want to work on (and base their idea on). The proposal includes a short description of the need, why they want to study this and how they will proceed with the actual work (see Table 4.1 for an example of the group project).

At the beginning of the course, some students question the time spent on group formation and project start-up. They argue that they have worked on pro-jects in teams before and want to get started on the "real content". Later on, however, most of them come to value the importance of project planning, and of getting a common understanding of the project aim, idea and work. Furthermore, there are always some students who question why the groups are formed based on interdisciplinarity, to get as diverse groups as possible, but later on almost all students highlight the interdisciplinary work as one of their most important lessons learned. We believe that this increased critical awareness occurs partly because the course design evokes elements of community-building in that the students engage with each other around the group project. However, for most students the project is something entirely new; it forces them to let go of their expectations and encourages them to work in new ways, which may run contrary to previous experiences.

> I have actually had a lot of use of the new ways to look at things e.g. the "turning everything inside out and upside down" in my daily work and it has already improved the projects I am working on.

Table 4.1 Group project example – understand

The first step for the team in the course project is deciding on a challenge to work with. This is an important step as all team members share their interests and perspectives. The first decision has to be taken together as the team members are still getting to know one another. One team chose the challenge of ensuring emotional wellbeing in elderly homes, with the difficulty of the elderly not being able to express their needs strongly enough and the lack of time of the staff to engage with the patients to identify problems early enough to prevent an effect on their health. The team especially focused on the caregivers' experience and were able to accompany a nurse during her work at an elderly nursing home and while she was interacting with elderly patients.

As a result of the observations and interviews the team identified one root problem that they wanted to work on further: The "handover" from one nurse to the other. Given the high workload of the staff in the home, they discovered that it was frustrating for them not to be able to perform their duties of observing patients for signs of concern and properly maintain records of patient's activities, incidents and behaviours. The high amount of paperwork to be done at the end of a shift worsened this situation.

Source: Cecilie Hilmer, co-course director 2016.

Having a 6-year working experience in hospitals and diagnostic centres as biomedical analyst I now see a different approach of how problems in the healthcare sector can be solved. Innovative ideas coming from people with different backgrounds seem to be the answer.

(Anonymous students, 2015)

Create – develop, test and evolve

A central method within service design is prototyping, "anything tangible that lets us explore an idea, evaluate it and push it forward" (Brown, 2008). Prototyping is something completely new for most students, and the course takes them through many practical examples and two full sessions that are devoted to the prototyping and testing of ideas (Table 4.2). In the first session we introduce the concept of prototyping, what it is, why it is important for service innovation and how you do it. The students discuss what they want to test, how to include the user perspective and which interaction points are crucial for the user. They end up formulating critical questions to be addressed. In the second session, the students test their prototypes in a "prototyping market" engaging in role play while acting as each other's users (Figure 4.2).

At the beginning of the prototyping sessions, it is not uncommon that the creative methods and exercises are questioned. Many students think that they are simple and rudimentary. Furthermore, the students almost always start brainstorming without further direction, coming up with ideas for how to solve the problem. This is something that we see from year to year, and it is most common among the students with a natural science background. Another important part of the second step is the role play, where the students have to test their prototypes when acting as each other's users. This is not easy for the students, and the teachers need to remind them that they should test each other's prototypes and

Table 4.2 Group project example – create

Based upon the previous work the teams have developed one or more potential solutions to the described/identified problem. Most of the time these solutions only exist in the minds of the students. This is one of the most challenging phases of the process, as the idea will have to be brought to life in order to test whether it really meets the identified needs. This is particularly challenging due to the nature of healthcare, where solutions will very likely be service based. The previously described team from the course in 2016 decided to focus on the "handover" between shifts, and developed a tool that simplifies the administrational work and includes the possibility to add other forms of information beyond facts that need direct follow up, making the tool work like a diary where information can be included during the shift and shared according to need. A "Wizard of Oz prototype" was build out of cardboard [Figure 4.2], where one team member made sure the testee saw the right interface at the right time. Other team members acted out the roles of the patient and the nurse of the following shift. One team member acted as a pure observer, took notes on the testee and his/her actions. After each test, the complete team would take some time to interview the testees about their experience.

Source: Cecilie Hilmer, co-course director 2016.

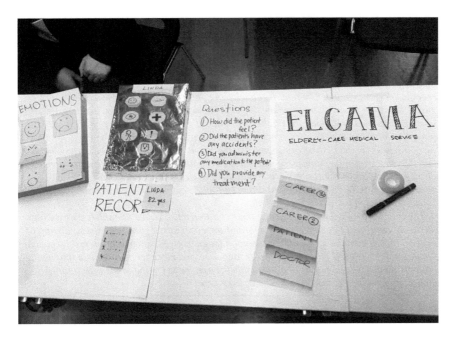

Figure 4.2 Preparing for role play, testing of prototypes and collecting user feedback.

Source: photo by Cecilie Hilmer, co-course director 2016.

give each other feedback from the tentative user perspective. They should criti-cally question their own experience as users and should not evaluate each other's ideas based on entrepreneurial tools and previous knowledge. After completion of the course's second step, the students have often embraced the user-centred way of working. They see the value of the creative methods when exploring the present situation for the user, or patients within health innovation, and reveal all possible challenges before going into the creation of ideas to solve the problem.

Deliver – disseminate and reflect

The third and last step is to deliver the final project reports and presentations. The different service ideas (Table 4.3) are presented orally as a short speech, or "pitch", to the whole class and a panel of teachers and professionals in the field. This is followed by a general discussion. The focus of the pitch is to com-municate the need the group have analysed and the functionality of the service they have developed. They are expected to present their service with the help of visualizations such as prototypes, movies, illustrations and images. Each group acts as critical reviewers for another group, reading the process report of the other group as well as preparing and asking questions and giving feedback after the presentation.

Table 4.3 Group project example – deliver

At this point the teams have ideally gone through two iterations or more, meaning rounds of testing and improving their proposed solution, or even changing the solution completely, if the feedback showed that the prototype did not meet the user's needs. The presentation takes place in the form of a pitch but with background about the users and their needs. It is important to understand which insights lead the team towards this specific service product. The final feedback from the opposition, course teachers and guests helps the teams to improve the project report that they will hand in a few days later. We decided on having the pitches without a digital presentation and we wanted to see all members involved in some way. The only digital tool allowed was video material. Also, this was an interesting experience for the teams as it required more arrangement and practice within the teams. We were able to create a safe space in the classroom to allow this experimental atmosphere and had teams presenting with a variety of approaches, mixing role play, storytelling, self-made props out of cardboard, and showing videos. The students enjoyed it.
The aforementioned team presented their solution as software on tablets that enables the healthcare staff to enter specific information, especially concerning the wellbeing of the patients. It combines this with the usual administrative documentation tasks, reducing the paperwork needed by adding simpler language and more icons and including the patients themselves as points of input. In their case, more testing in the real setting, the elderly nursing home, would be the ideal next step.

Source: Cecilie Hilmer, co-course director 2016.

The group project is summarized in a process report, where the students describe in five chapters how they have developed their service step by step. These chapters explore and describe: (i) the initial challenge that they set out to solve, (ii) the intended user, (iii) prototyping and testing, (iv) the application of entrepreneurial tools and (v) future possible steps to further develop the service idea. The practical work is also summarized in a written individual reflection on their experience and learning. The reflection should revolve around the work process itself and one's personal contribution to the project. The team dynamics, including one's personal role in the team (the position one took, what felt good, what went wrong and what one would do differently next time) are also discussed, as is their critical understanding of the field of "service innovation within healthcare" and its relation/relevance to the students studies/work. The students are asked to describe what they have learned during the course and use their prior experiences to situate the course in a wider context.

The group project is assessed by capturing the entrepreneuring, not the end result. The group process is described and discussed vis-à-vis three levels of understanding, where the students (i) show understanding for the process (the different steps, etc.), (ii) apply methods and theories and (iii) reflect on their experience and learning (the process, individual contribution, the team and the context). This approach enables the students to review and critically reflect on their own process as well as their own assumptions and values that they brought with them into the project. On completion of the third step, the students have developed a more critical awareness of entrepreneurship within healthcare. Even though the focus for the group project was to design and develop a service idea, the opportunity of transforming healthcare through means other than a start-up become more evident and is an idea that the students bring with them in their future profession.

Towards an entrepreneuring self

In working with the I2S course we have come to view habitus as an important concept, forcing us to rethink and reappraise, and together with the students engage in critical self-reflection about what it means to be a healthcare professional, what innovation and entrepreneurship is and how entrepreneuring can be a natural part of healthcare professionals' education and practice. As such, habitus is two-dimensional, forcing us as teachers and course and programme leaders to rethink the concepts and nomenclature we use in the course, framing development in terms of services and not solely in terms of products, and, perhaps even more importantly, by critically reviewing the notion of the entrepreneur as someone who accomplishes heroic acts and instead evoking the notion of the healthcare entrepreneuring and the entrepreneuring self as a facet of every healthcare worker's daily practices (Berglund & Johansson, 2007; Steyaert, 2007; Johannisson, 2011). Furthermore, using the concept of habitus as a sensitizing device encourages us to consider students' assumptions and expectations of engaging in entrepreneuring in the context of medical and life science education. The use of DT when designing the course has meant that the students encounter uncertainty and need to take responsibility for their own learning. This uncertainty is revealed, as they are required to identify innovations and changes in relation to their practices, which may run contrary to the traditional knowledge acquisition, and socialization processes they may be accustomed to. In other words, it situates the students in unknown territory. As this is new for many students, we need to talk about it throughout the course. Our focus is on targeting the symbolic capital inherent in the way medical and healthcare education is taught to students today, and also to promote critical reflection on the socialization process (Brosnan, 2010; Witman, Smid, Meurs & Willems, 2011). By asking the students to question their own expectations we create opportunities for them to critically reflect on their previous thoughts and assumptions on entrepreneurship. Our experience is that, most of the time, the students initially hold a more traditional view of entrepreneurship and see the entrepreneur as a superhero but this typically changes during the course, which is evident in their reflective assignment. Questioning this preconception is a way that allows us to tackle the second challenge outlined above, developing a pluralistic view of EE, not only corresponding to the traditional view of the entrepreneur as starting a new for-profit business but also acknowledging other forms of entrepreneurship(s). The course aims to teach the students about many different topics and disciplines, from identifying needs to designing and testing solutions and packaging the proposed solution as a service idea. Ideally the course will also empower the students to view entrepreneuring as part of the practice of healthcare in their future occupations. The students research in depth the topics that they need to know more about and/or find especially interesting. At the same time, they learn from and with each other in their interdisciplinary teams by sharing knowledge and experiences from their own discipline, which enables them to work on "bigger" problems than those they would be able to tackle on their own (Ledford, 2015). This is essential in the process of healthcare entrepreneuring.

Each year we find that the non-business students gain the most from hands-on supervision from teachers and peers as regards how to develop the entrepreneuring self.

> The most rewarding thing about working in a group was to be able to benefit from the combined knowledge of all my group members. Being a KI student I was glad to be able to contribute with my own knowledge (thinking a lot about the elderly people and how they can use our service in an easy way). The course made me see areas in the healthcare that need development, and hopefully I might come up with ideas that produce improvements. As a healthcare professional, I will have many patients every day, and with new ideas about for example journal writing and queuing systems we might be able to work more effectively and help more people.
>
> (Anonymous student, 2015)

The business students gain most from the different cases that illustrate the healthcare perspective of business, with its context-specific challenges and opportunities.

> To be honest, during the course I was sometimes frustrated that I was not learning anything new about business. However, now that I reflect back on the course I realize I have learned a tremendous amount of new things that at first are seemingly unrelated to business but, when I come to think of it, are very much business, and what's more, they open up new doors to my understanding of business.
>
> (Anonymous student, 2014)

So what comes out of all this, what have students embraced and what have we as educators learned? With the I2S course, we aimed for a course that was based on the broad definition of entrepreneurship, which reaches students from basic study programmes and where healthcare entrepreneuring is brought into focus. Through the new focus on services (in contrast to highly technological, tangible, often patented products) and the specific focus on challenges and opportunities within healthcare (in contrast to commercialization of research results, and drug development within the healthcare industry), the course takes a broader view of entrepreneurship in the medical context into account. In the process reports we see repeated examples of how the students have embraced the medical context when presenting the process of developing service ideas, often packaged as social ventures. By using these foci, we find that more and more of the basic study programmes leading to a professional qualification offer the I2S course as an elective programme for their students. With the foundation in DT the course captures the essence of healthcare entrepreneuring, having the students work and focus on process and not merely the end product. In the individual reflections, we see examples of how the students link their new knowledge to their ongoing studies and to their future careers.

Furthermore, during the development of this course the importance of co-development has been evident to us as educators. The course idea was initially developed with a student who questioned the technical product-oriented focus of existing courses. The student wanted a course with a more general approach to the packaging of knowledge, methods and processes generating products such as consultancy services, websites, applications etc. In collaboration with this "user", we decided to develop a course about service ideas. As already described, we used the concept of DT to capture the essence of service innovation. Again we co-developed the content with a designer to fully be able to fully embrace the design thinking process, and after two years a designer was recruited as the co-course leader. We find that the work on this course has increased our under-standing of the advantages and disadvantages of working with interdisciplinary courses. We have discovered that laying the foundation for the group work is very important. We have also seen that early communication is key. Most important however is the transition and a shift in focus from entrepreneurship to entrepreneuring as something always happening, a state of being (Johannisson, 2011). A course like this needs to continually improve and develop, and the next step in this journey would be to incorporate new learning outcomes and examinations that explicitly emphasize critical aspects of entrepreneurship. We like to think that we practise what we preach and that in each iteration of the course we ourselves are healthcare entrepreneuring.

In conclusion, we view ourselves as brokers of change (McGrath & Bolander Laksov, 2014), and acknowledge that it is important when discussing healthcare entrepreneuring with students we do it in a way that students are forced to question their own assumptions and perceptions about what it means to engage in entrepreneuring in the healthcare context. At the same time, we can see how our brokering role works in at least two different ways; in the SSES context we are able to question the strong business-oriented discourse and in the healthcare context we introduce and encourage the idea of healthcare entrepreneuring which has been outlined above. EE is still treated as a peripheral subject in relation to the other subjects at our university. Emphasizing healthcare entrepreneuring instead of entrepreneurship may be a way of tackling the challenges we addressed in the introduction to the chapter. Consequently, a pluralistic and nuanced conceptualization of EE could also mean that the concept of healthcare entrepreneuring permeates the medical and healthcare programmes. Although we are still on the periphery in the medical and life science university, we feel that the different aspects of how we work outlined in this chapter demonstrate some of our efforts at moving in from the periphery, and we feel confident that we are moving in the right direction.

References

Albert, M., Hodges, B. & Regehr, G. (2007). Research in medical education: Balancing service and science. *Advances in Health Sciences Education, 12*(1), 103–115.

Berglund, K. & Johansson, A.W. (2007). Constructions of entrepreneurship: a discourse analysis of academic publications. *Journal of Enterprising Communities, 1*(1), 77–102.

Brosnan, C. (2010). Making sense of differences between medical schools through Bourdieu's concept of "field." *Medical Education, 44*(7), 645–652.

Brown, T. (2008). Design thinking. *Harvard Business Review, 86*(6), 84–92.

Carlgren, L. (2013). *Design thinking as an enabler of innovation: Exploring the concept and its relation to building innovation capabilities*. Thesis, Chalmers University of Technology.

D.school. (2009). *Steps in a design thinking process*. Retrieved from https://dschool.stanford.edu/groups/k12/wiki/17cff/.

da Costa, A.D.S.M. & Silva Saraiva, L.A. (2012). Hegemonic discourses on entrepreneurship as an ideological mechanism for the reproduction of capital. *Organization, 19*(5), 587–614.

Design Council. (2005). *Design Council*. Retrieved from www.designcouncil.org.uk.

Eckerlund, I., Johannesson, M., Johansson, P.O., Tambour, M. & Zethraeus, N. (1995). Value for money? A contingent valuation study of the optimal size of the Swedish health care budget. *Health Policy, 34*(2), 135–143.

Gartner, W.B. (1990). What are we talking about when we talk about entrepreneurship? *Journal of Business Venturing, 5*(1), 15–28.

Jaye, C. & Egan, T. (2006). Communities of clinical practice: implications for health professional education. *Focus on Health Professional Education: A Multi-Disciplinary Journal, 8*, 2.

Johannisson, B. (2011). Towards a practice theory of entrepreneuring. *Small Business Economics. 36*(2), 135–150.

Karolinska Institutet. (2013). *Important discoveries made at KI*. Retrieved from http://ki.se/en/about/important-discoveries-made-at-ki.

Kenny, K. & Scriver, S. (2012). Dangerously empty? Hegemony and the construction of the Irish entrepreneur. *Organization, 19*(5), 615–633.

Ledford, H. (2015). How to solve the world's biggest problems. *Nature, 525*(7569), 308–311.

McGrath, C. & Bolander Laksov, K. (2014). Laying bare educational crosstalk: a study of discursive repertoires in the wake of educational reform. *International Journal for Academic Development, 19*(2), 139–149.

Mutch, A. (2003). Communities of practice and habitus: A critique. *Organization Studies, 28*(4), 546–563.

Reay, D. (2004). "It's all becoming a habitus": beyond the habitual use of habitus in educational research. *British Journal of Sociology of Education, 25*(4), 431–444.

Steyaert, C. (2007). "Entrepreneuring" as a conceptual attractor? A review of process theories in 20 years of entrepreneurship studies. *Entrepreneurship and Regional Development, 19*(6), 453–477.

Wacqyabtm, L. (2005). Habitus. In *International Encyclopedia of Economic Sociology*.

Witman, Y., Smid, G.A.C., Meurs, P.L. & Willems, D.L. (2011). Doctor in the lead: Balancing between two worlds. *Organization, 18*(4), 477–495.

Part III

On moving

5   A space on the side of the road

Creating a space for a critical approach to entrepreneurship

Pam Seanor

Opening narrative

This is a story of a narrative "space on the side of the road" (Stewart, 1996) that draws upon my practices, as a teacher/researcher in a business school, in the United Kingdom. As such, the story takes place in light of the ways in which critical entrepreneurship is taught in business schools and the roles for students in society and in how I create and cultivate critical approaches to teaching in entrepreneurship.

This critical approach makes it "other" than the story of how entrepreneurship is taught. This chapter arose from conversations with both Karen and Karin, the editors of this volume, as researchers and teachers, about what it means and how to evoke an "other" way of thinking about and facilitating a critical approach to entrepreneurship education. Johannisson (2016, p. 404) spoke of the limits to and prospects for teaching entrepreneurship – his story of the "other" being a critical approach of the "gap" between the "traditional" and the "everyday". When I began teaching five years ago, there was just such a gap in a module I inherited from those teaching it prior to me. It took the first year to recraft the narrative and practice of the module. One of my first actions was to rename the module Entrepreneurship: Ideas & Practices (it was previously called Advanced Entrepreneurship), as I was interested in facilitating a view of the processes of entrepreneurship and negotiating between differing ideas and practices. At my first field board, the external examiner complimented me for having what he termed "bridged this gap between theorizing and practice", which, for a time, offered legitimacy to my approach and enabled me to create a space to continue to develop the module. However, I find I am involved in working with – and against – meaning making and knowledge of entrepreneurship. Though Down (2013, p. 3) argued that problems are common, as "we live the same society", in conversations there appears a divide in how notions such as "enterprise" and "society" are interpreted; there are those colleagues who assume a more functionalist approach, what is termed the US tradition, and those of us attempting to engage with the wider issues and sensibilities embodied in the European tradition (Down, 2013). The feelings of frustration are palpable on both sides when words are not shared, and where some seek to encourage pluralism and others see only one view.

So, it is not my story alone but of the differing stories I experience, as module leader in devising and facilitating lectures and workshops, as well as the academic administration and evaluation of the module. One narrative stream is of taking a critical approach and of a pluralization of narrative in entrepreneurship as of differing stories with different degrees of intellectual and practical elements and implications. Interwoven with this stream is a second narrative, informed by the metaphor of being on the move (Steyaert & Hjorth, 2003; Down, 2010; Hjorth, 2011). I too seek to move students from an area they know, to encourage them to look at the world and its problems from more than the traditional vantage point and to look again from an alternative approach as a way of seeing entrepreneurial processes. When entrepreneurship is viewed as such a process it initially seemed inevitable that it will be seen to hold contradictions, tensions and clashes.

Yet, the more I mulled, the more my thinking was not only of movement in teaching practices of a critical approach to entrepreneurship but at the same time feeling of being sidelined to Stewart's (1996, p. 26) "space on the side of the road" and of the need to "give pause" and create a space for critique of how we as educators-researchers are grappling with theorizing and developing an "other" way in practices, within the constraints and demands in our institutions within a range of higher education policies globally. As such, the structuring of the chapter draws upon Stewart's (1996, pp. 29–30) writings of meaning of images and objects, which lies in a space of searching and of how things happened encountering "interruptions" of how stories are portrayed at once as two contradictory things. I offer two such "encounters" to begin a conversation. I then speak of the challenges in an interpretative space of provocations, tensions and surprises of teaching entrepreneurship in a critical way. I conclude with a discussion where I take a step back to "re-present" and to "generalize" my own experience, e.g. speculating about the extent to which my own experience is indicative of how difficult it is to introduce a critical course on entrepreneurship into a business school context since students might experience this as overly disruptive.

Encounter: dread and desire. What is a critical approach to entrepreneurship?

As a venture point, in searching to address what is it we mean by critique, I approach it as building awareness that there is never just one reality of entrepreneurship and of creating sensitivity for the differences in entrepreneurship. In reopening stories of others, these appear based upon their experiences with their master degree students – experiences of undergraduate teaching seem missing from these stories. And yet, like these writers, I too desire a critical approach and feel it is crucial to consider change and of the need to problematize conventional ways of thinking in entrepreneurship, which these other writers argue constrain creativity and to consider different ways of thinking from what is seen as "legitimate" in this domain.

Figure 5.1 Searching.

The notion of what being critical is of course open to differing and seemingly contradictory definitions (Śliwa *et al.*, 2013). Added to which, as teachers how we express critique and how students see it differs. As Leah Tomkin and Eda Ulus (2015, pp. 596–597) stated:

> Once we have gone past basic statements, such as "critical reflection is not the same as criticism, i.e., finding fault," we often struggle to articulate what it is we want our students to do. In our experience, we have found that students often interpret criticality as the requirement (or opportunity) to give their own opinion, which tends to result in ungrounded assertions and a certain disdain for theory.

Eda and Leah were colleagues and we often spoke of our experiences of teaching critical studies with students: theirs from organization studies; mine from entrepreneurship.

Throughout the module, I draw upon paradox, stories, watching movies collectively and the notion of "becoming" and how this notion links to movement. To pull these together, I use the imagery of the fable *The Story of All Wisdom*, sometimes called *The Story of the Elephant and the Blind Men*. This approach follows much of Gartner's (2001) story of the elephant in entrepreneurship and blind assumptions in theorizing and others taking the "alternative approach" (Down, 2013).

I want to offer a brief history of organizing the module for final-year management and business undergraduates at Bristol Business School, Bristol, UK. It was delivered over two terms but now runs for approximately four months in the final year in the spring term. This changed with the introduction of semesterization and this time factor is of note as I feel it takes time to develop relations with students and to encourage them to rethink. For instance, a student who was on other modules I delivered said he did not know where it was going but he knew from having me in other modules that I had an intention to do what I did and he "trusted" me and was willing to "make a leap".

The module is an optional choice as part of the final year (capped at 50 undergraduate students). To inform their choices, students can look at the module specification, as well as the module handbook; both clearly state that a "critical approach" is taken and include the following as learning outcomes that on successful completion of this module students will be able to:

1   Engage in critical discussion of differing perspectives of entrepreneurship processes.
2   Develop critical skills to effectively inform research and analysis of entrepreneurial processes through how differing theories relate to "everyday" practice.

Yet, when I ask students "Why did you choose to take this module?" for the majority it is as simple as "there is no exam".

In the introductory lecture, I draw upon the thinking of Bill Gartner that there is no one story of entrepreneurship; instead it is a space where multiple stories sit alongside one another. In the accompanying first workshop I have said we would break off the two-hour class-based session after the first hour. I ask my students to go to the Bristol floating harbour before the next workshop, to walk around and possibly talk and take notes and/or photographs with three differing examples of entrepreneurship to bring back to discuss in the next workshop. I ask them to do this with another student from the module. The intention is for them to look again at something in everyday practice. This session is to begin our conversation and by working in groups in the workshop for them to make sense for themselves and to hear how others make sense of a similar experience. Encouraging peer-to-peer discussion has at times created a space for "aha" moments and/or where you can see a student's eyes light up when they "get it".

Twenty-four students, approximately half the cohort, return to the second workshop. I ask "Honestly, who went to the harbourside?"; half hold up their hands. I ask them to form in to small groups and to ensure someone in each group has been to the harbourside to discuss their experiences. Even so, when I go round to speak with each group, participation proves tricky; in one group, a student who had gone to the harbourside begins the conversation by challenging my approach:

STUDENT: I went and did not find what you said in the lecture. The entrepreneur said he was only interested in money. It was just economics.

ME: [A pause for breath and relax the tensions creeping in to my shoulders] First, I'm glad to hear you went to the harbourside and spoke with someone. Tell me, whom did you speak with?

STUDENT: It was the guy running the ferry.

ME: Ah, is that the one going back and forth to the SS *Great Britain*?

That makes sense, considering that money would be a concern as one of the other ferry companies went bankrupt. Remember, I never said money wasn't a deal to be concerned about.

ME: So, did he say anything else when you were chatting?

STUDENT: He said they needed to think of new ways of working, not just going back and forth in a linear way from one side of the harbour to the other. And how they might interest more tourists to use them.

ME: OK – so say that again for the group.

STUDENT: More or less repeats what he said.

ME: What you just said sounds more than about money. By nature, a ferry has to work within the boundaries of the harbour and he's saying they have to rethink their work. So, might that in some way link to what we are speaking of as beyond economic views and of being creative?

STUDENT: [*Shrug*].

As part of the assessment for the module, I include a "portfolio of practices" where students are to comment on set questions and tasks from workshop activities and ideas from the lectures. Only one student commented on the above exchange as informing his learning and of rethinking and the need to move about to see things differently; of note, it was not the student who offered the above experience.

In offering the above anecdote of the difficulty of getting students to pause and reimagine their views, I in part highlight the importance of adopting a socially situated account of entrepreneurship. But I also want to emphasize there is more often no quick solution, no moment of illumination, but at times there appears a reluctance for the student to let go of the initial orientation, or perhaps more of a desire to seek cover.

There is an additional note, when I have mentioned this workshop activity of asking students to get out of the classroom to consider differing views, various colleagues have laughed and told me this is "unimaginable" activity and "of course students will not do this – what are you thinking?".

To sum up this encounter, the "desire" is of attempting differ ways to engage students. I offer the above exchanges, as there are also moments where what I felt was dread mixed with melancholy of carrying on and delivering the module. I appreciate that at some point many others have felt at odds or dissatisfied with the approaches of traditional entrepreneurship education. As Ball (2003) noted, "dread" was a common emotion associated with performance measures in education, though I smile to myself: he was speaking of the student, not of the lecturer.

Encounter: creativity and reality. A space for watching a film collectively and practitioner voices

This encounter addresses "moving away from the hitherto narrow paradigm" (Gibb 2002, p. 234) and of what I feel as crucial to a critical approach to bringing "creativity" into my teaching practices (Draycott & Rae, 2011). This approach is in part to be seen in the QAA (2012, p. 13) guidance to teachers of developing an entrepreneurial mindset as follows:

> This *might* include recognizing themselves, for example, as a creative or resourceful person; or as someone who can translate ideas into actions; or as a person who is prepared to challenge assumptions through investigation and research.

The "might" aspect of the excerpt, which I highlight, appears to advocate a critical approach. Penaluna *et al.* (2014) posed that the art side of creativity is crucial to understand how students engage in learning. So saying, they do not share experiences of how they enact such creativity in the classroom. Inspired by an email from Miguel Imas, who sent the link to the short film *Improbable*", I have for the last few years used it as a collective exercise to watch a movie together in the second workshop of "Re-thinking assumptions". The following excerpt from the accompanying workshop worksheet:

> Ideas explored: There are tensions and dilemmas in entrepreneurship, which will seem contradictory and "…you will often be left in a perplexing situation where you must make your mind up on paradoxical perspectives. You must be critical and decide for yourself."
>
> (Nielsen *et al.*, 2012, p. xx)

> This workshop is designed to think of things a bit differently – in part to take you a little out of your comfort zone by taking the first step in exploring the comment above, which was the thinking point at the end of lecture 1.

> Beginning to work with those in the workshop – sharing views and developing a tolerance for and ability to handle ambiguity.

> Activity: Watch the 24-minute Improbable clip
> www.youtube.com/watch?v=DQ2zlIPSsGk&feature=youtu.be

> Make notes

> • What did you think of what was said of teaching entrepreneurship as "subversive" and as changing "the rules of the game"?
> • What student's experiences and phrases caught your attention?

> Hint: For instance of the creative process and of not destroying everything but challenging ideas.

In groups

Using your notes – Discuss your immediate reactions how this film links to creativity in entrepreneurship.

The questions and tasks are to inform their notes for their "portfolio of practices". The point of the exercise is establishing an emphasis on otherness, as it involves living with contradiction and ambivalence, avoiding premature closure and not taking things for granted. This aspect is especially what students appear to struggle with and many often sit silently. Some looked bemused and had no idea of what to do. After a few moments a few will ask "What was the question?" or "What do you want us to do?". Hence, why I attempt to offer "hints". As I moved round the small groups, some slowly began to engage in talking about how they see the film; a few said they wished we taught classes in a similar manner. Though others said that they saw this film as about art and not about entrepreneurship. I have repeatedly found that students comment that creativity is associated with the arts – not entrepreneurship.

I turn now to inviting practitioners, as central to the critical approach, to facilitate workshops and to share their experiences. My intention was to show how these practitioner stories relate to creativity in everyday practices. I think carefully and invite practitioners who are engaging speakers and also those who will challenge student views of who is an entrepreneur and of what he/she does. As Hjorth (2011, pp. 59–60) said, such a storyteller:

> challenges students' imaginations of what a business can be or how it can be created. Such stories often provide an affect that can uproot students from existing systems of thinking.

This "uprooting" has sometimes worked, as Hjorth suggested, and the following are some of the comments of students who have said they welcomed practitioners being invited to speak of their everyday experiences: "guest lectures and lots of encouragement to think outside the box"; "Bringing in guest speakers in to lectures because it was better to relate to real life experiences/ theories".

The following is a brief sketch from a two-hour workshop between a visiting practitioner and student responses.

I met with Joe Constant prior to his coming in for the workshop. We chatted over cappuccinos and discussed what his work aims to achieve and how this might be part of his session, which would focus upon creativity and his experiences in everyday practices. The meeting was much of playing and exchanging ideas where we would challenge student's views. We agreed that before the workshop students would be asked to come prepared to discuss how they conceive success. I posted the following announcement on Friday, 4 March 2016:

Figure 5.2 Playing and exchanging ideas.

Dear all

Tuesday is the 3rd practitioner workshop. Joe Constant, founder of Kickstart and a former UWE award-winner, will be with us to share his ideas and practices of creativity. Two things to do to prepare before the workshop:

1   Look at the above embedded links above, especially the short video "seven lessons I did not learn from my business degree" (Kickstart-enterprise, n.d.); and
2   Joe has asked that each of you considers the question – What does success look like to you?

Please come prepared to engage in the conversation: Take a few minutes to think on this question and then write your thoughts down and bring to the workshop.

See you next week

Pam

On the day of the workshop, Joe's question was met with silence.

Initially not one of the students wanted to engage in the conversation. They seemed to have come more to be part of an audience than to participate in an exchange. None appeared to have looked at the link and/or raised any questions.

It seemed that none had engaged in the thinking prior to the workshop, at least, none had anything jotted down on paper.

Rather than leaving that question hanging in the air, Joe moved round the room and asked students individually. Tentatively each offered his/her idea of success as "doing what I want to do" or as "being able to travel". When asked what these comments meant for them, one student's comment seemed to sum up those of the group – it was a way to "put off" having to make a decision about getting a job. But there was another side to this discussion of what success looks like as being able to look after the families and children they hoped to have one day. In some ways these images of success were between putting off the immediacy of what each does after university and at the same time meeting the needs for a future imagined family.

He also asked a second question, "Do you identify yourself as being creative?". Not one student initially put up her/his hands. One though slowly raised his hand – but only part way up in the air. When I asked what he meant in this action, he replied "I hope that one day I will feel I have the potential to hold up my hand and say 'yes' and to be creative". This is such a hesitant action and such a complex sentence to unpack, and one, which has stuck with me. As an aside, neither the student nor others reported this story in their reflections from the workshop.

The space of story

In this section I turn to these encounters with students and the experiences in provoking the process of learning. I reflect on de Certeau (1984, p. 81):

> The story does not express a practice. It does not limit itself to telling about a movement. It makes it. One understands it, then, if one enters into this movement itself.… The storyteller falls in step with the lively pace of his fables. He follows them in all their turns and detours, thus exercising an art of thinking.

In my thinking and the use of the elephant, as my fable, and in encouraging the "art of thinking" in others, I want to highlight not so much the "lively" pace of the movement but the potential influences and rhythms of the steps from Stewarts' view from "the side of the road".

Bochner (2014, p. 231) stated that "without students there is no teaching or learning" and that it is what you learn from these exchanges that may assist in carrying on in academic life. Every year I actively review the module in a workshop – One question I pose is "What did you find most challenging?". After the previous runs, I have invited and met with a few students over a coffee to ask their views: "From your experiences, what would you share with someone just beginning the module? From what you know now, what would you see as they need to know?". Thus, I begin the introductory lecture offering the comment most voiced by students: "be prepared to have your thinking challenged". I add that these students found being challenged to be key to their learning. For the last two years, I have also invited in a former student, who has recently become a colleague, to share his experiences of the module; he offers a voice, which I feel that they might better relate to, a means of translating what I mean by challenging their views, particularly as he was not that long ago in their position. This message that entrepreneurial processes in everyday life are a challenge seems to me to underpin what I am attempting in the module.

Tensions

There are those writers who have placed the onus of taking a critical approach on the critical researcher/teacher. There is of course a much wider context and at times it feels like forces at play in this complex story between the dominant and alternative versions of entrepreneurship education.

With over 28,000 students and nearly 22,000 undergraduates, Bristol Business School is one of the largest business schools in the south-west of England. The official university narrative offers an account of the changing nature of entrepreneurship and enterprise education in the university to one with more "practice-based" modules. Like various other universities in the UK, it has recently begun to promote itself as the university for enterprise and entrepreneurship. As such, it appears to be responding to the long-standing debate over the need to change education delivered in the business school to make it more relevant for managers and organizations. Various writers have spoken of the

Figure 5.3 Forces at play.

"tensions" in this approach (Contu, 2009; Pittaway & Cope, 2006, 2007; Hjorth & Johannisson, 2006).

My module is listed as part of the 2020 UWE Enterprise Strategy. In the framework outlining plans to promote more students to start up enterprises, a briefing guide of the strategy focuses on students having access to enterprise and entrepreneurship modules. The single reference on the A4 plan which might be interpreted as critique is that an outcome will be graduate attributes of "decision making supported by critical analysis and judgement". Though this "outcome" offers hope, it would be naïve to suggest that my approach is within the university "practice-based" learning path, moreover that the Enterprise 2020 Strategy might entertain helping students "unlearn managerial convictions" (Johnson, 2016). The experience appears much in line with what Berglund and Holmgren (2006, p. 2) observed, namely that the social aspect of entrepreneurship education can be viewed as a "discursive construction" where there are dominant and alternative versions to be interpreted. As they argue that "in practice entrepreneurship has not yet become what has been hoped for" and in light of the need to be mindful to the tensions which they interpret as a political conflict of what is perceived as the role in the education system. I highlight here the nature of my experience of such conflict of what is "hoped for" refers to the differing practices and implications of those practising, or hoping to practise, a critical approach to entrepreneurship. Yet, it almost feels too simple to state that a critical approach to entrepreneurship education can be viewed as where dominant and alternative versions are to be interpreted. It is so much more and, as in the above encounter of "creativity and reality", seems more akin to the contradictions of "dread and desire" where meanings and ideas collide and there appears no way to resolve this story satisfactorily.

I spoke of movement as informing my approach and I linked this to the notion of "becoming". Alternating between my mulling over creativity and the notion of "becoming" an entrepreneur with my students, I struggle as to how to facilitate, perhaps enact, teaching entrepreneurship critically in a meaningful way for my students. Not one student commented upon the creativity episode with Joe Constant, the practitioner – as sketched out in the above encounter. Perhaps it is simply that they did not register creativity – or lack of it – as important or unusual. Hitherto, students' retrospective essays, part of their "portfolio of practices", entirely sidestep talk of "becoming". Many instead write of what we have covered in lectures and workshops. A few each year offer a traditional view of entrepreneurship and how the entrepreneur is born. And, while I seek acknowledgement of "other" stories in their essays, including, of course, the dominant narrative, I specify in the assessment brief that they are to write from the view of the alternative approach to entrepreneurship (Down, 2013). So saying, I do not expect students to embrace this approach.

What I remind myself of is that this is not an entirely comfortable place to be as this space is not simply a complex story, it rather "isn't something that can be gotten right" (Stewart, 1996, pp. 6, 211). I do though appreciate when writers speak of problems of critical approaches including "superior moralising" and "insistence on remoulding students' views in line with those of the educators" (Śliwa *et al.*, 2013, p. 244) and/or of remoulding those of colleagues (Ford *et al.*, 2010). I simply do not presume the (my) critical approach is better than that of others. I am more betwixt and between. On the one hand, I am very careful not to get caught up in thinking that I can influence students to be "creative" and/or to change their world views. What I can offer is differing views and a language for them to voice their views in relation to differing views that exist at the same time. It is, of course, for them to figure out, and to articulate, their views. And I come to think, perhaps, that this notion of "becoming" might simply be one step too far. On the other hand, given the dictate to get out of our academic spaces and to be creative in our teaching, in doing so, I feel like the critical teaching of entrepreneurship has "lost reverberation and resonance with everyday life" (Steyaert & Hjorth 2003, p. 785). In considering Chris and Daniel's comment in terms of the everyday life of my students, the following were notes I jotted down at the end of the of last term:

> This knowledge – or way of thinking – is not seen as static and is of movement – but it felt like something shifted significantly last year. This is of student's receptivity and resistance to the module. It seemed relevant to their lives; many said it was interesting – so it did not appear as apathy. So, what are the views of undergraduates in a business school about societal conscience, the realities of their world? I need to again revisit the relevance to students. What am I attempting to address and put in to practice? And can I do this with undergraduates and in a space where much is "practice-based"?

At times, the experience does not feel like creating a critical space where students explore "what lies beyond the limits of their experiences" (Hjorth, 2011, p. 57). Instead, a more apt metaphor feels that getting students to explore the possibilities of adopting a view of the process of entrepreneurship is more like asking them to go over to the margins of knowledge (with the discomfort in looking over the edge) and having a look to get a new view of the phenomena of entrepreneurship. Many appear not to want to engage in grasping differing ideas of theorizing or to hear differing stories, or simply resist seeing differing views, even when they repeat what was related in everyday practices. In relating ideas and experiences around the question "what is a critical approach?", it seems to relate back to Stewart's "place on the side of the road" as being both of a place being passed by but also of hope.

Provocation

Hjorth (2011) advocates provocation as a critical approach in the knowledge-creation process. I too have experienced such "movements" (p. 57) as reflected by numerous student "thank-you" cards and emails as illustrated in the following:

Sent: 10 June 2014 21:00
To: Pam Seanor
I thoroughly enjoyed the module and think it has perhaps been my most challenging, but also most useful module with regards to my interests and future career. So thank you for delivering such an inspiring and stretching module.
Kind regards
Kristine

I relate a part of the student's story here; she stated that she felt at the beginning of the module that I was saying that everything she had learned before that point was wrong. She moved from that early view to saying that "The most challenging has been how frustrating it is to be taught for 2 years and then try to see it from another viewpoint". This comment of "challenging" illustrated a key part of the process of provoking questioning and unlearning in order to think in different ways and to open up new possibilities – that it is not the case that one is right and the other wrong.

I have also asked questions in the workshops, as a mid-module review, and students commented positively of the module as being "different", or thought "provoking" and/or "stretching", by which they are speaking of how they have moved out of their previous states and understandings, of what was familiar, and modified their understandings. Yet, at the same time, as above, they also often voice the service nature of the enterprise culture (e.g. in relation to the mark achieved and how their experiences might have an impact on their future career prospects). As mentioned previously, I have also spoken with students after the module ends to find their experiences and of how they pose I might alter my teaching to better fit with student views. The following are fragments of their comments written down in response to the following question:

What do you feel is the most relevant aspect of the module to your learning?:

"The most useful thing about the course is looking at entrepreneurship from different perspectives outside the traditional norm"; "certainly a different way of learning. I think it's challenged my typical way of taking on info and knowledge"; "opening up my way of thinking- apparently it is not all about money" and to keep "the imagery and story of the elephant and the blind men – The story of all wisdom" [as the] "trademark" of the module.

However, by no means are my provocations all positive. Many do not appear to want to leave the comfort zone. Various students repeatedly say the challenge is that there were "No right or Wrong answers!!", though many, like this student with a double exclamation for emphasis, framed their comments as a complaint. Another commonly repeated comment was that students found the approach "wishy-washy", with some specifically stating they preferred using structured frameworks to examine written case studies (e.g. *Harvard Business Review*), as is practice in other modules. A number of students said that other modules set a problem and then lecturers state which theory to draw upon in solving it. Hence, my approach they say is "different" – again, "different" – not seen as a good thing.

There is another encounter to offer. I facilitate seminars on a module running in the first term with final-year undergraduates where I speak of the need to consider differing views and to critique. However, last year a couple of the students in the seminar, with some force, spoke against my approach. The next morning, when I walked out my front door, I was confused as to why there were broken eggs at my feet. It took many moments to look and see signs that my home had two dozen eggs smashed against the windows, stonework and front door. In sharing with a colleague she too had had a physical/verbal encounter with these students – though no eggs were thrown at her home. I cannot be sure that these students were involved, yet none of my neighbour's homes was "egged". Colleagues, neighbours and local police were greatly concerned; my next door neighbour pointed out there was a concentrated effort by whomever threw the eggs, as he showed me how they had to have stood back to hit my second storey and then move nearer to hit my front door yet entirely miss their door. In removing egg white from stonework, it enters the stone and the signs cannot be washed off; after the stone being sanded and layers removed, there remains a trace of this incident. This feels far, far beyond "resisting provocation" (Hjorth 2011, p. 58). To end this section, these are private narratives and not captured in the university performance matrix, which leads to the performance appraisal.

A space for performance appraisal

I turn to how the complex story is publicly told based upon the questions and indicators. I grasp the challenges of monitoring performance and offering evaluation. As Gibb (2002, p. 240) queried, there seems to be little of "what questions really ought to be asked and why and what we expect students to become as a result of exploring them". Or:

> What do they need to know, why do they need to know it and how do they need to be able to adapt and develop themselves to cope with, create and perhaps enjoy uncertainty and complexity are key questions to be addressed?
>
> (p. 244)

The following framework (Table 5.1) is part of the generic questions devised by the university to frame the "student voice". Students formally evaluate my performance; this opportunity is offered at the end of the term for those enrolled in the module to complete by an electronic evaluation feedback. It is anonymous – for the student. However, the teacher can be named. The feedback response is

Table 5.1 The student voice

N = 7	Strongly agree/ agree	No opinion	Strongly disagree/ disagree
I thought the module was well planned and organised.	3		4
I found the module intellectually stimulating.	3		4
Module teaching staff were knowledgeable and good at explaining.	3	1	3
This module supported me to understand my strengths and weaknesses and to plan for my future development.	2		5
Overall, I am satisfied with the quality of the module.	3		4
I would recommend this module to my fellow students.	2	1	4
The range and balance of approaches to teaching has helped me to learn.	3		4

viewed and used by the university management potentially as a management tool. As a public document with questions generated by the university, as part of my role as a module leader I must address negative student comments in my annual module report:

> Last year, of the seven students who completed the electronic evaluation feedback, this document is not representative of the 30+ students enrolled on the module. For those who took the time to fill in the form, it is almost equally divided and reflects two very different positions: seemingly those students who did very well and those who did not do very well.

There is also an opportunity for students to offer qualitative comments. I also need to include such comments in my module report. I highlighted that:

> those making comments appear to have negatively responded to the questions above. Whilst acknowledging these comments, to repeat they offer a specific voice:

> > *Please comment on the best aspects of the module*
> > "I have no positives about this module; None"; "That it's now over";
> > "This is easily to worst module I have taken since at University, and

has failed to enrich or enhance my learning like all other modules have"; "This module was the difference between me achieving a 1st and a 2:1 in my degree. The grades I achieved did not reflect my hard work and dedication within my final year of university. I would consider picking this module to be the worst mistake of my university tenure. I would consider her marking to be extremely harsh"; "3 of us on this module have achieved high 2:1s and First class grades in all other modules and assignments, yet we all received mid to low 50's in this module". "This is the first time I have commented on a module. I would accept myself achieving a poor grade if I did not work hard, but this course NEEDS to be looked at. [It needs] Different module leaders. Not a sole focus on alternative philosophy, and more real world business entrepreneurship stand points".

I include these excerpts of student comments on the electronic review to show how my decision to take a critical approach has a sharp edge. Some students take the opportunity to voice what might be seen as "back talk", and their words become their weapons, especially when not getting the marks they anticipated. It is also of note that they appeared not to believe that the ideas or the practitioners that that came in to the module were "real world business entrepreneurship stand points".

My afterthought is that in a small module it also becomes personal, not simply to me but also since these comments of receiving marks in the "50's" meant that I could identify those students. Hence, I was aware that they had not engaged or regularly attended lectures or workshops. This though they neglected to mention. There appears no responsibility for their learning in this process of evaluation.

Moreover, the questions appear more in line with thinking of the student as a consumer of our services in education and to assess satisfaction rather than their engagement in a dialogue of how challenging students is part of the learning process. I feel that this is a crucial aspect in taking a critical approach, which "challenges" and "provokes" understanding, their choice not to engage does not appear publicly. This encounter seems to resonate with Bragg's (2007, p. 343) argument that such evaluation was initially seen as an "emancipatory project" to empower students and while seen as playing "a more central role in educational policy, guidance and thinking", she posed a disquiet in that:

Such perspectives, however, seem reluctant to engage with the shifting power relations that have accorded students their new authority to speak, or to be critically reflexive about the means used to shape and channel what can be recognised as "student voice."

The questions above are those devised by the university to ensure all modules have the same questions. As Hjorth (2011, p. 59) warned:

Provocative–imaginative "moves" are likely to be "denied the minimum consensus, precisely because it changes the rules of the game upon which consensus had been based". So-called "real questions", questions that go after the rules of the game, need a pedagogues" protection in order to stay alive and initiate learning.

As a module leader, I can add one question; I have as yet chosen not to do this. In part, I felt my small module might quietly run along with little or no notice. And, I ask my own questions in a mid-module review and informal meetings with students – some used in this chapter's narrative. To, as Hjorth (2011) advocated, "guard" against this formal evaluation, is that I include in my module report external examiners' comments, which have been that the quality of feedback to students is seen as "top drawer" and the module has managed to "bridge" the theory–practice divide.

There is though another change from the Teaching Excellence Framework (TEF) by the UK government in 2017/18 academic year with the focus on preparing students for work. While emphasis on graduate employability is not new to universities, its current importance is amplified by being part of the key metrics outcome of TEF, which will be linked to student fees chargeable by universities in subsequent years. However, the TEF appears to also focus upon satisfaction and market mechanisms (Johnson, 2016) and neglect other goals of understanding and society:

> Low student satisfaction might merely mean that they are being challenged and tested in ways that they find uncomfortable. The truth is that good teaching is always challenging and often uncomfortable. There is no reason to suppose that the majority of students recognise it when they receive it. Many are more likely to prefer unchallenging teaching leading to unjustifiably high grades.
>
> (THE, 2017)

Concluding thoughts: the space of the gap

To return to where I began, the space on the side of the road in which the meaning (feeling) of a gap between theory and everyday can be dwelt in and on and the search for meaning begins with an impact. The above is of the encounters, reflections and illustrations presented as critique from the margins of the centre's ordering of things and attempts to exclude them (Stewart, 1996).

I do not opt for the safety of 'elsewhere' but spoke of my own experiences. Students appear to both accept and reject the critical approach, leaving a place seemingly where critique is within the accepted practice and there is also resistance against taking this approach to teaching entrepreneurship. But taking some students out of their comfort zones by provoking requires sensitivity for their responses. Much like Stewart, the stories are speaking at the same time of "dread and desire" of "highs and lows", "absence of and also of hope of redemption"

(1996, pp. 118–119). There is no whole from these fragments but they are offered here as a story as the moments that interrupt the flow of the official narrative.

Thus, I am again drawn back to Stewart's narrative when she speaks of the act of transgression and of how "stepping over a line remains an always seductive possibility in a doubly occupied place where parameters were long ago set by encompassing forces and yet there's no telling *what* people might do" (p. 61, emphasis in original). For others it might initially seem a leap to imagine university teaching in Bristol, England, as being in any way similar to the Appalachian communities where coal-mining was once the way of life, but the more I read, the more her story resonated with my experiences. My reading was not simply in the sense of an academic abstract – in the head – manner but really bringing these ideas to life in ways I had not considered before. And so, I have drawn upon Stewart's use of narrative of spaces to explore everyday practices of teaching and to also make a space to give a glimpse of the rift in a university between the official progress of teaching entrepreneurship and what feels more like a backwater in my attempting to keep a critical stream in my module.

In arguing a critical approach, the following questions, which arise from this space, are at the heart of the chapter as a means of seeing and challenging assumptions, including my own:

How might we reimagine entrepreneurship with our students and colleagues?

How can theory and practices of movement, in particular notions of "becoming" be used to open up debates about critical approaches to entrepreneurship with our students and colleagues? And what types of spaces and how might we facilitate such spaces in workshops?

And how, when and in which contexts, or perhaps stages of study, are critical approaches to the critical study of entrepreneurship valued? Is a critical approach possible at undergraduate level – even with the final year of student experience, especially when teaching is more "practice-based learning" for "the real world".

I have used Stewart's analogy of a space on the side of the road, as I am not interested in closing these questions down or seeking to stop the movement of this story to suggest one best practice approach. Nor have I attempted to romanticize these accounts. Instead, I have shown a glimpse of my story by following along its path so others might be "marked" by the impression to create a "mutual impact" that these queries seem to present more complex issues than are outlined in the guidance materials above such as the QAA and/or the institutional narrative. The point of drawing upon the space at the side of the road is to make something of the "gap" to present where ideas and meanings collide; that there is the possibility of hope, of another way, but at the same time of questioning if taking a critical approach has stagnated or is in decline, waiting.

Note: I want to thank the editors of this volume for their encouragement in crafting and sharing this story and to Pascal Dey for his comments on an early draft of this chapter. Also, my thanks to students, who have agreed to my using the module and their comments. Finally, I want to thank my son Ben Walker for allowing me to use his images; these are from how he made sense of my telling him bedtime stories and how his views of fairy tales shifted as an adult.

References

Ball, S.J. (2003). The teacher's soul and the terrors of performativity. *Journal of Education Policy, 18*(2), 215–228.

Berglund, K. & Holmgren, C. (2006). *At the intersection of entrepreneurship education policy and practice: on conflicts, tensions and closures.* Paper presented to the 14th Nordic Conference on small business research, Stockholm.

Bochner, A. (2014). *Coming to narrative: A personal history of paradigm change in the human sciences.* Walnut Creek, CA: Left Coast Press.

Bragg, S. (2007). "Student Voice" and Governmentality: The production of enterprising subjects? *Discourse: Studies in the Cultural Politics of Education, 28*(3), 343–358.

Contu, A. (2009). Critical management education. In M. Alvesson, T. Bridgman & H. Wilmott (Eds), *The Oxford handbook of critical management studies* (pp. 536–550). Oxford: Oxford University Press.

Down, S. (2010). *Enterprise, entrepreneurship and small business.* London: SAGE.

Down, S. (2013). The distinctiveness of the European tradition in entrepreneurship research. *Entrepreneurship & Regional Development, 25*, 1–4.

de Certeau, M. (1984). *The practice of everyday life.* Berkeley, CA: University of California Press.

Draycott, M. & Rae, D. (2011). Enterprise education in schools and the role of competency frameworks. *International Journal of Entrepreneurial Behavior and Research, 17*(2), 127–145.

Ford, J., Harding, N. & Learmonth, M. (2010). Each the other's other? Critical reflections on business schools and critical management studies. *British Journal of Management 21*(1), 71–81.

Gartner, W.B. (2001). Is there an elephant in entrepreneurship? Blind assumptions in theory development. *Entrepreneurship Theory and Practice, 25*(4), 27–39.

Gibb, A. (2002). In pursuit of a new "enterprise" and "entrepreneurship" paradigm for learning: Creative destruction, new values, new ways of doing things and new combinations of knowledge. *International Journal of Management Reviews, 4*(3), 233–269.

Hjorth, D. (2011). On provocation, education and entrepreneurship. *Entrepreneurship and Regional Development, 23*(1–2), 49–63.

Hjorth, D. & Johannisson, B. (2006). *Learning as an entrepreneurial process, The International handbook of research in entrepreneurship education.* Cheltenham: Edward Elgar.

Johannisson, B. (2016). Limits to and prospects of entrepreneurship education in the academic context. *Entrepreneurship & Regional Development, 28*(5–6), 403–423.

Johnson, J. (2016). *Success as a knowledge economy: Teaching excellence, social mobility and student choice.* London: Department for Business Innovation & Skills.

Kickstartenterprise. (n.d.). *Who we are.* Retrieved August 2017 from http://kickstart enterprise.com/who-we-are.

Nielsen, S.L., Klyver, K., Evald, M.R. & Bager, T. (2012) *Entrepreneurship in theory and practice*. Cheltenham: Edward Elgar.

Penaluna, A., Penaluna K. & Diego, I. (2014). The role of education in enterprising creativity. In R. Sternberg & G. Krauss (Eds), *Handbook of research on entrepreneurship and creativity* (pp. 360–397). Cheltenham: Edward Elgar.

Pittaway, L. & Cope, J. (2006). *Entrepreneurship education: A systematic review of the evidence. National Council for Graduate Entrepreneurship Working Paper 002/2006.* Retrieved November 2016 from http://ncge.org.uk/research.php.

Pittaway, L. & Cope, J. (2007). Entrepreneurship education – A systematic review of the evidence. *International Small Business Journal*, *25*(5), 477–506.

QAA. (2012). *Enterprise and entrepreneurship education: Guidance for UK higher education providers*, Gloucester: QAA. Retrieved November 2012 from www.qaa.ac.uk/Publications/InformationAndGuidance/Pages/enterprise-entrepreneurship-guidance.aspx.

Śliwa, M., Sorensen, B. & Cairns, G. (2013). You have to choose a novel: The biopolitics of critical management education. *Management Learning 46*(3), 243–259.

Stewart, K. (1996). *A space on the side of the road. Cultural poetics in an Other America.* Chichester: Princeton University Press.

Steyaert, C. & Hjorth, D. (2003). *New movements in entrepreneurship*. Cheltenham: Edward Elgar.

Times Higher Education. (2017). *HE Bill: why universities are not supermarkets*. Retrieved February 2017 from www.timeshighereducation.com/features/he-bill-why-universities-are-not-supermarkets.

Tomkin, L. & Ulus, E. (2015). Is narcissism undermining critical reflection in our business schools? *Academy of Management Learning & Education*, *14*(4), 595–606.

6 Conceptual activism

Entrepreneurship education as a philosophical project

Christian Garmann Johnsen, Lena Olaison and Bent Meier Sørensen

Introduction

> Philosophy is back in business.
>
> (Seidman, 2010)

In recent years, entrepreneurs have increasingly turned to philosophy for solutions. The above statement about the value of philosophy emerged from what Dov Seidman, CEO of the ethics and compliance management firm LRN, perceives as a need to rethink business as an intertwined field in which "Credit, climate and consumption crises cannot be solved through specialized expertise alone" (Seidman, 2010). Seidman is not alone in this observation. Christine Nasserghodsi, director of innovation at GEMS Education, discovered while developing an entrepreneurship programme that quite a few of the entrepreneurs she met had studied philosophy. After interviewing them, Nasserghodsi concluded that, although the entrepreneurs who had studied philosophy were not "likely to reference Foucault in a meeting", they nevertheless felt that their ability to use philosophical ideas when faced with challenges allowed them to "bring a unique set of skills to new businesses" (Nasserghodsi, 2012).

If entrepreneurs who have studied philosophy take advantage of their educational background, then we should think about how philosophy can be utilized in entrepreneurship education. Against this backdrop, we ask: how can philosophy become a productive force in the teaching of entrepreneurship in business schools? In this chapter, we discuss what philosophy might bring to entrepreneurship education by exploring our own practices in the classroom, which we call "conceptual activism". We understand conceptual activism as a way of teaching that aims to utilize philosophical concepts in the classroom for the purpose of unlocking alternative viewpoints on phenomena that remain central to entrepreneurship, such as agency, organization creation, success and failure.

The method presented and exemplified in this chapter, which we call conceptual activism, invites students into the contextually embedded discourses and practices associated with entrepreneurship. In the first part of the chapter, we present the philosophical foundations of our approach and discuss how our method allows us to engage with entrepreneurship in business education. In our work or, at least, as a guiding idea in our practice of teaching, we seek to deploy philosophical concepts in order to sensitize students to their own experiences and to discourses on entrepreneurship. This guiding idea is based on a particular understanding of philosophy, one often regarded as standing in contrast to the default interpretation of the role of philosophy in the social sciences. Philosophy has had a long history of being an "under labourer" (Spoelstra, 2007) in the social sciences, but we believe that it should be assigned a more active role in entrepreneurship education. Inspired by Deleuze and Guattari (1994), we see one aspect of our role as scholars as creating concepts that enable us to understand entrepreneurship in new and different ways. Moreover, we argue that such concept creation can be deployed in entrepreneurship education. On this basis, we develop a pedagogical approach that can both challenge and contribute to the teaching of entrepreneurship.

To support our claim, we share two examples from our own teaching experience in the second part of the chapter. These examples illustrate how it is possible to philosophically engage with dominant narratives, discourses, cultural expressions and visual images of entrepreneurship in the classroom. In this regard, we show how we can use philosophical concepts to challenge our own conceptions of entrepreneurial practices as well as those of our students. The first example uses art to problematize entrepreneurship and organization. We use a juxtaposition of two paintings of Saint Paul's conversion by Caravaggio to discuss how certain practices of creating organization can be rendered visible "with" the students rather than "to" the student. The second example focuses more directly on entrepreneurial practices, especially the issue of what constitutes success and failure. With the help of Julia Kristeva's (1982) concept of "the abject", we analyse how our view of entrepreneurial failure has shifted from being repressed to being included. Moreover, we look at what kinds of failure we can talk about and what kinds of failure remain repressed. We also examine how such philosophically informed analyses may support students and teachers in the creation of new conceptualizations of entrepreneurial failure in the classroom. In the concluding discussion, we propose that although the main role of philosophy in entrepreneurship education may be critique, philosophy can also play a role that lies closer to practice. Philosophy may spark the students' abilities to reflect upon their own entrepreneurial practices, and we argue that it may help develop such practices in the classroom and beyond.

Conceptual activism

We begin our discussion by reflecting on ourselves as teachers. What philosophical questions could we pose about the very institution of teaching of which we are part? In other words, how can we problematize pedagogy in our own teaching? Clearly, Deleuze, who studied philosophy at the Sorbonne, had his share of self-absorbed teachers. Deleuze suggests that we do not gain much from people who instruct us to replicate them. Instead, he believes that learning occurs when we do something together. In *Difference and Repetition*, Deleuze writes that:

We learn nothing from those who say: "Do as I do". Our only teachers are those who tell us to "do with me", and are able to emit signs to be developed in heterogeneity rather than propose gestures for us to reproduce. In other words, there is no ideo-motivity, only sensory-motivity.

(1995, p. 23)

Here, Deleuze outlines his basic view of pedagogy. For Deleuze, learning does not occur when we mechanically reproduce what others have already done – learning is not an act of repetition without change. As Deleuze remarks, when we study the history of philosophy, we tend to admire philosophers' achievements, accomplishments and concepts. However, if we simply repeat their words, thoughts and ideas, then we basically do what they do, as our efforts consist of emulating their procedures and confirming their insights. Deleuze elaborates that a different approach entails using the concepts developed by other thinkers for new purposes by trying "to send them in other directions, even if the distance covered is not astronomical but relatively small" (1995, p. xv). For Deleuze, learning is not a passive process of receiving transmitted information that the student registers, incorporates and acknowledges. On the contrary, learning is an active process in which the student engages in activities together with his or her teacher in a larger group of peers, who are all learners. In this way, the students and the teachers take part in a collaborate effort wherein the fundamental pedagogical principle is not to judge "go" or "no go" but to "go with us" (Deleuze & Guattari 1988, p. 177). It is important to emphasize that Deleuze's philosophy of concept creation involves a specific pedagogy. Gane talks about the "pedagogy of the concept" (2009, p. 86) and defines concepts as "experimental tools" (2009, p. 86) that allow us to gain new perspectives on the world.

This particular pedagogy is concerned with proactively partaking in activities that allow us to learn philosophy by utilizing it in concrete contexts. According to Deleuze, the act of "doing philosophy" consists of creating concepts in response to problems. In this regard, we believe that philosophy can offer imaginative approaches to conceptualizing problems and solutions, as philosophy, according to Deleuze and Guattari, is "the art of forming, inventing, and fabricating concepts" (1994, p. 2). A new concept gives us a prism from which we can gain a new perspective on the world. Therefore, philosophy is an activity that consists of pragmatic engagement with concepts in order to "enable more useful descriptions of the world" (Patton 2003, p. 58). Although Deleuze and Guattari stress that concepts are created, "doing philosophy" does not necessarily require us to invent novel concepts from scratch. On the contrary, if we look at Deleuze's own work, we can see that his concepts often stem from other thinkers. For example, Deleuze's concept of "multiplicity" originates from Riemann's differential mathematics, while his concept of "simulacrum" emerges from of his reading of Plato. As such, the creation of a concept may involve development of an established concept, transmutation of a concept from one context into another or the revision of the understanding of a well-known concept. As Gane elaborates, Deleuze's project of creating concepts opens up the "possibility of reinventing or reworking older concepts so that they are lifted from their historical settings and are pushed in directions that pose us problems today" (2009, p. 95).

In this chapter, we investigate how philosophical concepts can be useful for engaging students in entrepreneurship. Deleuze's insistence on the importance of creating concepts that allow us to think and act differently in the world applies equally to the entrepreneurship domain. As Hjorth *et al.* argue, "new concepts of entrepreneurship enable us to think differently and practice the world differently" (2008, p. 82). Based upon our reading of Deleuze, we propose "conceptual activism" as a method for advancing critical entrepreneurship education. Within critical entrepreneurship studies, there has been a persistent call to question the assumptions of entrepreneurship theory and practice (Tedmanson, Verduijn, Essers & Gartner, 2012; Verduijn, Dey, Tedmanson & Essers, 2014). Conceptual activism is a "problematisation" technique (Alvesson & Sandberg, 2011) but our goal is not simply to criticize underlying assumptions of current entrepreneurship research and practice. Rather, conceptual activism involves the proactive creation of new concepts that allow us to understand entrepreneurship in new and different ways.

As the word "critical" has become de rigueur in the social sciences, let us clarify its meaning in relation to our conceptual activism approach. We do not criticize simply in order to disclose false presuppositions. We use critique to demonstrate how dominant understandings of entrepreneurship overlook or neglect crucial or relevant insights (Olaison & Sørensen, 2014). Through the use of conceptual activism as a teaching strategy, we invite students to explore what entrepreneurship might become rather than accepting it as a phenomenon that is a given with established content that can be empirically "covered" and theoretically portrayed. Our concepts should not "recognize" what "everybody knows" (Deleuze, 1995), or confirm our prior suspicions and "common-sense" ideas (Spoelstra, 2007). On the contrary, concepts need to become the tool with which teachers and students explore alternative ways of conceiving entrepreneurship together. Ideally, a concept should allow us to be surprised, as it makes us sensitive to how we encounter those phenomena that perplex us. A concept is a form of "para-sense" because it challenges common sense (Spoelstra, 2007). In what follows, we give two examples of how we have used conceptual activism to explore entrepreneurship, one focusing on two paintings of Saint Paul's conversion by Caravaggio and the other on entrepreneurial failure.

Philosophizing about art and entrepreneurship

Entrepreneurship teaching often revolves around finding appropriate business cases that either exemplify stories of success, or present students with challenges or problems to solve. Such cases tend to be derived from contemporary ventures that engage in commercial practices with the aim of creating new products, services or manufacturing processes. Clearly, much can be gained from studying such cases of success or failure. At the same time, it is important to recognize that business cases are not the only way to learn about entrepreneurship. Many other sources may offer inspiration (for a discussion, see Beyes, Parker & Steyaert, 2016; Hjorth & Johannisson, 2007). In this regard, we come face to face with the common-sense assumption that to learn about business one must study business. Is this assumption worth challenging? Could we teach entrepreneurship in different ways? In other words, can we imagine entrepreneurship education being based upon alternative examples?

Let us begin with the widely accepted definition of entrepreneurship as the "creation of organization" (Gartner, 1988: 57; see also Hjorth *et al.*, 2015; Katz & Gartner, 1988). We pose a seemingly simple question: what is organization? In order to address this question, we draw on the teaching of art and explore how artwork itself contains organization (Sørensen, 2010, 2014). It is important to recognize that neither art nor organization are neutral. Throughout the course of history, art has been deployed as a means of exercising and confirming given societal distributions of power. As such, art is relevant for teaching entrepreneurship critically, as such regimes of power are often negated in great art. Thus, great art inevitably transcends given distinctions and shows forces at work that we normally cannot see. In explicit reference to Paul Klee's artworks, Deleuze and Guattari argue that: "The visual material must capture nonvisible forces. *Render visible*, Klee said; not render or reproduce the visible" (1988, p. 342). With this in mind, we recall that entrepreneurship involves inventing new ways

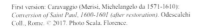

First version: Caravaggio (Merisi, Michelangelo da 1571-1610): *Conversion of Saint Paul, 1600-1601 (after restoration).* Odescalchi Coll., Rome. © 2017. Photo Scala, Florence.

Second version: Caravaggio (Merisi, Michelangelo da 1571-1610): *Conversion of Saint Paul, 1601.* Church of Santa Maria del Popolo, Cerasi Chapel, Rome. © 2017. Photo Scala, Florence/Fondo Edifici di Culto - Min. dell'Interno.

Figure 6.1 Juxtaposition I.

of seeing and acting by relating to currently nonvisible forces. At its best, art is a collective encounter that can generate a radically different experience in the recipient. You do not "teach" art or, at least, you should not. Instead, you should say "come with us" into a work of art.

Caravaggio offers a good place for educators engaged in art and entrepreneurship to start, as his paintings contain an almost infinite amount of "nonvisible forces". Consider the two Caravaggio paintings above. They allegedly depict the same event – Saint Paul's conversion on the road to Damascus. However, they construct two profoundly different versions of the same event. Moreover, the two versions express radically different ideas of organization creation. In fact, this may explain why the Catholic Church, which had commissioned the piece, rejected the version from the year 1600 but accepted the version from 1601. In the dire straits of the Counter-Reformation, the Church sought new ways to capture the souls (and the work) of modern citizens in seventeenth-century Europe. The 1600 version seems chaotic and retains the sense of shock experienced on the road to Damascus, when the learned, Roman citizen (hitherto known as Saul) fell off his horse and was lying on the ground, lost, blind and bewildered. Although Christ tries to rescue the fallen man in the painting, the soldier in the middle uses his spear to prevent this from happening, keeping calm in the high-alert situation. The accepted 1601 version, on the other hand, depicts the event in a very different manner. This latter painting became one of the hallmarks of world art, and parts of its masterfulness lies in the fact that it both depicts something central about the event – the change of heart and mind – while also bringing the event back to the well-known organization of the mother church.

With these two versions of the paintings in mind, we return to the question: what assumptions are involved when we say "organization" and when we define entrepreneurship as the creation of organization? Which versions are being promoted and which are left out? The Church could only accept the version of the painting that represented the Church's ideal of organization. If we turn the masterpiece on its head and juxtapose it with another classic visual expression – Henry Mintzberg's (1983) model, the Six Basic Parts of the Organization, from his book *Structure in Fives* – this becomes even clearer.

From this perspective, Paul is not a bewildered man on a horse headed towards Damascus. Saint Paul is, to use Mintzberg's expression, the "strategic Apex" of the new Christian Church. In short, Saint Paul is the entrepreneur insofar as he is the creator of organization. At the bottom of the painting, we now find the poor peasant and the horse. In Mintzberg's terms, they comprise the "operating core", which is illuminated by the divine light of Christ. Christ remains in the frame, but is now depersonalized and without a body. Nevertheless, Caravaggio renders the force of this master visible. The appropriate organization and its inherent class distinctions are now in place, and the mission of the convert is now clearly to confirm the practice of the one, undivided Church. The message becomes: "Get up, go into the city, and see that the believers affirm their allegiance to the Church and its strategic apex who, in the absence of Paul,

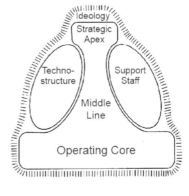

Conversion of Saint Paul, 1601 (the second version).   H. Mintzberg's (1983) 'Basic model of the organization'.

Figure 6.2 Juxtaposition II.

is the Pope in Rome". The second version consecrates and sacralizes the organization of the Church. In this case, entrepreneurship is not disruptive but conservatory.

The initial idea of juxtaposing Caravaggio's second version of *The Conversion of Saint Paul* (1601) with Henry Mintzberg's (1983) model of the Six Basic Parts of the Organization emerged as Sørensen completed his PhD dissertation in 2004. However, more than six years passed before this juxtaposition was published (Sørensen, 2010). Between the completion of the PhD and the publication of the 2010 paper, the juxtaposition was presented to numerous students in the master's programme in business administration and philosophy at CBS as well as to colleagues. The purpose of presenting this juxtaposition to the students was not simply to make them reproduce the teacher's analysis – that is, to teach them to "do as I do" – thereby confirming what the teacher already knew about art and organization. Instead, it was meant to provide a point of departure for a mutual discussion around art and organization. Thus, the juxtaposition was displayed with the intention that the teacher and the student could engage in a productive dialogue about the relationship between Caravaggio, Mintzberg, aesthetics, art, entrepreneurship and other topics that might spring to the participants' minds. In this way, the teacher invited the students to "do with me" – to visit the world of art and explore its relationship with organization. In turn, the classroom became a space for discussion and a space in which different opinions could be heard. The result was a productive dialogue that allowed for new insights to come to light. This was also acknowledged in the published paper (see Sørensen, 2010, p. 323).

One might assume that it would be easy for observers to articulate what Caravaggio is expressing on his canvases. However, in our experience, this is not the case. Indeed, some find it unsettling to be exposed to a piece of figurative art. Arguably, the modern viewer is more prone to see the shapes and contours of a Picasso or the entrepreneurial qualities of a Warhol than to contemplate a Caravaggio, whose paintings appear mystical, enigmatic and alien. However, this is part of the experience. After Paul was back on his horse and had become an apostle, he confessed to the Corinthians that "the visual is puzzling, and not only because ancient glass was less clear than today's transparent technology", because what we confront in art is an "*i*" an "enigma" – a riddle (Sørensen, 2013, p. 45). In this light, it is not surprising that students typically remain silent when they are asked about how they conceive the first version of *The Conversion of Saint Paul*. For most contemporary spectators, the figures displayed in Caravaggio's paintings do not seem to make much sense, and we have a hard time sensing them.

As suggested by Agamben (2007), the pedagogical strategy that may be used here is to profane the sacred – that is, return to use that which has been elevated to a transcendent sphere. In other words, Caravaggio's paintings must be used in a new way. Many students initially experience Caravaggio's paintings as representing a sacred table – an ancient piece of high art that should not be touched. The silence that befalls them is therefore the same silence that befalls people in a church, at a cemetery or at the start of a game. However, it is important to intervene in this silence by asking apparently mundane questions, such as "What is the little angel doing in the upper-right corner?" or "Why does the soldier hold a spear in his hand?" Such questions can help in deciphering the paintings, such that we return "to use what the sacred had separated and petrified" (Agamben, 2007, p. 74). Through the mist of highbrow art history and bourgeois pretentiousness, the characters may stand forth. The narrative unfolds for the students: a man has fallen off his horse, but why? Has he been struck by a seizure, torn by violence or hit by panic? The significance of the event is signalled by the presence of Christ. We must then ask: "what holds Christ back?". "Well," some might remark, "the soldier's spear." The conversation continues: "Why would Christ be afraid of a little spear?" "Fair point", some might think, while another might remark, "he had recently been pierced in the side at the cross". More comments often follow. Herein lies the learning. Teacher and student begin to do something together – to use the painting to engage in a mutual discussion and move the piece of art to a new use, including a new reading of Mintzberg (1983).

We suddenly ascertain that the students actually know a lot about analysing Christian art, the very art that at first might appear opaque to them. They are seldom encouraged to exercise these skills. When we juxtapose the two versions of *The Conversion of Saint Paul*, students often discover that the spear is the defining feature of the first version, as it holds all human, natural and cosmic forces in check. The placement of Caravaggio's second version of *The Conversion of Saint Paul* (1601) alongside Henry Mintzberg's (1983) model of the Six Basic Parts of the Organization also allows us to return Mintzberg's celebrated model to use. We can ask: "Does the "ideology", as expressed in the aura around the model, really signal the sacred status of the model and provide it with a halo?". This juxtaposition has sparked various reactions among students. Yet, contrary to what one might expect, the greatest impact on the students is not caused by the comparison of the two paintings by Caravaggio. Rather, what unsettles the class is turning the second version on its head. Such a profane act is not easily embraced. However, if the students accept this move, they see that Mintzberg's model does not necessarily collide with the piece of art in the juxtaposition – *the two coalesce*. At this stage, the paintings often become "clearer" to the students, and they are able to voice their experiences and contest them. However, as Caravaggio's paintings gain clarity, Mintzberg's Six Basic Parts of the Organization develop a monstrous, enigmatic and alien appearance. The students start to wonder: "why does the model shine? Why does it look like a body? *Where is its missing head?*". These questions and experiences all pertain to the question of entrepreneurship and organization. Discussions of such questions might make students of entrepreneurship sensitive to different versions of creating organization by showing them that representations of organization are always socially, culturally and historically embedded.

The abject failure of entrepreneurship

The previous example shows how art can be used to question the assumptions of entrepreneurship education. We can also demonstrate how philosophical concepts can be utilized to problematize and transform current practices or discourses. To do so, we use the concept of the abject to discuss entrepreneurial failure (see Olaison & Sørensen, 2014). Participants in education are increasingly required to cultivate an entrepreneurial self in order to make themselves employable (Berglund, 2013). Traditionally, entrepreneurship research and education have been premised on the assumption that entrepreneurship is a winner's game. Although approximately 90 per cent of all entrepreneurs experience failure in financial terms (Stevens & Burley, 1997), the phenomenon of entrepreneurial failure has been largely overlooked, perhaps because failure is treated as a kind of taboo (McGrath, 1999). Gradually, this aversion to failure has been moderated, such that failure is now seen as an integral part of entrepreneurship. In fact, when entrepreneurs give a speech or an interview today, they will invariably mention their failures in some form. Questions useful for addressing entrepreneurial failure in the classroom include: "What do entrepreneurs talk about when they talk about failure? What do they leave out?". Together with students, we can analyse our understanding of entrepreneurial failure, the outcomes of failure and the elements that are left out of this process. To facilitate the discussion, we use Kristeva's (1982) concept of the "abject", which describes the processes of incorporation and repression.

For Kristeva, the repressed is something that is unmentionable but is still an integral part of our thoughts. The philosophical concept of the abject can be used as a "tool" for unlocking discourses on entrepreneurship, thereby broadening students' understanding of entrepreneurship and sensitizing them to their own practices. According to Kristeva (1982), the abject is constructed in a delimitation of the subject. Thus, the abject is imbued with a threat of violence that "lies there, quite close, but it cannot be assimilated" (Kristeva 1982, p. 1). The concept of the abject draws attention to what which is simultaneously incorporated and repressed within a phenomenon. Thus, the abject highlights how the repressed is incorporated into a sanitized version, which, in turn, represses other aspects or keeps certain versions hidden. This is relevant for entrepreneurship discourse and practice because we can use this concept to elucidate what is incorporated and repressed in conceptions of entrepreneurship. The objective is not to make students experts in Kristeva's philosophical thinking, but rather to help them learn to use abjection as a tool for analysing phenomena and critically reflecting on their own practices and experiences.

Entrepreneurship is widely viewed as an engine for economic growth. Students often hear that our society needs more entrepreneurs like Bill Gates, Steve Jobs or Richard Branson. As a starting point for discussion, we can ask: How do we describe entrepreneurs and their failures? They often have many stories to share. Students of entrepreneurship are often introduced to Drucker, who suggests that it is not the economy that fails, but rather individuals who fail owing to their "greed, stupidity, thoughtless bandwagon-climbing, or incompetence" (1985, p. 46). In our experience, many students find this view shocking, especially as they identify themselves as entrepreneurs and hold different views on failure. Typically, students hold the view that failure is necessary for entrepreneurship because failure is a step to success. For this reason, students commonly state that failure is now out in the open and considered an integral part of the entrepreneurial process. Against this backdrop, we can use the concept of the abject to reflect on what we mean when we talk about entrepreneurial failure. We can ask: what kinds of failures are being sanitized and what kinds are repressed within our conception of entrepreneurship? For this discussion, we can utilize quotes collected from the Facebook group entitled "Famous Entrepreneur Quotes":

> Don't worry about failure, you only have to be right once.
>
> (Drew Houston, Dropbox)

> As an entrepreneur, you have to be OK with failure. If you're not failing, you're not trying hard enough.
>
> (Alexa Von Tobel, LearnVest)

> Learn from failure. If you are an entrepreneur and your first venture wasn't a success, welcome to the club.
>
> (Richard Branson, Virgin)

Students often recognize themselves in these quotes. Moreover, using the concept of the abject, it is not difficult for them to see that the quotes follow the same storyline: great entrepreneurs initially felt that no one believed in them, and they faced a series of failures that eventually led to success (Johnsen & Sørensen, 2017). This analysis can be supported by policy documents, such as the European Commission's report on "Business Failure and Starting Afresh", which states that "failed entrepreneurs learn from their mistakes and are more successful at the next attempt" (Reichenbach & Herrero Rada, 2005). When analysing the prevalent discourse on entrepreneurial failure, it quickly becomes apparent that failure is typically articulated as a "lifelong learning process" (European Commission, 2012), making failure "a potential for improvement" (Gosh, in Nobel 2011). When we discuss these quotes, personal stories and more formal documentation with students, we usually arrive at the conclusion that underlying this view is an assumption that there is a right kind of failure – failure that we can learn from – which serves as a stepping stone towards success. Using the concept of the abject, we can start to discuss the idea that, if there is "good failure", there must also be "bad failure". We can then ask students about what might constitute "bad failure". Some students may propose that bad failure involves not taking responsibility for one's own mistakes, especially in financial terms, and letting someone else "take the hit". This may provide an opportunity to return to Drucker's account of entrepreneurial failure from the 1980s, with which students often initially disagree. For example, echoing Drucker's view, Gosh (in Nobel, 2011) differentiates between venture failures and personal failures. Gosh asserts that venture failure is a "fiasco" that can be forgiven, while a personal failure implies moral degradation, such as when an entrepreneur is a fraud. In Reilly's (2012) words, when done right:

> Failure is not a reflection of self. It is completely objectified and isolated, believed to be an experience from which to learn, a measure of the inability to accomplish one specific task at a single moment in time, or the result of variables that likely have little to do with the individual in question. Nothing more.

With the help of Kristeva's concept of the abject, we can help students see how failure is repressed, as it cannot be considered a reflection of the subject's essence and the character of the entrepreneur. Thus, what makes an entrepreneur successful is his or her ability to cultivate an "unemotional relationship with failure" (Reilly, 2012). In this regard, failure is sanitized and compartmentalized. It is rendered into something that exists independent of the entrepreneur with the exception of the learning experience. Nevertheless, when faced with concrete examples of entrepreneurs, retaining such a clean-cut distinction is difficult because we do not know whether the entrepreneur is honest or dishonest. In order to illustrate this difficulty to students, we can use the example of Stein Bagger, a well-known entrepreneurial swindler in Denmark who suddenly disappeared after a trip to Dubai. On 6 December 2008, Bagger walked into the

Central Division of the Los Angeles Police Department in downtown Los Angeles. He was wearing jeans and a casual jacket, and carrying backpack. He walked up to the counter, where the following occurred:

> "I am Stein Bagger," the man said, putting his hands on the counter. "I'm a fugitive from Europe and I'm here to turn myself in."
>
> Sceptical officers took the lean, 6-foot man back for questioning.
>
> "We've had several people come in and tell us they were the king of Denmark," explained Officer Jack Richter.
>
> But as Bagger leaned across a desk, the sleeve of his black Armani jacket crept up to reveal a Rolex watch. A computer search turned up an Interpol warrant for his arrest on charges of counterfeiting, forgery and fraud, according to the LAPD.
>
> (Lin II, Blankstein & Larrubia, 2008)

Bagger's arrest in Los Angeles appeared to be the end of the line for the Danish IT star, whose company, IT Factory, had won Ernst & Young's national Entrepreneur of the Year Award just nine days earlier. Bagger had not attended the awards ceremony, as he and his wife were in Dubai on a luxurious vacation. In Dubai, Bagger left a restaurant where he was dining with his wife and several companions. He would never return to the restaurant or to his wife. Instead, Bagger withdrew US$5,000 from an ATM, procured a car, drove across the desert to Abu Dhabi and flew to New York. When he arrived in New York, he borrowed a friend's car and drove 4,000 kilometres across the United States to Los Angeles, where he eventually turned himself in to the police. Meanwhile, Ernst & Young Denmark regretted awarding the entrepreneur prize to Bagger's IT Factory and it refused to award the prize to any other company in 2008. Bagger was subsequently convicted of fraud in excess of DKK200 million and received a prison term of seven years. The money has never been recovered.

The media typically presents the Bagger case as a spectacular event. Although this event had tremendous economic and social consequences for everyone involved in IT Factory, the focus is almost always on "the story of Stein": his troubled family background, his persuasive manner, the fascinating world-spanning getaway and the epic ending. Clearly, Stein Bagger is an "empty signifier" – a man who is all too susceptible to being engulfed by stronger forces. One such force is Ernst & Young, which, as one of the Big Five accounting firms, confirms the title of the "entrepreneur" through its annual awards. On Ernst & Young's website, one finds a list of award winners throughout the years. For the year 2008, it says "No winner". This, of course, is a fabrication on the part of Ernst & Young, as there *was* a winner in 2008. Ernst & Young played a central part in elevating Bagger and turning his apparent success into a mystical, transcendent event, a signature of the sublime. However, Bagger turned out to be criminal. Ernst & Young's webpage bears witness to the fact that the failed entrepreneur is now an abject whose name cannot be mentioned without degrading the legacy of *other* winners. In the encounter between Stein Bagger and Ernst & Young, we can grasp the abject – that which cannot be included or mentioned. Ernst & Young cannot accept the fact that it had lifted up the very same abject whom they now place "beyond the scope of the possible" or beyond what exists. However, the fact that there was a winner and that the winner later confessed to being an embezzler can teach us something about failure in entrepreneurship.

The Stein Bagger example shows how the discourse of entrepreneurship involves two versions of failure: good failure and bad failure. While the former is associated with heroic struggle and learning from one's mistakes in attempts to become successful, the second is associated with fraud and criminal activity. Although these two versions are often contrasted, they are not as different from each other as one might think. Both versions of failure are, to use Kristeva's terminology, "sublime" and "spectacular". As such, both versions of failure offer normative accounts of how to behave or how not to behave, and they are often expressed through clichés, which are invoked so often that they become virtually meaningless. The use of such cases in entrepreneurship education might serve as a point of departure for discussing how we tend to portray and think about failure. In other words, teachers and students can discuss what is left out of "good failure" and "bad failure". This is not only a critical exercise that aims to disclose what is left out but also a creative endeavour that allows us to imagine different versions of entrepreneurial failure. In this discussion, we should not instruct students to "do or think as we do" but rather invite them to take part in a discussion of how failure in entrepreneurship is predominately represented in the media and in scientific discourse.

Based on such an analysis of the discourse and practice of entrepreneurial failure, we then have an opportunity to invite students to reflect on how they talk about entrepreneurship and failure. With the help of philosophical concepts as analytical tools, we have found that students often not only become invested in the cases that are presented to them in class, but they also welcome the opportunity to examine their own experiences in new ways in the classroom, where they can co-create new accounts and concepts of, for example, failure. Some may propose that when we talk about failure, we mostly do so in an optimistic and positive fashion, referring to such ideas as resilience, recovery, redemption, personal growth and lessons learned, all of which we feel compelled to communicate to others. Others may highlight the fact that, despite the extremely personal and often risky experience of an entrepreneurial failure, we often present it as being devoid of emotional aspects. This may encourage others to explore the affective states involved in failure, including fear of moving forward, despair, and anger at those who betrayed us or failed to warn us. Such exploration may lead to considerations of the consequences of failure for others and the necessity of being sensitive to all who are affected by entrepreneurial failures. The creation of a new understanding of entrepreneurial failure as including its effects on others, rather than as an individual learning experience, may lead to almost shocking revelations for students who, similar to many entrepreneurs, receive start-up funding from family and friends rather than from banks. The development of concepts of entrepreneurial failure together with students in the classroom might also lead us to reflect upon questions related to equality, the distribution of wealth and environmental sustainability. It is in this arena that philosophy shows its potential. Our experience with addressing these issues in the classroom has shown us that the students are concerned about these issues. They normally demonstrate an acute interest in questions related to entrepreneurial failure that go beyond common sense and ready-made solutions.

Concluding discussion

In recent years, the focus on entrepreneurship as a complex phenomenon has increased (Fayolle, Landstrom, Gartner & Berglund, 2016). This complexity emerges because entrepreneurship is always socially, culturally and historically embedded. To account for these aspects, scholars have suggested that entrepreneurship must be studied and taught from a cross-disciplinary perspective that includes history, philosophy and anthropology (Minniti & Bygrave, 2001; Gartner, 2013; Hjorth, 2011; Hjorth & Steyaert, 2006). Hjorth and Johannisson argue that interdisciplinary approaches are not only desirable but necessary in entrepreneurship education because conventional curricula are often overloaded with abstract economic models. They maintain that entrepreneurship educators together with students "need to be sensitive to local/temporal specificities" and "cultivate an openness before the event of sense, the power of becoming, the possibilities of creation" (Hjorth & Johannisson, 2007, p. 50).

In this chapter, we have explored what philosophy can offer entrepreneurship education. In line with Hjorth and Johannisson, we believe that "[t]hinking with management concepts will keep [entrepreneurship] out of reach" (2007, p. 50). In response, we have proposed that philosophy consists of creating concepts that allow us to explore different viewpoints. In other words, concept creation intervenes in our usual manner of thinking about the world. In research and education alike, we should play with concepts and experiment with what they enable us to do. Philosophy is not simply concerned with "the way things are" – it is also entails a "concern for how they may become" (Massumi, 2010, p. 13). To understand what the world may become, we need to experiment with what we can do. Deleuze learns from Spinoza that "[w]e do not know what a body can do" (1988, p. 17). According to Deleuze, the point is that the body is not a pre-given entity with fixed capabilities. Quite the contrary – the body contains unexplored potential from which we can gain knowledge only by experimenting with it can do. The notion of "the body" is, of course, itself a concept and, in Deleuze's account, a very dynamic one – even the earth is a body (although "without organs"; see Deleuze & Guattari, 1988). We can paraphrase Deleuze, stating that "we do not know what the concept can do". Thus, a concept is not something given in advance of an encounter of certain bodies, such as an encounter between a concept and a social practice of entrepreneurship. Instead, Deleuze believes that we need to experiment with what a concept can become and what it might allow us to think. This is the task of the philosopher – to explore what a concept might become in conjunction with the problem that it explores. On this basis, we believe that philosophy has much to offer entrepreneurship education.

In order to elaborate on our perspective, we proposed a philosophical approach that we call conceptual activism and examined how stretching concepts allows us to challenge conventional assumptions about entrepreneurship. We acknowledge that philosophizing about entrepreneurship might be demanding for some students, especially those who are new to the discipline. In addition, we realize that the relation between philosophy and entrepreneurial practices may seem abstract. Nevertheless, in our own teaching of entrepreneurship, we have discovered that even the most abstract philosophical concepts can be a productive force. When practised in the form of conceptual activism, philosophy applies concepts as experimental tools (Gane, 2009, p. 86). Therefore, the relationship between practice and theory is not passive – it is a creative process. Deleuze describes this activity as "relays" that open up new pathways and new understandings: "Practice is a set of relays from one theoretical point to another, and theory is a relay from one practice to another" (Deleuze, in Bouchard, 1977, p. 206). Learning, in turn, is an ensemble of relays. We used two examples to demonstrate how such relays might work and how we can use conceptual activism to rethink entrepreneurial practices. In so doing, we also create new concepts and understandings of entrepreneurship.

In our first case, we used art as a relay between philosophy and organization. In this context, art serves as a relay for thinking philosophically about organization (what is organization?) and entrepreneurially about organization (how can we rethink organization?). The case we presented has been used on several occasions in the master's programme in business administration and philosophy at Copenhagen Business School, where entrepreneurship is one of the practical contexts that students are required to analyse philosophically. Although we have not yet used this case with more traditional business-oriented students, we have used art in several other teaching situations. If used appropriately, art can be a great asset in teaching in general and, in particular, in critically oriented teaching (Sliwa, Sørensen & Cairns, 2015). Every human being, including students and researchers, has or can be motivated to have an opinion about a work of art, while an interest in philosophy or entrepreneurship cannot be taken for granted. Moreover, with great art a student does not need knowledge of art history or a generalized education, as great art relates directly to one's own life and community and addresses how life is lived in the world today. Indeed, the world is a given in a great piece of art not as a representation of the world as it appears at the time of the artwork's creation but as a certain experience that opens up to a world yet to come. Of course, art is about learning, an insight that was only recently lost. In this way, we believe that art can function as a relay between philosophy and entrepreneurial practices for business school students.

While students who are trained in philosophy can use conceptual activism as a tool for connecting philosophical concepts with business phenomena, such as entrepreneurship, the challenge for students who lack a background in philosophy and who are enrolled in programmes primarily focused on business is somewhat different. In our second example, our point of departure was a teaching situation in which few students were familiar with philosophy. In such situations, conceptual activism can be used as a tool that allows students to reflect on and experiment with their own entrepreneurial practices, and to examine the phenomena associated with entrepreneurial failure. In other words, philosophy can help students become sensitive to their own experiences in practical business activities. For this purpose, the philosophical concept becomes a relay between entrepreneurial practices. When illustrated with a case of entrepreneurial failure, students can make use of the philosophical concept of the abject to create relays between their own experiences with new business ventures. The concept then becomes a tool for understanding practice, for analysing what is taken for granted within their own understandings of the world and for reflecting on what is excluded from conventional conceptions of entrepreneurship. On this basis, students can explore the possibility of creating new practices and using (new) concepts in order to facilitate change in practice.

In our experience, modern students are taught to think and draw conclusions quickly. Quick thinking, gut feelings, intuition and "just do it" seem to be the pedagogical messages regarding what is required in order to succeed in business. Slow, reflective thinking is viewed as a waste of valuable time. Therefore, students often question the value of philosophy and remain sceptical about the utility of engaging in conceptual reflections. To address this concern, it is important to emphasize how concepts can become tools and to highlight the practical value of concepts. As we have argued, philosophical concepts are experimental tools that can create relays between practices. Deleuze pushes this line of thinking even further, arguing that concepts and practices are inherently connected, as the activity of creating concepts is a practice itself. For this reason, he insists that "theory does not express, translate, or serve to apply practice: it is practice" (Bouchard, 1977, p. 208). Undoubtedly, engaging in the creation of concepts as a practical endeavour is a challenging task. However, if the concept is practice and practice involves a concern for concepts, then we need to prepare our students for this task, as this is where an encounter may take place. In line with Deleuze, we see the teacher's challenge as being the person who says, "Engage in the philosophy of entrepreneurship with me". In line with Hjorth, we believe that philosophy and conceptual activism could become a useful approach "for thinking and practising entrepreneurship education" (2011, p. 60). Conceptual activism allows the classroom to be turned into a site where students can work with concepts and seek encounters. This is a collective project of "doing with me" and of co-creation, where encounters of becoming perplexed are merged with radical experimentation with philosophical concepts.

Acknowledgement

We would like to thank the Velux Foundation, Denmark, and the Bridge Program at Linnaeus University, Sweden, for supporting our research. As well, we would like to thank Tina Pedersen, who has provided indispensable language editing support.

References

Agamben, G. (2007). *Profanations*. New York, NY: Zone.

Alvesson, M. & Sandberg, J. (2011). Generating research questions through problematization. *Academy of Management Review*, *36*(2), 247–271.

Berglund, K. (2013). Fighting against all odds: Entrepreneurship education as employability training. *Ephemera*, *13*(4) 717–735.

Beyes, T., Parker, M. & Steyaert, C. (Eds) (2016). *The Routledge companion to the humanities and social sciences in management education*. London: Routledge.

Bouchard, D.F. (Ed.) (1977). *Language, counter-memory, practice: Selected essays and interviews by Michel Foucault*. Ithaca, NY: Cornell University Press.

Deleuze, G. (1988). *Spinoza: Practical philosophy*. San Francisco, CA: City Lights.

Deleuze, G. (1995). *Difference and repetition*. London: Continuum.

Deleuze, G. & Guattari, F. (1988). *A thousand plateaus: Capitalism and schizophrenia*. Minneapolis, MN: University of Minnesota Press.

Deleuze, G. & Guattari, F. (1994). *What is philosophy?* London: Verso.

Drucker, P.F. (1985). *Innovation and entrepreneurship: Practices and principles*. New York, NY: Harper & Row.

European Commission (2012). *Entrepreneurship 2020 action plan – Reigniting the entrepreneurial spirit in Europe*. Brussels: Enterprise Publications, European Commission.

Famous Entrepreneur Quotes. Retrieved 27 September 2016 from www.facebook.com/pg/famousentrepreneurquotes.

Fayolle, A., Landstrom, H., Gartner, W.B. & Berglund, K. (2016). The institutionalization of entrepreneurship. *Entrepreneurship & Regional Development*, *28*, 477–486.

Gane, N. (2009). Concepts and the "new" empiricism. *European Journal of Social Theory*, *12*(1), 83–97.

Gartner, W.B. (1988). "Who is an entrepreneur?" is the wrong question. *American Journal of Small Business*, *12*(4), 11–32.

Gartner, W.B. (2013). Creating a community of difference in entrepreneurship scholarship. *Entrepreneurship and Regional Development*, *25*(1–2), 5–15.

Hjorth, D. (2011). On provocation, education and entrepreneurship. *Entrepreneurship & Regional Development*, *23*(1–2), 49–63.

Hjorth, D. & Johannisson, B. (2007). Learning as an entrepreneurial process. In A. Fayolle (Ed.), *Handbook of research in entrepreneurship education: A general perspective* (pp. 46–66). Cheltenham: Edward Elgar.

Hjorth, D., Holt, R. & Steyaert, C. (2015). Entrepreneurship and process studies. *International Small Business Journal*, *33*, 599–611.

Hjorth, D., Jones, C. & Gartner, B. (2008). Introduction for recreating/recontextualising entrepreneurship. *Scandinavian Journal of Management*, *24*(2), 81–84.

Johnsen, C.G. & Sørensen, B.M. (2017). Traversing the fantasy of the heroic entrepreneur. *International Journal of Entrepreneurial Behavior & Research*, *23*(2), 228–244.

Hjorth, D. & Steyaert, C. (2006). American psycho/European schizo – stories of managerial elites in a hundred images. In P. Gagliardi & B. Czarniawska (Eds), *Management education and humanities* (pp. 67–97). Cheltenham: Edward Elgar.

Katz, J. & Gartner, W.B. (1988). Properties of emerging organizations. *Academy of Management Review*, *13*(3), 429–441.

Kristeva, J. (1982). *Powers of horror: An essay on abjection*, New York, NY: Columbia University Press.

Lin II, R.G, Blankstein, A. & Larrubia, E. (2008). *Fugitive ends global trek in L.A.* Retrieved 29 August 2013 from http://articles.latimes.com/2008/dec/07/local/me-danish7.

Massumi, B. (2010). What concepts do: Preface to the Chinese translation of *A thousand plateaus. Deleuze Studies, 4*(1), 1–15.

McGrath, R.G. (1999). Falling forward: Real options reasoning and entrepreneurial failure. *Academy of Management Review, 24*(1), 13–30.

Minniti, M. & Bygrave, W.D. (2001). A dynamic model of entrepreneurial learning. *Entrepreneurship Theory and Practice, 25*, 5–16.

Mintzberg, H. (1983). *Structure in fives: Designing effective organizations.* New York, NY: Prentice Hall.

Nasserghodsi, C. (2012). *The value of philosophy.* Retrieved 27 September 2017 from www.huffingtonpost.com/christine-nasserghodsi/the-value-of-philosophy_b_1853333.html.

Nobel, C. (2011). *Why companies fail – and how their founders can bounce back.* Retrieved 29 August 2013 from http://hbswk.hbs.edu/item/6591.html.

Olaison, L. & Sørensen, B.M. (2014). The abject of entrepreneurship: Failure, fiasco, fraud. *International Journal of Entrepreneurial Behaviour & Research, 20*(2), 193–211.

Patton, P. (2003). Concept and politics in Derrida and Deleuze. *Critical Horizons, 4*(2), 157–175.

Reichenbach, H. & Herrero Rada, S. (2005). *Entrepreneurship, business failure and starting afresh: The work of the European Commission.* Retrieved 29 August 2013 from www.europeanrestructuring.com.

Reilly, J.M. (2012). *Embracing failure on the path to success.* Retrieved 29 August 2013 from www.entrepreneur.com/article/223366.

Seidman, D. (2010). *Philosophy is back in business.* Retrieved 27 September 2016 from www.fastcompany.com/1521847/philosophy-back-business.

Sliwa, M., Sørensen, B.M. & Cairns, G. (2015). "You have to choose a novel": The biopolitics of critical management education. *Management Learning, 46*(3), 243–259.

Sørensen, B.M. (2010). St. Paul's conversion: The aesthetic organization of labour. *Organization Studies, 31*(3), 307–326.

Sørensen, B.M. (2013). The method of juxtaposition: Unfolding the aesthetic turn in organization studies. In E. Bell, S. Warren & J. Schroeder (Eds), *The Routledge companion to visual organization* (pp. 46–63). London: Routledge.

Sørensen, B.M. (2014). Changing the memory of suffering: An organizational aesthetics of the dark side. *Organization Studies, 35*(2), 279–302.

Spoelstra, S. (2007). *What is organization?* Lund: Lund University Press.

Stevens, G.A. & Burley, J. (1997). 3,000 raw ideas = 1 commercial success! *Research Technology Management, 40*(3), 16–38.

Tedmanson, D., Verduijn, K., Essers, C. & Gartner, W.B. (2012). Critical perspectives in entrepreneurship research. *Organization, 19*(5), 531–541.

Verduijn, K., Dey, P., Tedmanson, D. & Essers, C. (2014). Emancipation and/or oppression? Conceptualizing dimensions of criticality in entrepreneurship studies. *International Journal of Entrepreneurial Behavior & Research, 20*(2), 98–107.

Part IV
On challenging

7 Bringing gender in

The promise of critical feminist pedagogy

Sally Jones

Introduction

[C]lassroom learning embodies selective values, is entangled with relations of power, entails judgement about what knowledge counts, legitimates specific social relations, defines agency in particular ways, and always presupposes a particular notion of the future.

(Giroux, 2011, p. 6)

Entrepreneurship has developed as highly masculinized over hundreds of years (Ahl, 2004), underpinning the mainstream, contemporary emphasis on individualism and creative destruction that positions successful entrepreneurs as white, Western males (Ogbor, 2000), modern-day warriors (Gomez & Korine, 2008) and the new heroes of the economy (Marchesnay, 2011). This chapter explores the dilemmas and tensions of challenging such accounts through actively acknowledging gender in entrepreneurship education (EntEd). During my PhD research (focused on EntEd in the UK) I became increasingly uncomfortable with the gender dynamics – or, rather, the *lack* of awareness of such dynamics – in the university EntEd classrooms that I observed. I have subsequently written about the potential damage that a gender-blind and/or gender-neutral approach can do to both male and female students and have argued for gender to be foregrounded in EntEd (see Jones, 2014, 2015).

Gendered notions create a template of the ideal entrepreneur, linked to practical or vocational outcomes and to developing an entrepreneurial mindset, a mindset that has been criticized as highly masculinized (Ahl, 2002; Ahl & Marlow, 2012; Jones, 2015). Traditional EntEd also reifies particular activities and behaviours and is arguably institutionalized as a belief system in universities (Farny, Frederiksen, Hannibal & Jones, 2016). Lewis (2006) describes how decisions to keep gender out of a particular domain can result in a gender-blindness which suggests neutrality but which reproduces the masculine norm of entrepreneurship. However, bringing gender in may also reinforce negative gendered perceptions of "deficient entrepreneurial femininity" in relation to "efficient entrepreneurial masculinity". Both approaches run the risk of perpetuating suggested essentialist differences between men and women. "Efficient entrepreneurial masculinity" may feel as tight and uncomfortable to some as "deficient entrepreneurial femininity", emphasizing behaviours and attitudes that women must change in order to be deemed successful (Bird & Brush, 2002; Ahl, 2006; Hughes, Jennings, Brush, Carter & Welter, 2012). If gendered orders are interpreted as an individual shortcoming, this may also result in a requirement for individuals to change to adapt to the gendered entrepreneurship order, rather than changing this order. Such concerns have led to calls for feminist approaches to entrepreneurship research (Ahl & Marlow, 2012; Calas, Smircich & Bourne, 2009; Henry, Foss & Ahl, 2016). Thus, creating awareness for how to address the gendered entrepreneurship discourse requires reflection. This chapter outlines a critical feminist approach to teaching, which draws upon critiques of entrepreneurship research and experiences of bringing these debates into the classroom.

To explore these issues, in this chapter I outline my educational philosophy, some of the ways that I bring gender into the classroom and some dilemmas this poses for me. My main concern is my (and my students') engagement with the mainstream entrepreneurship literature, which is seemingly unavoidable given the context. Such literature often uses gender as a variable, comparing men and women as homogeneous groups (with women traditionally positioned as deficient). Entrepreneurial success is often linked to economic imperatives and, in this respect, women are positioned as underperforming (Marlow & McAdam, 2013). There *is* an emerging critique of the gender-blindness and evacuation of historical and cultural context in such narrow framings (Calas *et al.*, 2009; Marlow & McAdam, 2013) and I draw on such critiques in my teaching. However, I am mindful that the criticism, discussion and debate that I encourage in class could be undermined by the "lessons learnt offstage" (Miller, 1998), when students are continuously confronted with mass media constructions of entrepreneurship via, for example, television programmes like *The Apprentice* and *Dragons' Den*. I argue that employing critical feminist approaches, and actively reflecting on our current practices, can help us and our students to challenge mainstream accounts of entrepreneurship that underpin much traditional teaching and begin to alter the gendered entrepreneurship discourse.

The critical tensions of entrepreneurship education

> [F]eminist and Freirean teachers raise conflicts for themselves and for their students, who also are historically situated and whose own subjectivities are often contradictory and in process. These conflicts have become increasingly clear as both Freirean and feminist pedagogies are put into practice.
>
> (Weiler, 1991, p. 451)

I am relatively new to lecturing, having completed my PhD in 2011, when I got my first lectureship. However, I had spent many years working as an educator in community arts and adult education contexts (many of which involved working with all-woman cohorts and other marginalized groups such as the long-term unemployed and young offenders). This sensitized me to the underlying gendered (and classed, and raced) assumptions of students, employers, local government and welfare services, and social institutions more broadly. In the late 1990s and early 2000s I trained women returners in formal ICT qualifications. This context challenged women's position as less interested in technology, while at the same time acknowledging that mainstream college computer classes were often all-male by default.

Critical reflection on my role as an educator, with the potential to reproduce mainstream assumptions and attitudes, prompted my interest in critical pedagogies. Freire (2000), Shor (1996), Giroux (2011), hooks (2014) and McLaren (2015) argue that educators can and *should* challenge unreflexive, neutral and ahistorical representations and teach students to transgress the institutional positioning to which they are subjected (hooks, 2014). Such approaches also align with feminist pedagogy. Indeed, feminist pedagogy is "critical, oppositional, and activist" and "grounded in a vision of social change" (Weiler, 1991, p. 456).

As a critical feminist educator I seek to develop teaching approaches that allow spaces for students to challenge the gendered, normative assumptions inherent in traditional approaches to entrepreneurship. This chimes with the broader feminist view that gender binaries are based on socially constructed differences between men and women, which have developed to the disadvantage of women (Stanley & Wise, 1990). I do not want to be party to the reproduction of damaging gendered discourses and am mindful of Naidoo's (2004, p. 9) argument that:

> (university) education establishes a close correspondence between the social classification at entry and the social classification at exit without explicitly recognizing and in most cases denying, the link between social properties dependent on social origin.

As such, far from challenging gendered assumptions, universities can reproduce them. Margolis, Soldetenko, Acker & Gair (2001, p. 18) further argue that education systems perpetuate "an uneven distribution of cultural as well as economic capital. In the process, they endorse and normalize particular types of knowledge, ways of speaking, styles, meanings, dispositions and worldviews". In my engagement with critical pedagogy I seek to actively resist such normative approaches. Doing so involves encouraging students to share their life-world and experiences in the classroom, and in their engagement with the reading and debates as they progress through my courses. I actively encourage them *not* to suspend their disbelief (Jones, 2012) and to honestly engage with the concepts and theories I present.

Mainstream accounts of men and women's entrepreneurial aspirations and/or success often use gender as a variable – something which is increasingly criticized by feminist researchers (Hughes *et al.*, 2012; Henry *et al.*, 2016). Using gender as a variable has the potential to homogenize women's experiences, attitudes and abilities as it actively searches for and emphasizes differences between men and women. Such approaches disappear the social context and structures that may constrain or enable different men and women in this domain. The construction and reproduction of gender binaries and essential differences between male and female entrepreneurs also chimes with Steele and Aronson's (1995) concept of stereotype threat. Stereotypes have the potential to interfere with performance in the stereotyped domain by increasing self-consciousness, and encouraging an over-cautious attitude and low expectations in those positioned as inferior.

Such concerns also underpin my reflections on bringing gender into the classroom and how, as educators, we can consciously consider gender. I argue that mainstream EntEd has kept gender out, in its positioning of entrepreneurship as gender-neutral, value-free and meritocratic (Jones, 2010). Indeed, many educators consider EntEd an unsuitable context for consideration of gender and/or ethnicity (McKeown, Millman, Sursani, Smith & Martin, 2006). Thus, the neutrality and value-free status of EntEd is preserved, so as not to trouble mainstream notions of the primacy of agency in entrepreneurship and entrepreneurial success.

Stereotype threat and entrepreneurship education

Stereotype threat theory developed from studies in social psychology and is concerned with abilities linked to particular groups such as black students (Steele & Aronson, 1995; Aronson, Fried & Good, 2002), women (Murphy, Steele & Gross, 2007), and the working class (Croizet & Claire, 1998). It represents a threat to the social identity of an individual and occurs "whenever individuals' behaviour could be interpreted in terms of a stereotype, that is, whenever group members run the risk of substantiating the stereotype" (Croizet & Claire, 1998, p. 589). In this context the social identity is that of woman, and women's suggested deficiencies within the setting of entrepreneurship.

Allied to stereotype threat is the concept of stereotype lift (Walton & Cohen, 2003), whereby those identified as belonging to a superior group are emboldened in their expectation of success. This results from awareness that there is an *outgroup* who are positioned negatively in relation to a particular domain. Those who belong to the *ingroup* gain a boost in performance and confidence from their positioning (Steele & Aronson, 1995). Aronson *et al.* (2002) argue that ongoing exposure to stereotype threat can lead to the domain in question (in this case entrepreneurship) being perceived as less valuable or desirable by groups stereotyped as underachieving in that domain (in this case women). It has also been suggested that, when women suspect they may be one of only a few, or the *only* woman, involved in an activity they experience stereotype threat. Sekaquaptewa and Thompson (2003, p. 68) argue that "being the only member of one's gender in a group is a different experience for women than it is for men" and this negatively affects women's desire to enter careers or sectors that are perceived as male-dominated.

Of course, many educators are already informed and concerned about the impacts of gender. However, Drudy and Chathain (2002) suggest that teachers' concerns about gender are often located in the structural and curriculum levels rather than in classroom practice. Indeed, feminist educational theory is historically grounded in practice. This is because:

> interest in a feminist pedagogy, arose initially not from theoretical debate in education or teaching, but rather from practical concerns of feminist school teachers and university lecturers, wishing to address gender and other equality issues in the class- and lecture-rooms.
>
> (Weiner, 2004, p. 2)

To support reflection on critical, feminist teaching practices and to offer some practical examples, the following section outlines some of the approaches I take and how students respond to these.

Insights from a gender and entrepreneurship classroom

In 2012 I developed an undergraduate module, Gender and Entrepreneurship. It is based on my PhD research (Jones, 2011) and my ongoing research on gender, entrepreneurship and EntEd. The module explores the gendered dynamics of entrepreneurship in different contexts. It is based on feminist ideas, drawing upon social constructionism and sociology. Each week we look at a different aspect of entrepreneurship, e.g. history and definitions, the role of education, different business sectors, and international contexts. I take a social feminist perspective, focused on the role of social structures such as the family, education and the media, and how these can shape the opportunities, experiences, aspirations and motivations of men and women differently. Social feminism therefore "[recognizes] difference but in a context of equality. This difference arises essentially from socialization processes which shape gendered forms of behaviour" (Marlow & Patton, 2005, p. 721).

I also draw on a social*ist* feminist perceptive, which critiques the "historical reproduction of patriarchal capitalism" (Calas *et al.*, 2009, p. 562), framing entrepreneurship as: "gendering processes under patriarchal capitalism; gendering knowledge/subjectivities; interconnecting gender/ratioethnic/class processes reproducing global neoliberalism" (Calas *et al.*, 2009, p. 565). As such, the module is highly theoretically driven, with the underpinning perspectives becoming clearer as students progress through engagement in class activities and discussion. I also employ the principle of "deliberate vagueness", which "allows and requires the [student] to impose their own system of relevancy" (Wengraf, 2001, p. 122).

It is a level two, 10-credit module (aimed at second-year students). As a university-wide elective it attracts a range of students. This year I had students from psychology, communication studies, management, modern languages, economics, computing and philosophy. I also have many international students and this year welcomed students from Australia, Austria, China, France, Italy, South Korea, Taiwan and the US. Such student diversity enriches the discussion and debate as we progress through the module.

However, although it is an elective, students are not always initially invested in its focus. I do an anonymous exercise in the first class, which encourages honesty about reasons for taking the course, and students' concerns and hopes. Many students enrol because there are no exams and/or because it runs towards the end of the teaching day and is the only class that does not clash with their core modules (and they *have to* take electives). This year the majority of my students chose the module because of timing. Giving space for honesty and openness right from the start sets the tone for the rest of the course. As they progress, students are also encouraged to be honest about their responses to the reading, classroom resources and tasks, and also to bring in their own artefacts[1] to share and discuss with the group (this might be a TV programme they have watched or a blog they have read which resonates with them). They are also encouraged to share their own personal experiences and to reflect on whether and how the debates and research we explore, might affect them in their day-to-day lives, now and in the future. In many respects, I see this course as a rehearsal for some of the gender dynamics and institutional structures students may encounter as they progress through their careers. It offers opportunities for students to learn how to recognize and analyse such dynamics and to respond to them in a critical but thoughtful way.

The students are predominantly female, with around 20 per cent being male. I am always aware, in bringing in statistics about gender and entrepreneurship (which invariably benchmark women against men) that I am in the position of promoting stereotype threat for my female students, while potentially promoting stereotype lift for my male students. For this reason, I bring in exercises (two of which are outlined below) that support critical engagement with the gender stereotypes underpinning entrepreneurship. This encourages them to consider not only individual characteristics of entrepreneurs but also to engage with the sociopolitical, historical and cultural context within which entrepreneurship takes place, and how these might be influenced by gendered structures and institutions. I always offer counter arguments to any theories that I present, to highlight the lack of certainty and stability in these debates and to draw out *what* students think and *why* they think the way they do. This involves highlighting the debates and contestation of theories we engage with, such as Bem's Sex Role Inventory (1974) or Hakim's Preference Theory (2000). Students can find this destabilizing but I emphasize the need to navigate this area and come to their own, informed conclusions, rather than me being the "expert".

In the following I outline some incidents and interventions that I have found useful over four years of teaching the course. In some respects, they can all can be viewed as forms of feminist consciousness-raising, as I use them to support students in developing a critical awareness of culture (Sowards & Renegar, 2004).

Separating biological sex from gender

This is a typically feminist approach and supports exploration of common gender stereotypes associated with men and women which, although often based upon biological essentialism, can be separated from cultural constructions of masculinity and femininity. I use an exercise early on, based on Bem's (1974) Sex Role Inventory (SRI), to explore student perceptions of the gendering of entrepreneurship. However, instead of calling it the Sex Role Inventory I call it the Entrepreneurial Personality Index and ask students to score their perceptions of entrepreneurs using a 1–7 score (with 1 being almost never and 7 being almost always). Bem's SRI consists of socially gendered characteristics that are commonly associated with men and women, in the form of traditional ascriptions of masculine and feminine behaviours.[2] Most students score the masculine characteristics as highly congruent with entrepreneurship, and the feminine as least congruent. However, it is worth noting that students from Chinese and other East Asian backgrounds often identify feminine-typified behaviours as congruent with entrepreneurship. This has led to illuminating discussions about whether collective cultures encourage more communal and collaborative approaches to entrepreneurship than Western ones.

This exercise acts as a starting point to explore whether students subconsciously view entrepreneurship as masculine and leads to discussions about where these perceptions have come from (often it is the lessons learned offstage). We also consider, given that the SRI is over 40 years old, if any of these have changed over time and why. We discuss the argument that they are often based on biological distinctions, which drive socially gendered distinctions based on expectations of what it is to be male or female and, in turn, masculine and feminine. This also opens up opportunities to identify potentially damaging stereotypes for both men and women – e.g. masculinity (and men) seen as aggressive and femininity (and women) seen as weak.

The exercise usually causes tension and disagreement. Often students will argue that the suggested gendered behaviours are outrageously sexist and outdated and they question the relevance of using the SRI today. Male students can be offended by the proposed masculine behaviours of individualism and insensitivity, while female students challenge the view that they lack leadership ability and independence. This leads us to consider feminine *men* and masculine *women*, highlighting the importance of separating biological sex from gender (in terms of masculinity and femininity). It can take a while to work through the notion that these *are* stereotypes and represent societal *perceptions* of masculinity and femininity and prescribed gender roles as they commonly (uncritically) relate to men and women. This fruitful discussion lays the foundations for bringing in theories of stereotype threat and stereotype lift later in the module. Student feedback suggests that this has a significant impact, and many of them draw on these debates in their individual assignments.

To further emphasize the separation of biological sex from gender, I then ask them to use the SRI to reflect upon two business case studies: a social enterprise and a for-profit business, both focused on children,[3] to see if the words they use to describe the entrepreneurs here are different from those previously chosen. Here students tend to focus on traditionally feminine characteristics. I then reveal that both businesses were founded by men and we discuss the pros and cons of presenting a masculinized or feminized business brand to the world, and whether this might have different consequences for men and women. Often discussion turns to whether these are simply human characteristics that have been ascribed to men and women owing to binary, essentialist approaches and how notions of femininity or masculinity may vary historically and between cultures.

Sometimes students will share their own experiences of friends or family members who have been affected. For example, one male student's brother wanted to take time off to care for his new son but was actively discouraged by his family and work colleagues, who thought it would damage his career and he would not enjoy it. This personal example provided a lightbulb moment. Why is it then considered a *good* thing for women to "damage their careers"? "Ah! because, as the SRI suggests, femininity (and in an uncritical sense, women) 'love children' and are not ambitious and men, in their conferred masculinity, are 'insensitive to others' needs' and 'individualistic'"! This then prompted recognition that, although many people conflate women with gender, men are also gendered subjects. Indeed, this theme develops throughout the module, with male students often disclosing their hopes and fears for fatherhood.

In both of these exercises I try to subvert the symbolic power of language (Bourdieu, 1991), which combines with official discourses from the field of entrepreneurship to mask taken-for-granted gendered constructs and position them as neutral (Bruni, Gherardi & Poggio, 2005). Throughout our lives, we internalize expectations linked to prescribed gender roles and this informs our aspirations and expectations (Bourdieu, 1998). This internalization of gendered discourses informs individual choices and shapes societal norms, resulting in the arbitrary structures of society being accepted as somehow natural. The exercises also emphasize students' experiences and the cultural assumptions that they bring with them from *outside* the classroom. It starts to sensitize them to the debates and what they mean for *them*, as well as for entrepreneurship more broadly. Furthermore, it builds a sense of trust and experience-sharing within the group, while also emphasizing that there are no right or wrong answers and many different views exist on the subject. Students also begin to appreciate and understand how theory (which many of them *do* struggle with, initially) can be an explanatory device, which is very much linked to the "real world" and can help them make sense of it.

The "F" word

Student understanding and/or mistrust of feminism varies from cohort to cohort. Last year's cohort was particularly wary of feminism. Indeed, in my opening "hopes and fears exercise" several students disclosed that they hoped it wouldn't be "too feminist" or "trying to turn us all into feminists". Female students may argue feminism smacks of "special pleading" and "victimhood", suggesting they are not good enough to succeed without special support. They often argue that supposedly feminist literature and policy positions women as underperforming. I must admit this is something that I struggle with too, especially given my concerns about stereotype threat. I do feel that, in engaging with mainstream entrepreneurship research, I could be seen as suggesting my female students will only get so far and then there will be barriers in their way (often linked to motherhood, or motherhood potential). Some male students view feminism as a form of man-hating that belittles men's success and positions men as "bad". Both male and female students consistently argue that "times have changed" and that there is more gender equality, with more women in senior positions, than ever before and so feminism, or consideration of the impacts of gender inequality, is outdated and not wholly relevant to them.

It seems that many students experience "gender fatigue", a result of "[n]avigating the ideological dilemma around gender neutrality and discrimination" (Kelan, 2009, p. 167), with a major aspect being "a reluctance to acknowledge the persistence of gender inequities" (Kelan & Dunkley, 2010, p. 28). As a result, considering gender seems passé and/or is reduced to an individualized level rather than being a pervasive, structural concern (Gill, 2014). Such responses also suggest a post-feminist response, which is seen as a backlash against feminism. McRobbie (2004, p. 255) argues that "by means of the tropes of freedom and choice which are now inextricably connected with the category of 'young women,' feminism is decisively aged and made to seem redundant". In this context it is presumed that women have the freedom to choose their careers and are free from any structural constraints in doing so, given legislation to address sexism and gender-discrimination. Post-feminism presumes that " 'all the battles' have been won" (Gill, 2014, p. 511), echoing the sentiments expressed by many students, both male and female.

To think through these ideas, I use an article from the *New York Times* (Miller, 2014), which presents research by Correll, Benard and Paik (2007) and states that: "employers rate fathers as the most desirable employees, followed by childless women, childless men and finally mothers. They also hold mothers to harsher performance standards." Students are usually surprised that childless women would be preferred over childless men, and start to think about how it might underpin opportunities and choices to pursue entrepreneurship (and their own careers). This is particularly linked to the motherhood "penalty". Furthermore, being seen as more valued employees (and potentially better remunerated) might actually *discourage* fathers from leaving companies to pursue entrepreneurship, as they potentially have more to lose. It is also a way of thinking about the effects of gender as it links to social identity and the life course and, therefore, how its effects change as people progress through their lives.

The mistrust of feminism is an issue I have to address in the classroom, given the module's theoretical underpinning. It is an opportunity for me to explain my social feminist perspective and, again, for students to challenge, debate and discuss feminism as politically, theoretically and personally diverse. I offer an overview of different types of feminism to illustrate that it is not monolithic, although at its most basic level it simply seeks to promote equality between men and women. We also explore postcolonial and black feminisms, which critique other forms of feminism as Western, white and middle class. Indeed, later in the module I facilitate a session on intersectionality and entrepreneurship drawing on the work of Crenshaw (1989) and others to explore multiple inequalities and heterogeneous perspectives.

Bringing theory to life

The module is highly theoretically driven and I am eager for students to critique and apply these theories. I start encouraging this early on, based on the premise that we often uncritically engage with mass media and accept many of the headlines and discussions on social media about men and women, and gender. In order to help students become more critical media consumers, and to support engagement with developing issues around gender and entrepreneurship, I ask them to bring in artefacts to share.[4] Anything and everything is acceptable if it resonates with them and their engagement with the module. As well as news articles, students have shared YouTube videos, blogs, photographs, advertisements and TV programmes such as *The Apprentice*.

This supports both their group and individual assignments. In their group assignment they research and develop a case study of two entrepreneurs to compare and contrast though a gender lens. These are not necessarily a man and a woman and many groups choose to analyse two women or two men and how they might "do gender" (West & Zimmerman, 1987). To support this, I run a workshop on different ways of analysing gender in the media such as content analysis and semiotic analysis (see Gill, 2007). They can choose who they analyse and how they analyse, and the format and structure of their case study.

For their individual assignment students are asked to identify and critically engage with five artefacts that link to our discussions and debates. I stress that they do not have to agree with the theories we cover. However, I am "deliberately vague" about exactly what type of sources they should use and also the way that they might relate these back to the module and their own reflections.

This does seem to develop critical reflection and female students often choose sources that support disclosure of concerns about their future within an organization, or the impact of motherhood on their career. Likewise, male students often consider the impact of masculinity and their perceived role as a future breadwinner and/or father, who wants to be involved with his children's upbringing.

Most students suggest they leave the module with a more critical approach to the gendered discourses they may encounter. Our students are future leaders, employers and employees and I hope that my approach will also help them to feel more confident and assertive if they encounter situations that they do not agree with. I also hope they have different shared and personal experiences, and a new vocabulary to draw on, to help them challenge gendered discourses (and other forms of) overt and covert discrimination.

Student reflections

At the end of the module students complete a feedback survey. Here are some of the most recent comments, which give me hope that my critical, feminist approach does help them link theory and practice to develop a critical approach to gender:

> Really improved my critical thinking on this module and came across things I otherwise wouldn't have, even in a topic I am so passionate about outside uni.

> I enjoyed the content of this module especially as there is a lot of current news which is related to the content of the module which made it a lot more enjoyable as the theory is relevant.

> I enjoyed … the encouragement to voice our opinions on any part of the module.

> I liked the magazine/newspaper articles we read as it helped put the theory we had learnt into practice.

> It was interesting because it was very relevant to the real world.

However, in their individual assignments I do sometimes see manifestations of stereotype threat. This is particularly obvious where female students mention that "if I became an entrepreneur, I am likely to be less successful" or "women do worse than men at entrepreneurship". However, both male and female students seem determined to challenge gender bias when they enter the workplace and/or reach positions of power. That said, many still argue we should not focus too heavily on gender, as this is becoming less important in the workplace; we should judge people by what they have achieved and what they do, rather than their social identity. However, I do feel that it is my duty to open up these areas, so that students can engage with them and think about how they might respond if they encounter them in the future. I also hope that they become more critical of the gendered, neo-liberal construction of the "ideal worker" (Acker, 1990) and the "entrepreneurial self" (Bröckling, 2016).

The promise of critical feminist pedagogy

The term pedagogy refers to "deliberate attempts to influence how and what knowledge and identities are produced within and among particular sets of social relations" (Giroux & Simon, 1989, p. 23). It is argued that dominant (or mainstream) pedagogy "provides a complex system for the production of 'goods' – that is, forms of recognised and legitimate affect, meaning and value" (Worsham, 1998, p. 241). Critical pedagogy is "nourished by a strong dissatisfaction with things as they are" (Masschelein, 1998, p. 521) and recognizes that education is *not* a natural, ahistorical phenomenon but should be understood in its socio-historical and political context (Biesta & Tedder, 2007). The central aim of critical pedagogy is therefore, to challenge and transform wider society for justice and equality. In doing so it raises

> questions about inequalities of power, about the false myths of opportunity and merit for many students, and about the way belief systems become internalized to the point where individuals and groups abandon the very aspiration to question or change their lot in life.
>
> (Burbules & Berk, 1999, p. 50)

In advocating exploration of the historical and sociopolitical context of the curriculum, and by placing student knowledge and experience firmly at the centre of teaching, feminist (and other) debates can be brought in, in a way that actively supports feminist goals. Indeed, Avis and Bathmaker (2004, p. 308) argue that:

> a rethinking of critical pedagogy that draws upon feminism ... would ... refuse an essentialist reading, and would recognise the complexity, contradictions and messiness of educational practice.

Others such as Oberhauser (2002) suggest that critical pedagogy can help students think critically about knowledge production, countering ahistoricism and supporting them to negotiate their own positioning on their own terms. This acknowledges the "importance of position and identity in the creation and dissemination of knowledge" (Johnston, 2000, p. 271) and supports educators and students to recognize that "human possibilities are not fully occupied by the dominant forces or trends of any age" (Shor, 1996, p. 3).

Critical pedagogy also seeks to expose the *hidden* curriculum, defined as the lessons learned, which are not necessarily explicit or consciously intended by educators (Martin, 1983), including the reproduction of wider values, beliefs and unspoken, social norms (Margolis *et al.*, 2001). This involves not only lessons learned in class, but also lessons learned from students' engagement with wider society. As such, the hidden curriculum deals with the "forces by which students are induced to comply with dominant ideologies and social practices related to authority, behaviour and morality" (McLaren, 2003, p. 86). In this way it reflects "deeply held beliefs" (Bain, 1990, p. 29), which can have unintended negative consequences linked to gender (Myer, 2010), ethnicity (Hartlep, 2010) and/or class (McLaren, 2007). Therefore, without a critical, reflexive approach an unintended consequence of bringing gender in might be that we perpetuate and reproduce the very stereotypes that we seek to challenge. A critical, reflexive approach includes acknowledging the effects our conscious pedagogic choices may have on our students. It requires acknowledging our own beliefs and values about entrepreneurship, as this underpins our teaching (Bennett, 2006). Critical educators have moved from reflective practice (after Schon, 1983) to *reflexive* practice; "an 'unsettling', i.e. an insecurity regarding the basic assumptions, discourse and practices used in describing reality" (Pollner, 1991, p. 370). Furthermore, reflexive praxis requires "self-conscious and ethical action based on a critical questioning of past actions and of future possibilities" (Cunliffe, 2004, p. 408). To ignore such concerns risks *conferring* gender identity upon certain students (Holt, 2012), underpinned by mainstream consensus that the symbolic links between masculinity and "real" entrepreneurship represent a true and fair identity (Hamilton, 2013).

However, there is a danger that uncritically and unreflexively acknowledging differences between men and women, particularly where they are traditionally underpinned by essentialist notions linked to biological sex, could further entrench taken-for-granted, masculinized notions of entrepreneurship. To mitigate this, Kenway and Modra (1992, p. 142) argue for a feminist imperative in revising curricula (and, I would argue, education practices) to include and value:

> the range of experiences of girls and women, while at the same time recognizing that the definitions of femininity and masculinity which are formed and promoted ... should encompass a wide range of possibilities which make (men and women) not only "equally human" ... but equally free in the public and private sphere.

The implication is that education systems contribute to the closing down of possibilities for both men and women and that this is linked to "curricula steeped in Anglo-Saxon, middle class, male values which deny multiple aspects of [students'] home and community culture" (Kenway & Modra, 1992, p. 144).

I therefore argue that teaching that is predominantly based on research that benchmarks women against men is particularly damaging, especially where the context, historical background, structural and societal issues are ignored. Current mainstream entrepreneurship text books and literature can actively and uncritically perpetuate the gendered and neo-liberal discourses that I seek to highlight and challenge in the classroom. Indeed, given the very real failures of the neo-liberal market-based system and the resulting economic crisis, it is imperative that we do not continue with business as usual. It is ethically suspect to continue to present entrepreneurship as a universally "good" thing (Tedmanson, Verduijn, Essers & Gartner, 2012) or as a meritocratic form of "inclusive" capitalism (Dolan, 2012). To engage with mainstream literature and theories uncritically and in isolation, without acknowledging the social, political and historical context, risks individualizing "failure", while positioning female students as inherently deficient. Such accounts imply that women need to change rather than seeking to change the social, political and economic structures within which women are positioned. Unsettling such commonly held beliefs can provide cognitive jolts for our students (Massumi, 2009), opening up new areas for debate and discussion and emphasizing that there is more than one "it" when we talk about entrepreneurship.

As such, a critical feminist approach not only helps us to challenge and highlight gender roles and stereotypes but, more importantly, acts as a theoretical/analytical lens that broadens thinking about entrepreneurship and questions its settlement. It also invites us (perhaps, even compels us) to be innovative in our teaching, and to support the emergence of new practices of doing gender/doing entrepreneurship. Indeed, Calas *et al.* (2009) call for the reframing of entrepreneurship from a focus on economic imperatives to a focus on social change. They argue that entrepreneurship theory has been consistently delimiting and reductionist in its development, which has disappeared multilevel, pluralist and socially embedded understandings. Social (and socialist) feminist approaches therefore, broaden conceptualizations of entrepreneurship to account for the "power-laden, contested, and ever-changing social terrains where diverse interests play out" (Calas *et al.*, 2009, p. 555). This helps us to account for the gendered social embeddedness of entrepreneurial aspirations, opportunity recognition, resource acquisition, business growth etc., and acknowledges the historical, political and cultural dimensions of entrepreneurship (rather than just the economic). Feminism's focus on social change is therefore a powerful pedagogic lens to bring to entrepreneurship education, for educators seeking to challenge and broaden current mainstream conceptualizations.

Furthermore, critical, feminist pedagogies seek to broaden debates, understanding and critique *beyond* the classroom setting. They encourage students to think critically about their own prejudices and those of wider society, and the suggested roles of men and women, more broadly. In particular, a social feminist approach highlights how societal institutions, such as the family and education, perpetuate gendered roles and expectations. It turns a spotlight on how society positions men and women differently, within different cultural and societal contexts, and how such positions, while appearing natural and common-sense, are often based on socially constructed assumptions. In doing so it questions the rationales for entrepreneurship and explanations for suggested difference between men and women's career trajectories more broadly.

Concluding thoughts

In our current neo-liberal and, apparently, post-feminist Western society it may seem to us, and to our students, that gender should be kept out of the classroom. However, to bring gender in requires both educators and students to challenge and rethink their previous position on the choices that individuals make – in relation to entrepreneurship but also in relation to broader society. Subsequently, in actively bringing gender in, we may face resistance and resentment from both male and female students. However, a sensitive and critically engaged approach can help students to consider the debates within entrepreneurship, while also exploring their wider beliefs, assumptions and social position(s).

Ultimately, I see my module as a set of co-created discussions, critiques, knowledge and resources that everyone (myself included) can draw on as we progress through our careers and lives. University students are positioned as future leaders and it is therefore important that they engage with and consider the impact of gender (and other socially constructed forms of difference) for individuals and organizations. My hope is that a lasting outcome of the module will be students who can recognize and mitigate for gendered practices in their own lives and also act as agents of change when they can identify, articulate and challenge gender bias in the future. The promise of alternative perspectives, also challenges increasingly individualized accounts of "success" or "failure", which promote gender-evacuated meritocracy and the primacy of agency. Whatever the long-term outcomes, I *am* dissatisfied with current gendered conceptualizations of entrepreneurship and I hope that my approach helps students see that "things could always be other than they are" (Barnett, 1990, p. 155).

Notes

1 In this context an artefact is defined as "An object made by a human being, typically one of cultural or historical interest" (Oxford English Dictionary).
2 It also includes androgynous characteristics.
3 The examples used are Mary's Meals – a social enterprise that provides free school meals to students in disadvantaged communities worldwide – and Ella's Kitchen, a company that makes organic food for babies and toddlers.
4 See Berglund and Wigren-Kristoferson (2012) for a more detailed account of using artefacts in EntEd.

References

Ahl, H.J. (2002). The construction of the female entrepreneur as the "Other". In B. Czarniawska-Joerges & H. Hopfl (Eds), *Casting the other: Maintaining gender inequalities in the workplace* (pp. 52–67). London and New York, NY: Routledge.

Ahl, H.J. (2004). *The scientific reproduction of gender inequality: A discourse analysis of research texts on women's entrepreneurship.* Malmo, Koege, Herndon, VA, Abingdon: Copenhagen Business School Press.

Ahl, H.J. (2006). Why research on women entrepreneurs needs new directions. *Entrepreneurship Theory and Practice, 30*(5), 595–621.

Ahl, H. & Marlow, S. (2012). Exploring the dynamics of gender, feminism and entrepreneurship: advancing debate to escape a dead end? *Organization, 19*(5), 543–562.

Acker, J. (1990). Hierarchies, jobs, bodies: A theory of gendered organizations. *Gender and Society* 4(2), 139–158.

Aronson, J., Fried, C.B. & Good, C. (2002). Reducing the effects of stereotype threat on African American college students by shaping theories of intelligence. *Journal of Experimental Social Psychology, 38*(2), 113–125.

Avis, J. & Bathmaker, A. (2004). Critical pedagogy, performativity and a politics of hope: Trainee further education lecturer practice. *Research in Post-Compulsory Education, 9* (2), 310–313.

Bain, L. (1990). A critical analysis of the hidden curriculum in physical education. In D. Kirk & R. Tinning (Eds), *Physical education curriculum and culture: Critical issues in the contemporary crisis* (pp. 19–34).

Barnett, R. (1990). *The idea of higher education.* Buckingham and Bristol, PA: Open University Press.

Bem, S.L. (1974). The measurement of psychological androgyny. *Journal of Consulting and Clinical Psychology, 42*(2), 155–162.

Bennett, R. (2006). Business lecturers' perceptions of the nature of entrepreneurship *International Journal of Entrepreneurial Behaviour and Research, 12*(3), 165–188.

Berglund, K.A.E. & Wigren-Kristoferson, C. (2012). Using pictures and artefacts in a PAR process to disclose new wor(l)ds of entrepreneurship. *Action Research*, *10*(3), 276–292.

Biesta, G. & Tedder, M. (2007). Agency and learning in the lifecourse: Towards an ecological perspective. *Studies in the Education of Adults*, *39*(2), 132–149.

Bird, B. & Brush, C. (2002). A gendered perspective on organizational creation. *Entrepreneurship theory and practice*, *26*(3), 41–66.

Bourdieu, P. (1991). *Language and Symbolic Power* (G. Raymond & M. Adamson, Trans.). Oxford: Polity.

Bourdieu, P. (1998). *Masculine domination* (R. Nice, Trans.). Stanford, CA: Stanford University Press.

Bröckling, U. (2016). *The entrepreneurial self. Fabricating a new type of subject.* London: SAGE.

Bruni, A., Gherardi, S. & Poggio, B. (2005). *Gender and entrepreneurship: An ethnographic approach.* Abingdon and New York, NY: Routledge.

Burbules, N.C. & Berk, R.R. (1999). Critical thinking and critical pedagogy: Relations, differences, and limits. In T.S. Popkewitz & L. Fendler (Eds), *Critical theories in education* (pp. 45–66). New York, NY: Routledge.

Calas, M.B., Smircich, L. & Bourne, K.A. (2009). Extending the boundaries: Reframing "entrepreneurship as social change" through feminist perspectives. *Academy of Management Review*, *34*(3), 552–569.

Correll, S.J., Benard, S. & Paik, I. (2007). Getting a job: Is there a motherhood penalty? *American Journal of Sociology*, *112*(5), 1297–1338.

Crenshaw, K.W. (1989). Demarginalizing the intersection of race and sex. *The University of Chicago Legal Forum*, 139–167.

Croizet, J.C. & Claire, T. (1998). Extending the concept of stereotype threat to social class: The intellectual underperformance of students from low socioeconomic backgrounds. *Personality and Social Psychology Bulletin*, *24*(6), 588–594.

Cunliffe, A. (2004). On becoming a critically reflexive practitioner. *Journal of Management Education*, *28*(4), 407–426.

Dolan, C. (2012). The new face of development: The "bottom of the pyramid" entrepreneurs. *Anthropology Today*, *28*(4), 3–7.

Drudy, S. & Chathain, M.U. (2002). Gender effects in classroom interaction: Data collection, self-analysis and reflection. *Evaluation and Research in Education*, *16*(1), 34–50.

Farny, S., Frederiksen, S.H., Hannibal, M. & Jones, S. (2016). A CULTure of entrepreneurship education. *Entrepreneurship and Regional Development*, *28*(7–8), 514–535.

Freire, P. (2000). *Pedagogy of the oppressed.* London: Bloomsbury.

Gill, R. (2007). *Gender and the media.* Cambridge and Malden, MA: Polity.

Gill, R. (2014). Unspeakable inequalities: Post feminism, entrepreneurial subjectivity, and the repudiation of sexism among cultural workers. *Social Politics: International Studies in Gender, State & Society*, *21*(4), 509–528.

Giroux, H.A. (2011). *On critical pedagogy.* New York, NY: Continuum.

Giroux, H. & Simon, R. (1989). Popular culture as a pedagogy of pleasure and meaning. In H. Giroux & R. Simon (Eds), *Popular culture, schooling and everyday life* (pp. 1–29). Granby, MA: Bergin and Garvey.

Gomez, P.Y. & Korine, H. (2008). *Entrepreneurs and democracy: A political theory of corporate governance.* Cambridge and New York, NY: Cambridge University Press.

Hakim, C. (2000). *Work–lifestyle choices in the 21st century: Preference theory.* Oxford: Oxford University Press.

Hamilton, E. (2013). The discourse of entrepreneurial masculinities (and femininities). *Entrepreneurship and Regional Development, 25*(1–2), 90–99.

Hartlep, N. (2010). *Going public: Critical race theory and issues of social justice.* Mustang, OK: Tate.

Henry, C., Foss, L. & Ahl, H. (2016). Gender and entrepreneurship research: A review of methodological approaches. *International Small Business Journal, 34*(3), 217–241.

Holt, B. (2012). Identity matters: The centrality of "Conferred identity" as symbolic power and social capital in higher education mobility. *International Journal of Inclusive Education, 16*(9), 929–940.

hooks, B. (2014). *Teaching to transgress.* Abingdon and New York, NY: Routledge.

Hughes, K.D., Jennings, J.E., Brush, C., Carter, S. & Welter, F. (2012). Extending women's entrepreneurship research in new directions. *Entrepreneurship Theory and Practice, 36*(3), 429–442.

Johnston, R. (2000). Authors, editors and authority in the postmodern academy. *Antipode, 32*(3), 271–291.

Jones, S. (2010). Stuck in neutral? HE entrepreneurship and enterprise education and gender. *Assessment, Learning and Teaching Journal, 8*, 42–44.

Jones, S. (2011). *The gendering of entrepreneurship in higher education: A Bourdieuian approach.* Unpublished PhD thesis, Leeds Metropolitan University, Leeds, UK.

Jones, S. (2012). *Beyond (dis)belief? Gender and the suspension of disbelief in HE entrepreneurship education.* Institute for Small Business and Entrepreneurship (ISBE) 35th International conference, November 2012, Dublin.

Jones, S. (2014). Gendered discourses of entrepreneurship in UK higher education: The fictive entrepreneur and the fictive student. *International Small Business Journal, 32*(3), 237–258.

Jones, S. (2015). "You would expect the successful person to be the man": Gendered symbolic violence in UK HE entrepreneurship education. *International Journal of Gender and Entrepreneurship, 7*(3), 303–320.

Kelan, E.K. (2009). Gender fatigue: The ideological dilemma of gender neutrality and discrimination in organizations. *Canadian Journal of Administrative Sciences/Revue Canadienne des Sciences de l'Administration, 26*(3), 197–210.

Kelan, E.K. & Dunkley Jones, R. (2010). "Gender and the MBA". *Academy of Management Learning and Education, 9*(1), 26–43.

Kenway, J. & Modra, H. (1992). Feminist pedagogy and emancipatory possibilities. In C. Luke & J. Gore (Eds), *Feminisms and critical pedagogy* (pp. 138–166). London and New York, NY: Routledge.

Lewis, P. (2006). The quest for invisibility: Female entrepreneurs and the masculine norm of entrepreneurship. *Gender, Work & Organization, 13*(5), 453–469.

Marchesnay, M. (2011). Fifty years of entrepreneurship and SME: a personal view. *Journal of Small Business and Enterprise Development, 18*(2), 352–365.

McRobbie, A. (2004). Post-feminism and popular culture. *Feminist Media Studies, 4*(3), 255–264.

Margolis, E., Soldetenko, M., Acker, S. & Gair, M. (2001). Peekaboo: Hiding and outing the curriculum. In E. Margolis (Ed.), *The hidden curriculum in higher education* (pp. 1–19). New York, NY, and London: Routledge.

Marlow, S. & McAdam, M. (2013). Gender and entrepreneurship: Advancing debate and challenging myths; exploring the mystery of the under-performing female entrepreneur. *International Journal of Entrepreneurial Behaviour & Research, 19*(1), 114–124.

Marlow, S. & Patton, D. (2005). All credit to men? Entrepreneurship, finance, and gender. *Entrepreneurship Theory and Practice, 29*(6), 717–735.

Martin, J. (1983). What should we do with a hidden curriculum when we find one? In H. Giroux & P. David (Eds), *The hidden curriculum and moral education* (pp. 122–139). Berkeley, CA: McCutchan.

Masschelein, J. (1998). How to imagine something exterior to the system: Critical education as problematization. *Educational Theory, 48*(4), 521–530.

Massumi, B. (2009). National enterprise emergency: Steps towards an ecology of power. *Theory, Culture and Society, 29*(6), 153–185.

McLaren, P. (2003). Critical pedagogy: A look at the major concepts. In A. Darder, M. Baltodano & R. Torres (Eds), *The critical pedagogy reader* (pp. 69–96). New York, NY: RoutledgeFalmer.

McLaren, P. (2007). Critical pedagogy and class struggle in the age of neoliberal globalization. In E.W. Ross & R. Gibson (Eds), *Neoliberalism and Education Reform* (pp. 257–288). Cresskill, NJ: Hampton.

McLaren, P. (2015). *Life in schools: An introduction to critical pedagogy in the foundations of education* (6th edn). Abingdon and New York, NY: Routledge.

McKeown, J., Millman, C., Sursani, S.R., Smith, K. & Martin, L.M. (2006). *UK graduate entrepreneurship education in England, Wales and Scotland.* National Council for Graduate Entrepreneurship working paper.

Miller, R. (1998). The arts of complicity: Pragmatism and the culture of schooling. *College English, 61*(1), 10–28.

Miller, C.C. (6 September 2014). *The motherhood penalty vs. the fatherhood bonus.* Retrieved 3 March 2017 from www.nytimes.com/2014/09/07/upshot/a-child-helps-your-career-if-youre-a-man.html?_r=0.

Murphy, M., Steele, C. & Gross J. (2007). Signalling threat: How situational cues affect women in math, science, and engineering. *Psychological Science, 18*(10), 879–885.

Myer, E.J. (2010). *Gender and sexual diversity in schools.* Dordrecht, Heidelberg, London, New York, NY: Springer.

Naidoo, R. (2004). Fields and institutional strategy: Bourdieu on the relationship between higher education, inequality and society. *British Journal of Sociology of Education 25*(4), 457–471.

Oberhauser, A.M. (2002). Examining gender and community through critical pedagogy. *Journal of Geography in Higher Education, 26*(1), 19–31.

Ogbor, J.O. (2000). Mythicizing and reification in entrepreneurial discourse: Ideology-critique of entrepreneurial studies. *Journal of Management Studies, 37*(5), 605–635.

Pollner, M. (1991). Left of ethnomethodology: The rise and decline of radical reflexivity. *American Sociological Review, 56,* 370–380.

Schon, D. (1983). *The reflective practitioner: How professionals think in action.* Aldershot: Arena.

Sekaquaptewa, D. & Thompson, M. (2003). Solo status, stereotype threat, and performance expectancies: Their effects on women's performance. *Journal of Experimental Social Psychology, 39*(1), 68–74.

Shor, I. (1996). *When students have power: Negotiating authority in a critical pedagogy.* London, Chicago, IL: University of Chicago Press.

Sowards, S.K. & Renegar, V.R. (2004). The rhetorical functions of consciousness-raising in third wave feminism. *Communication Studies, 55*(4), 535–552.

Stanley, L. & Wise, S. (1990). Method, methodology and epistemology in feminist research processes. In L. Stanley (Ed.), *Feminist praxis: Research, theory and epistemology in feminist sociology* (pp. 20–60). London and New York, NY: Routledge.

Steele, C.M. & Aronson, J. (1995). Stereotype threat and the intellectual test performance of African Americans. *Journal of Personality and Social Psychology, 69*, 797–811.

Tedmanson, D., Verduijn, K., Essers, C. & Gartner, W.B. (2012). Critical perspectives in entrepreneurship research. *Organization, 19*(5), 531–541.

Walton, G.M. & Cohen, G.L. (2003). Stereotype lift. *Journal of Experimental Social Psychology, 39*(5), 456–467.

Weiler, K. (1991). Freire and a feminist pedagogy of difference. *Harvard Educational Review, 61*(4), 449–474.

Weiner, G. (2004). Learning from feminism: Education, pedagogy and practice. In *An invited seminar: Beyond Access, Pedagogic strategies for Gender Equity and Quality Basic Education in schools, Nairobi, Kenya* (pp. 2–3).

Wengraf, T. (2001). *Qualitative research interviewing.* London, Thousand Oaks, CA, and New Delhi: SAGE.

West, C. & Zimmerman, D.H. (1987). Doing gender. *Gender and Society, 1*(2), 125–151.

Worsham, L. (1998). Going postal: Pedagogic violence and the schooling of emotion. *JAC: A Journal of Composition Theory, 18*(2), 213–245.

8 Entrepreneurship and the entrepreneurial self

Creating alternatives through entrepreneurship education?

Annika Skoglund and Karin Berglund

Introduction

Entrepreneurship has spread via an abundance of organizations and people that embrace the prosperity its logic currently promises. Apart from the generation of new companies and market places, this promise also entails a flexible invention of entrepreneurial subjectivities and self-investment via alternative choices (Bröckling, 2016). We have recently seen a diversification of the contexts in which entrepreneurial subjectivities are invited to undergird entrepreneurship, for example in social entrepreneurship (Dey, 2014) and ecopreneurship. A peculiar pluralism of "entrepreneurial selves" is advancing, which makes it necessary to question how we, as educators in entrepreneurship, are offered to join in and become abiding facilitators of students' empowerment and subjectification to entrepreneurship, now in its rejuvenated forms. Our concern is thus in line with others who have turned to Foucault to study the potential effects teaching has on student subjectivities, either positively (Sliwa, Meier Sørensen & Cairns, 2015) or negatively (Simons & Masschelein, 2008).

This chapter presents the development and implementation of a critical entrepreneurship course, "Entrepreneurship and the Entrepreneurial Self" (EES), designed for masters students. The purpose of the course is (i) to deconstruct the basic ontological assumptions of entrepreneurship and explore the extension and reformulation of these assumptions for alternative forms of entrepreneurship, such as social entrepreneurship and ecopreneurship, (ii) to analyse the broadening of entrepreneurial subjectivities that unfold hand in hand with these forms of entrepreneurship, and (iii) to go beyond these forms of entrepreneurship and subjectivities to touch upon the (im)possibility of collectively constructing new worlds.

To address these issues we chose to introduce basic readings and developments of Foucault's work to the students (e.g. see Rose, 1999; Vrasti, 2012) and thereby enable their deconstruction of the basic assumptions and understanding of the socially and environmentally advanced entrepreneurial logic (Albrecht, 2002; Costea, Amiridis & Crump, 2012; Dempsey & Sanders, 2010; Goss, Jones, Betta & Latham, 2011; Jones & Spicer, 2009; Pastakia, 1998; Peredo & Chrisman, 2006; Pongratz & Voss, 2003). The theoretical focus for their reading is guided by a historical understanding of liberal and neo-liberal advancements and shifts in the provision of security – continuously aiming for self-regulating citizens (Foucault, 1979/1997; 1997/2004) – visible in how variegated entrepreneurial selves of today are cultivated by the enabling state and its handymen.

The perspective provided on the course presents entrepreneurship in relation to Foucault's notion of "productive power", where the capacities of the individual are empowered on behalf of the whole population, i.e. a "biopolitics" fascinated with life improvements (e.g. see Wallenstein, 2013). The theoretical framework emphasizes how self-regulation and the optimization of life itself, "making live and letting die" (Dillon & Reid, 2001), followed on from how liberal philosophy prioritized individual freedom in contrast to state rule (Lemke, 2001). We explain to the students how "freedom" has been linked to a construction of "the social" and "the economic", to open up possibilities for self-creation and self-regulation. Du Gay, Salaman and Rees (1996, p. 270) have even suggested that "the character of the entrepreneur can no longer be represented as just one among a plurality of ethical personalities but must be seen as assuming an ontological priority". At the same time, we emphasize how the promise of entrepreneurial freedoms and belief in individual capacities seductively speaks to and utilizes your "own" power to "[b]e the architect of your own future" (Pongratz & Voss, 2003, p. 248). By extension, we ask the students to critically reflect on political dimensions, human limits, alternative ideals and the collective efforts that are part of entrepreneurial endeavours (see further Costea *et al.*, 2012) and entrepreneurial education (Berglund, 2013).

The course consists of two parallel streams, one analytical and one practical. In the analytical stream, students read about entrepreneurship from the above-mentioned liberal and neo-liberal philosophy perspectives and apply this to analyse the emergence of new forms of entrepreneurship, what we call "alternative entrepreneurships" (Berglund & Skoglund, 2016). Recognizing new forms of entrepreneurship in late liberal societies brings up questions such as: How has "life" been optimized and vitalized through entrepreneurship? How does expertise call on the human to become entrepreneurial? How are new contexts cultivating entrepreneurial freedoms and self-regulation? And how do these contexts offer the entrepreneurial subject a reinvestment in the self?

In the practical stream of the course students engage collectively in a social mission of an imaginary company. Taking inspiration from the Hungarian/US IT company Prezi, this project, called "The entrepreneurial self of a company", invites students to shape a philanthropic project. Although their student project company is fictional, the students are required to carry out a social mission and solve a social problem of their own choice. In the final presentation, the students can either utilize their theatrical skills, for example by role-playing, or show photographs, film clips, and interviews with organizations and people affected by their social mission.

This practical, creative, learning process and cultivation of the students' imagination is later problematized in a final turn to theory, where the pedagogy applied is interrogated and questioned (Hermann, 2000). The students' ability to take the last theoretical turn is tested in the take-home exam, designed as a reflective essay, where students are able to apply the concepts related to the entrepreneurial self to critically reflect on the foundations and effects of their social missions.

This chapter illustrates the design of the course in detail, with the hope of inspiring others to take two critical turns, one in relation to entrepreneurship as enterprising, and the next in relation to alternative entrepreneurship*s*, i.e. social entrepreneurship, ecopreneurship, cultural entrepreneurship, sustainable entrepreneurship, etc. To end, we outline how entrepreneurship educators can take these two critical turns. The first step is to problematize how critical approaches to entrepreneurship as enterprising affects students. The second step is to question the teacher's role as facilitator of less enterprising forms of entrepreneurship and the interpellation of a plurality of entrepreneurial selves.

Towards critical perspectives on alternative entrepreneurship

In this section we start by outlining the emergence of critical perspectives within entrepreneurship studies before we introduce the specific pedagogical approach applied on the EES course. We show how the first critical turn has pointed to possibilities of redirecting entrepreneurship in various ways, while a second critical turn has taken a more sceptical approach to the plurality of entrepreneurial subjectivities produced by this redirection.

The first critical turn – against enterprising

Entrepreneurship has historically been constituted as an engine in the production of surplus value in capitalist societies (Schumpeter, 1934). Research on entrepreneurship has also been keen to provide knowledge about processes that lead to either new, or the growth of, companies and organizations to secure the production of surplus value. Typically, researchers have focused on explaining or understanding how entrepreneurship functions are delimited in one way or another, and can be improved in order to be better executed. The belief is that entrepreneurship, in this enterprising form and preferably with as little bureaucratic involvement as possible, is necessary for our economic well-being.

Entrepreneurship as enterprising has, however, been debated and contested, and new directions have been suggested. Ogbor (2000) argues that entrepreneurship research relies on a Western ideology, which renews the primacy of the market for building the good society (see further Harvey, 2005). And with this Western idea of entrepreneurship follows gender bias (Ahl & Marlow, 2012; Wee & Brooks, 2012), ethnocentric determination (Al-Dajani & Marlow, 2010) and a classed society (Gill, 2014). In their theoretical critique of the enterprising culture, Spicer and Jones (2005, p. 229) show the complexity of subjectification processes, and especially so for the "phantasmic character of the entrepreneur" (Jones & Spicer, 2005, p. 229). A character that seems odd when applied to

Berglund and Johansson's (2007b) illustration of how entrepreneurship has been introduced to marginalized groups such as immigrant women, cultural workers and people with disabilities.

Moreover, entrepreneurship has been discussed as contextually conditioned (Welter, 2011). It cannot be directly translated from one setting to another, but requires an understanding of the particular social relations and contexts in which it is performed, for example in the developing world (Naudé, 2010) or in depleted settings (Johnstone & Lionais, 2004). Lately, it has also been argued that entrepreneurship research in general needs to acknowledge the grand challenges of the global society (e.g. poverty, environmental degradation) since entrepreneurship is well suited to respond to these threats (Shepard, 2015). Shepard points to the possibility to go beyond the production of incremental research, to "crowd out more transformational research" instead (p. 489). Hence, more focus on social engagement (Nicholls, 2010) and environmental considerations (Pastakia, 1998) has been requested.

The abovementioned criticism of conventional entrepreneurship research has led to a rewriting of entrepreneurship (also coined by Hjorth in 2001) and several special issues. In 2004, for example, Steyaert and Katz (2004) "reclaimed the space of entrepreneurship" with focus on how it shapes societies. Another example is Jennings, Perren and Carter (2005), who called the predominant positivist and normative take on entrepreneurship into question. And in 2007 Gartner (2007) invited researchers to engage with narrative perspectives to lay the ground for entrepreneurial narrative as a "science of imagination". In addition, Rindova, Barry and Ketchen (2009) suggested a reconceptualization of entrepreneurial activity as "entrepreneuring as emancipation". Entrepreneurship has thus been researched in new settings, in new ontological and epistemological domiciles, expanding the categories of entrepreneurship. This has broadened the contexts wherein entrepreneurship is supposed to bloom and give rise to new alternatives, at the same time as this expansion is fed by new critical perspectives.

Even if the darker sides of entrepreneurship have been pointed out (Tedmanson, Verduijn, Essers & Gartner, 2012) and entrepreneurship has been problematized beyond its possibilities for redirection (Verduijn, Dey, Tedmanson & Essers, 2014), it nevertheless remains difficult to question entrepreneurship and its promises. Instead, entrepreneurship scholars have turned to how entrepreneurship can be redirected to provide more ethically thought-through solutions that focus both on how alternative values can be studied by researchers and created by entrepreneurs. The more or less normative research approaches taken have introduced discussions and debates with the wish to avoid the tendency to reconstruct a one-dimensional view of entrepreneurship. As a result of this first critical turn, we are now offered a plethora of directions for breeding new entrepreneurs. Likewise, at the beginning of the EES course, we provide the students with a theoretical background and empirical examples that help them to take the first critical turn, against enterprising entrepreneurship, in a move towards alternative entrepreneurship.

The second critical turn – against entrepreneurial selves

In the wake of the first critical turn, there have been pleas for social entrepreneurship, ecopreneurship, cultural entrepreneurship and community entrepreneurship, to mention a few prefix versions. These often address the errors of conventional entrepreneurship and its effects, and even speak about suppressed groups (women, the young, immigrants, ex-criminals, the poor etc.) as having been previously excluded but now possible to make into entrepreneurs. Based on entrepreneurship as a futuristic discourse (Berglund & Johansson, 2007a), full of promises, alternative entrepreneurship thus seeks to secure future progression through the repositioning of entrepreneurial selves.

The entrepreneurial self

The EES course introduces literature on the "entrepreneurial self" to scrutinize what type of qualities that are to be cultivated in the creation of these new, "better" entrepreneurs. The aim is to let the students problematize the interpellation of a pluralism of entrepreneurial selves that was mobilized by the students themselves when they went through the first critical turn. That is, a neo-liberal fostering of self-regulation has not only thrived on the will of economic subjects to be such, where entrepreneurship equals "enterprising" and a carving out of the competitive class; neo-liberalism has also thrived on entrepreneurship as "freedom to" an individualist and flexible way of life, nevertheless, for an efficient management of life itself through "freedom" (Rose, 1999). This exemplifies how entrepreneurial freedoms come at the cost of an overall attempt to manage the immense capacity of the human to freely shape itself and its social relations. It is a management of freedom, via talk about freedom, that seeks bearing in knowledge production about life itself (Rose, 1996), and thus has abiding effects on our social existence (Read, 2009). Lemke (2001, p. 202) shows how "neo-liberalism encourages human beings to give their lives a specific entrepreneurial form". In contrast to Schumpeter's (1942) worries, the entrepreneurial logic thus feeds into everyday life, as the entrepreneur has come to provide "a general guideline for individual life management" (Bröckling, 2005, p. 15), and indirect management of employees at a distance (Pongratz & Voss, 2003). This entrepreneurial way of being has gained an increased foothold via an abundance of organizations that take alternative routes to solve social and environmental problems.

Alternative entrepreneurships are not clear in their contours, and emerge in different guises and with repositioned promises. By providing the students with concepts such as "discourse", "biopolitics", "governmentality", "neo-liberalism" and "the entrepreneurial self", the course aims to give them an analytical distance. The students are by extension asked to analyse *how* the positive connotations of alternative entrepreneurship, and the promises made by its proponents, often correlate with moral investments in the outbreak of entrepreneurial selves. They are exposed to the double meaning of "subject", simultaneously subjugating yourself to and productively creating a subjectivity, to be able to focus on their collective subjectification during the practical project work with the social mission.

Social entrepreneurship

The exposure to neo-liberal economic crisis and the lack of state security are regarded by social entrepreneurship proponents as positive for the constitution of new "social" opportunities. While making a profit, creating wealth, or serving the desires of customers may be part of social entrepreneurship, these are only presented as a means to a social end and not as an end in itself (Hjorth, 2013). Even if social entrepreneurship takes different legal forms (for-/not-for-profit, NGO, public sector, hybrid organization), market-based skills and principles are applied and reinforced (Eikenberry & Kluver, 2004). Social entrepreneurship transfers the tenets of capitalist entrepreneurship to non-profit organizations, where it is seen as a way to create a more meaningful path to traditional corporatism (Dempsey & Sanders, 2010).

The often implicit baseline is that social entrepreneurs do not perceive a difference between making money and doing good. "Save the world and make money" is also the illustrative title of a Swedish book that encourages people to explore the social entrepreneurship route (Augustinsson & Brisvall, 2009), presenting social entrepreneurship as the only way to raise people out of poverty and despair and achieve social change (e.g. Bornstein & Davis, 2010; Yunus, 2007). Rather than maximizing profit, social entrepreneurs are expected to focus on creating social value and tackling evil problems, whereby their form of entrepreneurship takes on social and moral value. Social entrepreneurship is thus constructed as superior to conventional entrepreneurship, and the social entrepreneur becomes a more moral entrepreneurial hero who is vigilant in adapting to capitalistic disturbances. Social entrepreneurship thus fosters an entrepreneurial self who is inclined to believe that the only way to prosper in the world we inhabit is to subject others to socially entrepreneurial endeavours.

Through the first critical turn against entrepreneurship, "the social" has been re-established as a good arena for inventing innovative solutions when structures of the welfare state fall apart. Social entrepreneurship has thus come to include a transformation of those groups and individuals that are seen as a burden for the rest of society. There is, however, a need to paint a more nuanced picture of this turn to "the social". Interrogating social entrepreneurship with the help of the second critical turn highlights how the individual, the social and the economic are linked in new ways through which neo-liberal self-regulation is reproduced. Interrogating the repositioning of entrepreneurship to "the social" requires an analysis that recognizes the shift from direct state interventions to a neo-liberal ideal of indirect governing, here via the responsibilized social entrepreneur. Social entrepreneurship is believed to demonstrate flexibility and more local responses to social problems, which goes hand in hand with an outsourcing of risk management. Through social entrepreneurship, freedom is transformed from the "freedom of the businessman to take risks" (Easterbrook, 1949) to the social entrepreneur's freedom to address social and environmental risks (Berglund & Skoglund, 2016). Dempsey and Sanders (2010) show that social entrepreneurship celebrates a troubling account of work/life balance centred on self-sacrifice, underpaid and even unpaid labour. This privileges the commitment to social entrepreneurship endeavours by a renegotiated entrepreneurial self, at the expense of health, family and other aspects of social reproduction.

Green entrepreneurship

The concept of green entrepreneurship, or "ecopreneurship", has recently emerged to exemplify and spread ecologically entrepreneurial ways of living (Pastakia, 1998). The concept introduces various practices depending on the specific environmental problem, or lack of sustainability, that is targeted. Ecopreneurship often merges ecological and social problems, with the ambition to create self-reliance and sustainable development. However, we do not yet know what is required of those who are to accomplish ecologically entrepreneurial ways of living. Some ecopreneurship scholars propose that the ecopreneur is a change agent who acts in the name of biospheric life, thereby suggesting that the ecopreneur is best qualified to vitalize biospheric life and produce socio-ecological fit (for a summary of different positions, see Skoglund, 2017).

In this section of the EES course, ecopreneurship literature is first introduced and contextualized with the help of Schumpeter's accounts of entrepreneurship and anti-capitalistic predictions (Albrecht, 2002). The course then situates different types of ecopreneurship in relation to conventional green business ideas and market solutions to environmental problems, such as carbon offsets (Böhm & Dabhi, 2009; Böhm, Misoczky & Moog, 2012; Böhm, Murtola & Spoelstra, 2012). Extracts from a documentary by Adam Curtis are thereafter presented to provide an archival perspective on how ideas of green living have been implemented. These implementations are later compared with more contemporary forms of ecopreneurial endeavours, at the same time as the students are asked to explore how ecopreneurship still speaks about "life" with help of evolutionary accounts. The students are taught to recognize and problematize ecological systems theory and complex systems theory, with the emphasis on how these are reinforced within ecopreneurship literature. This leads up to a meta-perspective on the role ecopreneurship plays in contemporary forms of biopolitics (Reid, 2012, 2013). The students are encouraged to ask questions about the moral (and often financial) investments made in the ecopreneurial self. They are also encouraged to interrogate how ecopreneurship partakes in resilience-assembling, and to problematize political subjectivity, particularly in cases where the ecopreneur is asked to embed herself within a social-ecological system and adapt to the environment.

The theoretical framework of the EES course is mainly based on the second critical turn described above. The chosen literature is intended to make the students aware of their own willingness to criticize enterprising entrepreneurship, and thus subjectify to alternative entrepreneurship and a more moral investment in their entrepreneurial self. By providing a meta-perspective on their voluntary engagement in the outsourced social and green problems, the course finally problematizes the repositioning of entrepreneurial selves.

The course in entrepreneurship and the entrepreneurial self

The course in entrepreneurship and the entrepreneurial self (EES) was developed at Stockholm Business School, Stockholm University, in 2012. The aim of this course is for students to develop an understanding and knowledge of different forms of alternative entrepreneurships and of the entrepreneurial self (see Table 8.1 for the learning goals of the course).

EES consists of 7.5 credits and comprises one of the courses in a two-year masters programme in management studies, which is presented on the website as follows:

> The programme is firmly rooted in the belief that contemporary as well as future corporations need individual employees who understand how business is both affected by and affects society – politically, economically and culturally. It is through this approach, which focuses both on the practice and issues of organizations and on how these relate to broader societal concerns, that the programme aims to provide students with knowledge and skills to critically analyze and deal with the forces and practices that shape and change the future of management and organizations.

The EES course was taught for the first time in November 2012 and has been offered every autumn since then for the past three years. The course runs over a period of five weeks, with the focus on lectures, seminars and the course project during the first four weeks, since the last week is dedicated to the take-home exam. In the take-home exam, students use the theoretical perspectives applied

Table 8.1 Learning outcomes in the EES course

Knowledge and understanding	Judgement and approach	Skills and abilities
Analyse and discuss entrepreneurship from the notion of discourse and the entrepreneurial self.	Evaluate the production of different forms of entrepreneurship and identify alternative entrepreneurships.	To be able to creatively develop an entrepreneurial idea and enact a social entrepreneurial endeavour.
Apply theories and concepts to the different forms of entrepreneurship and analyse how entrepreneurial selves are constituted.	Reflect upon one's self as entrepreneurial by using applied theories and the different forms of entrepreneurship encountered in the course.	To be able to plan, present and perform an imaginary case and/or role play of the entrepreneurial idea/endeavour.

on the course individually to reflect analytically upon the project pursued on the course, the guest lectures and other examples of alternative entrepreneurships provided within the course.

The course consists of a combination of lectures, seminars and group work and requires a significant portion of self-directed study. All teaching and learning activities are carried out in English since the language of instruction is English. EES is divided into a "theoretical" and a more "practical" path (see Figure 8.1).

While the theoretical path is thematized and strongly supported by lectures, guest lectures and seminars, the practical path is based on the entrepreneurial skills of the students to collectively organize a social engagement within a fictive company. We will now give some insight into (i) the introduction to the course, (ii) the theoretical path, (iii) the practical path and (iv) completion of the course.

Introduction to course

Students are introduced to the course in a letter of welcome in which they are briefly informed about the course site/study guide etc. In addition, they are asked to bring a picture of entrepreneurship to the first lecture. Five hours of lectures and a workshop are allocated for the introduction of the course, the outline of which is presented in the morning. This is followed by a collective exercise, where students are divided into groups of six to eight participants, and where they present their pictures to each other, agree upon five key words and create a collage of entrepreneurship (using paper, glue, coloured pencils, crayons, stickers etc.). The students are given one hour to complete the exercise and then another hour to present their results. Usually the key words create a mix between

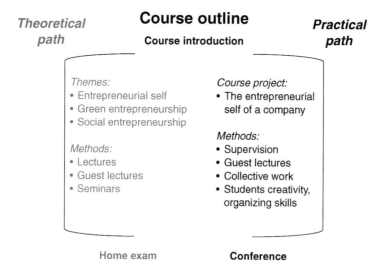

Figure 8.1 Course outline for entrepreneurship and the entrepreneurial self.

"conventional" and "alternative" entrepreneurship discourse (see Figure 8.2 from 2014's class).

In the afternoon the students' presentations are followed up with a lecture on discourse, which aims to open up for an understanding of entrepreneurship as a concept that it is possible to "define" in various ways. At the same time the students are provided with some space to reflect upon their own discourse and the assumptions they use for entrepreneurship.

At the end of the introduction day, the group project assignment is introduced and we have a Skype meeting with a manager from Prezi, the case company that sets the model for how to pursue their own group project, i.e. social mission. The students are at this point informed that they are to work in the same groups as during the morning session. Owing to the total number of students in the class, there has sometimes been a discussion about the relatively large project groups.

Theoretical path

The theoretical part of the course revolves around the three themes of: (1a/b) entrepreneurial self, (2) green entrepreneurship and (3) social entrepreneurship. While green and social entrepreneurship exemplify two contexts where alternative entrepreneurship has emerged, the entrepreneurial self is the theoretical perspective that is to be used by students to understand the emergence of alternative entrepreneurship. Green and social entrepreneurship are thus to be analysed by using concepts such as governmentality, neo-liberalism, biopolitics, the entrepreneurial self and entrepreneurial subjectivity, to engage analytically in a reflection on the effects of alternative entrepreneurship.

Figure 8.2 Student's discourse at the start of the course (example from 2014 course).

Each theme consists of a lecture (where key concepts are introduced and discussed), a guest lecture (to include different voices of social/green entrepreneurship) and a seminar to which students bring a prepared text that summarizes their reading (where students are engaged in analytical exercises). Students are strongly advised to read the literature in advance of lectures; this is particularly important in preparation for the lecture on the entrepreneurial self, where the teachers introduce the analytical concepts that will be used throughout the course. During the course the students are provided with questions to reflect upon entrepreneurship with the help of the second critical turn (see Table 8.2). The students are further encouraged to formulate their own questions to pose to the guest lecturers and at the seminars. The seminars take different forms in the three themes. Sometimes students present their writings/thoughts/questions in a study circle, at other times the student group (around 20 students in each

Table 8.2 Questions posed in relation to the three themes

Theme 1a: The entrepreneurial self: a historical perspective	How has life been optimized and vitalized? What qualities are required to "live well"? How has the expertise offered (hu)mans to become entrepreneurs/entrepreneurial? How is this connected to self-regulation and a moral identity?
Theme 1b: The entrepreneurial self: in contemporary society	What is the connection between the entrepreneur and the entreployee? What is the connection between the entrepreneurial self and the entreployee? Where and how are entreployees recruited? What is the connection between entreployee and employability? How is the principle of potentiality enacted by the entreployee?
Theme 2: Green entrepreneurship	How is the eco-entrepreneurial self being shaped? How is the individual ecopreneur coupled to the optimization of biospheric life (i.e. the reconfigured biopolitics)? How are the boundaries blurred between commercial and social forms of ecopreneurship?
Theme 3: Social entrepreneurship	How is social entrepreneurship represented? What kind of interventions can be discerned in social entrepreneurship? In what ways is social entrepreneurship described as emancipating/empowering? How is critique of capitalism incepted in knowledge processes of social entrepreneurship? How does social entrepreneurship support the circulation of freedom? Use a case of social entrepreneurship and describe how it works as a security technology.

seminar) are split up into smaller groups and given questions/tasks to complete collectively. We have experimented with these different seminar forms to spur all students to engage in the discussions and found that a mix between small groups (where students seem to talk more freely with each other) and a larger seminar group (where students can share their insights with each other) contribute to students' critical reflections.

The course then introduces the second critical turn, with the help of which the students can now start to reflect on the enforced creativity, freedom and "doing good" promised by alternative entrepreneurship. For example, the students often react to the im/possibilities of reaching a state of satisfaction, and how that leads to new forms of self-management (life balance, mindfulness etc.). Some are concerned with the difficulties of reaching a state of satisfaction when "the entrepreneurial" is a moving target where individuals can always become "more" in some way (cf. Costea *et al.*, 2012). The students thus become aware of how this may produce a work ethic of continued improvement, with the flip side of being subjected to a continuous struggle where we are encouraged to become incessantly better and where it may be difficult to reach satisfaction with who we presently are. Another example of "dark sides" discussed on the course is how the moral investment in social entrepreneurship goes hand in hand with a sacrificing subject (Dempsey & Sanders, 2010). This kind of entrepreneurial self puts the care of others ahead of the care of the self. The students also debate how they take on increased responsibilities, and take it upon themselves to solve former governmental problems. Some like to bear the outsourcing of risks, while others call for state security. This debate typically leads to further discussions about the effects of alternative entrepreneurship, and how it triggers new problems of inequality, injustice and social exclusion.

Practical path

The "shaping the entrepreneurial self of a company" project is a group assignment in which a social entrepreneurial endeavour is to be developed (see Table 8.3). The students are instructed to collectively create a social mission for a fictive company. To get their creative process started, in the introductory lecture a manager from Prezi presents how they work with their social missions. The students then shape a philanthropic project to be performed as if it had been realistically carried out. The students are expected to focus on how they can be both creative and authentic, since at the end of the course they are to present their social accomplishment using photographs, film clips, and interviews with the people they have helped. The students can also choose to do a role play, and theatrically tell the story of how they form an entrepreneurial self of the fictive company.

The purpose of the project is to gain insight into how entrepreneurship is a continuous practice that is underpinned by some sort of subjectification by the group members. The project also works as practical experience and a backdrop to the take-home exam and the more abstract discussions of entrepreneurial

Table 8.3 Case description to "shaping the entrepreneurial self of a company"

Prezi, a start-up located in the US and Hungary, has each year substituted their company Christmas party for a collective philanthropic project with the aim to "get together" and show that change is possible. In theoretical terms, they have together shaped a social entrepreneurial self of the company. In the perimeter of the Hungarian capital, Budapest, they have renovated an apartment of a poor family with a cancer sick father, as well as helped a Roma collective with their community school. As the company has expanded, with more employees and more diverse operations, these social entrepreneurial projects have also required more planning and management. The wish of the CEO has been contextualized, not only in relation to the company preferences, but in relation to the basic conditions of a family, and of a Roma population, in Hungary with its specific politics.

Your mission is to create one case of social entrepreneurship, inspired by Prezi. With descriptions of who you are, shortly what your company is doing and what type of collective philanthropic project you want to pursue. You are also to describe and present the plans for your project, from background information to how you decided, in detail, to perform it. Since this will be an imagined project, it is also to be performed as if it had been realistically carried out. Thus, in the end, you are to present the project to your friends in a form which makes it as authentic as possible. For example as a presentation with photographs, film clips, interviews with the people you pretend to have helped, or alike. Thus, this highly creative process could be organized as a "role play".

To facilitate your work, we point out some traditional and some important aspects that you might want to address. However, these aspects should not be considered as mandatory. Use what you find fruitful and add other aspects that you find suitable for shaping the specific entrepreneurial self of your company.

The course does however not support any illegal activities or missions that could lead to arrest.

- Core business idea, branch, number of employees
- Company history and vision
- Different roles, backgrounds, personalities in the company
- Area of operations, countries, cities
- Collective imagination of what a social entrepreneurial project is
- Planning of the project
- Background information of the context around your project
- Political questions of the relation between a company, society, state
- Management of the project (who is doing what, when and how)
- Costs involved in the project
- Internal conflicts between employees
- External conflicts
- Outcome of the project
- Successful and unsuccessful aspects

You will be evaluated on:
1 overall ambition of the entrepreneurial idea,
2 creativity in formulating, planning and presenting the idea,
3 authentic presentation ("real-life situation"),
4 collective timesheet (who did what, when and where and the time it took),
5 individual reflection of participating in the project (1 page)

selves. Overall, the project and the activities that the students need to pursue in order to accomplish a social or green mission can teach them what forming an "alternative" entrepreneurial self actually entails. This pedagogical approach also facilitates a discussion about power relations and effects of their social mission, mainly before and after their creative process.

Completion of course

At the end of the course the students are given a take-home exam in which they reflect on how they have been activated through alternative entrepreneurship, and how this relieves the state from direct intervention. They have one week to work with this assignment, guided by three questions in their writing of five to six pages. The students are encouraged to get into a circle of writing–reading–thinking–rewriting and also to base their analysis on the parts of the seminar discussions that they find to be of relevance.

In their reflective essays we can witness an analytical engagement with neoliberal management techniques and alternative entrepreneurships. Generally, the students know how to account for different contexts of entrepreneurship and they can distinguish between moral and financial investments in the entrepreneurial self. They can explain why a critique of entrepreneurship as enterprising has triggered the unfolding of alternatives. The students are also well aware of the problems that alternative entrepreneurship attempts to address (e.g. gender bias, exclusion, unemployment, social needs and environmental urgencies) and the promises that fail. They use key concepts from the course to analytically discuss the emergence of a plurality of entrepreneurial selves, visible in the examples provided on the course and in the meta-perspective on their group project.

Discussion

Entrepreneurship education often points to the benefits of "practical learning" to enhance innovation, commercialization and solutions to real problems. When entrepreneurship education was first introduced, it was also its value for the economy that was stressed (Berglund & Holmgren, 2013; Leffler, 2009). Both students and teachers were inserted in a market rationality as facilitators (Peters, 2001), whereby the activity and productivity of individuals became expressly linked to global competitiveness (Dahlstedt & Hertzberg, 2012). However, when entrepreneurship education gained terrain as a pedagogical approach that included other than economic missions, conventional capitalistic logics were deemphasized. This also meant that the cultivation of an active, responsible individual full of initiative was temporarily dethroned but quickly repositioned to new contexts. This revitalized the entrepreneurial self, who now hosts broader qualities than those ascribed to the conventional entrepreneurial self. The entrepreneurial self is a subject who wishes to change their own or even others' worlds, fundamentally convinced about the freedom to bring about social change by taking on risks outsourced by the state.

While other studies have criticized how the conventional entrepreneurial self has been fostered via entrepreneurship education in neo-liberal societies (Ball & Olmedo, 2013; Bendix Petersen & O'Flynn, 2007; Bragg, 2007; Connell, 2013; Down, 2009; Komulainen, Korhonen & Räty, 2009), the EES course described in this chapter goes beyond such criticism by tracing the effects of that criticism. That is, the EES course applies a pedagogical approach that is based on a second critical turn in entrepreneurship studies. This means that analytic interest is paid not only to the emphasis on the economic sphere in neo-liberal societies, but also to how alternative entrepreneurship emerges as a way to govern us whereby an abundance of entrepreneurial selves unfolds. Thus entrepreneurial freedom does not escape neo-liberal governing techniques but is, rather, re-inserted at their centre. Students of alternative entrepreneurship are still governed *through* entre-preneurial freedom, but to accomplish an expansion of responsibility and self-reliance. This productive power invites us yet again to subjectify as active and responsible, but as initiators of forms of entrepreneurship that are said to do good, often in opposition to the market and its ethical defects. Consequently, the first critical turn against conventional entrepreneurship has produced alternative subject positions that flourish on criticism of the greedy, socially and environ-mentally irresponsible, to-be-retired conventional entrepreneurial self. This previous hero is to be dethroned by a supposedly better version of the entrepre-neurial self, an upgraded hero of the enabling state.

Through a mix of lectures, guest lectures, seminars and a student-driven project, the course provides the students with both analytical distance and prac-tical closeness to how neo-liberal management techniques work through altern-ative entrepreneurship. The course thereby opens up for an exploration of how advanced liberal management thrives on criticism, sometimes posed by civic society but taken over by social or green entrepreneurs. Hence, it is the trans-formation from (one) entrepreneurship to alternative forms of entrepreneurships and the effect this has on the entrepreneurial self that constitutes the terrain of investigation for the students. That is why the EES course introduces the history of liberal thought to the students, and asks them to reflect upon their own posi-tion within its more contemporary manifestations of productive power and "freedom to" (e.g. see Foucault, 1978/91).

Turning to our own pedagogical development as educators, this experimental course taught us several things. The first lesson we learned came when the stu-dents performed the practical social engagement project. While we wanted the students to critically reflect upon what kind of entrepreneurial selves they became, the students were (at least initially) much more focused on solving a specific problem in the most innovative way. Thus, at this stage of the course, the students were more prone to assimilate only the first critical turn. It appeared to be difficult for them to be both engaged in the project and to be able to inter-rogate and reflect upon its assumed goodness. The students were unable to ques-tion their social or green engagement and the "grand solution" to the problem they sought to solve. The tendency to defend their entrepreneurial endeavours, rather than to reflect upon them, was also a recurrent discussion during the final (examination and) conference where other students in class (often addressed as stakeholders) pointed to the potential dark sides of the presented project. The dark sides have thus often remained a blind spot for students when they have engaged in making up their (fictive) company, developed the entrepreneurial idea and enacted their social project. The tendency to become passionately engaged in developing an alternative is also discerned in social entrepreneurship (Berglund & Schwartz, 2013) and among those engaged in developing an entrepreneurial education in compulsory schooling (Holmgren, 2015).

The second lesson we learned is linked to the evaluation of the practical project. Many students found that the practical project was much harder work than they expected. What they found most difficult was organizing a group of six to eight students, raising awareness of social problems, feeling empathy and facing the vulnerability of the other in need (see Chapter 11). They considered a two-grade scale of pass or fail to be unrewarding, for which reason the initial scale was amended to pass, pass with merit or fail. However, when this new scale was launched in the second version of the course, the standard of the final presentations deteriorated drastically. This left us with unanswered questions on how to grade the practical project and how to "reward" the students for actually trying to process their selves through the social or green mission they pursued. There is a need to continue experimenting with the pedagogical design of the group project and its grading as well as its aim to make the students aware and reflective of their possible subjectification to "doing good".

Lastly, during the years we have also learned which phases the students normally go through and at what point during the course. This has given us the ability to be more prepared to meet their needs. While we were much more nervous when the course was launched about how it would be received by the students, we now know that during the first week they look bewildered and have difficulty following the take on entrepreneurship provided on the course. During the third week they start to formulate questions inspired by the second critical turn, and during the fifth week they make impressive use of the concepts provided to develop an analytical stance towards entrepreneurship in their individual home exam. At the end of the course the students often comment on how their scepticism during the first week has transformed into satisfaction. They express surprise at the unexpected perspective of entrepreneurial selves, especially useful for their reflection on entrepreneurship studies as entailing more than practical "do it yourself" lessons. In the end, they have finally and conclusively been rewarded – with a more diverse understanding of entrepreneurship, especially in comparison to the usual fix given to economic subjects within business schools.

Conclusion

Entrepreneurship education has predominantly called on economic subjects to foster competitive, self-regulating and responsible citizens, i.e. conventional entrepreneurial selves. What we have shown is that criticism of such indoctrination, coming from various academic and public camps, has been appropriated with the effect that the identity of the entrepreneur is undergoing radical change. Historically speaking, entrepreneurship has always come hand in hand with a flexible invention of entrepreneurial subjectivities, and as many others before us have stated: neo-liberalism is a moving target. This requires a new educational agenda that problematizes "alternative entrepreneurship" and its effects. If universities are to introduce new forms of entrepreneurship, such as social, green or sustainable, we should, as teaching-oriented researchers, together with the students, at least try to interrogate the emergence of rejuvenated and upgraded entrepreneurial selves that secure the spread of these alternative forms so often taken for granted.

References

Ahl, H. & Marlow, S. (2012). Exploring the dynamics of gender, feminism and entrepreneurship: Advancing debate to escape a dead end? *Organization, 19*(5), 543–562.

Albrecht, J. (2002). Environmental issue entrepreneurship: A Schumpeterian perspective. *Futures, 34*(7), 649–661.

Al-Dajani, H. & Marlow, S. (2010). Impact of women's home-based enterprise on family dynamics: Evidence from Jordan. *International Small Business Journal, 28*(5), 470–486.

Augustinsson, E. & Brisvall, M. (2009). *Tjäna pengar och rädda världen: den hållbara ekonomins entreprenörer*. Stockholm: Bookhouse.

Ball, S.J. & Olmedo, A. (2013). Care of the self, resistance and subjectivity under neoliberal governmentalities. *Critical Studies in Education, 54*(1), 85–96.

Bendix Petersen, E. & O'Flynn, G. (2007). Neoliberal technologies of subject formation: A case study of the Duke of Edinburgh's Award scheme. *Critical Studies in Education, 48*(2), 197–211.

Berglund, K. (2013). Fighting against all odds: Entrepreneurship education as employability training. *Ephemera: Theory & Politics in Organization, 13*(4): 717–735.

Berglund, K. & Holmgren, C. (2013). Entrepreneurship education in policy and practice – On tensions and conflicts in processes of implementing entrepreneurship education. *International Journal of Entrepreneurial Venturing, 5*(1), 9–27.

Berglund, K. & Johansson, A.W. (2007a). The entrepreneurship discourse – Outlined from diverse constructions of entrepreneurship on the academic scene. *Journal of Enterprising Communities: People and Places in the Global Economy, 1*(1), 77–102.

Berglund, K. & Johansson, A.W. (2007b). Entrepreneurship, discourses and conscientization in processes of regional development. *Entrepreneurship and Regional Development, 19*(6), 499–525.

Berglund, K. & Schwartz, B. (2013). Holding on to the anomaly of social entrepreneurship dilemmas in starting up and running a fair-trade enterprise. *Journal of Social Entrepreneurship, 4*(3), 237–255.

Berglund, K. & Skoglund, A. (2016). Social entrepreneurship: To defend society from itself. In A. Fayolle & P. Riot (Eds), *Rethinking entrepreneurship: Debating research orientations* (pp. 57–77). New York, NY: Routledge.

Bornstein, D. & Davis, S. (2010). *Social entrepreneurship: What everyone needs to know*. Oxford: Oxford University Press.

Bragg, S. (2007). "Student voice" and governmentality: The production of enterprising subjects. *Discourse: Studies in the Cultural Politics of Education, 28*(3), 343–358.

Bröckling, U. (2005). Gendering the enterprising self: Subjectification programs and gender differences in guides to success. *Distinktion*, 11, 7–23.

Bröckling, U. (2016). *The entrepreneurial self – Fabricating a new type of subject*. London: SAGE.

Böhm, S. & Dabhi, S. (2009). *Uppsetting the offset, the political economy of carbon markets*. London: MayFlyBooks.

Böhm, S., Misoczky, C.M. & Moog, S. (2012). Greening capitalism? A Marxist critique of carbon markets. *Organization Studies*, *33*(11), 1617–1638.

Böhm, S., Murtola, A.M. & Spoelstra, S. (2012). The atmosphere business. *Ephemera: Theory & Politics in Organization*, *12*(1–2), 1–11.

Connell, R. (2013). The neoliberal cascade and education: An essay on the market agenda and its consequences. *Critical Studies in Education*, 54(2), 99–112.

Costea, B., Amiridis, K. & Crump, N. (2012). Graduate employability and the principle of potentiality: An aspect of the ethics of HRM. *Journal of Business Ethics*, *111*, 25–36.

Dahlstedt, M. & Hertzberg, F. (2012). Schooling entrepreneurs: Entrepreneurship, governmentality and education policy in Sweden at the turn of the millennium. *Journal of Pedagogy*, *3*(2), 242–262.

Dempsey, S.E. & Sanders, M.L. (2010). Meaningful work? Nonprofit marketization and work/life imbalance in popular autobiographies of social entrepreneurship. *Organization*, 17, 437.

Dey, P. (2014). Governing the social through "social entrepreneurship": A Foucauldian view of the "art of governing" in advanced liberalism. In H. Douglas & S. Grant (Eds) *Social entrepreneurship and enterprise: Concepts in context* (pp. 55–72). Ashwood: Tilde.

Dillon, M. & Reid, J. (2001). Global liberal governance: Biopolitics, security and war. *Millennium – Journal of International Studies*, *30*(1), 41–66.

Down, B. (2009). Schooling, productivity and the enterprising self: Beyond market values. *Critical Studies in Education*, *50*(1), 51–64.

Easterbrook, W.T. (1949). Possibilities for a realistic theory of entrepreneurship – the climate of enterprise. *The American Economic Review*, *39*(3), 322–335.

Eikenberry, A.M. & Kluver, J.D. (2004). The marketization of the nonprofit sector: civil society at risk? *Public Administration Review*, *62*(2), 132–140.

Foucault, M. (1997/2004). *Society must be defended*. London: Penguin.

Foucault, M. (1978/1991). Governmentality. In G. Burchell, C. Gordon & P. Miller (Eds), *The Foucault effect – studies in governmentality with two lectures and interviews with Michel Foucault* (pp. 87–104). Chicago, IL: University of Chicago Press.

Foucault, M. (1979/97). The birth of biopolitics. In P. Rabinow (Ed.), *Michel Foucault, ethics: subjectivity and truth, Essential works of Michel Foucault 1954–1984* (pp. 73–79). New York, NY: New Press.

Gartner, W.B. (2007). Entrepreneurial narrative and a science of the imagination. *Journal of Business Venturing*, *22*(5), 613–627.

Gay, P.D., Salaman, G. & Rees, B. (1996). The conduct of management and the management of conduct: Contemporary managerial discourse and the constitution of the "competent" manager. *Journal of Management Studies*, *33*(3), 263–282.

Gill, R. (2014). "If you're struggling to survive day-to-day": Class optimism and contradiction in entrepreneurial discourse. *Organization*, *21*(1), 50–67.

Goss, D., Jones, R., Betta, M. & Latham, J. (2011). Power as practice: A microsociological analysis of the dynamics of emancipatory entrepreneurship. *Organization Studies*, *32*(2), 211–229.

Harvey, D. (2005). *A brief history of neoliberalism*. Oxford: Oxford University Press.

Hermann, S. (2000). Michel Foucault. In S. Gytz Olesen & P. Møller Pedersen (Eds), *Pedagogik i ett sociologiskt perspektiv* (pp. 83–114). Lund: Studentlitteratur.

Hjorth, D. (2001). *Rewriting entrepreneurship: Enterprise discourse and entrepreneurship in the case of re-organising ES*. Thesis, Växjö University.

Hjorth, D. (2013). Public entrepreneurship: Desiring social change, creating sociality. *Entrepreneurship & Regional Development, 25*(1–2), 34–51.

Holmgren, C. (2015). *The governing of teachers in the name of entrepreneurship: the problem-creating and the solution creating subjectivities*. Presented at the CMS, 2015.

Jennings, P.L., Perren, L. & Carter, S. (2005). Guest editors' introduction: Alternative perspectives on entrepreneurship research, *Entrepreneurship Theory and Practice, 29*(2), 145–152.

Johnstone, H. & Lionais, D. (2004). Depleted communities and community business entrepreneurship: Revaluing space through place. *Entrepreneurship & Regional Development, 16*(3), 217–233.

Jones, C. & Spicer, A. (2009). *Unmasking the entrepreneur*. Cheltenham: Edward Elgar.

Jones, C. & Spicer, A. (2005). The sublime object of entrepreneurship. *Organization, 12*(2), 223–246.

Komulainen, K., Korhonen, M. & Räty, H. (2009). Risk taking abilities for everyone? Finnish entrepreneurship education and the enterprising selves imagined by pupils. *Gender and Education, 21*(6), 631–649.

Leffler, E. (2009). The many faces of entrepreneurship: A discursive battle for the school arena. *European Educational Research Journal, 8*(1), 104–116.

Lemke, T. (2001). "The birth of bio-politics": Michel Foucault's lecture at the Collège de France on neo-liberal governmentality. *Economy and Society, 30*(2), 190–207.

Naudé, W. (2010). Entrepreneurship, developing countries, and development economics: New approaches and insights. *Small Business Economics, 34*(1), 1–12.

Nicholls, A. (2010). The legitimacy of social entrepreneurship: Reflexive isomorphism in a pre-paradigmatic field. *Entrepreneurship Theory and Practice, 34*(4), 611–633.

Ogbor, J.O. (2000). Mythicizing and reification in entrepreneurial discourse. Ideology critique of entrepreneurial studies. *Journal of Management Studies, 37*(5), 605–635.

Pastakia, A. (1998). Grassroots ecopreneurs: Change agents for a sustainable society. *Journal of Organizational Change Management, 11*(2), 157–173.

Peters, M. (2001). Education, enterprise culture and the entrepreneurial self: A Foucauldian perspective. *Journal of Educational Enquiry, 2*(2), 58–71.

Peredo, A.M. & Chrisman, J.J. (2006). Toward a theory of community based enterprise. *Academy of Management Review, 31*(2), 309–328.

Pongratz, H.J. & Günter Voss, G.G. (2003). From employee to "entreployee': Towards a "self-entrepreneurial" work force? *Concepts and Transformation, 8*(3), 239–254.

Read, J. (2009). A genealogy of homo-economicus: neoliberalism and the production of subjectivity. *Foucault Studies, 6*, 25–36.

Reid, J. (2012). The disastrous and politically debased subject of resilience. Development dialogue – the end of the security–development nexus? *The Rise of Global Disaster Management, 58*, 67–80.

Reid, J. (2013). Interrogating the neoliberal biopolitics of the sustainable development–resilience nexus. *International Political Sociology, 7*(4), 353–367.

Rindova, V., Barry, D. & Ketchen, D.J. (2009). Entrepreneuring as emancipation. *Academy of Management Review, 34*(3), 477–491.

Rose, N. (1996). Governing enterprising individuals (chapter 7). In *Inventing our selves: Psychology, Power, and Personhood* (pp. 150–170). Cambridge: Cambridge University Press.

Rose, N. (1999). *Powers of freedom – reframing political thought.* Cambridge: Cambridge University Press.

Schumpeter, J. (1934). *The theory of economic development: An inquiry into profits, capital, credit, interest, and the business cycle* (Redvers Opie, Trans.). Cambridge, MA: Harvard University Press.

Schumpeter J.A. (1942). *Capitalism, socialism, and democracy.* New York, NY: Harper.

Shepard, D. (2015). Party on! A call for entrepreneurship research that is more interactive, activity based, cognitively hot, compassionate and prosocial. *Journal of Business Venturing, 30*, 489–507.

Simons, M. & Masschelein, J. (2008). The governmentalization of learning and the assemblage of a learning apparatus. *Educational Theory, 58*(4), 391–415.

Skoglund, A. (2017). Deconstructing ecopreneruship. In C. Essers, P. Dey, D. Tedmanson & K. Verduijn (Eds), *Critical perspectives on entrepreneurship: Challenging dominant discourses.* New York, NY: Routledge.

Sliwa, M., Meier Sørensen, B. & Cairns, G. (2015). "You have to choose a novel": The biopolitics of critical management education. *Management Learning, 46*(3), 243–259.

Steyaert, C. & Katz, J. (2004), Reclaiming the space of entrepreneurship in society: Geographical, discursive and social dimensions. *Entrepreneurship & Regional Development, 16*(3), 179–196.

Stockholm Business School (2016). Retrieved from https://sisu.it.su.se/search/info/SMANO.

Tedmanson, D., Verduijn, K., Essers, C. & Gartner, W.B. (2012). Critical perspectives in entrepreneurship research. *Organization-Interdisc Journal of Organization Theory and Society, 19*(5), 531.

Verduijn, K., Dey, P., Tedmanson, D. & Essers, C. (2014). Emancipation and/or oppression? Conceptualizing dimensions of criticality in entrepreneurship studies. *International Journal of Entrepreneurial Behavior & Research, 20*(2), 98–107.

Vrasti, W. (2012). *How to use affect in late capitalism.* Retrieved from http://citation.allacademic.com/meta/p_mla_apa_research_citation/4/1/7/0/3/pages417031/p417031-1.php.

Wallenstein, S.O. (2013). Introduction: Foucault, biopolitics, and governmentality. In J. Nilsson & S.O. Wallenstein (Eds), *Foucault, biopolitics, and governmentality* (pp. 7–34). Stockholm: Södertörn University.

Wee, L. & Brooks, A. (2012). Negotiating gendered subjectivity in the enterprise culture: Metaphor and entrepreneurial discourses. *Gender, Work & Organization, 19*(6), 573–591.

Welter, F. (2011). Contextualizing entrepreneurship—Conceptual challenges and ways forward. *Entrepreneurship Theory and Practice, 35*(1), 165–184.

Yunus, M. (2007). *Banker to the Poor.* New Delhi: Penguin.

9 Between critique and affirmation

An interventionist approach to entrepreneurship education

Bernhard Resch, Patrizia Hoyer and Chris Steyaert

Introduction

The grand narratives of creativity and entrepreneurship, hailed as highly promising elements for growing the economy, have flowed, even flooded, into the lecture halls and curricula of business schools and management programmes around the globe (Steyaert & Dey, 2010). Hence, enacting critical approaches in entrepreneurship education means rowing hard against the tide. In fact, one could argue that any critique – no matter how enlightening or emancipatory – risks being perceived as either detached or hopeless in the face of such a powerful force. Still, we contend that it is naïve, if not potentially dangerous, to be overly optimistic about these twin notions, because they can distort and minimize the complexity that surrounds them.

Therefore, in the master's-level course "Entrepreneurship and Creativity" that we have developed iteratively since 2009, we try to stimulate critical understandings of and alternative perspectives on the relationship between creativity and entrepreneurship. While a critical approach to entrepreneurship education can take different forms, our particular twist on the theme is grounded in the tension between critique and affirmation (Germain & Jacquemin, 2017), what Hjorth (2017) has called a "critique nouvelle". More concretely, we argue that it is not enough to simply question the optimistic politics of entrepreneurship education. Instead we call for a critique of critique, which in our view requires affirmation (Weiskopf & Steyaert, 2009). According to Nietzsche's (1969 [1886]) parable of three metamorphoses, critique is needed to make space for creation, yet critique without affirmation can become sterile (see also Weiskopf & Steyaert, 2009). In the spirit of Michel Serres's "Troubadour of Knowledge" (1997), we believe that what makes imaginative learning possible is engaging in the unsettling practice of swimming in an ocean of "thirdness", between the antipodes of critical reflection and creative affirmation.

In this course, the oscillation between critique and affirmation eventually takes the form of an interventionist pedagogy which integrates a series of sociomaterial and affective enactments. According to Fenwick and Edwards (2010), actor network theory (ANT) in particular offers the potential "for fresh and productive interventions within educational issues" (p. 1). More concretely,

ANT-ish interventions destabilize existing associations among material and human actors by introducing new elements from the outside. Assuming that educational work unfolds through the assembling and disassembling of complex human and non-human relations, intervening in this process holds the potential for altering common perceptions and activities around learning pedagogy, curriculum and assessment. Therefore, we tactically intervene in the well-practised educational "assemblage" that typifies management education (Steyaert, Beyes & Parker, 2016) and (business) universities (Izak, Kostera & Zawadzki, 2017). Typically, our interventions aim at disentangling and reassociating time and space, bodies and motions, people and materials, and we constantly add new elements to the equation in sometimes curious ways: chairs are arranged in circles or removed altogether; students engage in improvisational theatre or visit a nightclub during the daytime; PowerPoint is banned while theoretical models become embodied in slogans, storyboards and soundscapes.

Such "reshuffling" opens up unusual learning formats which push towards critical reflection as well as experimentation with aesthetic, material, spatial and embodied ways of learning. At the same time, our interfering with the established assemblage of the business school classroom does not proceed without frustrations. In fact, it is often accompanied by (somewhat untypical) affective intensities. Students, for their part, have to step out of their usual comfort zone and class routines as they engage in a process of close collaboration. This requires them to disclose strengths and weaknesses, making it likely to trigger critical self-reflection. For us as instructors, the course requires an elusive balance between deliberate planning and flexible improvisation. Meanwhile, we also become the moderators of, and the projection screens for, all sorts of emotional intensities, both positive and negative, that students experience as they progress through their own learning journey.

In the following we will first describe the course in more detail by situating it in the context of the university and by zooming in on the opening session. As we share more details about the course process, we will describe more carefully our take on the modes of critique and affirmation and their interplay – which informs our interventionist approach to critical entrepreneurship education. By focusing on two particular course sessions that are vital in the overall learning journey, and by reviving a final presentation by one of the student groups, we try to exemplify and enliven this interventionist approach at the intersection of critique and affirmation in and beyond the classroom. We then discuss the theoretical groundwork and broader potential of an interventionist pedagogy in the context of critical entrepreneurship studies, and conclude this chapter by reflecting on the learning outcomes that this course can culminate in (or not) for both students and instructors.

Setting the scene

Any take on critique in entrepreneurship education, we argue, must begin with an assessment of its contextual conditions to determine how to proceed with a critical intervention. Over the past decade, the university where we teach the master's course "Entrepreneurship and Creativity" has – like many business schools – increasingly built up an entrepreneurial emphasis by giving it priority in teaching and extra-curricular activities. These efforts range from a week-long "founders' garage" and a "founder of the year prize" to the appointment of several professors in the field of entrepreneurship. This might be considered a fairly dramatic transformation for a business school that built its reputation on developing managerial experts in finance and consultancy but has increasingly incorporated disciplines and courses from the humanities and social sciences (Eberle & Metelmann, 2016) into its educational profile. In the university's vision (as stated on its website), it engages in training "our students to become entrepreneurs whose actions are informed by social responsibility".

Not surprisingly then, among the main attitudes that students bring to the course – usually filled to the maximum of 30 students – are enthusiasm about creativity and belief in entrepreneurship. Both concepts have become imperative signifiers of a post-industrial knowledge society, endowed with the promise of altering organizations, cities, communities and ourselves. Given this beginning, we know it will be a stretch to develop and maintain a critical edge in our course on entrepreneurship and creativity.

As students come in with a primarily positive view of entrepreneurship and creativity, our first challenge is to inquire more thoroughly into these preconceptions and to question their positive "bias". One of the core mantras of the course is that we not only talk about creativity in the context of entrepreneurship, but also practise and experience it; that is, we "do" creativity, to understand how creation is the core of the process of entrepreneuring (Steyaert, 2007). Hence, what we as instructors try to "do" from the very beginning is disturb the familiar classroom through intervening in its spatial arrangements, learning formats, comfort zones and modes of presentation.

So, in the first session of the course we already pry into some student expectations, by removing all the tables and arranging the chairs into a circle (Steyaert, Hoyer & Resch, 2016). This might seem a rather minor deviation, but it launches us all on a different "entry" into the course. Since the circle of chairs creates a big opening in the middle, students are immediately drawn to the fact that the class has no real beginning or end but actually unfolds "in the middle" (Steyaert *et al.*, 2016). Rather than validating new structures, though, we go on to re-arrange the classroom for each session according to the day's programme. In the final session – when student groups enact their projects – the room is cleared out entirely and each group is responsible for arranging the empty space according to its needs. Sometimes a group even takes us to an entirely different space on campus, illustrating that they have internalized the "permission" to stray from the script.

Another way we try to alter some stabilized preconditions in the rigid context of the university is to tweak expectations around time. Instead of 12 sessions of two hours, we make it six sessions of four hours. This provides us with the possibility to create repetition and intensity. We also encounter other limits, to which we try to give a different twist. For example, we cannot stop the buzzer from going off at the start and end of every 45-minute teaching unit, but we can agree with the students to relocate the pre-scheduled break to a point in time when it fits the actual flow of the session. Likewise, though we must adhere to examination and grading policies that underpin the legitimacy of academic degrees at the business school, we are still free to ban the use of PowerPoint in students' final group presentations, pointing out how this medium of supposedly professional communication extends its "genre-inherent characteristics even in the face of contradictory organizational requirements" (Schoeneborn, 2013, p. 1777).

Critique

Enacting critique

Once we have successfully fiddled with some of these taken-for-granted structures – thereby enacting a subtle yet material critique of the usual boundaries – we quickly schedule a first critical text. This reading – Rehn and De Cock (2009) – deconstructs creativity with its celebration of "the useful" and "the new", namely by showing that creativity does not necessarily contain original properties. Moreover, we ask "what is meant by useful?" and "useful for whom?" to get students to reflect upon the startling idea that creativity per se does not yield positive results. More generally, the critical texts that we draw upon in the course mingle elements of various critical approaches such as denaturalization, use of critical theory and reflexivity. In particular, they provide interesting directions for two activities: expanding the prevailing individualized conception of creativity, and deconstructing the dominant image of the entrepreneur as an individual heroic male, who is granted flashes of God-given genius. We contrast this with a relational perspective, which regards entrepreneurial creativity as inherently embedded in cultural systems, material objects, and discursive formations; from this perspective creativity is socio-materially attributed and cannot be found inside certain objects or persons (Glăveanu, 2010).

More fundamentally even in terms of enacting a critique that goes "against the grain", we engage with relational changes, by connecting to different worlds: the world of choreography and (dance) theatre, the world of artistic creation and public intervention, and the world of entrepreneurial networks and urban renovation. In the following we will zoom in on one particular course session where students get a first impression of how – through strange encounters – an (affirmative) critique can play out beyond the boundaries of the classroom, as they engage in a four-hour city walk in a neighbouring city.

Taking a critical walk

Course session two: the class is on a field trip. We are on a train to visit a buzzing entrepreneurial neighbourhood in a city one hour away. Some students use this travel time to mingle with their groups and discuss the final presentations, while others casually engage with the tutors and share their excitement about the trip. Upon our arrival at the train station we are welcomed by an entrepreneur who is known for his alternative bookshop – also a café, event location and publishing house – which he initiated in a neighbourhood long before it became trendy (Deckert, 2016). Today he will show us his new project, near the station, part of the site of a huge urban renewal project the size of 10 soccer fields. As we enter the area of the former freight terminal into which the main investor has poured €1 billion, we immediately sense the tension between attempts to create an entrepreneurial third space and the blunt face of commercialization.

And so it continues. Walking in the shadow of the skyscrapers, all of them planned by big-name international architects, we witness the promise of the grand narrative: vegetarian restaurants, stylish bars and individualist designer stores – an evocation of the global and gentrified city. This project is surely part of the city's effort to brand itself as a creative and entrepreneurial hub in close connection but also fierce competition with other cities to attract the global "creative class" (Florida, 2002). This political narrative of urban creativity (Steyaert & Beyes, 2009) urges city planners to engage in intensely challenging image production and marketing to attract the most promising creative talents, innovative technologies, and diverse lifestyles. Simultaneously, though, the counter-narrative lurks behind the corners of a deserted plaza of the newly built pedagogical university and other aseptic boulevards and atriums. The overall feel is of dystopia; it warns of precarious working conditions, gated communities and an economy based on surveillance.

Our guide embodies this tension. We see the excitement in his eyes as he leads us to the busy construction site for his new venture: an arthouse cinema turned bar turned cultural centre. While the construction workers are preparing their chicken thigh barbecue, he tells us about how the main investor, the public railway company, is now divided into a transport division and the profit-making real estate division. The latter has to make high annual adjustment payments to finance the public mandate of its sister. Unfortunately, this type of mega-project leads to a focus on profits and largely ignores social inclusion. This situation is also exemplified by his new neighbour, our guide tells us. Only recently Google decided to transfer one of its European headquarters from the periphery of the city to this location. In an attempt to open itself to the city, it rented the bulk of the office space in one fell swoop, jeopardizing access for smaller initiatives or investors.

Then we leave the area of the mega-project, which abruptly opens out into a vibrant neighbourhood caught in the early stages of gentrification. Shabby discount stores meet ethnic food restaurants; design meets demolition. We perceive the traces of pulsating nightlife, from galleries and student bars to venues of a more delicate sort. Our destination is a co-working space, a hub and salad bowl for socially minded freelancers, entrepreneurs and tech people. We enter through a colourfully and creatively designed café and wander through several floors of casually busy office space, including a joint kitchen, meditation room, sleepover area and digitally equipped workshop rooms.

During our guided tour we learn that this former atelier of the local art school has been recently refurbished in a collaborative effort and that the growth of this community-building organization is staggering. What we can't hear though are the silent and solitary struggles of the emerging class of digital freelancers and entrepreneurs, their struggle for customers and a fair income, their long working hours and their precarious position in the social security system. How are these "entrepreneurial selves" (Bröckling, 2015) navigating their working lives between the poles of self-realization and self-exploitation?

Cohendet, Grandadam and Simon (2010) would conceptualize this hub as an example of the "middleground", an intermediate structure that links the informal underground culture to the formal organizations and institutions of the upper-ground. Informed by this article, the students are asked to compare their immediate experiences during the city walk with the example of Montréal and its creative behemoths Cirque du Soleil and the game designer Ubisoft. The authors pick up a major shortcoming of the "creative class paradigm" (Florida, 2002): it deals merely with "who" the creative actors are in a city, rather than "how" they achieve creativity. In turn they were able to identify three different layers of urban creativity. On top is the "upperground", the level of established innovative firms and institutions that market ideas. On the other end of the spectrum is the "underground" of adventurous individuals who are not well connected to the commercial scene but launch and develop these new ideas. The decisive layer, though, is the so-called "middleground": communities, which function as intermediaries, facilitating learning between the actors and generating common knowledge as well as "grammars of use" (Cohendet *et al.*, 2010, p. 92) that ultimately allow jointly exploiting and commercializing new ideas.

Later that afternoon we wander deeper into the same district, a former industrial area characterized by busy arterial roads, a freeway exit ramp, major turn-of-the-century industrial buildings, modern skyscrapers and a prominent S-Bahn viaduct, which houses bars, boutique shops and even a summer garden. Groups of students "lead the sightseeing" at distinctive landmarks that we have assigned beforehand. The highlights of the walk are marked by unexpected encounters like this one:

> We meet a local artist, who was given the task of building something out of a truckload of bulky waste – a prime example of the interplay between critique and affirmation, one could argue. The artist is frustrated with the "ghost town" around her. In her view the newly built business parks and hotels – but also the recently opened art university – gradually grind down the many charming places of autonomy and self-organization. Consequently, her artwork resembles a city map, but at the same time a landscape of cracked and broken earth.

The tour ends in one of the city's most popular (electronic) night clubs, which is famous for its artfully crafted decorations that carry its trembling crowd of visitors off into surreal worlds. Over a beer with one of the founders we have

Figure 9.1 The contours of an entrepreneurial cluster or cracks in a community's soil?
Source: Artwork by Muriel Baumgartner

time to learn more about the entrepreneuring of night life and to reflect on the unfolding nexus of atmospheres and encounters that made our day.

Returning to the two struggling narratives of urban creativity and entrepreneurship (Steyaert & Beyes, 2009), we propose a third narrative or rather a heterotopic set of little narratives that takes into account the many sites that set city politics in motion. This is a performative perspective that acknowledges resistant artistic performances, and neighbourhood initiatives that pay attention to homeless people and others who may fall through the grids of the creative city. Whether it is critical theory or personally motivated indignation that informs such initiatives, what we emphasize is their potential to reveal alternative realities, to make them felt by exploring the weak points and fissures of the urban neighbourhood, eventually nudging it into and affirming a different constellation.

Affirmation: making space for affirmative practice

After this encounter with critique, or actually in parallel, we invite students to also engage in affirmative practices. For, as Weiskopf and Steyaert (2009) note, it is not enough to merely become "lionesque" – Nietzsche's (1969) aphorism of emancipation – through questioning or refusing one's own received views of creativity and entrepreneurship. Even if critique makes space for creative, different and entrepreneurial activities, more childlike transformations will be needed in the form of play, improvisation and experimentation. In fact, the affirmative mode presupposes a radical "ground clearing" (Hardt, 2002). It is less concerned with judgement, condemnation and silencing and more with "bringing an oeuvre, a book, a sentence, an idea to life" (Foucault, 1997, p. 323). It is grounded in a spirit of creation and invention. Learning, in other words, becomes a matter of metamorphosis, and thus a commitment to "going all the way" in a *Full Monty*-like fashion (Steyaert, 2014): starting with an imaginative idea, forming a team, overcoming doubts, improvising, practising and, finally, taking the risk to perform and thereby be transformed.

In practical terms, through a range of group exercises students get to experiment and play around with different socio-material resources for enacting an affirmative critique of creativity and entrepreneurship. Going back to the very first session, we undertake a playful exercise based on four questions that elicit dominant conceptions around creativity and entrepreneurship, at the same time stirring up the affective flows in the classroom. We ask the students to quickly name three words they associate with creativity, and then ask three surprising questions: about their favourite failure, their earliest memory of doing something creative, and creative skills they have never applied in the classroom. As a result, each year we as a group are seized by flows of tension, excitement, timidity and relief, but each time these resonances evolve differently. In some cohorts, single acts of whistling, acrobatics or intimate story-telling immediately flush away a collective layer of self-protection; in others, suspicions about the unusual pedagogy actually harden.

Either way, engaging in affirmative activity is not just "optional" in this course, so some students will have to stretch as we gradually introduce different practices of "playing". These variations of play are meant to prepare students for their final enactment of an entrepreneurial case in a creative group performance. Already in the first session we announce that PowerPoint is not a viable medium in this course. Instead we ask students to perform their final group presentations in a more imaginative format (Bohannon, 2011). This usually triggers an interesting cycle of headache, thrill, frustration and adrenalin, so we choose to support students in the unsettling process of "getting there" by continuously adding small exercises borrowed from movie makers, improvisational theatre and team-building seminars. These exercises often create relational and affective intensities.

In small groups, students are prompted to crystallize their understandings of creativity by drawing a triptych, sketching a story-board, preparing a five-minute performance in "musical" style, or writing a poem. While students prepare for their creative presentations, we occasionally interrupt the process again, asking them to integrate seemingly random objects into their narrative, or incorporating the perspective of a clown or a blind man into their performance. Moreover, with the help of brainstorming exercises, case studies, movie fragments and site visits, we investigate various practices of creative collaboration, ranging from industry giants like Pixar (Catmull, 2014) to the rather undocumented entrepreneuring of nightlife.

This series of smaller and larger interventions into the ordinary assemblage of a course process provides the students with a rich and intimately personal wealth of experience in collaborative-creative group dynamics to be taken up in their course papers. In addition to these fun and equally nerve-racking exercises, we dedicate various other resources into the build-up to the final presentations, such as inviting established local artists into the classroom to provide feedback on some work-in-progress elements of the student presentations. Interestingly, the latter intervention often leads to paradoxical outcomes. In most cases, the atmosphere in the room heats up when student groups present a preliminary scene or sneak preview of their planned presentations to us or an external "jury" – almost as if they were auditioning for one of the notorious TV talent shows where entrants get either a thumbs up or a thumbs down.

Here's the routine. The student group enters an emptied classroom. They have a few minutes to perform. Then they receive feedback. Usually there is scant time for discussion. Some students have performed amazing scenes that promised to convey a subtle yet clear message (and we applauded them). Paradoxically, to our dismay, during the actual presentation of the final project these promising beginnings fell flat as they turned into unreflective celebrations of the creativity paradigm. In other cases we felt we offered our critique in the right tone, but for whatever reason the group never implemented it. In yet another scenario, some student groups have grown angry and hostile as we criticized their overly naturalistic roleplays, their static use of space or their lack of multiple perspectives and narrative layers. These students left the encounter irritated, disheartened and somewhat demoralized, while we felt guilty at having broken the chain of resonances. Astonishingly then, out of the latter experience – probably the most frustrating one – students have developed some of the most memorable final presentations. In this respect, Bjerg and Staunæs's (2011) study of "appreciative management" in a school reminds us that self-determined and inspired learning emerges not only from positive affect, but also from experiences like going through an emotional rollercoaster between excitement at performing and shame at not having performed up to one's own expectations.

The lesson we take from this is that affirmation is not to be mistaken for blind approval or a struggle-free journey towards novel creations. Instead, affirmation can well be driven by the power of negative affectivity, unpleasant intensities and a harsh learning process. Just like critique, affirmation can confront and can be very disturbing. To illustrate this, we deliberately arrange for a number of unsettling encounters with the strange worlds of not only urban renewal, but also art performance and modern dance. For the latter, we leave the assigned classroom again and go work in a dance performance space. During a workshop with a dance choreographer – including the practices and affects that this brings with it – we hope to provide yet another alternative in the ongoing assemblage of the learning process.

Inviting students to dance

This session, where we invite students to move and dance, has become a kind of blockbuster over the years. It is hosted by an independent dance choreographer, who is a former dancer at the local dance theatre company, and an artist-entrepreneur par excellence. Every year we observe students going out of their way to tap along with this considerable intervention in the assembling process. Students often mirror their experiences in their final group presentations.

The first unique element of this intervention is that we change locations and move to the local multi-art centre, an old yet refurbished train depot in an up-and-coming area of the city. It is only a 10-minute walk downhill from the university, but this change of location transforms the atmosphere considerably. While the industrial prehistory of the place is unmistakable, the art centre was completely renovated in 2009/10; today it hosts a bar and restaurant, a cinema and an art exhibition centre, as well as several dance and theatre performance spaces. For this session we book one of the two performance halls; this offers plenty of room for students to move around freely, unseen by outside spectators. In terms of materiality, the dress code for the session is also different as we encourage students to show up in sports clothes; this invites them to loosen up from their general habitus (of dressing) and disciplined postures.

Instead of tables, chairs and projection screens, students encounter only the empty space, with water bottles and some apples for the break. Instead of lectures and discussions, there is mostly just music or silence. Instead of pulling out, and hiding behind, their laptops, students have very different instruments for this session: their own bodies, their own sweat, their own intuition. Most importantly, working with an artist and dance choreographer rather than university lecturers (who are now participating in the exercises along with them) changes their self-awareness and their conception of what they can learn today.

During the first session of the course we have alerted students to a lethal danger: the danger of sitting on one's butt. As Nilofer Merchant (2013) claims, "sitting is the new smoking" in the sense that a lack of movement may be considered the greatest cause of illness today, especially for people who spend their entire (working) day in front of a computer. This warning aligns well with a more general critique of how the body has become disciplined and docile in Western civilization (Foucault, 1977). As Ken Robinson (2006) explains in one of the most circulated TEDTalk videos – our invitation message to students prior to the start of the course – we educate our children "progressively from the waist up. And then we focus on their heads. And slightly to one side" (2006: 9'10"). The hierarchy of subjects in all educational systems worldwide, he notes, is mathematics, natural sciences and languages on the top, then the humanities, and at the bottom we find the arts. Robinson even identifies a further hierarchy within the arts: art and music occupy a higher status than drama and dance. This is a pity, we think, as dancing has an untapped capacity to stimulate, among other things, (creative) thinking.

Therefore, the maxim of the session is: move! We do not accept excuses such as "but I cannot dance"; we follow Twyla Tharp (2003), the award-winning dance choreographer and author of several books, on her dictum that *everyone* can be creative. Vlad Glăveanu (2010, p. 81) refers to this understanding as the "democratization" of creativity (see also Bilton, 2007; Hulbeck, 1945; Weiner, 2000), presenting a critique to the long-held and elitist assumption that creativity is the "métier" of only a few gifted talents. Instead, according to the so-called "I-paradigm" of creativity (Glăveanu 2010, p. 81), everyone can be creative. And thus, taking it step by step (Coutu, 2008), students are gently "seduced" to practically rediscover their bodily talents and some ingredients of play that they had forgotten about and almost unlearned in the context of the business school.

After some warm-up moves and breathing exercises, students delve into their first affirmative lesson: "touch". Ironically, even though the sensory experience of touch is one of the earliest and most instinctive ones, in the world of work and higher education the notion of touching has become one of those taboos that embarrass us to the core. So, to avoid breaking with conventions too drastically, we have students first experiment with touching the floor beneath their feet. Despite the fact that walking is one of our most habitual activities, people rarely consider it a sensual experience. This (un)consciousness changes, however, as students are asked to concentrate on the way their feet touch the floor. Next they are instructed to either "receive" or "conquer" the floor with their feet. As we observe the students' changing postures, we can tell that they now walk around with much more awareness of self and other.

The next challenge then is to get into tactile exchange with others. At the university, exchanges of touch are normally reduced to a narrow repertoire – the occasional shaking of hands or a contextually justified pat on the shoulder. But this is drastically expanded in today's dance and improvisation workshop. In a first step, the class is divided into pairs, and one of each is instructed to give the other person a massage, from the neck to the lower back and up again; then they give them a gentle to medium strong tapping from the neck to the feet, ending on the butt. We are still in the first hour of this dance improvisation session, but students have already come a long way.

The next affirmative lesson focuses on embodied trust. "Close your eyes and let yourself be guided through the room by the other person – but without the use of words, only a gentle yet firm grip on the arm and/or the back. Ok, start walking" … "And now faster" … "And now run". Even though the space is big enough to spread out, when 14 dyads, a total of 28 people, start running around at the same time, the sound of the stampede itself may become intimidating to the blindfolded person. Or it may in fact not intimidate, depending on the trusting bond that is just in the making. What the trust building leads up to in the end is the formation of small groups of four to five people who are asked to develop a short dance choreography.

Curiously, while this should pose the biggest challenge of the course up to this point, mostly students deal with it well, even when the instructions are given that the choreography has to be developed without any talking among the group members. And then we observe something beautiful: Instead of falling into their usual work habitus of discussing things to the point of exhaustion, we see students trying something out, improvising, demonstrating something, watching others do their tricks, imitating, trying again, discarding, repeating, tweaking and twisting a bit here and there and then: rehearse, rehearse, rehearse. When it is time to perform their choreography in front of the class, students can hardly believe what they do: they move and dance together.

Performing

Even though we do not explicitly ask students to incorporate dance elements into their final group presentations, many of them – still influenced by the workshop – do so anyway. To give a little impression of what this can look like, below we describe a final group presentation entitled "freedom of speech" performed by a group of five students in 2015. In this presentation the audience is invited to revisit and to a certain extent re-experience the tragic events at *Charlie Hebdo*, the French satirical magazine, which in January 2015 fell victim to a terrorist attack that killed a large number of its editorial team. This time, however, the "story" is presented in a different way: through music, silence and percussion. In the entire presentation, the only person speaking in a series of short video clips, is a student acting as a French reporter who gives some context around the events in Paris. The story, which is centred on the theme of freedom, starts with a group of four *Charlie Hebdo* caricaturists performing a self-composed rap, each courageously taking the lead in one of the four verses.

Then, frighteningly, after this enchanting ode to freedom, the audience witnesses the "breaking of pens" – the shooting of all protagonists. They learn from the breaking news that this was an assault on the freedom of speech, notwithstanding – or maybe especially due to – the magazine's controversial reputation

Figure 9.2 Presentation on the relationship between creativity and freedom in the *Charlie Hebdo* tragedy.

for touching upon issues that are (supposedly) too sensitive for satire. Much of the happenings we have already seen before, but what happens then?

In the presentation, the caricaturists are resurrected, but this time they are muted with tape across their lips. A non-verbal, yet physically intense, fight breaks out over which direction to take from here. From the reporter we learn that this fight is symbolic of the chaos that has broken out in the streets of Paris, fusing feelings of solidarity and fear, and marking a loss of rhythm. A period of silence is needed, for both the performers and the audience, to be ready for the next phase. Then music is played, but this time without singing. The focus is clearly on the beat, which is taken up by one person at a time but then slowly becomes contagious. With the help of percussion a new collective rhythm is found again, one that seems to be even stronger than anything we have heard so far. The *Charlie Hebdo* editors remain muted, but now their jingle of freedom is taken up by the audience. The message gets multiplied: four times, five times, six times. For a moment it seems like the peaceful freedom fighters have won the war as they managed to bring their creativity and entrepreneurial spirit, which originally flourished in their work as free caricaturists, to a new and much broader level: one that has actually been fired up by this attack on freedom.

The presentation reminds us that the romantic notion of freedom can quickly flip into its opposite when the carefree feeling around it gets lost and freedom becomes something to fight for. In addition to the pointed enactment of the complex relationship between freedom, creativity and entrepreneurship, we are also struck by the aesthetic quality of the presentation. Not only do the students provide a beautiful variation between different elements and forms, such as video, singing, being muted, using percussion and engaging the audience; they also perfectly time and orchestrate the flow of action and the smooth blending from one scene into the other. This turns the presentation into one coherent piece of art with all its different layers: a performance that echoes well into the future.

An interventionist pedagogy

As we have tried to illustrate in this chapter, our approach to conveying a critical understanding of entrepreneurship is to playfully enact it at the intersection of critique and affirmation. We do so by interfering, in various ways, with the taken-for-granted educational assemblage process, which ideally then cascades into a multilayered learning journey. Since we consider this approach as above all a "practice" of holding a learning space between the stimulation of critique and the enactment of alternative views on the relationship between creativity and entrepreneurship, we also theorize the pedagogy of this course foremost as a series of practices.

Or, as Mulcahy (2012, p. 82) explains it with reference to Garfinkel, critical knowledge and imaginative thinking are "practice all the way down". More concretely even, we consider the course pedagogy to be an in(ter)vention (Steyaert, 2011) in the playful way we scale and enact the learning situation through smaller and bigger inventions. An interventionist pedagogy, we argue, can offer a "powerful counter-narrative to the conventional view of developmentalism that dominates the pedagogical gaze, positioning learners in continual deficit and learning activities as preparation for some imagined ideal" (Fenwick & Edwards, 2010, p. 22). As we have also tried to illustrate in this chapter, the affectual flows that such an interventionist pedagogy can generate in the classroom may even result in a fumbling reinvention of teaching itself.

An important inspiration of an interventionist pedagogy – understood as an associative process – is an actor network theory approach to education which perceives learning as continuously performed into material reality through webs of association (Fenwick & Edwards, 2010, 2012; Fenwick, 2016). As Fenwick and Edwards (2010) explain, ANT is not a theory of what to think but a way to "intervene". The focus here, as Mulcahy (2012) asserts, is on how knowledge comes to be produced – also materially – into "tangible knowledge" (Gherardi, 2006). The question is how heterogeneous resources are mobilized and assembled through networks of association to establish an object of knowledge in practice. To answer this question it is vital to look at educational work as ontological, even if knowledge and learning are dominantly seen as an epistemological issue. The ontological stance, however, privileges knowledge and learning as always performed. Mulcahy (2012, p. 82) elaborates: "[t]he assumption is made that nothing has reality, or form, outside its performance in webs of relations with performances being defined as 'material processes, practices, which take place day by day and minute and minute'" (Law & Singleton, 2000, p. 775).

Through this performative approach, "teaching a class" becomes a form of world-making that occurs as the classroom process unfolds minute by minute, but also through the range of entanglements that co-produce the process, some even from a distance: the school buzzer and water bottles, light and temperature; students' bodies and teachers' experiences; tables, chairs, computers and video players; session outlines and current readings, exercises and instructions; the day's moods and the university's reputation, and more. In this (dis)assembling process, it is important not only to alter human–human relations but also to acknowledge the materiality of ongoing associations that "make visible the rich assortments of things at play in educational events and how they are connected" (Fenwick & Edwards, 2010, p. 22).

An interventionist pedagogy follows a tactical approach (de Certeau, 1984) as it tries to infiltrate the grand narrative of creativity and entrepreneurship through its cracks and fissures. The assemblage thinking of Deleuze and Guattari helps us to grasp a processual and socio-material perspective on the world, in which agency is derived from the precarious associations of human and non-human bodies into emergent wholes (Müller, 2015). For the educator, then, the task – in terms of both inviting critique and enabling affirmation – is one of bricolage. One gathers multiple resources – people, motion, spaces, materials, theories, time and exercises – and engages in constantly reassociating these elements in a broad spectrum of interventions as documented in this chapter.

By deploying interventions, one can create an empty or third space (Steyaert, 2006), which allows for material alternatives to be performed. This requires improvising, experimenting, taking risks and inviting external actors to the "playground" in order to form new associations. In the course we therefore try to intervene in the traditional assemblage of the classroom through play and through confrontation with unfamiliar elements. We hold that an interventionist pedagogy becomes "productive" when it brings along new translations and trans-formations not just on the level of critical ideas but also in the form of new enactments, collective experiences and unfamiliar affective intensities. For instance, the walk around the city oscillates between two kinds of experience: the usual process of ushering one's way through the city, following planned routes, and another, less usual, of wandering around and becoming immersed in the city's other feelings and little narratives.

Also, the improvisation workshop unfolds along a plethora of intensities and feelings: between being reserved and feeling enthusiastic, between staring in dis-belief and going for it, between feeling unable and sensing the magic of your group improvisation. Likewise, both interventions – walking/strolling and dancing/moving – are embodied practices (Beyes & Steyaert, 2015); students' bodies-in-interaction shape joint waves of affect that also immerse them and make them enact sessions in ways other than we had anticipated. In line with Deleuze and Guattari, we perceive affect as a "trans-individual force of organ-izing" (Michels & Steyaert, 2017). We stimulate its unfolding by exercising col-laborative creativity and drawing in new external relations.

In summary, three elements – learning as knowing in practice, assemblage thinking and a focus on collective waves of affect – are interwoven conceptually in the interventionist pedagogy we propose in the context of critical entrepre-neurship studies. Such pedagogy, if applied more broadly, requires sensitivity to the everyday performance of socio-material and affective webs of interrelating. The goal would be to enact imaginative performances that persuasively address weak points in the dominant assemblage of current academic education, while simultaneously relying on the performativity of embodied learning experiences that have an effect on the individuals as well as on the group on a collective level (see also Gilbert, 2013).

No critique without reflection

As students embark on their collaborative group work, somewhat vague but requiring intense rehearsal and interaction, we also try to offer spaces for them to reflect. In fact, as a little welcome gift to the course, all students get a colourful notebook as an important companion and material prop throughout the course, and we offer recurring diary moments where we encourage them to note down their experiences as they are happening. Based on their collection of reflections, students wrap up the course – usually a few weeks after the final session – in a reflection paper in which we hope to see the tension between cri-tique and affirmation enacted again. Some students feel intrigued and at the same time overwhelmed by the opportunity to write a course reflection paper in a crea-tive format.

Once the course is "over" (at least according to the academic calendar), it is time for us as instructors to also step back and take a moment to reflect. In their learning papers, students confront us – as much as themselves – with the questions "what is to be learned from this course?" and "how to make sense of this different learning process?" To provide a thorough answer to this question, one that cannot be easily summarized in three bullet points, students give us some insights into their own personal learning path throughout the course; some even speak of going through a notable transformation. Several students told us they had fundamentally departed from their pre-course conceptions of what the notions of creativity and entrepreneurship embody. We are praised for the unusual and creative format of the course and the unique assemblage process of each course session. A few students have even said this was their best course in four years of university education.

But there are doubts as well, all the way, which we notice as students do not spare us from their frustrations, struggles and hard lessons. Sometimes our feedback on their creative attempts was too blunt, we provided too little time in improvisation exercises, or they couldn't easily understand why we moved slowly at various points or built in repetition. Especially the work involved for the creative group presentations is described as emotionally intense and conflictual. Usually, individuals can work through these upsetting experiences in their learning papers, but we have also had to deal with interpersonal problems in groups; one student even quit over this.

We instructors can certainly relate to such dynamics. Working in a team of three, we find our own course preparations are also intense, mostly fun, but never trouble-free. We brainstorm, we negotiate, we get silly at times, we all have our "favourites", but there's never enough time to incorporate all our ideas. If we were to teach the course individually, we would probably be teaching three rather different courses. And yet, we never considered turning the course into a "one (wo)man show".

Prior to each of the course sessions, we spend a considerable amount of time and resources to carefully plan the "run of the session". That means mapping the unique set of interventions of each course unit: what (critical) readings will we draw upon and how will students engage with them? What exercises will we try out? What objects/materials do we need to bring to the session? Can we show a video (clip)? Can we go outside? Will we break the group up and work with them in separate classrooms? Who will say what? As we try to keep the course lively and alive, we also – sometimes zealously – try to avoid repeating session designs from the previous year(s).

Despite all these efforts, we are painfully aware of our weak points as well. It almost feels paradoxical to offer a course on creativity in which we prepare the sessions so meticulously, even developing a detailed schedule. We have learned that the group can come to a creative flow and instant improvisation only with a well-rehearsed scenario. Even then, we must constantly counter an inclination towards "safe execution", so we frequently try to break out of our own comfort zone. Otherwise this would thwart our pedagogic idea(l)s around collective improvisation and open risk. Along those lines we agree with Gilbert (2013) that the individual state of the teacher is as important as thorough preparation. By changing the bits and pieces of each session each year, we try to keep up our own sense of surprise, excitement and anticipation. Reacting to subconscious and bodily felt affective feedback loops requires a healthy mental and physical state as well as the confidence to speak freely about the "run" of the session. Taken together, all this results in a sense of awareness and presence that would easily dissolve if we stuck compulsively to a set scenario.

Accordingly, we also try to stay sensitive to the dynamics of the day, so we can make last-minute adjustments as the course unfolds. Indeed, whatever preparations we make, we can never predict the process through which a session will unfold, and especially the relations between sessions; after all, no one can design intensities, affects and atmospheres (Michels & Steyaert, 2017). In other words, the tension between critique and affirmation evolves with the moods and modes that colour the responses of the students; so, rather than sitting on our butts too comfortably, we too have to constantly seek to reimagine this course on entrepreneurship and creativity, a course that is constantly in the making.

References

Beyes, T. & Steyaert, C. (2015). Der Sinn der Lehre: Ethnographie, Affekt, sensemaking. In C. Maeder, A. Brosziewski & J. Nentwich (Eds), *Vom Sinn der Soziologie* (pp. 197–211). Konstanz: UVK.

Bilton, C. (2007). *Management and creativity: From creative industries to creative management*. Malden, MA: Blackwell.

Bjerg, H. & Staunæs, D. (2011). Self-management through shame-uniting governmentality studies and the "affective turn". *Ephemera: Theory and Politics in Organization*, *11*(2), 138–156.

Bohannon, J. (2011). *Dance vs. PowerPoint, a modest proposal*. TEDx Brussels. Retrieved from www.ted.com/talks/john_bohannon_dance_vs_powerpoint_a_modest_proposal.

Bröckling, U. (2015). *The entrepreneurial self: Fabricating a new type of subject*. Los Angeles, CA: SAGE.

Catmull, E. (2014). *Creativity, Inc*. London: Transworld.

Cohendet, P., Grandadam, D. & Simon, L. (2010). The anatomy of the creative city. *Industry and Innovation*, *17*(1), 91–111.

Coutu, D. (2008). Creativity step by step. A conversation with choreographer Twyla Tharp. *Harvard Business Review*, *86*(4), 47–51.

de Certeau, M. (1984). *The practice of everyday life*. Berkeley, CA: University of California Press.

Deckert, B. (2016). *Die Entdeckung des Kosmos: Autoethnographie einer urbanen Intervention.* Bamberg: Difo-Druck.

Eberle, T.S. & Metelmann, J. (2016). Integrating humanities and social sciences: Institutionalizing a contextual studies programme. In C. Steyaert, T. Beyes & M. Parker (Eds), *The Routledge companion to reinventing management education* (pp. 398–414). London: Routledge.

Fenwick, T. (2016). What matters in sociomateriality: Towards a critical posthuman pedagogy in management education. In C. Steyaert, T. Beyes & M. Parker (Eds), *The Routledge companion to reinventing management education* (pp. 398–414). London: Routledge.

Fenwick, T. & Edwards, R. (2010). *Actor–network theory in education*. London: Routledge.

Fenwick, T. & Edwards, R. (Eds) (2012). *Researching education through actor–network theory*. Chichester: Wiley-Blackwell.

Florida, R.L. (2002). *The rise of the creative class*. New York, NY: Basic.

Foucault, M. (1977). *Discipline and punish: The birth of the prison*. London: Penguin.

Foucault, M. (1997). The ethics of the concern for the self as a practice of freedom. In P. Rabinow (Ed.), *Michel Foucault. Ethics, subjectivity and truth*. New York, NY: New York Press.

Germain, O. & Jacquemin, A. (2017). Positioning entrepreneurship studies between critique and affirmation. Interview with Chris Steyaert. *Revue de l'Entrepreneuriat, 16*(1), 55–64.

Gherardi, S. (2006). *Organizational knowledge: The texture of workplace learning*. Oxford: Blackwell.

Gilbert, J. (2013). The pedagogy of the body: Affect and collective individuation in the classroom and on the dance floor. *Educational Philosophy and Theory, 45*(6), 681–692.

Glăveanu, V.P. (2010). Paradigms in the study of creativity: Introducing the perspective of cultural psychology. *New Ideas in Psychology, 28*(1), 79–93.

Hardt, M. (2002). *Gilles Deleuze: An apprenticeship in philosophy*. University of Minneapolis, MN: Minnesota Press.

Hjorth, D. (2017). Critique nouvelle: An essay on affirmative-performative entrepreneurship research. *Revue de l'Entrepreneuriat, 16*(1), 47–54.

Hulbeck, C. (1945). The creative personality. *American Journal of Psychoanalysis, 5*(1), 49–58.

Izak, M., Kostera, M. & Zawadzki, M. (2017). *The future of university education*. London: Palgrave Macmillan.

Law, J. & Singleton, V. (2000). Performing technology's stories: On social constructivism, performance, and performativity. *Technology and Culture, 41*(4), 765–775.

Merchant, N. (2013). *Got a meeting? Take a walk*. TED 2013. Long Beach, CA: Long Beach Performing Arts Center. Retrieved from www.ted.com/talks/nilofer_merchant_got_a_meeting_take_a_walk.

Michels, C. & Steyaert, C. (2017). By accident and by design: Composing affective atmospheres in an urban art intervention. *Organization, 24*(1), 79–104.

Mulcahy, D. (2012). Assembling the "accomplished" teacher: The performativity and politics of professional teaching standards. In T. Fenwick & R. Edwards (Eds), *Researching education through actor-network theory* (pp. 78–96). Chichester: Wiley-Blackwell.

Müller, M. (2015). Assemblages and actor-networks: Rethinking socio-material power, politics and space. *Geography Compass, 9*, 27–41.

Nietzsche, F. (1969 [1886]). *Thus spoke Zarathustra*. London: Penguin.

Rehn, A. & De Cock, C. (2009). Deconstructing creativity. In T. Richards, M.A. Runco & S. Moger (Eds), *The Routledge companion to creativity* (pp. 222–231). Oxford: Routledge.

Robinson, K. (2006). *How schools kill creativity*. TED 2006, Monterey, CA. Retrieved from www.ted.com/talks/ken_robinson_says_schools_kill_creativity.

Serres, M. (1997). *The troubadour of knowledge*. Ann Arbor, MI: University of Michigan Press.

Schoeneborn, D. (2013). The pervasive power of PowerPoint: How a genre of professional communication permeates organizational communication. *Organization Studies*, *34*(12), 1777–1801.

Steyaert, C. (2006). Cities as heterotopias and thirdspaces: The example of ImagiNation, the Swiss Expo02. In S.R. Clegg & M. Kornberger (Eds), *Space, organization and management theory* (pp. 248–265). Copenhagen: Liber and CBS Press.

Steyaert, C. (2007). "Entrepreneuring" as a conceptual attractor? A review of process theories in 20 years of entrepreneurship studies. *Entrepreneurship and Regional Development*, *19*(6), 453–477.

Steyaert, C. (2011). Entrepreneurship as in(ter)vention: Reconsidering the conceptual politics of method in entrepreneurship studies. *Entrepreneurship and Regional Development*, *23*(1–2), 77–88.

Steyaert, C. (2014). Going all the way: The creativity of entrepreneuring in the Full Monty. In C. Bilton & S. Cummings (Eds), *Handbook of management and creativity* (pp. 160–181). Cheltenham: Edward Elgar.

Steyaert, C. & Beyes, T. (2009). Narrating urban entrepreneurship: A matter of Imagineering? In B. Lange, A. Kalandides, B. Stöber & I. Wellmann (Eds), *Governance der Kreativwirtschaft. Diagnosen und Handlungsoptionen* (pp. 207–221). Bielefeld: Transcript-Verlag.

Steyaert, C. & Dey, P. (2010). The politics of narrating social entrepreneurship. *Journal of Enterprising Communities*, *4*(1), 85–108.

Steyaert, C., Beyes, T. & Parker, M. (2016). *The Routledge companion to reinventing management education*. London: Routledge.

Steyaert, C., Hoyer, P. & Resch, B. (2016). Playing and the performing arts. Six memos for the future classroom. In C. Steyaert, T. Beyes & M. Parker (Eds), *The Routledge companion to reinventing management education* (pp. 342–357). London: Routledge.

Tharp, T. (2003). *The creative habit*. New York, NY: Simon & Schuster.

Weiner, R. (2000). *Creativity and beyond: Cultures, values, and change*. Albany, NY: State University of New York Press.

Weiskopf, R. & Steyaert, C. (2009). Metamorphoses in entrepreneurship studies: Towards an affirmative politics of entrepreneuring. In D. Hjorth & C. Steyaert (Eds), *The politics and aesthetics of entrepreneurship* (pp. 183–201). Cheltenham: Edward Elgar.

Part V
On dialogues

10 Moving entrepreneurship

Karen Verduijn

Introduction

This chapter offers a description and evaluation of a course format seeking to familiarize students with processual thinking. Whereas typically "university courses approach learning processes from the point of view of stability as normal and change as its other" (Hjorth & Johannisson, 2007, p. 52), this course posits both learning and entrepreneur*ing* as fluid, and not necessarily intentional (or necessarily "planned"), but as an open and indeterminate ongoing process.

From a processual point of view entrepreneuring is seen as an active intervening in, and disruption of the spatio-temporal rhythms of everyday life (Verduijn, 2015). During the course, students design their own filming projects, an exercise conducive to making them:

1   question predominant, taken-for-granted ideas about entrepreneurship, and the entrepreneur, such as realizing that entrepreneurial "reality" may not be all that planned/plannable/straightforward as they perhaps originally thought), and
2   think "filmically"/visually (i.e. in (moving) images, with emphasis on observing, getting involved, playing with perspectives etc.).

The course aims to "open up" students' predominant frames of thought, to stimulate their curiosity and to make them look (and think) differently (literally, to *move* them). Since we view upon both learning and entrepreneuring as social endeavours, the students make the films in small groups and evaluate each other's films.

The purpose of this chapter is to describe how processual thinking underpins this particular course, and to reflect upon the challenges in guiding students in switching towards this "other" ontology, as well as in crafting and upholding such a stance given, among others, students' previous educational experiences and prevailing institutional and cultural norms regarding e.g. examinations and grades (which are counter-"productive" when it comes to seeing learning as an open, indeterminate process). The next sections will clarify the course's theoretical backbone (i.e. the processual approach), as well as the course set-up, and offer personal experiences with teaching the course, and reflections on the course format.

A processual approach

"Traditional" attempts at theorizing entrepreneurial processes have been guided by assumptions of determinism, emphasizing the entrepreneurial process as new venture creation, and positing the same as an intentionally planned activity, a linear trajectory. Most such conceptualizations assume that the "development" of a new venture proceeds through (identifiable) sequences of stages, or steps – depicting it as a road towards a pre-defined goal (e.g. Churchill & Lewis, 1983; Carter, Gartner & Reynolds, 1996). More and more contributions, however, question such assumptions (e.g. Görling & Rehn, 2008; Hjorth, 2004; Steyaert, 2004, 2007; Sørenson, 2006; Levie & Lichtenstein, 2010; Johannisson, 2011; Sarasvathy, 2012) and view upon entrepreneur*ing* as a process of becoming (Steyaert 1997, 2007; Boutaiba, 2003; Nayak & Chia, 2011). A processual approach (also called a *process metaphysics* (Chia, 1999)) finds its roots in the works of such philosophers as Whitehead, Heidegger, Bergson, James and, more recently, Deleuze and Guattari. The processual approach is predicated on a *becoming ontology*, in which movement is seen as the "primordial quality" (Nayak, 2008) in theory development. This entails moving away from conceptualizations in terms of taxonomies, hierarchies, dichotomies, segmentation, stages and (sequential) steps. It means letting go of any conceptualization featuring categories that temporarily "may make it easier for us to grasp reality but ... also hide ... underlying complexities" (Cooper, 2005, p. 1689). Becoming, change, creativity, disruption, and indeterminism form the main ingredients of a processual approach, which purports that we should "unpack" states, events and entities in order to be able to reveal the complex processes in and of everyday life. Indeed, such an approach entails letting go of linear conceptualizations of processes, "in which the present is a moment between the (now finished) past and the (yet to come) future" (Hosking, 2007, p. 14). Rather, it implies paying explicit attention to how we can view upon "future" as the realms in which becoming takes shape and develops (Adam & Groves, 2007, pp. 53–55).

In such a process view, predicated on *becoming*, "the world" is seen and understood as forever changing, in "flux", with flux and change thus forming the "standard" (and not the exception, or something that happens in-between states of stability; see for example Tsoukas and Chia (2002)). Process theorists decline thinking about phenomena in terms of "things" and (stable) entities; rather they actively purport a critique of "thingification", or reification (i.e. the tendency to see "things" as "fixed"). Consequently, process theorists prefer such words as "event" and "actual occasion" over "thing" or "substance" (Steyaert, 1997) and refuse prescriptions of "what we *should* become". This thus also points at particular emancipatory qualities of, and in entrepreneuring, a discarding of delimitations of the space(s) of our possibilities (e.g. Rindova, Barry & Ketchen, 2009; Verduijn, Dey, Tedmanson & Essers, 2014).

In the scope of this course, I connect processual thinking with its emphasis on what (may) become to Chia's (1996) thoughts on divergent/"upstream" versus convergent/"downstream" thinking. In teaching the course, I further link divergent/upstream versus convergent/downstream thinking to right-brain/left-brain thinking ideas (Kirby, 2004, 2007).

To elaborate, Kirby (2004) argues that entrepreneurs have a "right-brain" thinking preference. He draws on explanations of how, generally, the brain is seen as divided into two hemispheres: left and right. The left side of the brain is seen to be where language and logic are handled, whereas the right side of the brain is where information is processed intuitively, relying heavily on images. Right-brained thinking is explained as lateral, unconventional, unsystematic and unstructured (at least, when compared to left-brain thinking). According to Kirby, it is right-brained lateral thinking that is "at the heart of the creative process" (Kirby, 2004, p. 515):

> while the left brain requires hard facts before reaching a conclusion, the right is happier dealing with uncertainties and elusive knowledge. It favours open-ended questions, problems for which there are many answers rather than a single, correct solution.... The left specializes in precise descriptions and exact explanations; the right enjoys analogies, similes and metaphors. The left demands structure and certainty; the right thrives on spontaneity and ambiguity.
>
> (Lewis, 1997, pp. 38–39, in Kirby 2004, p. 515)

To illustrate, in left-brain thinking, as in convergent thinking, any problem (or set of problems) should ideally lead to one, overall solution. In right-brain thinking, as with divergent thinking, we would arrive at a number of plausible answers to any one problem (Kirby, 2007).

The latter in particular can be linked to Chia (1996). Chia (1996) adopts the metaphor of a river to discern between upstream and downstream thinking. In downstream thinking, as with a river moving towards the sea, ideas become more and more carved, and are tunnelled in one obvious direction (with the river: the sea). Downstream thinkers thus are those who attempt to relate every event to a single central vision, or (organizing) principle, with traces of past patterns of thought constraining and shaping the possibilities of future thinking (Chia, 1996, p. 417). Alternatively, in upstream thinking, we move towards where a river emerges, towards the 1,001 rivulets that eventually become that steady united stream heading towards sea. Upstream thinking means pursuing many ends, often unrelated, and even contradictory. Upstream thinking is literally divergent, crafting relationships between apparently disparate ideas. Chia argues that it is upstream thinking that we need in entrepreneuring, and that to switch from downstream to upstream thinking requires the "weakening of thought processes", a "paradigm-shifting mentality" (p. 409). It is upstream thinking that this course tries to stimulate in its aim to *move* students' thinking.

Film

Since "from a processual philosophy, entrepreneurship is closer to life in the sense that it is about creation" (Hjorth & Johannisson, 2007, p. 63), this is indeed what the course invites students to do. Since evidently we do not want to "capture"/freeze movement, we need a creative project that allows for movement, making film a suitable option. Given that – in relation to the processual approach adopted – it is the right-brain type of thinking that we want to stimulate during this course, it is important to note that film is also conducive in another way, i.e. the preference of right-brain thinkers for visuals/images. As well, living in "a world of moving images" invokes the need to not only communicate our ideas in writing, but also in sound and imagery. In that sense, the creating of their films also has "practical", hands-on value for the students involved in this course.

Apart from Claire (2009) and Verduijn *et al.* (2009), there is no extant literature on adopting film as pedagogical instrument in entrepreneurship education. There is literature on the adoption of film in studying management and organization. Especially notable in this respect is the work of Emma Bell (2008). She takes a pointedly critical stance towards reading film(s) in studying management, using deconstruction techniques. Yet what she mainly relates of is the analysis of extant (feature) films, not the adopting of film as a pedagogical instrument as such in (management) education.

The course's set-up

The first "aim" of the course is to create a distance from students' established ways of seeing and doing things (so as to (re-)create an "open mind" (e.g. Hjorth & Johannisson, 2007)). We do so by setting out to question predominant, taken-for-granted ideas about entrepreneurship, such as those associated with the heroic image of the entrepreneur, its connotation with (setting up) successful, profit-driven businesses, it being seen as a positive force towards a healthy economy, with as a central tenet the spotting of (profitable) opportunities etc. This is done by introducing them to deconstructions of the dominant images of the entrepreneur, and entrepreneurship (e.g. Ahl, 2004), and by unmasking the entrepreneurial process as consisting of such glorious, "grand" activities as "identifying an opportunity", "writing the business plan", "founding the business" etc. (Görling & Rehn, 2008). This is introduced in liaison with the course's assignment, i.e. to create a short film about entrepreneurship. As with process philosophy in general, the idea with the film is also that it is predominantly the process that matters. The filming process itself is conducive to students opening up their fixed ideas, "activating" their curiosity, improvising, and trying (playfully) to find out how *they* might come to think (differently) about entrepreneurship, what *their* images related to the entrepreneurship phenomenon are becoming, where they may find entrepreneurship literally "in the streets" etc. and then translate this into (moving) images. The students' films can be seen as their "works of art", literally the emergent result of their (creative) entrepreneurial journeys.

Since we conceive of learning from a dialogic perspective (which is seen to be "crucial in order to prevent the tendency to closure" (Hjorth & Johannisson, 2007, p. 53)), students assess each other's films. That is the second assignment students work on, and hand in at the end of the course: a 250-word assessment of the films made by their peers, listing its strengths and weaknesses in relation to the course's aims, and theoretical backbone, and providing their grades for the peers' films. The individual assessment papers inter alia provide an opportunity for me as a teacher to get an impression of if the students have actually come to understand the course's ideas, and "theory". The assessment papers are graded (by me) based on how thorough they are in their feedback, and if they relate their interpretation of the films made adequately to the theoretical ideas being adopted in the course (so I'm not "judging" the interpretations as such).

The course is taught at undergraduate level (third year), runs over eight weeks and has a total of eight ECTS (which equals 168 study hours). Typically, the course attracts 35–70 students. The students are being guided in their processes in a number of ways. We start with lectures (two per week), in which we introduce and explain the course ideas. The lectures are followed by weekly workgroup meetings in which students can generate feedback on their ideas-in-process. In these work group meetings they present their filming ideas and discuss them with their peers. Given that – as said – it is the peers who grade the films, these sessions are highly valuable in more than one way. Indeed, these sessions provide the opportunity for the teams to assess whether or not their ideas "work" in the eyes of their peers. My role is mainly to stimulate the dialogue (and not to tell them what I think about their ideas, although I do relate their projects back to the course's core ideas). The very final session is where we all view and discuss the films through "filming installations", with students literally walking from room to room to watch the films. Students also have to upload their films on YouTube so that everyone involved can (re)watch the films when preparing the assessments.

The course's content

The accompanying literature for this course is Jones and Spicer's (2009) "Unmasking the entrepreneur" as well as Chia (1996). I use them as a stepping stone towards moving the students' thinking, i.e. to "unfix" (loosen up) their previously obtained ideas about entrepreneurship (Chia calls this the "weakening" of thought processes). I do not use all of Jones and Spicer (2009), but I prepare lectures about a number of their intriguing ways of rewriting entrepreneurship and the entrepreneur. I tell them about how the entrepreneur may have come to be seen as a sublime and phantasmic object: desirable but eventually unattainable, and how entrepreneurship may be conceived as an apparition, an illusory mental image (a "heffalump", in Jones & Spicer, 2009, p. 35). I talk about how all the various definitions of entrepreneurship actually unveil an enormous variety of contradictory understandings and ideas, and that failing to come to one "essential" definition is not only impossible, but also points at how entrepreneurship has become an "empty signifier". I discuss Lacan's "mirror stage" (p. 31), pointing at how there is always a distortion in what we (think we) see, a "dynamic of misrecognition" (p. 32), so that nobody ever sees "reality" (because symbolism, wish and desire come in the way). I talk about how value and destruction are two sides of the same coin, thus also arguing how entrepreneurship is thus not only "of" the economy, connected with (neutral) principles of utility and exchange, but how creating new environments is not without its repercussions, for changing "the fabric of society" (Calas, Smircich & Bourne, 2009). Last but not least, I make a plea for how exploring extreme cases (such as Jones & Spicer's "treatise" of the case of Marquis de Sade, chapter 6) can push the boundaries of our thinking, not to create (even) more space in our understanding of entrepreneurship, but to literally take it to its limits.

As I see it, Jones and Spicer's ideas invite the students to look differently, and challenge the way(s) they have come to think about entrepreneurship. I stipulate how they offer "techniques" for doing so, and invite them to start playing with those techniques.

With Chia (1996) I provide the students with a framing for the course: given that the article is over 20 years old, it is nonetheless still very accurate in describing how a "standard" business school context does not necessarily stimulate students' imaginations, whereas in a highly versatile world that would be one of the things they would need, thus invoking other/new ways of thinking and educating. With the metaphor of the river it provides a vivid image for what process philosophy purports, and how trying to capture/freeze "reality" is not what we should want (for downright unattainable). And that exploring the "possibility of dramatically different ways of seeing the world" (Chia, 1996, p. 423) goes hand in hand with "complexifying", and the embracing of confusion, chaos and ambiguity. And that in particular is something most of the students (initially) resist doing, as I will narrate of below.

Experiences in teaching the course

The course's set-up is different from what the students have got used to – the "standard" science approach (Chia, 1996) – and it takes time for them to change their ideas, and views. In the beginning students inadvertently struggle to make sense of what is going on, and for sure fall back on that standard way of approaching things. To provide some examples: in providing feedback to peers (during the work group meetings), they feel the need to be "experts" before they have "an opinion". And they do want to look at "other sides" but feel they need "proof" of them ("hard facts"). As well, they continuously seek my approval, as "expert insight". This requires careful navigating on my part. Surely, I cannot (and do not) tell them what is "right" or "wrong". I do not tell them "this is how it's done" or "that's the kind of film you should be making". But I do refer back to the "techniques" and concepts as offered by Jones and Spicer (2009), and stimulate them to take up those techniques and concepts as thinking exercises, as well as to dare to experiment with what comes out of it. I do this among others by preparing a set of "tasks" that may help them to become more reflexive, and to "play" with their ideas. Examples of such tasks are watching and reflecting on particular video clips, and reflecting on certain questions, as well as on the literature provided. These tasks are designed to raise awareness, and guide them in their journeys towards discovering and forming new ideas.

After all, moving their ideas and their thinking requires the students feeling safe to do so, and – as said – initially they might think that their teacher telling them "what to do" (and what to think) is what will give them that sense of safety and security. In line with this, they do generally find it hard to accept that it is their peers who grade the film (and not the teacher), for that does not – initially – give them that sense of security. Rather, they see this as a highly insecure "factor" to take into their stride during the course (actually, this fact is continuously being met with disbelief, where students just cannot fathom that it will not be me who knows best, and thus provide them my "verdict"). Yet, I feel the peer grading is vital in them developing their own ideas – not only for themselves, in their filming projects, but also about other students' projects. In the end, there is usually some kind of "revelation" where they realize that they do have ideas about other students' projects, in relation to what the course offers. All in all, the eventual peer grading of the films not only aids in shifting the learning responsibility from the teacher alone towards the students but is also instrumental in the moving of their (own) ideas.

The students assessing each other's films is not only a way for me to "test" if they have come to understand the course ideas but also a way of meeting institutional grading requirements without compromising on the process philosophical ideas re indeterminism and multiplicity. Indeed, having that one final judgement by means of one (teacher-determined) grade would not do justice to the course's ideas. But what happens with the students assessing each other's films, and providing their grades, is that yes, we have some final number to pass on to admin, but the underlying "picture" is one of multiplicity since students vary (heavily) in their grading, and the reasons they provide as to arriving at that particular grade.

In their struggles to make sense of the filming assignment, students inadvertently ask for me to show them examples of previously made films. Yet I try not to show them until quite late in the course process because I feel this would provide too much of a closing-off (at least a number of students imitating the film I appear to like most). The work group meetings are vital in them jointly arriving at an understanding of what their films might (and might not) portray, and creates an awareness of how to look at, and assess them. Jointly, we develop and discuss such questions as: what is this film "up against"? What dominant images does it seek to abrogate? Does the film "push" any boundaries? Does it go "beneath the surface" (Jones & Spicer, 2009)? Does it "scratch off" (some of) that "shiny veneer" associated with entrepreneurship (ibid.)? What "other" image(s) of entrepreneurship is/are being created? This type of question, and the discussions we have around them, stimulate the dialogue about the filming projects, and awareness of the kind of process this course is trying to invoke.

As to teaching this course: it is a struggle to not fall back on the "traditional" ways of teaching, and just tell them what I think they should do (insofar as I would "know"). Yet, the authoritative teacher is what the students expect, and what I have easily got used to over the years. So, it is a constant struggle not to fall into the trap of just offering the students what they seem to expect (e.g. Fenwick, 2005 on the problematic role/positionality of the (critical) educator). Indeed, it is a dialogue. In teaching the course I am very open as to why I do not offer them a "checklist", why I do not set the stage by showing them previous years' best films, and I also sketch them my journey and my (ongoing) shifts in thinking. Indeed, the process philosophical stance is so different from the standard (scientific) approach, and that approach so omnipresent and taken for granted, that – as said – it is difficult for all involved to not fall back on it. I recall a discussion with two students about how "correctly executed scientific research" just simply "delivers" *facts*, and why would you question those facts? I tried to suggest that perhaps "facts" are only temporarily possible, partly interpretations, and that "correctly executed scientific research" may be somewhat overrated and not as nuanced as what a process philosophical stance might invoke, and the students augmentedly looked at me as if I came from planet Mars.

Referring back to the students' evaluations: if, at the very least, by the end of the course I have managed to "loosen" their perceptions, and challenge their thinking, I feel that the course's goals have been met. And fortunately this seems to be the case with the majority, also when reading the individual assessment papers. Although some students do provide remarks along the lines of "the course just didn't make any sense, I suggest they replace it with the original course (e-business)", "the assignment was vague" and "I think it was unclear what the films were supposed to contain", there are more students who claim such things as "I think the course was interesting in that it really challenged the perception of the entrepreneur and it made me think a lot about boundaries (if any) for entrepreneurship", "the course provides a new way of learning and making an assignment", "the course challenges the general view of entrepreneurship" and "the method used was very out of the box and interesting".

In the difficult learning process, it is a challenge not to "lose" the students, as with the example of the two students and the facts. It is a balancing act between providing them with the ambiguity, chaos and confusion needed to move their own thinking, and not push them too hard, for this might "close" the learning process (also see Hjorth, 2011). This is a matter of providing them with boundaries in the form of continuously making explicit the course's tenets.

Final reflections

I have been teaching this course over quite a number of years, in a number of variants, the latest one being the format I have introduced above. It started out as an introduction to entrepreneurship for graduate students. The very first time was when the filming project was conducive to students exploring and visually communicating their idea(s) about entrepreneurship (with less to no emphasis on abrogating dominant ideas). This already delivered quite interesting, entertaining films (for an evaluation of this particular format, see Verduijn *et al.*, 2009). For example, one of the films was kind of a portrayal of "a day out of the life of entrepreneur X". This was actually a very interesting, almost cynical film. In further developing the course, this particular film has led me to also adopt a less "arty" but more ethnographic/documentary style of film where students were asked to "capture" entrepreneuring in its everyday unfolding with an emphasis on the actual practices/"happenings" related to entrepreneurial initiatives (notably with as little emphasis on interviewing the individual entrepreneur as possible). This is in line with how Claire (2009) adopts film in teaching. The aim of this episode in my experiences in teaching with film was more towards the diving deeper into entrepreneurs' lived experiences (and enhancing the students' understanding of entrepreneurial real life) than in "weakening thought processes", as in the current format. This episode delivered a documentary style of filmmaking, which has actually – as an assignment in itself – proven to be the most "concrete" for the student (which is what they tend to like/prefer, in line with learning things that have "practical value"). The current course set-up adopts more of a performative approach of the visual (Steyaert et al., 2012), with less of a "realist" outlook on concrete "worlds" "out there" being reported about.

Over the years, I had students comment that "most films portray (some) ideas/concepts employed in this course, but all fail to really use them". I do not fully agree, but I can see how not all of them become fully immersed in the project, and not all of them start engaging with the course ideas in depth, nor really use them in their films. At one point I even tried to have an exam testing their knowledge of the course's theoretical ideas prior to making the film, but to no avail, and actually contrary to the course approach (indeed, suggesting that they should become "experts" before being able to make their films, rather than the filming itself being a way to discover, and uncover, new ideas).

As to the dialogic approach, it needs to be undertaken with care:

> the so-called dialogic process of critical education itself contains significant repressive potential, with its assumptions that "democratic spaces" for "voice" can actually be created within heterogeneous groups marbled with complex power relations and conflicting interests, simply by pronouncing it so.
>
> (Fenwick, 2005, p. 33)

Fenwick suggests that we need to be careful with regards to students' vulnerability, since a "critical" course format entails actively intervening in students' belief systems. So there is first and foremost a need to be aware of group dynamics, and the emergence of more, and less dominating voices and views.

Furthermore, there is a need to be aware that, as a *critical* educator, we run the risk of (re)creating our own oppression dynamics vis-à-vis students (Fenwick, 2005). Indeed, in critically educating, we set out to unveil the principles of oppression (Fenwick, 2005) in relation to the entrepreneurship phenomenon. This – in students' eyes – might come across as the educator taking on some kind of (hero) rescuer role: freeing them from bad/oppressive etc. ideas. This can create an image of the critical educator appearing as offering another ideologically superior stance (actually swapping the one dominant, taken-for-granted view with another). So, as Fenwick asserts, "even" with a dialogic approach, the educator's position is one with power, and this needs to be taken into consideration throughout the course process.

This chapter relates of a course format stipulating entrepreneur*ing* as a complex, non-linear phenomenon, breaking away from dominant frames of thought ("unfixing" stereotypical entrepreneurship thinking), introducing an imaginative rethinking of possibilities, by playing with the unexpected (and the yet-un-thought). The course invites students to become aware of their own thinking preferences, and to look differently. I see this course as an example of adopting a critical take on entrepreneurship in that it aims to open up predominant frames of thought, and unfixing fixed ideas. Dominant conceptualizations of entrepreneurship are being questioned, and students become reflexive of their own taken-for-granted ideas. And, yes, this invariably creates turmoil. They question general university educational policy (with courses usually setting out to tell them "what the world is like"), and some become angry. But that is what criticality is about, isn't it? It doesn't leave one untouched. For being critical is developing an awareness of what matters, and what matters should touch (if not *move*) you.

References

Adam, B. & Groves, C. (2007). *Future matters. Action, knowledge, ethics*. Leiden & Boston, MA: Brill.

Ahl, H. (2004). *The scientific reproduction of gender inequality; A discourse analysis of research texts on women's entrepreneurship*. Malmö: Liber AB.

Bell, E. (2008). *Reading management and organization in film*. Basingstoke: Palgrave Macmillan.

Boutaiba, S. (2003). *Becoming a company – Narrative temporalities in new start-ups*. PhD thesis, Department of Organization and Industrial Sociology, Copenhagen Business School.

Calas, M., Smircich, L. & Bourne, K. (2009). Extending the boundaries: Reframing "entrepreneurship as social change" through feminist perspectives. *Academy of Management Review, 34*(3), 552–555.

Carter, N., Gartner, W. & Reynolds, P. (1996). Exploring start-up event sequences. *Journal of Business Venturing, 11*, 151–166.

Chia, R. (1996). Teaching paradigm shifting in management education: University business schools and the entrepreneurial imagination. *Journal of Management Studies, 33*(4), 409–428.

Chia, R. (1999). A "rhizomic" model of organizational change and transformation: Perspective from a metaphysics of change. *British Journal of Management, 10,* 209–227.

Churchill, N. & Lewis, V. (1983). The five stages of small business growth. *Harvard Business Review, 61,* 30–50.

Claire, L. (2009). Advancing liberal arts values … entrepreneurially. In G.P. West, III, E.J. Gatewood & K.G. Shaver. (Eds), *Handbook of university-wide entrepreneurship education.* Cheltenham: Edward Elgar.

Cooper, R. (2005). Relationality, *Organization Studies, 28,* 1689–1710.

Fenwick, T. (2005). Ethical dilemmas of critical management education. Within classrooms and beyond. *Management Learning, 36*(1), 31–48.

Görling, S. & Rehn, A. (2008). Accidental ventures – A materialist reading of opportunity and entrepreneurial potential. *Scandinavian Journal of Management, 24,* 94–102.

Hjorth, D. (2004). Creating space for play/invention – concepts of space and organizational entrepreneurship. *Entrepreneurship & Regional Development, 16,* 413–432.

Hjorth, D. & Johannisson, B. (2007). Learning as an entrepreneurial process. In A. Fayolle (Ed.), *Handbook of research in entrepreneurship education* (pp. 46–66). Cheltenham: Edward Elgar.

Hjorth, D. (2011). On provocation, education and entrepreneurship. *Entrepreneurship and Regional Development, 23,* 49–63.

Hosking, D. (2007). Can constructionism be critical? In J. Holstein & J. Gubrium (Eds), *Handbook of constructionist research.* New York, NY: Guilford.

Johannisson, B. (2011). Towards a practice theory of entrepreneuring. *Small Business Economics, 36,* 135–150.

Jones, C. & Spicer, A. (2009). *Unmasking the entrepreneur.* Cheltenham: Edward Elgar.

Kirby, D. (2004). Entrepreneurship education: Can business schools meet the challenge? *Education and Training, 46*(8/9), 510–519.

Kirby, D. (2007). Changing the entrepreneurship education paradigm. In A. Fayolle (Ed.), *Handbook of research in entrepreneurship education* (pp. 21–33). Cheltenham: Edward Elgar.

Levie, J. & Lichtenstein, B. (2010). A terminal assessment of stages theory: Introducing a dynamics states approach to entrepreneurship. *Entrepreneurship Theory and Practice, 34,* 317–350.

Nayak, A. (2008). On the way to theory: A processual approach. *Organization Studies, 29,* 173–190.

Nayak, A. & Chia, R. (2011). Thinking becoming. Process philosophy and organization studies. *Philosophy and Organization Theory Research in the Sociology of Organizations, 32,* 281–309.

Rindova, V., Barry, D. & Ketchen, D.J. (2009). Entrepreneuring as emancipation. *Academy of Management Review, 34,* 477–491.

Sarasvathy, S.D. (2012). *Worldmaking in entrepreneurial action.* In A.C. Corbett & J. Katz (Eds), *Advances in entrepreneurship, firm emergence and growth* (pp. 89–123). Emerald.

Sørensen, B. (2006). Identity sniping: Innovation, imagination and the body. *Creativity and Innovation Management, 15,* 135–142.

Steyaert, C. (1997). A qualitative methodology for process studies of entrepreneurship: Creating local knowledge through stories. *International Studies of Management and Organization, 27,* 13–33.

Steyaert, C. (2004). The prosaic of entrepreneurship. In D. Hjorth & C. Steyaert (Eds), *Narrative and discursive approaches in entrepreneurships studies.* Cheltenham: Edward Elgar.

Steyaert, C. (2007). "Entrepreneuring" as a conceptual attractor. A review of process theories in 20 years of entrepreneurship studies. *Entrepreneurship & Regional Development, 19*, 453–477.

Steyaert, C., Martí, L. & Michels, C. (2012). Multiplicity and reflexivity in organizational research. Towards a performative approach to the visual. *Qualitative Research in Organizations and Management: An International Journal, 7*(1), 35–39.

Tsoukas, H. & Chia, R. (2002). On organizational becoming: Rethinking organizational change. *Organization Science, 13*, 567–582.

Verduijn, K. (2015). Entrepreneuring and process. A Lefebvrian perspective. *International Small Business Journal, 33*(6), 638–648.

Verduijn, K., Dey, P., Tedmanson, D. & Essers, C. (2014). Emancipation and/or oppression? Conceptualizing dimensions of criticality in entrepreneurship studies. *International Journal of Entrepreneurial Behavior & Research, 20*(2), 98–107.

Verduijn, K., Wakkee, I.A.M. & Kleijn, E.A.H. (2009). Filming entrepreneurship. *International Review of Entrepreneurship, 7*(3), 195–206.

11 On vulnerability and possibility in critical entrepreneurship education

Mutual learning between students and teachers

*Anna Wettermark, André Kårfors, Oskar Lif,
Alice Wickström, Sofie Wiessner and
Karin Berglund*

Introduction

Every time we go in to teach we take a deep breath before entering the classroom and remind ourselves that one or two students in there are likely to know more about the subject than we do. This could be because of their previous experiences and knowledge, or because their gaze from the outside is sharper than ours. At times this exposure of our vulnerability is intimidating for us – we want to be "good", knowledgeable teachers who make a real contribution. At other times we see outstanding students as a resource and a source of inspiration. Which interpretation comes more naturally depends, we think, on how secure we feel on the topic, but also on how the students function as a group – whether they are defensive and competitive, or curious and willing to share their learnings. In this chapter we will report on a course in which the latter state emerged, and we will suggest that it is precisely because of the presence of those outstanding students that we, as teachers, have the opportunity to learn and develop our courses. We will also suggest that a similar logic of seeing the encounter with others as an opportunity for development can, and should, be incorporated into the teaching of entrepreneurship – not least because entrepreneurship is often circumscribed as creative, curious and open-minded, as an activity to explore new paths or disclose "new worlds" (Spinosa *et al.*, 1999).

   A second aspect of vulnerability that we wish to discuss in this chapter is how to meet students who display the opposite tendencies, who do not want to embrace more reflective aspects of entrepreneurship but prefer to centre on issues of "how to be an entrepreneur". Their scepticism and reluctance to interrogate entrepreneurship exposes us to another kind of vulnerability: a feeling of behaving "wrongly", of not "giving" students what they want. In this chapter we will view these forms of vulnerability as interconnected, and will discuss them both. We will also invite students from a course in critical entrepreneurship that we taught to present their experiences and their impressions of vulnerability, in themselves and in others. From their voices we can follow how theories on the entrepreneurial self that we used on the course gave rise to queries and frustration, but also how they spurred students to reflect upon "others" as those whom social entrepreneurs strive to assist, their "beneficiaries".

We start this chapter with a description of the learning processes that evolved during the "Entrepreneurship and the Entrepreneurial Self"[1] course in which we wanted to encourage students to reflect critically on entrepreneurship, with a focus on vulnerabilities in selves and in others. We then present and discuss some essays that students handed in as part of their course exams, and in doing so reflect on the learnings students have extracted from the course. In the subsequent section we pass the word over to the students and invite them to elaborate on their experiences from the course, thereby adding the perspective of *learning*, not only teaching, entrepreneurship. In the final sections we reflect, as teachers and students, on our experiences from the course and what they tell us about vulnerability in ourselves and in the others of entrepreneurship. Our purpose with this chapter is thus twofold: we want to develop our thoughts on vulnerabilities and possibilities in teaching entrepreneurship, and we also wish to include the reflections of students who showed involvement during the course, as we believe that a focus on mutual learning is important.

Teaching entrepreneurship: standing still while moving reflectively?

In our course on critical perspectives of entrepreneurship there are no given answers; no one is right and no one is wrong, neither teacher nor student. That does not necessarily mean that vulnerability is "done away with", or that this would be one of our objectives – vulnerability, as we see it, is not finite but may take different shapes and have varying origins. On the contrary, we wish to create a social space for thinking about this amorphous vulnerability, a space that is reflective and honest, yet secure and respectful of others, and that thus invites and makes possible the posing of difficult questions. At the same time we want to prevent this space, our classroom, from turning into a venue for the expression of opinions or emotions that better belong in other fora – to ensure that no one is hurt and those who are willing to take on the challenges find a room for reflection. This implies that interpretations and experiences that we discuss in this space can be more or less theoretically founded, and our reflections more or less anchored in personal experiences. The aim of the course is to encourage the development of both these aspects in students: a theoretical awareness that includes individual reflections and insights, so as to enable students to not only be theoretically knowledgeable and assume critical perspectives, but also to develop an understanding about the practical and relational challenges that this may involve, that is to "embody" their knowledge.

Since we have previous experience of teaching the course, we enter classes with certain preconceptions. We are aware that, whereas some students are likely to respond positively to the challenges of the course and the creative possibilities it offers, others are likely to resist its theoretical approach. We are also aware that there are processual dimensions of learning in motion during the course; students who have previously started off in a constructive manner have then experienced confusion and disbelief in the middle of the course when more critical theories are presented, but most have been able to integrate their impressions at the end of the course. As teachers we have discussed these experiences and how we can accommodate students, so as to allow them to express their confusion, doubts and scepticism – and their vulnerability – while ensuring that they meet the performance criteria of the course. Building on the theories of Brown (2010, 2012), we developed a feeling that "standing still" was important, by which we meant both a belief that what we were doing was important and something we should pursue in the approach of the course, but also that we must provide room for students to resist and meet them as individuals. We thus engaged with Brown's ideas that vulnerability and shame are two sides of the same coin. When we feel students' questioning attitudes, this not only awakens our vulnerability as teachers but also triggers thoughts of shame. We may then experience feelings of "what did I do wrong?", "I should probably adapt to their requests?", "I need to pretend that they are on board" or "no one needs to know about this failure". We thus understand shame as a general human emotion that washes over us, making us feel small, imperfect and not good enough, and we see vulnerability as an exposure to others and to their validation or rejection of our ideas (Brown, 2010; Ibarra, 1999). Brown here uses the concept of "shame resistance", which can be expressed in three ways (see Hartling in Brown, 2010, p. 77). The first is to avoid the shame by "hiding" – becoming quiet, keeping things secret, e.g. by suggesting a break, or "running" from the classroom after the lecture, to make oneself inaccessible to students. A second way is to go with the shame, which means pleasing people and winning approval, e.g. by making a joke of the "troubling news" that has been addressed or asking what students want and moving along with their wishes. A third option is to protest, control others through aggressiveness, and fight shame with shame, e.g. by lashing out at a student for saying something "stupid". Brown does not argue for any of these responses, but for learning about one's own reactions of shame and vulnerability, and embracing them. Standing still. Allowing these bodily and emotional reactions to take place – within us – then, when they no longer have a hold on us, we can react with more awareness. This may take five minutes, or 15, or it may last until the next lecture. But, as both of us participated in all the sessions, it was easier for us to "stand still", feeling the silent support of a colleague.

We start our course "gently" with exercises focusing on popular images and narratives of entrepreneurship – exercises that are meant to be "fun" and to stimulate the creativity and collaboration of students. Soon, however, the teaching becomes more challenging and students are introduced to theories of, for example, Bröckling (2016) and Jones and Spicer (2009), and a number of scientific articles that examine entrepreneurship from critical, multidisciplinary perspectives. For many students these are novel ways of conceptualizing entrepreneurship, which they perhaps did not expect to come across on a management course. Before we begin teaching, students are therefore informed that the course is not about starting your own company, nor about what characterizes successful entrepreneurs. They are instead presented with the idea that the course builds on a philosophical approach to questions that affect large parts of our lives, whether working lives or private lives. We find this "forewarning" to students helpful as it calibrates expectations and prepares students for the fact that they are about to meet a different view of entrepreneurship. We also emphasize that the course may contribute to giving them a better grounding to deal with complex issues – and thus train them to engage in reflexive decision-making, similar to Schön's idea of the reflective practitioner (1984). At the same time, the importance of this philosophical approach is signalled, and it is underlined that the course is integrated into the master's programme and that students will have to relate to the content of the course further on in the programme. If, once we begin, students find the approach of the curriculum challenging, or that it extends beyond the normal scope of business school courses, we strive to confirm them in their impressions. Yes, this is a demanding course, covering areas that may be unfamiliar and controversial; areas that call into doubt the very conception of who we are as individuals and who we desire to be. But also, yes, you can do this, and one of the purposes of the course is to open up for an examination of societal issues from new perspectives. From these new perspectives you may be able to reflect on your experiences, see patterns in society and critically examine ideas taken for granted of who you strive to be and what forms you into that person. Vulnerability, or the subject's exposure to others, hence sneaks in through the back door, in a generic but nonetheless challenging way.

On the course, students are asked to problematize the two critical turns of entrepreneurship (see Chapter 8 in this volume) and to reflect upon the differences between a conventional reading of the entrepreneur and a more inclusive and socio-discursively based view of the entrepreneurial self. These ideas are put into a historical context by leaning on theories on power and neo-liberal governmentality (e.g. Foucault, 1978; Rose, 1989). Students are introduced to the principle of potentiality (Costea, Amiridis & Crump, 2012), to the concept of the entreployee (Pongratz & Voss, 2003) and to ideas of an inclusive and caring capitalism (Vrasti, 2012) that, through its flexibility and persuasiveness, becomes uncriticizable, and from which neo-liberal subjects may have difficulties in distancing themselves. Students are thus expected to develop a sociological understanding of entrepreneurship as a historically, culturally and socially contingent phenomenon that has taken different forms throughout history and in contemporary entrepreneurial society has exploded into multiple forms.

We then go on to suggest that conflicts, emotions and a sense of vulnerability are integral parts of entrepreneurship. From the notion of a socially inclusive entrepreneurship and from the suggestion that "everyone can be an entrepreneur" to the more imperative "everyone should be an entrepreneur", we encourage students to investigate distinctions between entrepreneurs and non-entrepreneurs and possible conflicts of interest between them. We ask the question that if everyone can be entrepreneurial, where then do we draw boundaries between selves (entrepreneurs) and others (non-entrepreneurs) and with what consequences? Through questions such as these, students are to consider ethical dimensions of inclusion and exclusion, and distinctions between selves and others. The relationships between the self (understood as the entrepreneurial self), the desired self (understood as the ethos of the endlessly active, capable and responsible ideal entrepreneur) and others (understood as the less entrepreneurial beneficiary who needs support from social entrepreneurs) are then explored in discussions and voluntary seminars that build on the course literature. The self is portrayed as subjected to a neo-liberal ideology, as striving towards the (impossible) fulfilment of external and internal expectations, reaching towards its potentiality, its desired self, or – to lean on Lacan – its Ideal-I (Jones & Spicer, 2009). We point out that during the first critical turn, when entrepreneurship becomes "green" or "social", conflicts tend to be external, located in clashes of interests between different actors. But when entrepreneurial identities and ideals are questioned, during the second critical turn, conflicts frequently transform and become internalized, related to ideals and values. In the complex and tension-ridden relationship between what one is and what one wishes to be, the literature that we lean on suggests that a discrepancy may emerge between the self-view of the entrepreneur and the idealized self. To use a Lacanian allegory, the self and the image of the self that appears in the mirror are never quite the same. The closing of this gap between self-understanding and self-aspiration then appears as somewhat of a mission impossible, and in the split mirror image the futile, illusionary quality of striving to reach the moving target of a neo-liberal ethos takes shape (Jones & Spicer, 2005).

Students are then introduced to the possibility that the relationship between the (entrepreneurial) self and its desired self (ethos) may be coloured by narcissist motives and emotional drive, by an ambition to prove oneself, to perpetually strive to become "more" (Costea *et al.*, 2012; Goss, 2005). Selves hence run the risk not only of overburdening themselves in their efforts at self-optimization (Bröckling, 2016) but also of "forgetting" others – others that are pushed to the margins of entrepreneurial attention, and that turn into a grey, faceless mass of "beneficiaries" of social entrepreneurship activities; mostly needy, unprivileged, far away, out of sight and reach. But this self-centredness, according to a neo-liberal ideology that treasures affective competencies and welcomes the initiatives of social entrepreneurs to alleviate social ills (Vrasti, 2012), is an inherent weakness, a crack in the image of the entrepreneurial self. In order to live up to the neo-liberal ethos, socially conscious entrepreneurs may have to venture out into society and find some others whom they can care about, so as to prove their entrepreneurial competence. By doing so, by responding to the call for a caring capitalism, social entrepreneurs find themselves entangled in an ideology that repeatedly and persuasively reproduces images of an ever more human, (com)passionate capitalism (Vrasti, 2012).

At this point, students are introduced to the ethics of Lévinas (1969) and a philosophy that purports to foster recognition, responsibility and an interest in the Other. The face of the Other must be seen, Lévinas argues, in real-life person-to-person encounters – encounters that overthrow and destabilize the self. The face of the Other in front of us, Lévinas contends, calls us into responsibility and into being. However, if the self is to be impacted by the Other, it must accept the Other in her alterity, without comparisons with the self and without expectations for reciprocity, or motives of self-confirmation (Spivak, 1987). The Other, then, holds an at least temporary primacy over the self, and the purpose of striving to understand the Other should not only be to get to know her, and to learn about her, but to learn *from* her (Spivak, 1987). If one succeeds in this, the Other may transform from the problem that she is often portrayed in the management discourse as being (e.g. Chakrabarty, 2002), from an obstacle to a smoothly running business, from a Lacanian object of dis-identification (Jones & Spicer, 2009) or from a security threat to society (Berglund & Skoglund, 2016) to an empowered entrepreneurial subject of identification and a potential source for the self's development and transgression (Butler, 2005).

In parallel with this theoretical trajectory, students engage in practical social entrepreneurship projects so as to have an opportunity to encounter others, "other" others, that they would possibly not have met in "normal" circumstances. By involving students in these practical projects, we want to make them think about what they can do for vulnerable groups, and to reflect upon their own vulnerability and how it may be linked to the strivings of the entrepreneurial self to reach her potential – and the potentiality of others. This attention to the vulnerabilities of others may not be explicitly expressed, in order not to evoke resistance, but nevertheless impels students to consider aspects of relations between entrepreneurial selves and their others. In previous courses, students have come into contact with societal issues through working in soup kitchens, preparing food for the homeless in collaboration with the Salvation Army, making a promotional video for an animal rights organization, visiting a home for the elderly to inform the residents about Internet security or encouraging newly arrived immigrants to join in sporting activities. These projects provide occasions for students to reflect on moral dilemmas and the (explicit or implicit) conflicts that the encounter with others may give rise to – aspects that we ask students to reflect upon in their project reports. In these reports, some students elaborate on dilemmas of priorities, reminding us of Derrida's undecidability (1993), in which they are left without guidelines on how to behave. Other students comment on how uncomfortable they feel in the encounter with the vulnerability of others – they note not only the gratefulness of others, but also their reverence, submissiveness and surprise that business students are interested in them (as others). In their projects, students thus catch glimpses of another set of subjectivities than those available to them, and encounter the idea of ethics as a practice, enacted in daily activities (Dey & Steyaert, 2016). In our discussions of the projects we strive to openly address the vulnerability that many of us sense when engaging in social entrepreneurship. We show students a TEDTalk by Brené Brown and discuss with them issues of emotions and conflicts in entrepreneurship in an effort to counteract the "numbing" effects of suppressed vulnerability and to support an acceptance for the fact that entrepreneurship may involve a willingness to risk oneself, to share one's emotions and to lay bare one's vulnerabilities (Brown, 2012).

Learning entrepreneurship: essays on the relationship between selves and others

In this section we focus on the work of the students and what they have learned during the course. We start by presenting the final essays of four top-scoring students; we describe the main themes of their individual papers and conclude with a short summary. Through this selection we obviously give a voice to those who have coped well with the requirements of the course and, while being aware of the bias this introduces, we feel it is important to underline the quality of these students' work. They are, however, not unique in their achievements, as the majority of students taking part in the course show an ability to reflect productively on the contents of the course. What makes these four students stand out is their ability to integrate theories and approaches of the course, and their willingness to take part in dialogues.

The four essays that we chose circle around an exploration of whether an ethically sensitive entrepreneurship is possible under a prevailing neo-liberal ideology. Wickström[2] (2016), for example, problematizes the relations between givers and receivers, or the entrepreneurial self and the Other, in social entrepreneurship. The question she asks herself is if the perspective of the Other, as a cognitive tool, is persuasive enough to challenge power dynamics within the entrepreneurial discourse. How, she wonders, do entrepreneurial acts affect the Other from a power-related point of view, and in what sense do they impact on the agency of the Other, or her ability to act differently than before? Wickström suggests that relations with others should, if one follows the ethics of Lévinas (1969), constitute a non-reciprocal relationship in terms of instrumental exchange, where the face of the Other calls one into awareness of the fragility of self while at the same time summoning the self through what it is not. In alternative entrepreneurship one must try to interrogate not only who the Other is but also how we epistemologically construct this Other, as a Western Eurocentric outlook could contribute to a construction tainted by a stereotypic framing shaped by societal discourse. This could then reinforce an asymmetrical relationship between the entrepreneurial subject and the Other, where the latter is prevented from constructing her own sense of subjectivity instead of rendering innovation "with, of, and by the Other" through exchange (Jones & Spicer, 2009, p. 108).

Wickström then continues:

> When exploring ethics in alternative entrepreneurship, Dey and Steyaert (2016) position this as a negotiation between the entrepreneur and the given context as they focus on the practices that form entrepreneurs into ethical subjects. From a Foucauldian perspective, they position this as individuals becoming subjects of their own knowledge by transgressing the subjectivity offered to them, by retaining a critical awareness of how technologies of power affect us. They connect this to a relational approach of the Other as they centralize how alternative entrepreneurship ought to protect the space of this Other, by moving away from instrumental and transactional relational models.

Wickström argues that, in a neo-liberal discourse, the subjectivities available to others become constrained in scope and in influence, as compared to subjectivities of the self, as do the possibilities of others to transgress subjectivities and become what Foucault (1978) calls subjects of their own knowledge. Protecting – and respecting – "the space of the Other", Wickström continues, is, then, no easy task, as the Other's voice is channelled through entrepreneurial selves shaped by personal values and with limited knowledge of the others with whom they interact. Wickström's reasoning here resounds with the theories of Spivak (e.g. 1987) when she calls our attention to the difficulties faced by others in speaking with their own voices, according to their own epistemologies, without being subsumed by politically stronger forces.

Wickström concludes that "the understanding of the Other, together with the overall socio-political context, is lacking within the entrepreneurial construct of self", and that there is a necessity for the self to demarcate herself through the construction of otherness; the otherness of the Other must thus be maintained. Building on Scharff (2015), Wickström further suggests that "[i]f the constitution of entrepreneurial subjectivities involves othering, exclusionary processes may lie at the heart of neoliberalism", implying that the neo-liberal discourse and the subjectivities it produces possibly undermine an ethical approach to the Other (Lévinas, 1969).

Kårfors (2016) approaches a similar dilemma when he tackles the question of whether alternative entrepreneurship and the emergence of a more caring entrepreneurial self have the potential to outweigh exclusionary dynamics in entrepreneurship. He writes that, within "conventional" entrepreneurship (Berglund & Skoglund, 2016), exclusion is highly observable.

> The principle of potentiality "[generates] more forms of individualistic hierarchy and elites" (Costea et al., 2012, p. 34), which hardly conforms to the concept of inclusion. Those who are not entreployees, and fail to exhibit adequate self-control, self-commercialization and self-rationalization (Pongratz & Voss, 2003) even exclude themselves by internalizing the guilt and shame stemming from this failure (Costea et al., 2012; Pongratz & Voss, 2003) – as argued by Scharff (2015, p. 9): "[T]he entrepreneurial self only has itself to blame if something goes wrong".

Do the egalitarian aspirations of a more caring, moral, humane entrepreneurship then have the necessary force to alleviate problems of exclusion and elitism in entrepreneurship? Kårfors continues:

> [T]he ambition to increase individual autonomy, an essential element of entrepreneurship and the entrepreneurial self (Pongratz & Voss, 2003; Gill, 2014) indubitably represents an effort to make entrepreneurship more inclusive. The power of this force appears to be quite formidable: by empowering those who are excluded from the entrepreneurial discourse, "who do not fit vital norms" (Berglund & Skoglund, 2016), it operates as a "security

technology" that has the potential to normalize deviating subjects, to eliminate "unwanted elements" and thereby "defend society from itself" (Berglund & Skoglund, 2016). Social entrepreneurship can therefore be seen as a protective effort made in self interest.

Kårfors then investigates the role of class, political law and power in the construction of otherhood, and when it comes to the empowerment of others suggests that beneath the "benevolent veneer" of this concept lies the exclusionary force of unequal power relations. By assisting socially marginalized people, he writes, we lessen a basic symptom of their poverty and direct our attention to their predicament, which may be seen as positive. This, however, may – contradictory to our intentions – contribute to a learned helplessness by "cementing [our] own authority and the dependency of [our] clients" (Bröckling, 2016), possibly evoking feelings of shame and weakness in others. Consequently, "an exclusionary counter-attack occurs", preventing the autonomy of others.

Kårfors's arguments complement the views of Wickström, as both authors argue that the logic and ideology of entrepreneurship are predicated on the deviance, inferiority and exclusion of the Other – cast as a distinctly different, non-entrepreneurial, antithetic Other. These assumptions then work against responsible and inclusive readings of alternative entrepreneurship and evoke a need to problematize by what means and through which mental mechanisms we demarcate boundaries between selves and Others, between entrepreneurs and non-entrepreneurs, between those who are "good enough" to uphold desirable societal functions in the wake of the welfare state and those who require "fixing" to be able to contribute to society (Ahl & Marlow, 2012).

Lif (2016), in his essay, examines the societal consequences of the prevailing image of the alternative entrepreneur. He conceptualizes the alternative entrepreneurial self as an outcome of a pastoral power that influences subjects to behave and think in ways aligned with the interests of those in power (Foucault, 1978):

> This "entrepreneurial self" is currently in the phase of the second critical turn, a phase in which a successful alternative entrepreneur constantly needs to strive to reach his/her full potentiality (Costea *et al.*, 2012) and use his/her emotional energy and passion for improving a socially good cause (Goss, 2005; Dempsey & Sanders, 2010). The alternative entrepreneur is in consistent struggle to gain the security affiliated with being a successful entrepreneur (Berglund & Skoglund, 2016). The alternative entrepreneur succeeds more or less in this endeavour by using its whole personality (Anderson & Warren, 2011; Scharff, 2015) and importantly by having a social ethos, i.e. an ability to use its affective and empathetic qualities in making the entrepreneurial pursuit successful (Rose, 1996; Vrasti, 2012; Bröckling, 2016).

Lif's alternative entrepreneur comes across as preoccupied with, and burdened by, striving to fulfil her potential to the extent that little energy is directed towards other relationships, or objectives that lie outside of the links between the self and the desired self. Lif continues by examining the consequences of this approach:

> When critically analysed, alternative entrepreneurship can be seen as using "the other" when it socially constructs itself. Because it is via the relationship with "the other" that the alternative entrepreneur can fully show his/her ethos and strive to achieve his/her full potentiality. I.e. "the other" is a critical part of how successful alternative entrepreneurs build up their organization and/or narrative about themselves.

Interactions with others, and the creation of social utility for the benefit of the Other, thus become desirable for an aspiring entrepreneurial self under a caring capitalism. The alternative entrepreneur, Lif reasons, needs "the other" to justify and legitimize itself, revealing not only a narcissist tendency but also a diversion away from an interest in societal and structural causes of inequalities to more individually focused explanations (Bröckling, 2016; Scharff, 2015).

Wiessner (2016), in a fourth and final essay, focuses on conflicts that arise when engaging in alternative entrepreneurship, such as the conflict between the interest, or space, of the Other and that of an entrepreneurial self, set on reaching self-optimization. She, like her student colleagues, relates changing demands on individuals to an increasingly persuasive neo-liberal ideology:

> Just as the entrepreneurial self was called upon by governments to meet the demand for self-regulating and competitive individuals, the social entrepreneur is now called upon by the same authorities to fill the shortage of social security which was previously distributed by governments, but lacking in today's downsized public welfare system.... The consequences of the state encouraging individuals to not only take full responsibility for their own well-being, but to help solve social issues in society inevitably leads to areas such as health and social care being impregnated with "business thinking" (Dey & Steyaert, 2016, p. 5) as social entrepreneurs become the new welfare providers in society.

This, she argues, results in entrepreneurial selves engaging in "showing the less entrepreneurial individuals in society how to take responsibility for their lives and enhance their entrepreneurial qualities". The use of empowerment as a "universal therapy" for inequalities in society, Wiessner cautions, may be illusionary and not actually concerned with distributing power to those who lack it. Rather, empowerment is based on the belief that by making people *feel* more powerful, they will choose to advance their entrepreneurial selves, making them less likely to cause problems in society. Again we see how alternative entrepreneurship is aimed at improving societal security, as a form of "defending society from itself". Wiessner here shows affinity to the reasoning of Kårfors as she relates to the combined neo-liberal interests of the state to govern through the subjectivities of individuals (Rose, 1989), and the interest of these individuals to prove their potentiality and to self-optimize (Costea *et al.*, 2012; Foucault, 1978). More pressure is hence accumulated onto entrepreneurial selves and, as social entrepreneurship is characterized by "individualism and marketing of the self" (Dempsey & Sanders, 2010, p. 454), Wiessner argues, this "begs the question if social entrepreneurship is just ultimately the sugar coated version of the entrepreneurial self in search of a new level of self-fulfilment".

If social entrepreneurs engage in social entrepreneurship as a means of reaching higher on a ladder of neo-liberal achievements, then "the motives of the social entrepreneurs become not just an internal conflict but an ethical one as well", she reasons. For, if social entrepreneurship is to be ethical, it must focus upon the interest of others, and how entrepreneurs, in the actual *doing* of social entrepreneurship, engage in moral dilemmas and try to find a balance between the interests of selves vis-à-vis those of others (Dey & Steyaert, 2016).

In our interpretation, as teachers, some common threads appear in these essays; all four students avoid getting stuck in "impossible" questions, such as what the "real" motives are for engaging in social or alternative entrepreneurship. Wickström, Kårfors, Lif and Wiessner skilfully navigate past this ground and instead take a step "outwards", directing their attention towards more structural aspects and their societal consequences. They identify tensions and inconsistencies in the entrepreneurial discourse and juxtapose narratives of an active, autonomous, competitive entrepreneur, fulfilling herself and the needs of society in one go, with claims that entrepreneurship should be responsible, respectful of others, socially inclusive and compassionate. "Are these two narratives compatible?" the students ask themselves, albeit from their individual analytical platforms. In what circumstances, in what respects, are they, or are they not, achievable? The students strive to go beneath the surface, they scrutinize "the benevolent veneer" or "the sugar coated surface" of entrepreneurial discourses, and search for different layers, and perspectives not usually adopted, such as those concerning the vulnerabilities of others. As teachers we note that the perspective of the course here equips students to develop a critical awareness, and, by extension, to act differently and make decisions that may alter social practices and relations between selves and others.

In the following section we pass the word over to the students, to the writers of the four essays analysed above, to let them express their reflections on their learning experiences from the course.

Students' reflections on their learnings

In retrospect, we feel that the course has made an impression by challenging our mainstream understanding of entrepreneurship. Instead of being considered as a highly desirable role by virtue of its embodying attractive traits such as creativity, ambition and business acumen, the figure of the entrepreneur may just as easily be conceived as an unattainable ideal. The course allowed us to further evaluate this by studying the notion of subjectivity and its connection to entrepreneurship, from the perspectives of authors such as Lacan and Foucault. While the aim of enhancing one's critical thinking abilities is embedded in the core of most business studies, the emphasis on one's own subjectivity is not. Being encouraged to adopt a critical lens when approaching the concept of the "entrepreneurial self", we were able to see how this ideal has become an alluring mirage that convinces us that there is always more, and, by logical necessity, never enough.[3] As we continue to analyse contemporary neo-liberal society and management from different perspectives in our studies, we are reminded that being entrepreneurial has become an imperative to which we may have to adapt in order to become successful. Indeed, our future employers will probably expect it of us. In the absence of critical awareness, the insidious nature of this striving for perfection is in danger of being obscured by the positive entrepreneurial personality traits.

The concept of the "entrepreneurial self" could be considered highly relatable for anyone in their twenties living in today's society. However, we came to interpret the concept in different ways. For one of us, the early phase of the course led to a strong urge to resist the effects of how the societal idea of the "entrepreneurial self" might have come to affect now internalized personality traits, such as being energetic, creative and hardworking. While these had previously been highly valued, they started to become the target of criticism in an attempt to escape the feeling of ideological manipulation. However, with time, the person experiencing these doubts realized that this was the wrong path to follow, since it only opened up for more self-criticism and internalized blame. Instead, the insights were used to make a thorough analysis of his own behaviour. And, because of the deeper understanding of this social construct, he holds that most (or all?) of these traits are virtuous, not only in the eyes of the "entrepreneurial self" but also from other moral foundations. Thus, it is important to point out that the general understanding of entrepreneurship as something positive can be highly beneficial for society, especially if one looks historically at other comparatives of dominant ideological ideal types. As the course touched upon some of the mechanisms connected to the underlying logic of the "entrepreneurial self" it opened up for further problematization. This led to a sense of distance towards the absurdity of how the term "entrepreneurship" is sometimes used and exploited in contemporary society, which also generated a sense of sadness when confronted with how subjects can suffer from problematic aspects of this discourse. From this perspective, the critical lens can be seen as useful for further interrogating some of the more problematic aspects of entrepreneurship, such as vulnerability. As we were encouraged to critically re-evaluate the discourse on entrepreneurship from our own subjective perspectives, a certain degree of vulnerability and openness to exploration of ourselves was required. One of us explicitly remembers when our lecturers introduced the concept by showing us a video of Brené Brown talking about her research and explaining that "we can't practice compassion with other people if we can't treat ourselves kindly". Vulnerability could thus be understood as a way to counteract the pressures of society by embracing our imperfections and being brave enough to show them.

Perhaps, then, entrepreneurship is inimical to vulnerability? The pressure to realize one's full potential, to constantly focus on cultivating one's entrepreneurial skills to perfection, a persuasive theme in the entrepreneurship discourse (Bröckling, 2016; Rose, 1996), naturally encourages self-elevation, which is arguably antonymic to the notion of recognizing one's limitations and imperfections. Juxtaposed with this backdrop, alternative entrepreneurship emerges as a potential means by which we externalize our own vulnerability. Entrepreneurship then becomes a psychological defence mechanism that projects this undesired vulnerability onto a specific target (e.g. the "Other"), which simultaneously allows us to add admirable traits of compassion and conscientiousness to our entrepreneurial personalities.

Students embracing vulnerability

The students' essays draw our attention to paradoxical and contradictory assumptions in the entrepreneurship discourse, and portray entrepreneurs as somewhat ensnared, caught in a web of expectations which they – so obviously from an outside perspective – cannot possibly fulfil. Entrepreneurs, under the interrogative lens of the students' essays, appear as squeezed between opting not to see inconsistencies, or "the space of the Other", continuing with business as usual, and rather uncritically accepting the credo of a caring, inclusive, second-turn form of entrepreneurship offered to them. In a sense, the vulnerabilities of alternative entrepreneurs are unveiled in a theoretical, but nonetheless revelatory way. From the angle of the students' work, an important question that emerges is whether it is feasible to be a successful entrepreneur, according to a neo-liberal ethos, and to simultaneously show respect for the alterity of the other. This is a question that lays bare the vulnerabilities of entrepreneurial selves, their desires and (emotional) risk-taking. It also leaves us with doubts concerning the Other and how we can see and "act on" the vulnerabilities of others without either reinforcing these vulnerabilities, or impelling others to tread in our own footsteps.

In the students' interpretations, social entrepreneurship then emerges as a practice of the self (Dey & Steyaert, 2016), and in this practice morality is enacted outside of the obedience to established codes of rule (Derrida, 1993). This we see, for example, in how entrepreneurs, in their daily lives, "bend and breach" norms that impel them to define themselves in particular ways. Entrepreneurs, thus conceived, instead of playing by the rules come across as playing *with* the rules of the capitalist game as they engage in practices of freedom (Foucault, 1978) in myriads of different ways. Resistance, accordingly and as suggested by Bröckling (2016), arises in an experimenting with how one can be "different differently": how one can, in conscious and morally informed ways, act on fissures in how things are normally done that make possible one's own subjectivities and re-interpretations of existing practices – and that embrace, albeit often tacitly, the vulnerabilities of both selves and others.

We think that many students show remarkable progress during the course, confirming our beliefs that students are able and reflective learners. With limited prior knowledge of entrepreneurship, students write essays with a high level of insight and critical awareness. One observation we made during the course, however, was that it seemed easier for students to identify vulnerabilities in others, and to imagine the consequences and reactions this may evoke in others, than to relate to their own vulnerabilities. When asked *after* the course and for the purpose of this chapter to elaborate on their reflections, the four students whose essays we selected, as we have seen, clearly address their own reactions and vulnerabilities. They also create a link between how the vulnerability of the Other is somehow always connected to "my vulnerability". Perhaps this mirrors a progression of thought, that we tend to identify vulnerabilities in others sooner than we allow them to surface in ourselves. It could also, we realize, be a consequence of how the course is designed, with little room for the exploration of individual psychological experiences – something that we will bear in mind for future versions of the course.

Teachers embracing vulnerability

There are several experiences that we, as teachers, take away from this course. The first is a reaction of relief: relief that the vulnerabilities that we "put on the table" were handled with care and respect by students. We believe that this relates to our "standing still", which might not be something that students recognize but which made it possible for us to act in a more thought-through manner – and for students to air their frustrations and feelings of discomfort without being met by defensive reactions from our side. Hence, through embracing shame and vulnerability, we created space for responses that it might be essential for students to express in their "progression" within the course – from enthusiasm to bewilderment and then back to a more integrated position, reflecting a combination of critical awareness and reflective insights, linking selves and others. Perhaps this also explains why, on this particular course, we experienced a greater willingness among students to "go along" with our perspective of entrepreneurship and to explore its consequences.

More importantly, students developed an openness and a willingness to work together. While we are proud of them and impressed by their work, we also bear in mind that this positive outcome has not always been the case. During previous courses, students' reactions to the curriculum were characterized not only by scepticism but also by internal competition. On occasions these negative reactions made us hesitate to continue with the course – our vulnerabilities as teachers were uncovered, shame was triggered and we were exposed to the vulnerabilities of students when they were unable to cooperate with each other. These experiences prompted us to anchor the course in our personal reflections and to try to foresee – and understand – student reactions. By acknowledging our vulnerability as teachers, by, in a sense, being "unmasked" before the students, we were at the same time aware that we implicitly asked them to do the same – to "unmask". This possibly created an unspoken, but nevertheless sensed, pressure on them to act and reason like us, which they may have felt unprepared for.

Scrutinizing one's vulnerabilities requires a certain courage and maturity, qualities that we may not expect that students have or are willing to share with us. But, in line with the reasoning of Brown, we simultaneously believe that the suppression of vulnerabilities leads to a numbness that impedes creativity and collaboration. Avoidance of vulnerability may then steer the individual into defensive positions in order to uphold a sense of security, which inserts a distance between selves and others, inhibiting the ability to develop sensitivity to others, and preventing openness towards learning. We also discern this when we strive to "boost" our own academic accomplishments, to enhance our careers, while neglecting to listen to others, such as students.

Perhaps paradoxically, we felt that when we developed an awareness of our vulnerability, shame and exposure to the potential criticism of students we became more sensitive towards their vulnerabilities. In meeting them as our others, a space for exploration emerged which did not encompass all students but enough to create a climate of trust and learning. The students made us realize that the course may be perceived as provocative and that, to a certain extent, we expose their vulnerabilities when we ask them to assume our perspective, to be critical and reflective. This vulnerability may have different sources; for many students, a questioning of the neo-liberal subject, of its active, autonomous, wealth-creating, American dream type of character may be deeply disturbing, and we came to realize that developing other perspectives of this ethos requires time. We have also learned that an exposure to the alterity of others, theoretically as well as in practice, may be emotionally trying. As teachers we may need to consider that we can only *invite* students to open up for thinking differently about themselves and about entrepreneurship – and to equip them with the necessary analytical means (and to a limited extent the practical opportunities) for doing so.

Experiencing a sense of vulnerability, we have argued, is embedded in entrepreneurship. Suppressing this vulnerability may not only hinder creativity but may also increase the very fear one seeks to handle. Instead, embracing vulnerabilities in the conviction that we have the resources to handle them creates possibilities and builds trust between selves and others. By recognizing vulnerability, and by practising it, we might reach a more balanced approach that opens up for new possibilities. This may not erase our individual drive for potentiality and self-fulfilment, but may transform this drive into a more relational force, into a mutually held principle of potentiality in which we do not focus (only) on individual achievement (Bröckling, 2016), or self-optimization (Foucault, 1978), but on joint efforts – an entrepreneurship "with, of, and by the Other" (Jones & Spicer, 2009), with the aim of bringing about a more collective seizing of opportunities. In the very mundane context of critical entrepreneurship education, such a process might create opportunities for working together with students in developing critical and reflective courses. We believe that such a cooperation can lead to a more profound understanding of how courses in entrepreneurship are perceived and how they can be further developed.

Notes

1 The course is described in more detail in Chapter 8 in this volume. In the version of the course presented in this chapter the themes of "social" and "green" entrepreneurship were replaced by themes of "conflicts" and "relations with others" in alternative forms of entrepreneurship.
2 Minor changes have been made in excerpts from the students' papers. These changes are mainly of an editorial nature.
3 However, one of us is sceptical to this conclusion and believes its epistemological assumptions do not fully support this normative claim.

References

Ahl, H. & Marlow, S. (2012). Exploring the dynamics of gender, feminism and entrepreneurship: advancing debate to escape a dead end? *Organization, 19*(5), 543–562.

Anderson, AR. & Warren, L. (2011). The entrepreneur as hero and jester: Enacting the entrepreneurial discourse. *International Small Business Journal, 29*(6), 589–609.

Berglund, K. & Skoglund, A. (2016). Social entrepreneurship: To defend society from itself. In A. Fayolle & P. Riot (Eds), *Rethinking entrepreneurship: Debating research orientations* (pp. 57–77). New York, NY: Routledge.

Brown, B. (2010). *The gifts of imperfection: Let go of who you think you're supposed to be and embrace who you are*. Minneapolis. MN: Hazelden.

Brown, B. (2012). *Daring greatly: How the courage to be vulnerable transforms the way we live, love, parent, and lead*. New York, NY: Penguin.

Bröckling, U. (2016). *The entrepreneurial self – fabricating a new type of subject*. London, Thousand Oaks, CA, New Delhi and Singapore: SAGE.

Butler, J. (2005). *Giving an account of oneself*. New York, NY: Fordham University Press.

Chakrabarty, D. (2002). *Habitations of modernity: Essays in the wake of subaltern studies*. Chicago, IL: University of Chicago Press.

Costea, B., Amiridis, K. & Crump, N. (2012). Graduate employability and the principle of potentiality: An aspect of the ethics of HRM. *Journal of Business Ethics, 111*, 25–36.

Dempsey, S.E. & Sanders, M.L. (2010). Meaningful work? Nonprofit marketization and work/life imbalance in popular autobiographies of social entrepreneurship. *Organization, 17*, 437.

Derrida, J. (1993). *Aporias: Dying—awaiting (one another at) the "limits of truth"* (T. Dutoit, Trans.). Stanford, CA: Stanford University Press.

Dey, P. & Steyaert, C. (2016). Rethinking the space of ethics in social entrepreneurship: power, subjectivity, and practices of freedom. *Journal of Business Ethics, 133*(4), 627–641.

Foucault, M. (1978/1991). Governmentality. In G. Burchell, C. Gordon & P. Miller (Eds), *The Foucault effect – studies in governmentality with two lectures and interviews with Michel Foucault* (pp. 87–104). Chicago, IL: University of Chicago Press.

Gill, R. (2014). "If you're struggling to survive day-to-day": Class optimism and contradiction in entrepreneurial discourse. *Organization, 21*(1), 50–67.

Goss, D. (2005). Schumpeter's legacy? Interaction and emotions in the sociology of entrepreneurship. *Entrepreneurship Theory and Practice, 29*(2), 205–218.

Ibarra, H. (1999). Provisional selves: Experimenting with image and identity in professional adaptation. *Administrative Science Quarterly, 44*(4), 764–791.

Jones, C. & Spicer, A. (2005). The sublime object of entrepreneurship. *Organization*, *12*(2), 223–246.

Jones, C. & Spicer, A. (2009). *Unmasking the Entrepreneur*. Cheltenham: Edward Elgar.

Kårfors, A. (2016). *Student essay, entrepreneurship and the entrepreneurial self course*. Unpublished report, Stockholm Business School.

Lévinas, E. (1969). *Totality and infinity – an essay on exteriority*. Pittsburgh, PA: Duquesne University Press.

Lif, O. (2016). *Student essay, entrepreneurship and the entrepreneurial self course*. Unpublished report, Stockholm Business School.

Pongratz, H.J. & Voss, G.G. (2003). From employee to "entreployee": Towards a "self-entrepreneurial" work force? *Concepts and Transformation*, *8*(3), 239–254.

Rose, N. (1989). *Governing the soul: Technologies of human subjectivity*. London: Routledge.

Rose, N. (1996). *Inventing our selves: Psychology, power, and personhood* (chapter 7). Cambridge: Cambridge University Press.

Scharff, C. (2015). The psychic life of neoliberalism: Mapping the contours of entrepreneurial subjectivity. *Theory, Culture & Society*, *33*(6), 107–122.

Schön, D.A. (1984). *The reflective practitioner: How professionals think in action* (Vol. 5126). New York, NY: Basic.

Spinosa, C., Flores, F. & Dreyfus, H.L. (1999). *Disclosing new worlds: Entrepreneurship, democratic action, and the cultivation of solidarity*. Cambridge, MA, and London: MIT Press.

Spivak, G.C. (1987/2012). *In other worlds: Essays in cultural politics*. London and New York, NY: Routledge.

Vrasti, W. (2012). *How to use affect in late capitalism*. Retrieved from http://citation.all academic.com/meta/p_mla_apa_research_citation/4/1/7/0/3/pages417031/p417031-1.php.

Wickström, A. (2016). *Student essay, entrepreneurship and the entrepreneurial self course*. Unpublished report, Stockholm Business School.

Wiessner, S. (2016). *Student essay, entrepreneurship and the entrepreneurial self course*. Unpublished report, Stockholm Business School.

Epilogue

Critical entrepreneurship education: a form of resistance to McEducation?

Ulla Hytti

Introduction

Universities are increasingly expected to strengthen their role in society (Jarvis, 2013). This also suggests a transition towards the "entrepreneurial university" (Etzkowitz, 2014; Foss & Gibson, 2015) and a reorientation of university strategies and policies to promoting entrepreneurship and societal impact (Siegel & Wright, 2015). One tenet in this development is increasing the supply of entrepreneurship education and training modules campus-wide, and making entrepreneurship topics mandatory or at least highly recommended to all university students irrespective of their discipline. This strong wind of entrepreneurship and entrepreneurialism into the universities is not without critics (also see Chapter 1 of this volume). The resisting voices are asking if the move towards the entrepreneurial university will erase any attempts to safeguard the traditional values and threaten the academic ethos of the Humboldtian university (Philpott, Dooley, O'Reilly & Lupton, 2011).

The advocates of the entrepreneurial university on the other hand are affirmative that the transition is inevitable and base their opinion on several arguments. First, youth unemployment is alarmingly high in several EU members states (Eurofound, 2015). This combined with the fact that educational attainment levels of the population have improved significantly over the last 30 years in the EU (Eurostat, 2016) is contributing towards the understanding that self-employment and entrepreneurship are also real alternatives for university graduates. This is also reflected in the fairly positive attitudes of young people towards entrepreneurship as a career option in many countries (Eurofound, 2015).

Second, the careers are also envisioned to be in change (Arthur, 2008; Rodrigues & Guest, 2010). On one hand the changes in organizations are suggested to provoke the "boundaryless career", where individuals move between firms and in and out of self-employment (DeFillippi & Arthur, 1994), and build up a "career" portfolio that includes different forms of paid, unpaid and voluntary work, and non-work (Clinton, Totterdell & Wood, 2006). On the other hand, recent analyses suggest the boundaries are not actually dissolving but rather there is a growing complexity and more subjective perspective on career boundaries (Rodrigues & Guest, 2010). Either way, it is suggested that universities need to equip students with new kinds of "employability skills" and "entrepreneurial skills" in order to manage their careers in the changing landscape (Sewell & Dacre Pool, 2010).

Third, new technologies in the form of digitalization and artificial intelligence, for example, are enabling new kinds of entrepreneurial opportunities (Grégoire & Shepherd, 2012) where the educated youth graduating from universities may have a particular advantage in making use of their knowledge in the entrepreneurial arena. Finally, many countries that have had a relatively strong role for the state in the society are trying to cut government spending. Thus, there is an increasing demand that social entrepreneurship and innovation are needed to combat social problems and address social challenges (Lawrence, Phillips & Tracy, 2012), in which the universities and university education have a role to play.

So are the critical voices towards entrepreneurship in the universities oblivious to or in denial from these emerging trends in their surroundings and societies? Are they embracing divergent worldviews coupled with the different sets of beliefs about the future where we are educating and preparing our youth? Or, where can we trace the source and location of resistance towards entrepreneurship?

McEducation – students as consumers for entrepreneurship (education)

I argue that the academics are not resisting the entry of entrepreneurship into the university per se but they are resisting the ways it is introduced and the ways entrepreneurship is understood. This book is not about criticizing and stopping entrepreneurship but about enacting it with more concerns for the context, aiming at reflexivity, and understanding the bigger picture. The resistance is targeted at the narrow interpretation of entrepreneurship, and at the implementation of entrepreneurship as a managerial, top-down project (Philpott *et al.*, 2011; Kolhinen, 2015), as well as at understanding university as a place of educational consumption and students as consumers. This is discussed also through the metaphor of the McDonaldization of higher education (Ritzer, 1998), that I find insightful for thinking about entrepreneurship and entrepreneurship education in universities.

"Employability" is introduced as a performance measure for universities, and possibly one of the main drivers for strengthening the entrepreneurship agenda (Berglund, 2013). The students as consumers have the right to education that guarantees their employability, jobs and careers in thriving industries (Ritzer, 1998), irrespective of any changes in the career landscape. Thus, university students not only in business schools but also in all other disciplines have the right to entrepreneurship education that transforms their arts or social sciences degrees into better "currency" from the perspective of employers. And if entrepreneurship is underlined as a career option, the responsibility for the employment is not with the university or the employers but with the individuals themselves.

Following this idea that every student has the "right" to entrepreneurship education (and an obligation to become entrepreneurial) in the university creates a massive demand for these educational services. With the current aspiration to respond to the need, the university responds by offering entrepreneurship courses campus-wide. They do not typically value academic achievement and theoretical abilities for entrepreneurship but emphasize practical and social competences and skills (Komulainen, Naskali, Korhonen & Keskitalo-Foley, 2014). Thus, there is a firm belief that experiential methods – learning from experience – will lead to better learning outcomes than other "more traditional" methods (Kozlinska, 2016), and practice is a more efficient vehicle for learning than theory. This is particularly demonstrated by the primacy of learning through/for over learning about approaches (Lackéus & Williams-Middleton, 2015). And indeed, students (consumers) are often satisfied with these "hands-on" courses, which has been taken as a signal of their usefulness. Yet, this may also signal that other courses are not intellectually comfortable (see Chapters 5 and 7 of this volume) or they may not be familiar with the alternatives (Parker & Jary, 1995; Chapters 9 and 10 of this volume).

These university entrepreneurship courses are typically run as venture creation programmes that represent standardized practically oriented courses ran in a similar fashion across the globe adopted from e.g. Junior Achievement models (n.d.). Through these courses the university fosters an approach to entrepreneurship education that shares a strong focus on profit-oriented start-ups and new venture creation, and fosters a consensus where "the core of entrepreneurship is related to the process of opportunities, new venture creation, growth, risk and acquisition and allocation of resources" (Kyrö, 2015, p. 610). Previously, business planning was the key content and the process to be learned (Honig, 2004) but now business plans have given way to business model generation (Osterwalder & Pigneur, 2010) or lean start-up models (Blank, 2013) as key content in entrepreneurship education, supported by practices of drafting canvases, pitching exercises and competitions (Brown, 2017). Hence, the conclusion from this is that higher education has become less of a human emancipation tool and more of a capital reproduction mechanism (Da Costa & Silva Saraiva, 2012).

Sometimes the demand from the consumers – the students – is so high that mass customization and use of technology is needed to meet the demand. Courses are run as online courses and make use of existing online resources. This is also helpful in meeting the students' expectations of education to be nearby and operating around the clock and saving money in comparison to the other forms of education. Thus, following Ritzer's (1998) ideas of McDonaldization, entrepreneurship education can be seen analogous to the fast-food restaurant as a highly cost-efficient machine for dispensing hamburgers and similar highly standardized foods.

While the venture creation programmes may not fully live up to the fast-food restaurant analogy in terms of being particularly cost effective since typically they will necessitate time resources from faculty, their reliance on standardized content and models embedded in the business model and lean canvas alleviates some of these problems. Since in terms of their content and methods they are so alike, the analogy may still be applicable.

In this McEducation version of entrepreneurship education the university takes a one-size-fits-all approach by claiming that once entrepreneurship courses and services are offered campus-wide and are open to all, they are available to all. Yet, this assumption has been questioned (Komulainen, Korhonen & Räty, 2009). Inclusion cannot be achieved simply by increasing numbers, and thus inclusion does not in itself bring greater equality (Delanty, 2003). The strong new venture creation focus, often combined with a technology or science bias, means that in reality the entrepreneurship becomes an elitist and narrow approach and the vast majority of students for example in humanities and social sciences become excluded from them. This one-size fits all model is also oblivious to the questions of gender, class or ethnicity (Berglund, Lindgren & Packendorff, 2017). Importantly, all axiological debates in entrepreneurship education are silenced, marked by the lack of "why" questions (Kyrö, 2015).

Where to from here? Bringing back the why!

I advocate that the success of the entrepreneurship agenda is strongly dependent on whether or not the university relies on its core Humboldtian values of criticality and reflexivity in introducing entrepreneurship into the university. In this sense my take on entrepreneurship education will not emphasize the dualism or the choice between the traditional academic and entrepreneurial values. Rather, I wish to join Fayolle (2013) and Kyrö (2015) among others in their call for more reflexive approaches and reflexivity as a necessary condition in furthering entrepreneurship education. In this book the reader can see how reflexive approaches are enacted in the classroom. The McDonaldization of education is not a guarantee of success for embedding entrepreneurship at the university, on the contrary, it has the risk of becoming a functionalist pervasive ideology that may be taken to mean anything to anyone, and it easily and often becomes a contested concept (an analogy developed based on ideas presented of "leaderism" in Alvesson and Spicer (2012).

Entrepreneurship education in universities will develop by bringing back the axiological debate (do we want to? should we? and how should we do it?) (Kyrö, 2015) and focusing on the why question, and continuously investigating what is happening, what kind of ideas we are offering either consciously or accidentally, how our approaches are inviting some and excluding others. How our students are accepting, applying and transforming entrepreneurship and what are the outcomes and consequences of these actions? We should question the one-size-fits all approach and reflect on different learning approaches and entrepreneurship education practices we could and should introduce for teaching and learning of entrepreneurship, which the contributors in this book seek to do.

Despite the popularity of the new venture creation approaches, it is necessary to remind ourselves that university (entrepreneurship) education should not be equalled to "pleasing customers, but about giving them the intellectual resources to challenge establish ways of doing things – however uncomfortable that may be for them and others" (Parker & Jary, 1995, p. 333). We must be sensitive to the polyphony within the universities (Kolhinen, 2015; Chapter 1 of this volume) and not to reproduce unreflexively normative ideas of entrepreneurship (Chapter 7), but allow the different voices (Chapter 9) and also use the different disciplines (Chapter 4) to develop their own approaches (such as in Chapter 6). Universities should facilitate active sense making both for faculty and students in order create room for developing their (and our) own understanding of – and also questioning – the content and meaning for entrepreneurship in the different disciplines. Following the contributors and colleagues in this book we should continue to invite our students to explore if they identify with various entrepreneurial identities and how they make sense of entrepreneurship and their entrepreneurial abilities and futures from their different social positions (such as gender, discipline, family wealth).

Thus, it is here where I believe that this volume will be an important resource to the extent that hopefully it will transition into becoming the "mainstream entrepreneurship education" or at least contribute to informing the "uncritical entrepreneurship education". To elaborate on the McEducation analogy, entrepreneurship need not to be consumed as fast-food between real meals ("real disciplines") but it could become one of the ingredients together with the other disciplines that are applied to create delicious meals. But it is equally important to cultivate an understanding that it may be possible to cook a nice meal without this one ingredient!

References

Alvesson, M. & Spicer, A. (2012). Critical leadership studies: The case for critical performativity. *Human Relations, 65*(3), 367–390.

Arthur, M.B. (2008). Examining contemporary careers: A call for interdisciplinary inquiry. *Human Relations, 61*(2), 163–186.

Berglund, K., Lindgren, M. & Packendorff, J. (2017). Responsibilising the next generation: Fostering the enterprising self through de-mobilising gender. *Organization*. doi:10.1177/1350508417697379.

Berglund, K. (2013). Fighting against all odds: Entrepreneurship education as employability training. *Ephemera, 13*(4), 717.

Blank, S. (2013). Why the lean start-up changes everything. *Harvard Business Review, 91*(5), 63–72.

Brown, T. (2017). Affärsmodellen är död! [Business models are dead!] Åsikten [Opinion], *Entré* 1/2017, 24.

Clinton, M., Totterdell, P. & Wood, S. (2006). A grounded theory of portfolio working. *International Small Business Journal, 24*(2), 179–203.

Da Costa, A.D.S.M. & Silva Saraiva, L.A. (2012). Hegemonic discourses on entrepreneurship as an ideological mechanism for the reproduction of capital. *Organization, 19*(5), 587–614.

DeFillippi, R. & Arthur, M. (1994). The boundaryless career: a competency-based perspective. *Journal of Organizational Behaviour, 15*(4), 307–324.

Delanty, G. (2003). Ideologies of the knowledge society and the cultural contradictions of higher education. *Policy Futures in Education, 1*(1), 71–82.

Etzkowitz, H. (2014). The second academic revolution: The rise of the entrepreneurial university and impetuses to firm foundation. In T.J. Allen & R. O'Shea (Eds), *Building technology transfer within research universities: An entrepreneurial approach.*

Eurofound, (2015). *Youth entrepreneurship in Europe: Values, attitudes, policies.* Luxembourg: Publications Office of the European Union.

Eurostat, (2016). *Educational attainment statistics.* Retrieved 5 April 2017 from http://ec.europa.eu/eurostat/statistics-explained/index.php/Educational_attainment_statistics.

Fayolle, A. (2013). Personal views on the future of entrepreneurship education. *Entrepreneurship & Regional Development, 25*(7–8), 692–701.

Foss, L. & Gibson, D. (2015). *The entrepreneurial university: Case analysis and implications.* London: Routledge.

Grégoire, D.A. & Shepherd, D.A. (2012). Technology-market combinations and the identification of entrepreneurial opportunities: An investigation of the opportunity-individual nexus. *Academy of Management Journal, 55*(4), 753–785.

Honig, B. (2004). Entrepreneurship education: Toward a model of contingency-based business planning. *Academy of Management Learning & Education, 3*(3), 258–273.

Jarvis, P. (2013). *Universities and corporate universities: The higher learning industry in global society.* London: Routledge.

Junior Achievement models (n.d.). Retrieved from www.jaworldwide.org.

Kolhinen, J. (2015). *Yliopiston yrittäjämäisyyden sosiaalinen rakentuminen: case Aalto-yliopisto.* [Social construction of entrepreneurial university: Case Aalto University], Acta Universitatis Lappeenrantaensis 659. Thesis, Lappeenranta University of Technology, Lappeenranta, Finland.

Komulainen, K., Korhonen, M. & Räty, H. (2009). Risk-taking abilities for everyone? Finnish entrepreneurship education and the enterprising selves imagined by pupils. *Gender and Education, 21*(6), 631–649.

Komulainen, K., Naskali, P., Korhonen, M. & Keskitalo-Foley, S. (2014). Internal entrepreneurship – a Trojan Horse of the neoliberal governance of education? Finnish pre- and in-service teachers' implementation of and resistance towards entrepreneurship education. *Journal for Critical Education Policy Studies, 9*(1), 341–373.

Kozlinska, I. (2016). *Evaluation of the outcomes of entrepreneurship education revisited.* Annales Universitatis Turkuensis, Series E, tom. 10 Oeconomica. Thesis, Juvenes Print, Turku.

Kyrö, P. (2015). The conceptual contribution of education to research on entrepreneurship education. *Entrepreneurship & Regional Development, 27*(9–10), 599–618.

Lackéus, M. & Williams-Middleton, K. (2015). Venture creation programs: bridging entrepreneurship education and technology transfer. *Education + Training, 57*(1), 48–73.

Lawrence, T., Phillips, N. & Tracy, P. (2012). From the guest editors: Educating social entrepreneurs and social innovators. *Academy of Management Learning & Education, 11*(3), 319–323.

Osterwalder, A. & Pigneur, Y. (2010). *Business model generation: A handbook for visionaries, game changers, and challengers.* Hoboken, NJ: John Wiley & Sons.

Parker, M. & Jary, D. (1995). The McUniversity: Organization, management and academic subjectivity. *Organization, 2*(2), 319–338.

Philpott, K., Dooley, L., O'Reilly, C. & Lupton, G. (2011). The entrepreneurial university: Examining the underlying academic tensions. *Technovation, 31*(4), 161–170.

Ritzer, G. (1998). *The McDonaldization thesis: Explorations and extensions.* London: SAGE.

Rodrigues, R.A. & Guest, D. (2010). Have careers become boundaryless? *Human Relations, 63*(8), 1157–1175.

Sewell, P. & Dacre Pool, L. (2010). Moving from conceptual ambiguity to operational clarity: employability, enterprise and entrepreneurship in higher education. *Education + Training, 52*(1), 89–94.

Siegel, D.S. & Wright, M. (2015). Academic entrepreneurship: Time for a rethink? *British Journal of Management, 26*(4), 582–595.

Index

Page numbers in *italics* denote tables, those in **bold** denote figures.

Achtenhagen, L. 7, 16, 64–6, 71
Acker, J. 141, 149
activism 37; national social movement 34; as personal commitment *76*; student, 1960s 34; *see also* conceptual activism
Agamben, G. 126
Ahl, H.J. 139–40, 160, 202, 219
Albrecht, J. 158, 164
Al-Dajani, H. 8, 160
Alvesson, M. 7, 65, 68, 122, 231
Armstrong, P. 7–8
Aronson, J. 142
Arthur, M.B. 228
assemblage 179; classroom, intervention in 192; of course process 186; dominant, of current academic education 192; educational process, taken-for-granted 190; of learning process, ongoing 186; process of each course session 193; thinking 191–2
assumption(s) 6, 84, 124, 219; blind 101; brought into project 92; common-sense 123; contradictory 223; about creating democratic spaces 207; deconstruction of 158; of determinism 200; dominant 8, 19; elitist 188; embodiment of 85; epistemological 226n3; gendered 141; implicit 9; insecurity regarding 150; no prior 26; ontological 158, 191; pedagogical 9; questioned 231; re-thinking workshop 104; right kind of failure 129; sets of 35–6; socially constructed 152; of student potential to reflect 67; taken for granted 9
assumption(s), challenge 104, 116; entrepreneurship, by stretching concepts 133; freedom to 38

assumptions, entrepreneurship: challenged by stretching concepts 133; education questioned by using art 127; ontological 158; theory and practice questioned 122
assumptions, students' 92–3, 152; cultural 146; forced to question 95; used for entrepreneurship 167

Bagger, Stein 129–31
Ball, S.J. 6, 10–13, 103, 172
Barnett, R. 33, 153
Barry, A. 10, 161, 200
becoming 6, 13, 16, 35–6, 38n1, *76*, 101, 109–10, 116; aware decision makers 14; best at what you are doing 72; clearer 143; entrepreneurial 10, 28; entrepreneurs 53–4, 62; future 65; images 202; immersed 192; informed decision maker **15**; less important in the workplace, gender 149; mainstream entrepreneurship education 232; mode 69–71; ontology of 66, 200; perplexed 134; personally involved 63; power of 132; quiet 213; reflexivity 74–5; risk of 231; subjects of own knowledge 217; world 64
being/becoming 16, 63, 70, 74
Bem, S.L. 144–5
Bendix Petersen, E. 11, 172
Berglund, K. 6–8, 11, 14, 18–19, 33, 43, 45, *47*, 48–9, 52, 67, 84, 93, 109, 127, 132, 153n4, 159–60, 162, 164, 171, 173, 216, 218–19, 229, 231
Beyes, T. 9, 123, 179, 182, 184, 192
Bill, F. 14
blog 144, 148; entries 72, 75, 77

blogging 77–8; activity 71; approach 63, 71; exercise 76–7; experiment 71; reflective 76; reflexivity achieved through 72
Bochner, A. 68, 107
Böhm, S. 164
Bouchard, D.F. 133–4
Bourdieu, P. 16, 82, 84–5, 146
Bragg, S. 11, 35, 114, 172
bright sides of entrepreneurship 45, 60
Bröckling, U. 149, 158, 162, 183, 213, 215, 219, 220, 223, 225
Brosnan, C. 85, 93
Brown, B. 213, 216, 222, 225
Brown, T. 86, 90, 230

Calás, M.B. 8, 140, 143, 152, 204
capitalism 15; acceptance of 33; caring 215, 220; critique of *168*; inclusive 151; inclusive and caring 214; patriarchal 143; pervasiveness of 36; raw 82, 84
capitalist anti-capitalistic predictions 164; disturbances 163; entrepreneurship 163; game 223; ideology 7; logic 10, 171; society 33, 160
challenge(s) 3–4, 74, 82, 84–5, 91, 95, 111, 188, 199, 212; to be addressed 78; to be overcome 54; common sense 122; discover all possible angles to 86; empowered to tackle *56*; enterprise as concept 38; established ways of doing things 231; existential 66; feminism 147; gender bias 149, 153; of global society 161; healthcare context-specific 94; health-related 85; of idea and working process 55; individualized accounts of success or failure 153; interpretative space of provocations 100; legitimacy of oppressive institutions 7; mainstream conceptualizations 152; of monitoring performance 112; opportunity to accept 11; outline 89, 93; preconceptions of creativity 180; project *89*, 92; purpose of the conference 33; received views 73; in reflexivity 63, 66; social *57*, 229; societal 60; society for justice and equality 150; solutions 55; stereotypes 150–1; understanding 114
challenge(s) assumptions 104; conventional, about entrepreneurship 133; gendered normative 141; of university teaching 38
challenge(s) educational 67; entrepreneurship 19; healthcare 82;

teacher's 134; university preconditions 18
challenge(s), entrepreneurial 46, *50–1*, 58; discourse, power dynamics within 217; processes in everyday life 108
challenge(s) entrepreneurs 52; societal 46
challenge(s) entrepreneurship *56*; conventional assumptions about 133; education 19; educators teaching 28; general view of 206; mainstream accounts of 18, 140; for societal change 46; student understandings of 19; teaching of 120
challenge(s) faced 119; in entrepreneurship education 19
challenge(s) gendered discourses 148, 151; normative assumptions 141
challenge(s) students 17; female 145; groups 53; imaginations 105; to rethink 17; solutions 45; to solve 122; thinking 204, 206; understandings of entrepreneurship 19; views 105
challenged 111; mainstream understandings and discourses of entrepreneurship 7; perception of the entrepreneur 206; students 17, 108, 111, 115; thinking 107; women's position 141
Chia, R.C.H. 8, 64–6, 77, 200–1, 203–4
Choo, K.L. 9
Claire, L. 202, 207
cognitive/emotional 16, 63, 69, 72
Cohendet, P. 183
conceptual activism 120, 122, 134
Connell, R. 10, 35, 172
conscientization 16, 63, 67, 71, 78n1
convergent thinking 200–1; *see also* downstream thinking
Costea, B. 11, 158–9, 169, 214–15, 218–19, 221
co-working space 182
creative class 182; paradigm 183
creativity 10–13, 64, 70, 104, 109, *170*, 180, 221; activity focused on 82; collaborative 192; constrain 100; course on 193–4; deconstructs 181; democratization of 188; dominant conceptions around 185; enforced 169; in entrepreneurship 105; individualized conception of 181; ingredient of processual approach 200; lay foundation for 87; numbness impeding 225; practices of 106; relationship with entrepreneurship 190; relationship with freedom **189**, 190; stimulate 213;

student **166**; unbounded 84; understandings of 185; unreflective celebrations of 186
creativity, narratives of 178, 191; urban 182–4
critical entrepreneurship 99; course 18, 158, 211; pedagogy 12, 14
critical entrepreneurship education (CEE) 3–4, 8, 12, **15**, 16, 19, 36, 122, 179, 225, 232; conceptual activism method to advance 122; interventionist approach to 179; mundane context of 225; positioned as periphery activity 36
critical entrepreneurship studies (CES) 3–4, 7–8, 12, 122, 179, 192; literature 12
critical management education 8–9, 12; institutions 9; literature 4
critical pedagogues 10
critical pedagogy 8, 10, 13, 141, 149–50; insights 11; literature 4, 8–9, 12
Croizet, J.C. 142

da Costa, A.S.M. 7–8, 84, 230
Dahlstedt, M. 6, 10, 12, 27, 29, 171
dark sides of entrepreneurship 8, 13, 45, 49, 52, 60, 169, 173
de Certeau, M. 107, 191
Deleuze, G. 120–3, 132–4, 191–2, 200
Dempsey, S.E. 158, 163–4, 169, 219, 221
Denmark 129–30
Derrida, J. 216, 223
Design Council 86
design thinking (DT) 82, 85, **86**, 88, 93, 95; *see also* thinking, thought
Dey, P. 6–7, 117, 122, 158, 161, 178, 200, 216–17, 220–1, 223
divergent thinking 200–1; worldviews 229; see also right-brain thinking
Down, B. 10, 27, 99–101, 109, 172
downstream thinking 200–1; *see also* thinking, thought
Drucker, P.F. 128–9
d.school **86**
du Gay, P. 8, 31, 159

eco-entrepreneurial self *168*
ecopreneur 164, *168*
ecopreneurial 164
ecopreneurship 158, 160, 162, 164, *168*
education 12, 14, 16, 25–7, 32, 132, 229–30; academic 62, 67, 77, 192; actor network theory approach 191; alternative conceptions of 36; of children in India

55; context, community arts and adult 140; employability from 29; enterprise culture governs 9; in entrepreneuring 65; feminist teachers and lecturers 143; formal 78; GEMS 119; generalized 133; goals of 31; instrument of economic development 33; investment of the individual 10; lower 3; management 9, 179, 202; McDonaldization of 14, 229–31; neo-liberal technology 11; participants in 127; performance measures in 103; perpetuating gendered roles 152; practices 15, 151; programmes 10; provocation in 5; services provided to students 35; shift the why of 6; stakeholders 4; student consumer of services 114; systems 141, 151; understood in socio-historical and political context 149–50; *see also* critical management education, healthcare education, higher education, McEducation
education, business 119; school ventures 67; need for change 108
education, university 29, 141, 193, 229, 231; traditional values 34
educational 12; background, take advantage of 119; challenge 67; concepts 19; context 5, 77; issues 66, 178; levels 35; neo-liberal practices 13; philosophy 140; policy 114; previous experiences 19; programmes 10, 82; reflective settings 66; settings 62, 76
educational agenda, new 174; assemblage process 190; assemblage, well-practised 179; attainment levels 228; events 191; feminist theory 143; policy, university 208; practice 150; previous experiences 199; profile 180; systems worldwide 187; work 191; work unfolds 179
educational consumption 229; services, demand for 230
Edwards, L.J. 46, 178, 191
emancipation 8, 67, 69, 161, 184, 230
enterprising self 4, 8–13, **166**
entrepreneurial cluster **184**
entrepreneurial education 159, 173
entrepreneurial self 4, 18, *76*, 78, 158, 160, 162, *165*, **166**, 167, *168*, 211–12, 215, 218, 220, 222; alternative 171, 219; of a company 159, 169, *170*; conventional 171–2; crack in the image of 215; fostered by social entrepreneurship 163; of the future 77; moral and financial

entrepreneurial self *continued*
investments in 171; neo-liberal
construction 149; participants required
to cultivate 127; relations with the Other
217; revitalized 171; socio-discursively
based view 214; striving to reach full
potential 216; version of 221; *see also*
enterprising self
entrepreneurial university 14–15, 28–30,
32–3, 35–7, 228
entrepreneuring 3–4, 19, 38, 64–6, 73, 78,
88, 92, 199, 208; capture 207; as
emancipation 161; enacted 74; engaging
in social 69; experience as relational 77;
healthcare 82–3, 87, 94–5; mundane
practices of 14; of night life 184–5;
practice 68; practices for societal 16;
process of 180; as process of becoming
200; responsible 71; self 93–4; social-
political 37; student understandings of
71; training 62, 67; upstream thinking
needed 201
entrepreneurs 8, 28–9, 73, 75, 82, 119, 128,
161, *168*, 180, 182–3, 217, 219; alternative
223; aspiring 64; becoming 53–4; better
162; challenges met 46, 52; children as 74;
compare and contrast though gender lens
148; differences between male and female
142; dilemmas 52; distinctions from non-
entrepreneurs 214; established 5;
experience failure 127; failed 129;
following social or environmental mission
45; green 172; individual characteristics of
144; inspirational meetings with 76; live
encounters with *76*; other than
stereotypical Western 7; potential 47;
practising 78; responsible 16, *50*, 62–3, 65;
right-brain thinking preference 201; social
69, 163, 172, 211, 215, 220, 221; socially
conscious 215; start-up funding from
family 131; students learn to behave as 35;
student perceptions of 145; successful 14,
139, 213; successful alternative 220
entrepreneurship: educators 3–6, 12, 14,
17, 19, 26–7, 29, 132, 160; in societal
change 16, 48; ENSO course 45, 49; *see
also* bright sides of entrepreneurship,
dark sides of entrepreneurship
Entrepreneurship and Business
Development (EBD) 67
entrepreneurship education (EE/EntEd)
4–6, 11–12, 14, 17, 36, 38, 45, 82, 84–5,
131, 139, 143, 171, 173, 229–31;
acknowledging gender in 139; action-
based 65; alternative versions of 108;
apparent contradictions in 27;
assumptions questioned 127; audience
and student perceptions of 47; based on
alternative ideas 123; in business schools
43, 64; challenges 82; concept creation
deployed in 120; conceptual activism
122; conceptualization in healthcare 16,
95; critical approach to 87, 99, 109, 178;
critical tensions of 140; designing 5;
enacting 13; entrepreneurial self 172;
feminist pedagogies 152; film as
pedagogical instrument in 202;
framework of 10; interdisciplinary
approaches 132; interventionist approach
to critical 179; mainstream 8, 142, 232;
optimistic politics of 18, 178; philosophy
utilized in 119–20, 132–4; pluralistic
view of 93; political conflict over role
109; primary purpose 35; programme 75;
resisting 13; responsible 66, 71; role of
reflexivity in 16, 62; social aspect of 109;
stereotype threat 142; students acquire
mētis and *phronesis* 64; student
preconceptions of 59; supply of 228;
traditional 83, 103; university emphasis
on 29; using artefacts in 153n4; *see also*
critical entrepreneurship education,
entrepreneurial education
episteme 62–4, 67
epistemological curiosity 63, 67, 74,
77–8
Ernst & Young accounting firm 130–1
Essers, C. 7, 43, 122, 151, 161, 200
ethical 217; action 151; approach
undermined 218; defects of market 172;
determination of what is right and
wrong 16, 62; dimensions of inclusion
and exclusion 214; investment of the
individual 10; personalities, plurality of
159; practices 12; social
entrepreneurship 221; solutions,
thought-through 161
ethically: sensitive entrepreneurship 217;
suspect 151; thought-through solutions
161
ethics 84, 119; in alternative
entrepreneurship 217; of Lévinas 215,
217; practice in daily activities 216;
university 35
ethnicity 142, 150, 231
Etzkowitz, H. 28, 31, 33, 228
Eurofound 228
European Commission 129

European Google headquarters 182; tradition 99; value of entrepreneurship 84
Eurostat 228
exploitation 14, 25–6, 32; entrepreneurial 27, 29; self 183; of workers in developing countries 44

failed 114, 131; entrepreneurs 129–30
failure 120, 213; affective states involved in 131; bad/good 129, 131; entrepreneurial 122, 127–9, 131–2, 134; experienced in financial terms 127; favourite 185; individualized accounts of 153; individualizing 151; internalizing guilt and shame stemming from 218; of neo-liberal market-based system 151; repressed 120, 128–9; step to success 128; treated as taboo 127; unemotional relationship with 129; venture or personal; versions of 131; 129; *see also* success and/or failure
Famous Entrepreneur Quotes 128
Farny, S. 27–9, 35, 139
Fayolle, A. 4–5, 132, 231
femininity 151; cultural constructions of 145; gendered perceptions of deficient entrepreneurial 139–40; varies between cultures 146
feminism 150; black 147; focus on social change 152; mistrust of 146–7; post-feminism 147; social 143
feminist 141, 143, 147; consciousness-raising 144; goals 150; imperative 151; literature and policy 146; post-feminist response 147; post-feminist Western society 152; researchers 141; theoretical perspective 8, 17
feminist approach 144; critical 149, 151; social 152; to teaching, critical 140
feminist, critical: approach 149, 151; approach to teaching 140; educator 141
feminist pedagogy/pedagogies 140–1, 143; critical 17, 149, 152
feminists 146
Fenwick, T. 38, 178, 191, 206–8
Fletcher, D.E. 7, 14
Florida, R.L. 182–3
Foss, L. 140, 228
Foucault, M. 10, 18, 119, 158–9, 172, 185, 187, 214, 218–19, 221–3, 225
fraud 129, 130–1
freedom to 172; address outsourced social and environmental problems 164; be

gained 12; challenge assumptions of university teaching 38; choose their careers 147; individualist and flexible way of life 162
freelancers 182–3
Freire, P. 63–4, 67, 74, 77, 78n1, 141
Freirean pedagogies 140
functionalist approach 99; pervasive ideology 231

Gane, N. 121, 133
Gartner, W.B. 7, 43, 55, 60, 84, 101–2, 122–3, 132, 151, 161, 200
gender 4, 17–18, *76*, 143, 147–8, 152, 231–2; bias 149, 153, 160, 171; binaries 141–2; bringing in 139–40, 142, 150, 152; conferring identity 151; critical approach to 149; dynamics 139, 144; evacuated meritocracy 153; prescribed roles 145–6; stereotypes 144
gender-blindness 139–40
gender-neutral 139, 142
gender neutrality 147
gendered 3, 143, 152–3; assumptions 141; behaviours 145; constructs 146; neo-liberal construction of ideal worker 149; perceptions, negative 139; practices 18; structures and institutions 144
gendered discourses 3, 148, 151; entrepreneurship 17–18, 140; internalization of 146
Gherardi, S. 146, 191
Gibb, A. 5, 29, 31, 33, 38, 65, 104, 112
Gilbert, J. 192, 194
Gill, R. 147–8, 160, 218
Giroux, H. 139, 141, 149
Glăveanu, V.P. 181, 188
Görling, S. 200, 202
Gorman, G. 43, 47
Goss, D. 158, 215, 219

habitus 16, 82, 84–5, 93, 187–8
Hannon, P.D. 29, 31, 33, 35–6, 38
Harvey, D. 10, 160
healthcare education 16; entrepreneurship put on the agenda 85; professional 84, 93; programmes 83; traditional notions challenged 82; transforming 88
Henry, C. 5, 43, 47, 140–1
hierarchy/network 16, 63, 69–70, 73
higher education 3–4, 11, 188; capital reproduction mechanism 230; entrepreneurship in 84; marketization of 9; policies 100; purpose of 15, 36

Hjorth, D. 4–8, 64, 100, 105, 109–10, 112, 114–15, 122–3, 132, 134, 161, 163, 178, 199, 200, 202–3, 206
Holmgren, C. 4, 109, 171, 173
Holt, R. 64, 77
hooks, B. 141
hub 183; creative and entrepreneurial 182
Hughes, K.D. 140–1
Humboldt, W. 33
Humboldtian university 228; core values 231

Idea to Service Business Transforming Healthcare (I2S) course 82, 85, 87, 93–4
IFTA (in, for, through, about) 4–6, 14, **15**
immigrants 162; encouraged to join in sporting activities 216; women 161
inequality/inequalities 6; gender 147; multiple 148; of power 150; problems of 169; societal and structural causes of 220; sources of 9
innovation(s) 11, 86, 217; business and market 43; to combat social problems 229; design thinking (DT) method 85; director at GEMS Education 119; economic development through 33; focus of entrepreneurship 84; government policy 30; within healthcare 82–3, 91, 93; impact through 26; managers of multinational corporations 14, 25; practical learning to enhance 171; service 82, 87–8, 90, 92, 95; strategies 28; units of multinational firms 28;
innovation(s), university 29, 31; forum on 68–9

Jamieson, I. 5, 49
Jaye, C. 84, 87
Jennings, P.L. 7, 161
Johannisson, B. 5, 8, 16, 43, 52, 62, 64–6, 69, 71, 73, 78n2, 83, 87, 93, 95, 99, 109, 123, 132, 199, 200, 202–3
Johnsen, C.G. 17, 129
Jones, C. 7–8, 13, 158, 160, 203–5, 213, 215–17, 225
Jones, S. 17, 27, 139, 141–3
Junior Achievement models 230

Kårfors, A. 19, 218–21
Karolinska Institutet (KI) 83, 87, 94
Katz, J. 65, 123, 161
Kelan, E.K. 147
Kenway, J. 151

Kickstartenterprise 106
Kirby, D. 4–5, 201
Kolhinen, J. 229, 232
Komulainen, K. 172, 230–1
Kristeva, J. 17, 120, 127–9, 131
Kyrö, P. 65, 230–1

lateral thinking 201
leaderism 231
leadership 70; view that women lack ability 145
Leffler, E. 4, 171
left-brain thinking 201
Lemke, T. 10, 159, 162
Lévinas, E. 215, 217–18
Lif, O. 19, 219–21
Löbler, H. 29

management education: educational "assemblage" that typifies 179; institutions enact other spaces 9; rethinking 9; *see also* critical management education
Margolis, E. 141, 150
Marlow, S. 8, 139–40, 143, 160, 219
masculinity 151; cultural constructions of 145–6; gendered perceptions of efficient entrepreneurial 139–40; impact for male students 148
Masschelein, J. 149, 158
Massumi, B. 132, 151
Mautner, G. 31, 33
McDonaldization of education 14, 229–31
McEducation 19, 229, 232; version of entrepreneurship education 231
McGrath, C. 16, 95
McLaren, P. 141, 150
mētis 62–4, 67, 73, 75–6
Michels, C. 9, 192, 194
middleground 183
Mintzberg, H. 124–7
moving 95, 212, 217; along with wishes 213; away from conceptualizations 200; away from the narrow paradigm 104; downstream thinking 201; entrepreneurship 19; forward, fear of 131; images 199, 202; intervention 192; student thinking 203, 205; target 169, 174, 215
Mulcahy, D. 190–1

Nasserghodsi, C. 119
Nayak, A. 8, 200
neo-liberal 172; achievements 221;

advancements 159; constructions 149;
discourse 218; displacements 3;
economic crisis 163; educational
practices 13; ethos 215, 223; fostering
of self-regulation 162; governmentality
11, 214; ideal of indirect governing 163;
ideology 215, 217, 220; interests of the
state 220; logic 10; management
techniques 171–2; market-based system
151; market connotations 33; narrative
of modernity 84; philosophy 35;
philosophy perspectives 159; pursuits 3;
self-regulation 163; societies 10, 18,
222; subjects 214, 225; technology 11;
Western society 152
neo-liberalism 10–11, 13, 167; moving
target 174; thrived on entrepreneurship
162
Nielsen, S.L. *47*, 48–9, 52, 104
Nietzsche, F. 38n1, 178, 184
Nobel, C. 129
nonvisible forces 123–4

Ogbor, J. 7, 139, 160
Olaison, L. 8, 14, 17, 122, 127
Olssen, M. 29, 35
otherness 105; of the Other 218
Other *see* the Other

Parker, M. 123, 179, 230–1
Pastakia, A. 158, 161, 164
Patton, P. 121, 143
Perkmann, M. 28, 31, 33, 38
Peters, M. 9–10, 29, 35, 171–2
Philpott, K. 228–9
phronesis 62–4, 67, 73, 75–6
Pittaway, L. 6, 28, 109
Pongratz, H.J. 158–9, 162, 214, 218
processual 8; approach 199, 200, 202;
dimensions of learning 212;
entrepreneuring 66, 87; nature of
entrepreneurship 83; perspective
through assemblage thinking 191
productivity 11, 13, 171
provocations 5, 111; as critical approach in
knowledge-creation process 110;
interpretative space of 100; resisting 112

QAA 104, 116

Rae, D. 45–6, 54–5, 58, 60, 104
Reay, D. 84–5
reflecting 14, 69, 205; critical awareness
and reflective insights 224; critically on

own practices and experiences 128; on
current practices 140; on entrepreneurial
process 54; entrepreneurs 16; on
involvement in projects 71; on learning
outcomes 179; organizational needs *57*;
on ourselves as teachers 120; on real-life
situations 62
reflecting on entrepreneurship: education
38; as individual vs collective
phenomenon *56*; what is excluded from
conventional conceptions 134
reflexivity 4, 62, 64, 76, 78, 181, 229, 231;
advancing 16, 63; among equals 72;
basis of 68; enhancing 63, 67, 77; social
dimension of 71
reflexivity: being/becoming 66, 69–70,
74–5
reflexivity: cognitive/emotional 65–6, 69,
72
reflexivity grid 16, 63, 75–6, *76*
reflexivity: hierarchy/networked 66,
69–70, 73
reflexivity modes 65, 69, 72, 75; of
enacting 16, 63
Rehn, A. 7, 181, 200, 202
Reid, J. 159, 164
Reilly, J.M. 129
right-brain 201–2
Rindova, V. 162, 200
Ritzer, G. 229–30
Robinson, K. 187
Rodrigues, R.A. 228
Rose, N. 158, 162, 214, 219, 221, 223

Sarasvathy, S.D. 69, 200
Scharff, C. 11, 218–20
Schön, D.E. 66, 150, 214
school/schooling compulsory 3, 173
Schumpeter, J. 160, 162, 164
Seidman, D. 119
self-employment 5, 228; self-employed 6
Sex Role Inventory (SRI) 144–6
Shepard, D. 161
Shor, I. 141, 150
side of the road 107; space on the side of
the road 99–100, 110, 115–16
Skoglund, A. 8, 18, 159, 164, 216, 218–19
Śliwa, M. 101, 110, 133, 158
SOcial Regional Innovation System
(SORIS) 68–9, 71, 76–8
societal 152; causes of inequalities 220;
challenges 60, 85; change 16, 45–6,
48–9, *50*, 53, 58; concerns 165;
conscience 110; consequences 219, 221;

societal *continued*
    discourse 217; distributions of power
    123; entrepreneurs 52, 54;
    entrepreneurship 44–6, *51*, 52, 60;
    functions 219; idea of entrepreneurial
    self 222; impact 228; issues 16, 43, 52,
    59, 151, 214, 216; norms shaped 146;
    perceptions of masculinity and
    femininity 145; problems *50*, 52–5,
    59; risks 55; sectors 48, 52; security
    220
Sørensen, B.M. 8, 17, 122–3, 125–7, 129,
    133, 158
SORIS *see* SOcial Regional Innovation
    System (SORIS)
Spicer, A. 7–8, 13, 158, 160, 203–5, 213,
    215–17, 225, 231
Spinosa, C. 37, 64, 66–7, 211
Spivak, G.C. 216, 218
Spoelstra, S. 120, 122, 164
Steele, C.M. 142
stereotype lift 17, 142; for male students
    144; theories of 145
stereotype threat 17, 142; concerns over
    147; for female students 144;
    manifestations of 149; theories of 145
Stevens, G.A. 45, 127
Stewart, K. 99–100, 107, 109–10, 115–16
Steyaert, C. 6–8, 18, 38n1, 64–5, 87, 93,
    100, 110, 123, 132, 161, 178–80, 182,
    184–5, 190–2, 194, 200, 207, 216–17,
    220–1, 223
Stockholm Business School 165
students 28, 208; assumptions 93; attempts
    to train *phronesis* and *mētis* 73; banking
    system 63, 67; belief systems,
    intervention in 207; blog entries 72;
    bodies-in-interaction 191–2; capabilities
    recognized 67; capacity for innovation
    29; changing postures 188; efforts in
    SORIS programme 77; empowerment
    158; engagement with mainstream
    entrepreneurship literature 140;
    engagement with wider society 150;
    essays 223; essays sidestep talk of
    becoming 109; established ways of
    seeing and doing things 202; evaluations
    206; evaluations of course outcome 55;
    familiarity with social media 63; films
    202; future occupations 87; home and
    community culture 151; impacts of
    social lives 78; influence of socio-
    cultural backgrounds 75; presentations
    167, 181; primary focus 49; professional
    and private lives 65; project reports 54;
    projects 16, 205; protests 15; quality of
    work 217; questioning attitudes 213;
    reactions to curriculum 224; reasons for
    taking the course 144; reflexivity 62, 71;
    societal engagement 45; solutions
    grounded in cultural context 44;
    understandings of entrepreneurship 4,
    19, 69, 128, 207; views remoulded 110;
    vulnerabilities 19, 207
students' assessments: of the course *56–7*;
    of learning 58
students' expectations 48–9, 59; of
    education, meeting 230; of learning
    needs *50–1*
students' experiences 146; in different
    learning contexts 63; experiential
    learning 64; previous educational 19,
    199; prior 72; voiced 127
students' imaginations: of business
    challenged 105; cultivation of 159;
    stimulated 204
student reflections: critical 169; upon
    entrepreneurial practices 120; on
    learning 221; on participation in SORIS
    71
students' thinking: frames opening up 199;
    moved 201, 203
success and/or failure 6, 122; dialectics 17;
    individualized accounts of 153;
    phenomena central to entrepreneurship
    119; what constitutes 120
Swan, E. 62, 65

Teaching Excellence Framework (TEF)
    115
techne 62–4, 67
Tedmanson, D. 7, 43, 122, 151, 161, 200
TEDTalk 187, 216
the Other 215–17; entrepreneurship with,
    of, and by 225; exclusion of 219; for the
    benefit of 220; space of 217–18, 220,
    223; vulnerability of 224
thinking 102, 132; art of 107; assemblage
    191–2; business 220; challenged 107,
    206; create a social space for 212;
    creative 187; critical 149; critical
    abilities 222; design 82, 85, 95; about
    effects of gender 147; entrepreneurial
    50, *56*; exercises 205; existing systems
    of 105; future-oriented process 16, 60;
    habitus 84; imaginative 190;
    managerialist 30; movement in teaching
    practices 100; norms that guide 85;

other/new ways of 204; philosophical 128, 133; point 104; prior to workshop 107; processual 199–200; push the boundaries of 204; reflective 134; right-brain 202; right-brain/left-brain 201; shifts in 87, 206; stereotypical entrepreneurship 208; sustainable *50*; tools 17; way of 110–11; what to create 69

thinking about entrepreneurship 151; education 99, 134, 229

thinking, student 171, 225; as consumer 114; moving 203, 205–6; preferences 208

thought: of children as entrepreneurs 74; entrepreneurship 5; independent 33; liberal 172; moral 65; patterns of 85, 201; processes weakened 201, 203, 207; progression of 224; provoking or stretching 111

thought, students' *113*; predominant frames, opened up 199, 208

thought-out solutions 13

thought-through 224; ethically 161

uncritical entrepreneurship education 232

upperground 183

upstream thinking 200–1

US 130, 143; Hungarian/US IT company Prezi 159, *170*; tradition 99

Verduijn, K. 7–8, 19, 43, 122, 151, 161, 199, 200, 202, 207

visible 17, 191; plurality of entrepreneurial selves 171; rendered 120, 123–4; shifts in provision of security 159

voiced 107; concerns 5; opposition view 33; student personal goals and aspirations 11

voice(s) 217, 232; alternative 38; back talk 114; concerns about control 44; critical towards entrepreneurship 229; democratic spaces for 207; less dominating 207; "other" entrepreneurs 7; the Other's 218; practitioner 104; resisting 228; service nature of the enterprise culture 111; of social/green entrepreneurship 168; student 108, 110, 112, *113*, 114, 149, 211; student experiences 127; for university staff 37

Vrasti, W. 7, 158, 214–15, 219

vulnerability 4, 19, 211–12, 214, 222; developed awareness of 225; embracing 223–4; exposure 211, 213; numbing effects of suppressed 216; of the Other 173, 224; of others 216; potential means to externalize 223; student 207

vulnerable groups 216

Weber, S. 9, 64

Weiler, K. 140–1

Weiskopf, R. 38n1, 178, 184

Welter, F. 7, 140, 161

Wickström, A. 19, 217–19, 221

Wiessner, S. 19, 220–1

Williams-Middleton, K. 62, 230

*For Product Safety Concerns and Information please contact
our EU representative GPSR@taylorandfrancis.com Taylor & Francis
Verlag GmbH, Kaufingerstraße 24, 80331 München, Germany*

T - #0223 - 160425 - C0 - 234/156/12 - PB - 9780367735357 - Gloss Lamination